T0328365

Re-Understanding Entrepreneurship

How do entrepreneurs make decisions in the real world? Why are entrepreneurs absent from mainstream economics? What functions do entrepreneurs play in the market? What type of institutional environment is needed for entrepreneurship to play a role? Neoclassical economics is a market theory that ignores entrepreneurship. This distorts our understanding of how the real market works, leading to a theory of market failure that forms the common foundation of various government interventions. The market is not only an allocative process but, more importantly, a discovery and a creative process. To understand the real market, Weiying Zhang argues that economics must shift from a price-centric to an entrepreneur-centric paradigm. Blending theory and narrative, Zhang intersects history with the present, supporting his theory with relevant case studies. He argues that once entrepreneurship in the market is correctly understood, the foundation for government intervention is undermined and the economy can sustainably flourish.

WEIYING ZHANG is Boya Chair Professor of Economics at the National School of Development, Peking University. The recipient of several prestigious awards, he is widely regarded as the leading advocate of the free market in China as well as an authority on the theory of the firm and ownership reform. Zhang has studied entrepreneurship for four decades and, through numerous articles, papers, and books, has almost single-handedly changed the public image of entrepreneurs in China.

Re-Understanding Entrepreneurship

What It Is and Why It Matters

WEIYING ZHANG
Peking University, Beijing

Translated by Matthew Dale

CAMBRIDGE
UNIVERSITY PRESS

Shaftesbury Road, Cambridge CB2 8EA, United Kingdom

One Liberty Plaza, 20th Floor, New York, NY 10006, USA

477 Williamstown Road, Port Melbourne, VIC 3207, Australia

314–321, 3rd Floor, Plot 3, Splendor Forum, Jasola District Centre,
New Delhi – 110025, India

103 Penang Road, #05-06/07, Visioncrest Commercial, Singapore 238467

Cambridge University Press is part of Cambridge University Press & Assessment,
a department of the University of Cambridge.

We share the University's mission to contribute to society through the pursuit of
education, learning and research at the highest international levels of excellence.

www.cambridge.org
Information on this title: www.cambridge.org/9781009453394

DOI: 10.1017/9781009453387

© Weiying Zhang 2024

Translated by Matthew Dale

First published 2024

A catalogue record for this publication is available from the British Library

*A Cataloging-in-Publication data record for this book is available from the Library
of Congress*

ISBN 978-1-009-45339-4 Hardback
ISBN 978-1-009-45336-3 Paperback

Contents

Figures

Preface

The entrepreneur is the key player in the market. However, entrepreneurship is totally absent from mainstream market economics. Neoclassical economics is a market theory without entrepreneurship. This misconception of the market distorts our understanding of the real market economy, leading to a theory of market failure that forms the common foundation of various government interventions. Once entrepreneurship in the market is correctly understood, so-called market failure is nothing but a failure of market theory, and the foundation of government interventions is undermined.

Neoclassical economics cannot understand entrepreneurship mainly because the rational decision making model is inconsistent with entrepreneurial decision making. Put simply, what neoclassical economics means by a "rational decision" is not what an entrepreneurial decision means in the real market. To understand the real market, economics must shift from the price-centric paradigm to the entrepreneur-centric paradigm.

This book primarily focuses on four issues: How do entrepreneurs make decisions in the real world? Why are entrepreneurs absent from mainstream economics? What do entrepreneurs do in the market? What type of institutional environment brings entrepreneurship into play the most? The four parts, including 16 chapters, of this book revolve around these four questions. The main contents of each part are as follows.

The four chapters (1–4) in the first part titled "The Nature of Knowledge and Entrepreneurship" discuss the mental model of entrepreneur decision-making. The first chapter primarily discusses entrepreneurship from the perspective of F.A. Hayek's theories of knowledge, holding that indescribable "soft knowledge" is the most critical to entrepreneurs. Without understanding the importance of soft knowledge, it is impossible to understand entrepreneurship. Chapter 2 uses three classic examples to explain what distinguishes entrepreneurial decisions from managerial/rational decisions and forms the core of the entire book. It is extremely important for our understanding of the market economy. Entrepreneurial decision-making is not scientific decision-making, it is not making a choice under given constraints, nor is it solely focused on profit. This re-understanding of entrepreneurial decisions implies that mainstream economics' externality theory, anti-monopoly theory, and corporate governance theory must all be revised. This also means industrial policy has lost its theoretical basis. Chapter 3 holds that the essence of central planning is a systematic negation of entrepreneurship. Big data (and even artificial intelligence) cannot displace entrepreneurial decision-making. The false belief that central planning is possible with big data is extremely naïve. Chapter 4 argues that envy and misunderstanding of knowledge are the two reasons for common prejudice and hostility toward entrepreneurs.

The four chapters (5–8) in the second part titled "The Entrepreneur in Market Theories" examine the reasons entrepreneurs should hold a central position in market theory. Chapter 5 points out the eight paradoxes of the neoclassical model. The neoclassical model is not a good market theory and its Market Failure Theory is wrong. The Austrian School of economics places entrepreneurs at the center of the market and has a better understanding of the market. A paradigmatic shift is needed for understanding the real market. Chapter 6 discusses the six standards of a good market theory. A good market theory should be a theory about how the economy develops and changes, not only a theory about how the market reaches equilibrium and stability. A market theory that lacks entrepreneurs and ignores the reputation mechanism is not a good theory. Chapter 7 discusses mainstream economics' misunderstanding of monopoly and competition. Mainstream economics' concepts of competition and monopoly are incorrect. Ignoring entrepreneurship is the primary reason for this misunderstanding. Entrepreneurship and competition are two sides of the same coin. Entrepreneurship is the best anti-monopoly law because it is more conductive to the breakdown of monopolies than any legal and regulatory provisions or policies. Chapter 8 discusses the relationship between entrepreneurial profit and income distribution. A misunderstanding of profit is largely responsible for the common misunderstanding of income distribution in the market economy. I argue that entrepreneurial profit is a responsibility system which makes possible trust between strangers in the market and value creation. With entrepreneurial profit, the market economy generates common prosperity and ordinary people are the biggest beneficiaries of the market economy. Competitiveness and entrepreneurship also imply a high mobility of income distribution, rather than deepening the gap between the rich and poor.

The four chapters (9–12) in the third part titled "The Uncertainty of Innovation and Industrial Policy" examines the entrepreneurial function in economic growth and its implications on industrial policy, from the viewpoint of innovation uncertainty. Chapter 9 first reviews the traditional theories (neoclassical growth theory and Keynesian economics) that economists use to explain economic growth. Their common shortcoming is ignoring the role of entrepreneurs. The chapter then outlines the entrepreneur-centric "Smith–Schumpeterian growth model" and the two functions of entrepreneurs (i.e. arbitrage and innovation), and finally uses this framework to analyze China's economic growth over the last few decades. Chapter 10 discusses the difference between arbitrage and innovation, the unpredictability of innovation, and the four uncertainties of innovation (referring to uncertainty of technological feasibility, uncertainty of commercial value, uncertainty of related technology, and uncertainty brought about by politics, culture, and policy). The uncertainty of innovation means there cannot be a unified and centralized plan for innovation. Instead, innovation relies on the special skills and expertise of various entrepreneurs, similar to the Eight Immortals in Chinese mythology. Chapter 11 further exemplifies the uncertainty and unpredictability of innovation through a detailed case study of the competitive process between airships and airplanes in the early stage of the aviation industry. This is the most detailed and complete case study in the book and is extremely illuminating for understanding entrepreneurship and innovation. Chapter 12 first clarifies the definition of industrial policy, then analyzes the challenges faced by industrial policy from the perspective of innovation uncertainty and the incentive mechanism. Overlooking entrepreneurship is the fatal weakness of industrial policy advocates. The basic conclusion of this chapter is that industrial policy is destined to fail.

The four chapters (13–16) in the fourth part titled "Institutional Ecology of Entrepreneurship" discuss the type of institutional ecology that is most beneficial to the emergence of entrepreneurs. Chapter 13 discusses the different allocation of entrepreneurial resources in government and in commerce and its impact on the economy and society. It also discusses the type of system that is most favorable to entrepreneurial talents choosing to engage in entrepreneurial activities. The evolutionary game methodology is then used to analyze the evolutionary equilibrium of entrepreneurial talent allocation and briefly analyzes the rise of China's grassroots entrepreneurs over the last 40 years. Chapter 14 analyzes the interdependency between entrepreneurs and capitalists, holding that the government can displace neither entrepreneurs nor capitalists. It is argued that the best corporate governance structure allows entrepreneurship to play the biggest role, as opposed to restricting professional managers. Chapter 15 discusses the relationship between the rule of law and innovation, holding that the rule of law protects rights, not interests. Protecting interests hinders innovation and entrepreneurship. This chapter compares Britain and France to show that the protection of rights is related to the rise and fall of a country. Innovation grows out of an ecosystem of free competition. Artificial prohibitions, or innovation zones, stifle it. Chapter 16 discusses the challenge for entrepreneurs brought about by value conflicts between different nations. The source of this challenge might be the government or the private sector. This chapter emphasizes the serious value conflicts that have always existed between China and the United States but obscured by the good wishes of both sides in the past. As opposing values have manifested themselves, both Chinese entrepreneurs and American entrepreneurs face bigger challenges than they did over the past 40 years.

Since I began engaging in economic research, entrepreneurs have always been the topic of my research. Appendix A of this book provides a brief outline of the course taken by my research on entrepreneurs and can be helpful for understanding the entire book.

Appendix B explains my process of understanding the Austrian School. I previously believed I was following the path cut by neoclassical economics but in fact I unconsciously deviated from this path early on. Entrepreneurship became the central topic of my research precisely for this reason. In spirit, I have been a disciple of Hayek for a long time.

This book is written for scholars, bureaucrats, and entrepreneurs. I hope my fellow colleagues in economics will read this book and reflect with me on the flaws in mainstream economics and correct misunderstandings of the market. Bureaucrats reading this book can have a little less "fatal conceit" and a little more reverence toward the market. Entrepreneurs reading this book will pursue less quick successes but more foresight. Entrepreneurs will only choose innovation if they pursue long-term interests. This book is also written for the general reader. I believe that any person who reads this book in earnest will have a new comprehension of entrepreneurship and the market economy, as well as a more rational judgment of economic policy.

This book is written in a way that blends theory and story. History intersects with the present. The theoretical views in this book are supported by relevant case studies. I avoided overly academic arguments. My goal in writing this way is to allow the reader to understand profound reason from relaxed reading.

We live in an era of rapid change. Grasping the unchanging things behind the phenomena is the best way to calmly deal with changes. I believe entrepreneurship is one of those things that creates change but itself does not change.

Weiying Zhang
February 1, 2023

PART I

The Nature of Knowledge and Entrepreneurship

1 | *Soft Knowledge and Entrepreneurship*

How big is the gap between an outstanding enterprise and a mediocre enterprise? It is less than 5%! I deeply believe the percentage is even smaller. This might seem a little sensationalist, but it is not. Remember that the genetic distance between humans and apes is less than 2% and the genetic distance between humans and most mammals is less than 5%. However, it is precisely this small gap that puts humans as the rulers of the earth, and not the other mammals.[1]

From this perspective, it is this small gap that leads to the success of some enterprises and to the failure of others. But what exactly causes this gap? I believe the most important cause is entrepreneurship. Entrepreneurship is crucial to success and without it many enterprises will definitely fail.

To understand this point, we must discuss the essence of knowledge.

Hard Knowledge and Soft Knowledge

During the 1930s Socialist Calculation Debate, F.A. Hayek described the essence of knowledge. He separated knowledge into two simple categories: scientific knowledge and practical knowledge (Hayek, 1937, 1945). We can simply refer to them as "hard knowledge" and "soft knowledge."[2] Hard knowledge refers to knowledge that can be disseminated using language, text, numbers, diagrams, formulas, and other ways. This type of knowledge is objective, anyone can obtain it, and it can be used intensively. Newtonian mechanics and Einstein's

---

[1] The shared genetic material of humans, chimps, and mammals actually refers neither to the number of chromosomes nor to the number of whole genes, but to the number of DNA "letters" (technically, base pairs) that match each other within the respective human, chimp, and mammal genes. See Dawkins (2009), chapter 10, p. 151.

[2] I prefer hard versus soft knowledge rather than scientific versus practical knowledge because not all hard knowledge is scientific and soft knowledge is more than practical knowledge.

theory of relativity are examples of hard knowledge. Soft knowledge refers to knowledge that cannot be disseminated using language, text, numbers, diagrams, formulas, and other ways. Know-how and intuition, for example, are subjective and personal. They can only be understood without words. This is the meaning of Laocius' saying: "The Dao that can be trodden is not the enduring and unchanging Dao. The name that can be named is not the enduring and unchanging name."

Michael Polanyi differentiated between tacit knowledge and explicit knowledge (Polanyi, 1958, 1959). *Tacit knowledge*, as opposed to formal, codified, or explicit knowledge, can be defined as skills, ideas, and experiences that are possessed by people but are not codified and may not necessarily be easily expressed. Explicit knowledge is know-what, and tacit knowledge is know-how. Scientific knowledge is explicit knowledge, but practical knowledge is primarily tacit knowledge. This means the person knows which actions to take but cannot tell which factors or parts constitute what he is doing or know if they are real or fake.[3]

The basic feature of soft knowledge is that it cannot be effectively transferred and copied but it is extremely important for decision making. It is especially important for creative decision making. Hayek told us people often forget that scientific knowledge is not the only knowledge relevant for decision making:

a little reflection will show that there is beyond question a body of very important but unorganized knowledge which cannot possibly be called scientific in the sense of knowledge of general rules: the knowledge of the particular circumstances of time and place ... The shipper who earns his living from using otherwise empty or half-filled journeys of tramp-steamers, or the estate agent whose whole knowledge is almost exclusively one of temporary opportunities, or the arbitrageur who gains from local differences of commodity prices – are all performing eminently useful functions based on special knowledge of circumstances of the fleeting moment not known to others. (Hayek, 1948[1980], p. 80)

Polanyi even believed that tacit knowledge is the "dominance principle" of all knowledge. Even the most formal and scientific

---

[3] For a detailed discussion of the differences between two types of knowledge related to economics, see Soto, de (2010). Collins (2010) develops a common conceptual language to bridge the concept's disparate domains by explaining explicit knowledge and classifying tacit knowledge (including relational tacit knowledge, somatic tacit knowledge, and social tacit knowledge).

knowledge follows a certain conscious or creative behavior, without exception, and embodies completely tacit knowledge (Polanyi, 1959, pp. 24–25). For example, Newton's universal gravitation and Einstein's theory of relativity are both hard knowledge, but why did other people not discover them? Newton and Einstein had tacit knowledge that others did not. We do not know how Newton discovered universal gravitation or how Einstein discovered the theory of relativity, and they themselves had no way of clearly explaining it to us.

Soft Knowledge Is Crucial for Entrepreneurial Decision Making

What is the difference between entrepreneurs and managers? Stated simply, the knowledge they base their decisions on is different. Entrepreneurial decision making primarily depends on soft knowledge whereas managerial decision making primarily depends on hard knowledge. Discussions of decision making in economics and most management studies are based on hard-knowledge decision making: "select among alternative" means to achieve given goals. Here, these goals and means can be clearly described, even quantifiable. This is far from real entrepreneurial decision making. True entrepreneurial decision making is not about selecting given means to satisfy given objectives. Instead, it is about actively and creatively seeking new goals and means. Entrepreneurship depends to a large extent on the ability to perceive and judge new goals and new means. In other words, managers use tools but entrepreneurs create tools. Managers achieve goals but entrepreneurs define goals.

From the perspective of decision making, if means and goals are given and similar, then with the same data all rational people will make the same choices. On students' tests and homework, there is only one standard answer for each question. If your answer is different from other students' answers, then either you are wrong, or they are. However, when making entrepreneurial decisions, even with the same data and hard knowledge, different entrepreneurs will make totally different choices. You cannot say *ex ante* who is right and who is wrong. The majority might be wrong.

Why? Because entrepreneurial decision making not only depends on data and hard knowledge, but also on soft knowledge. An individual's imagination, perception, and judgment related to market prospects, technological prospects, and resource availability are soft knowledge.

Judgment is not calculative. Entrepreneurial decision making is similar to a scientist's discovery but is different from so-called scientific decision making!

It is impossible to understand entrepreneurship without understanding the importance of soft knowledge. Hayek even believed it was the contempt for practical knowledge that, to a large extent, caused people to favor production over commerce:

> It is a curious fact that this sort of knowledge should today be generally regarded with a kind of contempt and that anyone who by such knowledge gains an advantage over somebody better equipped with theoretical or technical knowledge is thought to have acted almost disreputably. To gain an advantage from better knowledge of facilities of communication or transport is sometimes regarded as almost dishonest, although it is quite as important that society make use of the best opportunities in this respect as in using the latest scientific discoveries. (Hayek, 1948[1980], p. 81)

Israel Kirzner defined entrepreneurial knowledge as the "highest order of knowledge" – the ultimate knowledge needed to harness available information already possessed. "The kind of 'knowledge' required for entrepreneurship is 'knowing where to look for knowledge' rather than knowledge of substantive market information" (Kirzner, 1973, p. 68). He called it "alertness."

Entrepreneurship transcends data. Even though hard knowledge and data are very useful to entrepreneurs – both are certainly needed for entrepreneurial decision making – but that data can be obtained by anyone. True entrepreneurship certainly transcends this knowable data. Decisions made solely based on data are only scientific decision making, not entrepreneurial decision making. Entrepreneurs must see behind the knowledge and data, the things average people do not see. Also, different entrepreneurs will see the things very differently.

Traditional economics believes the primary function of the market is scarce resource allocation. Assuming that resources, technologies, and preferences are all given, then the next step is to select means according to objectives. Actually, the most important function of the market is not resource allocation, but instead is changing resources – creating new technologies, new products, and new forms of organization – to change the usefulness of resources or even obtain entirely new resources. These changes are what we call innovation. Social progress, to a large degree, is brought about by innovative entrepreneurs. This type of innovation cannot be provided by data. In terms of innovation, the help that data can provide is extremely limited.

The computer industry is an example. After International Business Machines (IBM) introduced the first computer for commercial use in 1954, computers progressed from large-scale computers, microcomputers, personal computers, laptops, and tablets to smart phones. These were disruptive innovations, but few of the new disruptors came from the original dominant producer.[4] IBM dominated large-scale computers but missed the microcomputer market. None of the microcomputer companies developed into the primary manufacturers of personal computers. Laptops were dominated by Japanese firms such as Sony, Sharp, and Toshiba. Why? Obviously, data was not a reason. The early companies did not have less data than the latecomers or focus less on customers' needs. Instead, the reason was that they judged incorrectly! Incorrect judgment is unrelated to the amount of data.

The reason for this is related to uncertainty. What does uncertainty mean? It means the future cannot be predicted based on past data. This is precisely the reason why we need entrepreneurs. If we can use data to predict the future, then we do not need entrepreneurs. We would only need managers, or even just robots. The entrepreneur's prediction of the future is not based on statistical models or calculation. Instead, it is based on imagination, alertness, self-confidence, judgment, and courage. Or, we should say that any decision that can be made with statistical models is not the function of entrepreneurs. Instead, that is the work of daily management. Therefore, it is no wonder entrepreneurial judgment cannot be understood by average people. During the Industrial Revolution, John Wilkinson, a British steel magnate, proposed building ships with iron. People believed he suffered from "Iron Madness" because getting iron to float on water was not in line with the "hard knowledge" of the time. Regardless of what other people said, Wilkinson created an iron boat and floated it on the River Severn. In a letter to friends, he said: "It answers all my expectations and has convinced the unbelievers who were nine hundred ninety-nine in one thousand. It will be only a nine days' wonder, and afterward a Columbus' egg."[5]

---

[4] See Christensen (1997), Forward. In the book, Christensen provides various detailed case studies to show that many disruptive innovations do not come from previous dominant firms.

[5] For Wilkson's innovative ideas of iron bridges and iron ship, see Mantoux (1964 [1929]), pp. 307–308.

How Did Ice Become a Mass Consumer Product?

Allow me to use a story related to ice to prove this point.[6]

Today, ice is an important consumer product. In Western countries, as soon as you enter a restaurant, the waiter will first bring you a glass of water with ice cubes. In ancient life, however, ice cubes were rare treasures. Usually, only emperors and dignitaries could afford to enjoy them. How did ice cubes become a mass consumer product? It was the creation of Frederic Tudor, an American businessman, in the first half of the nineteenth century.

Tudor was born in 1783 and came from a relatively wealthy Boston family. His father was a lawyer. Tudor's older brother suffered from arthritis, which caused extreme pain every winter. When he was 17, Tudor was asked by his father to accompany his older brother to the Caribbean, hoping the warmer weather would improve his brother's health. The result was counterproductive. The diseases caused by tropical heat and humid climate accelerated the death of his older brother.

Nevertheless, this disastrous journey gave Tudor a radical – even absurd – idea: if he could transport ice from the freezing north to the West Indies, he might be able to make money. Two years after the death of his older brother, Tudor went into business with his younger brother and cousin. They began transporting the worthless ice in the lake near their house to the hot south. In November of 1805, Tudor sent his younger brother to set up an outpost in Martinique. He also bought a brig called *Favorite* for $4,750 and began collecting ice blocks. In February of 1806, they set sail from Boston Harbor, loaded with ice, toward Martinique. After a three-week journey, the ice arrived in Martinique, but the venture proved to be a failure. The younger brother had not found a suitable place to store the ice, so it quickly melted. More trouble came from the residents of Martinique being disinterested in frozen blessings from foreign countries. They did not know what to use ice for. Tudor lost $4,500 in his first attempt, which was a large amount of money at the time.

This bleak situation repeated itself in the following years. Tudor also suffered the disastrous consequences of shipwrecks and customs embargoes. Everyone laughed at him. The *Boston Gazette* reported on his

---

[6] For the full story of ice becoming a consumer good and its implications, see Johnson (2014), chapter 2.

shipments of ice but told its readers it was "no joke!" In 1813, he was in so much debt that creditors had him thrown in prison. After he was released, he made another attempt. He managed to borrow $2,100 in 1815 and even borrowed $3,000 at 40% interest in 1816. He built a structure to store ice, then modified the design. He continuously improved the way ice was preserved during transportation and storage to reduce the rate of melting, which involved a series of innovations. Using three things that had almost zero cost on the market (ice, wood chips, and an empty boat heading south), Tudor was eventually commercially successful.

Fifteen years after his original hunch, Tudor's ice trade began to make profits. By the 1820s, his icehouses had spread all over the southern United States, filled with chilled water from New England. In the 1830s, his ice merchant ships traveled as far as Rio, Brazil, Madrid, Spain, and even Mumbai, India. By the time of his death in 1864, Tudor had accumulated a large fortune worth more than $200 million today. He was known as the "Ice King of Boston." Of course, later more and more people imitated him, and the ice trade became a new industry with considerable scale.

Ice becoming a mass product changed America's population and political map because the hot and humid south became more bearable. The ice trade also led to the invention of the refrigerator. A doctor in Apalachicola, Florida used ice transported from the north to cool down patients. A hurricane cut off his supply of ice, so he designed a machine that makes ice, thus inventing the refrigerator.

After the introduction of the refrigerator, man-made ice gradually replaced natural ice. Ice can maintain freshness, which made long-distance transportation of meat products profitable, which changed the role of Chicago in the United States. This also changed America's political map! (Johnson, 2014, chapter 2.)

The Four Points of Entrepreneurship

I used the above example to explain true entrepreneurship. If I must generalize qualities of entrepreneurship, I would like to emphasize the four points below.

Alertness to Profitable Opportunities

Entrepreneurs can sense opportunities where others do not. Many people traveled from the north to the Caribbean, but only an entrepreneur like Frederic Tudor recognized that transporting ice could be a profitable opportunity. Israel Kirzner even equated entrepreneurship with alertness: "The entrepreneurial element in the economic behavior of market participants consists ... in their alertness to previously unnoticed changes in circumstances which may make it possible to get far more in exchange for whatever they have to offer than was hitherto possible" (Kirzner, 1973, pp. 15–16).

Imagination of the Future

Imagination is the capability to see something that does not already exist or to think of a possibility that has not been recognized by others. Entrepreneurial innovation always starts with entrepreneurial imagination. The mass market for ice was imagined by Frederic Tudor. Joseph Schumpeter said that innovation is a new combination of production (or of different factors of production).[7] A product or technology is composed of something. A new combination is a type of imagination of the unseen future, not observation of the existing things. George Stephenson imagined a horse cart and a steam engine combined together, leading to the steam locomotive. Augusta Ada Lovelace was the daughter of English poet Lord Byron and is called the "mother of programming." In 1841, she wrote: "What is imagination? It is the combining faculty. It brings together things, facts, ideas, conceptions in new, original, endless, ever-varying combinations ... It is that which penetrates into the unseen worlds around us, the worlds of Science" (Isaacson, 2014, chapter 1, p. 8). When are most people the most "imaginative"? When they are sleeping, which is known as dreaming. To entrepreneurs, imagination is dreaming while awake and they believe that dreams can become reality.[8]

Simplification of Complexity

People often criticize economists for thinking issues are too simple. I believe entrepreneurs view issues as even simpler. Perhaps this is an

---

[7] Combination is the central concept in Schumpeter's theory of entrepreneurship. Schumpeter uses the term combination in two senses: There are new combinations as well as already existing combinations. New combinations are defined as innovations by Schumpeter. For a valuable discussion, see Becker, Knudsen, and Swedber (ed.) (2011), pp. 22–23. For the original idea of new combinations, see Schumpeter (1934), chapter 2.

[8] I will have more discussion on entrepreneurial imagination in Chapter 2.

important distinction between entrepreneurs and managers. Managers often view issues as more complex, but entrepreneurs view them as simple. A man becomes an entrepreneur precisely because he views issues as simple. A man that views issues as complex cannot possibly become an entrepreneur. Simplification encompasses a lot. It helps you grasp the essence of issues while at the same time giving you the courage to resolve issues. Frederic Tudor had the courage to start his ice business because, at the beginning, he thought he only needed to transport ice from Boston to the West Indies. What is so difficult about that? Why did Mr. Li Shufu dare to found the Geely Motor Company? Because he viewed automobiles in simple terms. He has two famous sayings. The first is: "What's so hard about a car? Isn't it just two motorcycles put together?" The second is: "Isn't a car just a sofa on four wheels?" These were the nature of cars as he understood them at the time. Simplified understanding led him toward automobile manufacturing, and he did not look back. Geely is now the most influential Chinese private-sector automobile manufacturer. I have heard many entrepreneurs say that if they had known how hard it would be, they would not have gone into business! But that is the entrepreneur!

Perseverance and Patience

Things appear simple but actually doing them is not that simple. All great entrepreneurs have experienced failure. Frederic Tudor spent two years in debtors' prison. Henry Ford tried three times and failed the first two. Without strong perseverance and great patience, you cannot become a successful entrepreneur. Probably we shall say that the entrepreneur is a person who pursues success even after failing over and over again, as shown by the case of Tudor. Even two years in jail did not defeat him. Chinese entrepreneur Feng Lun says that "greatness is boiled." Another Chinese entrepreneur, Mr. Duan Yongji, said that being in business means "holding on hard." Their sentiment reflects this characteristic.

Columbus' Egg

As a university professor, I must frankly admit that what school can teach students is mainly hard knowledge, knowledge that can be formalized, not soft knowledge that determines the fate of entrepreneurs. However, hard knowledge is also important. No entrepreneur can only rely on that 5% of soft knowledge to survive. No matter how that 5% plays out, the 95% is the foundation. There are three reasons for this. The first reason is entrepreneurs must also assume certain management functions. In reality, no entrepreneur only performs pure entrepreneurial functions. Although many management functions can be delegated, there are still some management functions that need to be undertaken by entrepreneurs. Moreover, finding suitable agents and supervising their behavior also requires some entrepreneurial qualities. The second reason is that soft knowledge is like a ship which rises with the tide. Soft knowledge floats on hard knowledge. Hard knowledge cannot ensure your success. But without hard knowledge, success will be very difficult. Especially in today's knowledge economy, if other people have knowledge that you do not, then you can hardly become a successful entrepreneur. The third reason is, if you accumulate more hard knowledge, then you can integrate it to improve your soft knowledge and improve your entrepreneurial ability. Without renewing hard knowledge, your soft knowledge will be exhausted.

One must remember that some soft knowledge may degenerate into hard knowledge as time goes on. The once uncodifiable may later be modeled and then everyone will be able to quickly learn it. So, imitating a successful entrepreneur cannot make an entrepreneur successful!

You might have heard the story of Columbus' egg. After Christopher Columbus returned from the Americas, he became a hero in the hearts of the Spanish people. The king and queen also regarded him as a guest of honor and made him an admiral. But some Spanish nobles were not happy with this. When God created the world, did he not create the land on the west side of the sea? Anyone that took a boat out to sea could find that piece of land! At a dinner, Columbus put an egg on the table and asked who could make it stand up. Many people tried, but no one succeeded. When the egg came back to Columbus' hands, he lightly tapped the tip flat and made it stand up.

This is entrepreneurship. However, if you were to use the same method to make the egg stand up after Columbus, it would not count as entrepreneurship!

2 | *Understanding Entrepreneurial Decisions*

People have much to say about entrepreneurship. They speak of the adventurous spirit, curiosity, creativity, self-confidence, decisiveness, paranoia, commitment, non-conformance, heroism, perseverance, etc. We are familiar with these descriptions of entrepreneurship.

After studying entrepreneurs for more than 30 to 40 years, I realized that to understand what true entrepreneurship is we must understand what entrepreneurship is NOT. This is particularly true for those who are accustomed to the rational decision model thinking. In this chapter, I will focus the discussion on what distinguishes entrepreneurial decisions from the rational decisions. I will start with some examples, analyze them, and then draw some conclusions I believe are universal. Each example I discuss is representative of reality.

Entrepreneurial Decision Making Is Not Scientific Decision Making

Paul Otellini (1950–2017) was Intel Corporation's fifth Chief Executive Officer (CEO). The first three CEOs of Intel joined the company when it was founded in 1968. They can be called true entrepreneurs. Their personalities complemented each other, and they turned Intel into the "engine" of the computer and information technology industries. Among them, Robert Noyce was one of the inventors of the integrated circuit and Gordon Moore was a proponent of "Moore's Law."[1]

In the Noyce era (1968–1975), Intel developed the microprocessor and manufactured random-access memory (RAM) and dynamic random-access memory (DRAM). In the Moore era (1975–1987), Intel was still a specialized manufacturer of DRAM, but in the face of

---

[1] For the story of founding Intel and complementarity of the first three CEOs' personalities, see Isaacson (2014), chapter 5.

Japanese competition, Intel rapidly lost market share. In 1984, Intel's market share dropped to 1.3%. At that point, the company decided to re-focus on microprocessors and decided to exit the DRAM business. In the Andrew Grove era (1987–1998), Intel focused on the personal computer (PC) processor business. The company, as a result, achieved tremendous growth. Intel and Microsoft became dominant in the PC industry. However, the company's business strategy became too rigid.

When Grove retired, he promoted Craig Barrett to CEO. Barrett had been Grove's right-hand man. He was a typical professional manager that had served as Chief Operating Officer (COO) for a long time, and was called "Mr. Inside." When Barrett came into the role in 1998, the Internet and cell phones were becoming common. Barrett began to acquire other companies on a large scale in an attempt to become a cell phone and Internet company. However, he failed and resigned in 2005.

Paul Otellini was also a "Mr. Inside" when he transitioned from COO to CEO as Barrett's replacement. Intel's performance was impressive during the Otellini era. Revenue increased from $38.8 billion to $54 billion. Surprisingly, on November 19, 2012, Otellini announced he would step down in May of the following year. He was only 62 years old, which was younger than the normal retirement age of 65 at Intel. Additionally, Otellini announced he was stepping down before a replacement had been identified, a first in the history of Intel.

The primary reason for Otellini's sudden departure was misjudging the response to the smart phone and tablet business. In an interview with *The Atlantic* magazine during his time as CEO, he stated that he had decided against the opportunity to be the supplier for the first-generation iPhone.

The story goes like this. In 2007 and 2010, Apple released the iPhone and iPad, respectively. Apple first considered contracting Intel to produce the first-generation iPhone's processor. Steve Jobs contacted Otellini and offered to buy processors for $10 each but not one cent more.

Otellini organized a team consisting of engineering, marketing, and finance experts to do a feasibility study. They calculated a series of estimates. Given a specific price, what production levels guaranteed profit? This was determined by iPhone sales. Intel's team ran the calculations and believed the massive amount of funding required to develop processors for the iPhone would cause big losses if each one was sold for just $10.

Otellini accepted the advice of his subordinates and turned down Apple's proposed deal. Apple then turned to Samsung. Samsung's CEO accepted the offer without hesitation. As a result, Samsung's rapid growth took it from tenth place to third place in the foundry industry. It also developed its own smart phone, the Samsung Galaxy, to compete with Apple. Apple later sued Samsung over intellectual property issues.

Intel's initial cost and sales estimates were wrong. iPhone production levels exceeded the Intel team's projections by over one hundred times. Intel's regrets came too late![2]

The point I want to make with this story is: *Entrepreneurial decision making is not scientific decision making!*

Entrepreneurial decisions are different from managerial decisions. Using the phrases of Rindova and Courtney (2020), managerial decision making is an adapting posture (based on scientific epistemologies focusing on truth seeking), while entrepreneurial decision making is a shaping posture (based on design epistemologies focusing on truth making).

Decision making in economics and management studies is managerial decision making, not entrepreneurial decision making. Managerial decision making is scientific decision making, which is based on data and calculation. Given data, the optimal choice is singular. Entrepreneurial decision making is based on alertness, intuition, imagination, and judgment.[3] People will have different thoughts and judgments about the same data, so choices will be different (Lachmann, 1986). Therefore, scientific decision making can form a consensus and has a standard answer but entrepreneurial decision making is non-consensus and does not have a standard answer. In other words, decisions with standard answers are not entrepreneurial decisions.

We can use tests or curriculum as examples to explain this point. On a test, you have the choice, such as A, B, C, or D, but there is only

---

[2] For a detailed description of Intel's development and misjudgment on the iPhone processor, see Takashi Yunogami's (2013) book published in Japanese by Bungeishunjū Ltd. A Chinese-language version was made available by the China Machine Press in 2015. Also see Chris Miller (2022), chapter 33.

[3] Different scholars of entrepreneurship emphasize different aspects of entrepreneurship. For instance, Kirzner (1973) emphasizes "alertness"; Shackle (1979a, b) emphasizes "imagination"; and Casson (1982) and Foss and Klein (2020) emphasize "judgment." In my view, these different aspects are complementary, rather than substitutive. Which one is more important depends on what kind of decision the entrepreneur makes. For innovation, imagination is the most important.

one correct answer. Imagine taking the test and then afterward asking your classmates how they answered. If most classmates chose A, but you chose C, you will feel conflicted because you are likely incorrect.

From the perspective of entrepreneurial decision making, the answer the majority of people believe is correct might actually be incorrect. We see that the most important decision making by outstanding entrepreneurs is often not originally acknowledged by the majority of people or is even considered preposterous. The decisions the majority of people agree with can only be scientific decision making; they certainly are not entrepreneurial decision making. Of course, we cannot say the opposite: that decision opposed by most people is certainly correct. What I mean to say is that entrepreneurs will not make decisions according to majority opinion. Of course, the opinion of the entrepreneur might be incorrect. Correctness is determined by an *ex-post* test in the market. We have no way to judge correctness before the future arrives. Majority opinion cannot be the standard for judgment.

I once had a student who first joined a multinational company with a high salary after graduation. One day he reached out to me and said he wanted to start his own business. He sought out my opinion. I said I did not have a way to determine if the idea would work or not. I asked him: "What do your parents think?" He replied, "My parents are totally opposed to it." I told him he might as well try! In my view, decisions that parents agree with are likely not entrepreneurial decisions. This student made the jump and is successful up to this point.

I once lectured at the Heima ("black horse") Seminar for young entrepreneurs. When I arrived, they were having a business plan competition, so I sat down and listened. Zhou Hongyi, founder of Qihoo 360 and an already successful entrepreneur, was evaluating a young entrepreneur's business plan. I heard a very negative attitude toward the feasibility of the idea. When I spoke, I said: "Young man, Zhou saying your idea was unfeasible does not mean your idea is unfeasible." When Zhou started his business, other people told him it was unfeasible. Those people at that time were more famous than even Zhou is today.[4]

---

[4] Zhou Hongyi repeatedly said "almost every idea I proposed since I started my businesses was opposed by all others." His earlier company "3721," the first internet service provider in China, was taken over by Yahoo! in 2004. Zhou was then appointed as CEO of Yahoo! China. He resigned 18 months later and started up Qihoo 360 which IPO'd on the New York Stock Exchange in

As German scholar and entrepreneur Dr. Rainer Zitelmann (2018) observed, entrepreneurs often do not act according to assumptions about rationality in classical economic theories. They do not base their decisions on probability or complex theoretical assumptions, but instead on intuition and perception.

The reason data and calculation do not play a key role in entrepreneurial decision making is because entrepreneurial decision making faces a high degree of uncertainty. So-called uncertainty refers to the subjective, unknown, and unique future affairs faced by entrepreneurial decision making. There are no statistical samples, probability distribution, or objective data available (Knight, 1921). In the terminology of economics, the state space – the set of states of the world that determine the consequences of an action – is incomplete. Under such an uncertain situation, as Keynes famously put it, "there is no scientific basis on which to form any calculable probability. We simply do not know" (Keynes, 1937, p. 214). Economists equate "uncertainty" with "risk" and then equate "risk" with statistical variance.[5] This is seriously misleading.

Further, uncertainty is not exogenous, but endogenous. It is influenced by current and future choices of various interactive players, not pre-determined by what happened in the past that is just waiting to be revealed. The same action brings about countless possible consequences. As pointed out by Shackle, "the sequel of any present choice of action which [a person] makes will be partly shaped by choices made, by others or himself, in time-to-come" so that the future "waits to be created, to be originated, by choices to be made, now and in time-to-come, by himself and others" (Shackle, 1979a, pp. 9, 27). In other words, the future is not only uncertain, but also indeterminate.[6]

March 2011. For the story of Zhou's business career, see *Subverter: Autobiography of Zhou Hongyi* .

[5] Although Knight distinguishes uncertainty from risk as early as 1921, mainstream economists still treat uncertainty as risk with probability distribution.

[6] Shackles (1979a) says, "Uncertainty conveys the suggestion that there is a determinate future, preexisting choice and independent of it, needing only to be found out ... It seems plain that if the future merely waits to be revealed, business of choice is merely a response to signals, a response which may be uncomprehending, even groping and blundering, but which is destined nonetheless to lead things into course laid down from some once-and-for-all-unique creation of history as an entirety" (p. 27). For Shackle, the future is indeterminate, and it is indeterminacy that "has its seat in men's power of

Because of the uncertainty and indeterminacy of the future, not only is the market a discovery procedure that continuously obtains information – instead of solving equations with given data – as said by F.A. Hayek (1978), the market is more like a creative process (Alvarez and Barney, 2007, 2010; Buchanan and Vanberg, 1991). It is the application of human imagination and creative potential (Shackle, 1979a, b; Littlechild, 1979). Entrepreneurs do not make decisions with available data. Instead, they discover data, imagine the possible future, and create things that did not exist before. Data for horse-drawn carriages is useless for predicting the automobile. Sailboat data is unlikely to tell us whether iron boats are feasible. Iron boats and automobiles were largely imagined by entrepreneurs like John Wilkinson and Carl Benz.

Under uncertainty and indeterminacy, imagination plays a vital role in entrepreneurial decisions. Indeterminacy implies that choice can make a difference in the history to come. What a person will choose depends on what that person imagines. "Choice that begets action cannot be induced by the reported result of that action, only by the imagination of its possible result. Many rival such imagination will form skein of conceived sequels of the action" (Shackle, 1979b, p. 25).

Imagination is not a prediction of the future, but a blueprint for the future; not what might be, but what should be; not possibility that will be determined by some external factors, but possibility that is dependent upon your choices; not something to be discovered, but something to be created; not something for you to adapt to, but something for you to move toward. For example, when Henry Ford imagined a mass market for automobiles in the early 1900s, he meant to make it happen. By cutting production costs substantially through standardizing parts and using the assembly line, he made automobiles affordable for ordinary families. Without his imagination, automobiles would not have become a mass market, and it would have been impossible for 60% of American households to have a family car by 1930. Similarly,

imagination" (p. 20). It is very unfortunate that Shackle's ideas of indeterminacy and imaginations are ignored by almost all economists, even including most Austrian School economists. For interesting discussions in economics literature, see Littlechild (1979), Buchanan and Vanberg (1991), Lachmann (1976, 1977), and Lewis (2017). For discussions in more recent management literature, see Griffin and Grote (2020), Arikan, Arikan, and Koparan (2020), Packard and Clark (2020), Rindova and Courtney (2020), Berglund, Bousfiha, and Mansoori (2020), and Lampert, Kim, and Polidoro (2020).

when Bill Gates imagined there would be a personal computer on every person's desk, he intended to make it a reality by creating the software industry.[7]

We must differentiate between entrepreneurial decision making and managerial decision making. I do not dismiss the importance of data and scientific decision making in the management of firms. Actually, in my view, more than 95% of decisions in well-established firms are ordinary management decisions that can rely on the scientific decision-making methods learned in management schools. However, entrepreneurial decisions that determine the fate of the firm are different from managerial decision making and are not scientific. For example, whether a restaurant should be opened in a specific location is an entrepreneurial decision. How many ingredients the restaurant should procure every day and how many cooks and servers should be employed are managerial decisions. Managerial decision making can be done with the help of data and calculation, whereas entrepreneurial decision making relies more on alertness, intuition, imagination, and judgment. Managerial decisions can be delegated to non-entrepreneurial people. In large hierarchical companies, people in top leadership positions primarily make entrepreneurial decisions while people in middle and lower management positions primarily make managerial decisions. Therefore, for high-level leaders, alertness, intuition, imagination, and judgment are critical. For middle managers, data and calculation are critical.

We must acknowledge that entrepreneurs in reality often simultaneously hold multiple roles, such as being a manager while at the same time being an entrepreneur. In addition to entrepreneurial decision making, they must also do a lot of managerial decision making. However, entrepreneurs must first determine what is an entrepreneurial decision and what is a managerial decision. Confusion between them and misjudgment can lead to fatal mistakes.

In the previous case, Otellini's error was to mistake an entrepreneurial decision for a managerial decision. Jobs' launch of the iPhone was a typical entrepreneurial decision. Accordingly, supplying the iPhone processor was also a typical entrepreneurial decision. It required

---

[7] Lecuna (2021) provides a very interesting and insightful case study on the role imagination plays in entrepreneurial decisions. Also see Orole, Gadar, and Nor (2012).

intuition, imagination, and judgment, not the calculations of corporate finance and marketing personnel. Samsung accepted Apple's offer without hesitation, precisely based on the entrepreneurial intuition of Samsung's chairman, Lee Kun-hee. When Otellini was interviewed by *The Atlantic*, he said: "My gut told me to say yes." This might be second guessing. The fact is he believed the data. He did not act according to his intuition. This is the difference between managers and entrepreneurs.

Entrepreneurial Decision Making Is Not Finding a Solution within Given Constraints, It Is Changing the Constraints Themselves

Du Sha is an old friend of mine. We first met in February 1982 at the National Conference on Quantitative Economics. At that time, he was a soon-to-graduate quantitative economics graduate student at Nanjing University and I had just started my M.A. in Economics at Northwest University in Xi'an. In September 1984, we met again at the Mount Mogan Conference. At that time, he was an associate professor at Nankai University in Tianjin. After the Mount Mogan Conference, he became more and more well-known. He organized the Second Annual Young Economic Reform Conference in Tianjin during the spring of 1985 and co-founded the academic journal *Young Economist Forum*. He became the guest of honor of Li Ruihuan (then the Mayor of Tianjin) to guide the city's economic reform and opening.

At the end of 1985, he participated in the "State Council Working Group on Study in the United States" organized by the State Education Commission. He visited America for 45 days, touring the country, speaking to Chinese students, and was well received. After returning to China, he was invited to lecture at many universities. However, the contents of his lectures made the people responsible at the State Education Council uncomfortable. When he applied to go to Britain for a visit, the procedures "got stuck." In a fit of anger, he decided to go into business.

In 1987, Du went to Shenzhen, the forefront of China's reform and opening. By the end of 1988, his company had accumulated three million yuan. He decided to invest two million yuan in the Hong Kong foreign exchange market. Within three months, he profited two million Hong Kong dollars. His confidence exploded and he was determined to be a financier, the George Soros of China.

With help from friends, he borrowed money from banks and did more and more foreign exchange transactions. He bet the Japanese yen would appreciate. However, he did not foresee the turbulence in Japanese politics that resulted in the Japanese yen depreciating against the US dollar from 145.69 to 158.46. After he was forced to close his position, not only were his profits gone, he also owed HK$14 million.

Du slipped into depression. He even thought about jumping off the 50-storey Guomao Building but lost his nerve. He had to earn enough money within 10 months to repay his HK$14 million debt. He owed money to the banks and his friends. Money from the banks was borrowed through relationships with friends. If he did not repay the money, not only would he offend and implicate his friends, he might also go to jail. How could he make that much money in such a short amount of time?

One afternoon in the summer of 1989, he was sitting on his bed watching television. Footage of Deng Xiaoping and Mikhail Gorbachev shaking hands came on the screen to announce the normalization of Sino-Soviet relations. Du suddenly had the idea that the normalization of Sino-Soviet relations would start with cultural exchange. If he could bring the Soviet State Circus to perform in China, he might be able to make a lot of money and repay his HK$14 million debt. In 1957, when he was nine years old, he saw the Soviet State Circus perform in Beijing. It was an unforgettable performance. The then Chinese leaders like Mao Zedong, Liu Shaoqi, and Zhou Enlai were also in the audience. At the time, Sino-foreign cultural exchanges were all handled between governments. A sole proprietor like Du could not take part, but he was still eager to try.

On the second day of the Lunar New Year in 1990, he took the train to Beijing. His goal was to have the Ministry of Culture formally invite the Soviet State Circus for a tour of China and give the business to him. With the help from the right relationships, he finally got to meet You Qi, Director of the Overseas Cultural Communication Bureau of the Ministry of Culture. He told Director You that allowing him to organize the event while Sino-Soviet relations were rapidly improving would not only provide the Ministry of Culture an opportunity to perform, but also save a lot of money for the Ministry of Culture while creating a new form of cultural exchange. From the Ministry of Culture's perspective, it meant killing three birds with one stone.

Director You was enthusiastic about the opportunity, but still hesitant. It would be great if Du could succeed, but if he lost money and canceled halfway through, then Director You's reputation within the Ministry would be ruined. She asked for a safeguard.

Du understood what the director meant. He blurted out an offer to provide an irrevocable guarantee of US$500,000 if the Ministry of Culture allowed him to organize the tour. With that guarantee, the director and the Ministry of Culture had nothing to worry about.

One week later, Director You called Du to tell him that the Vice-Minister of the Ministry of Culture, Gao Zhanxiang, had approved the recommendation to invite the Soviet State Circus to tour China, fully undertaken by Du's company. The premise was that he had to deliver the US$500,000 guarantee.

Where could he go to get the US$500,000 guarantee? Not only was Du broke, he was also in debt. No bank would be willing to issue this type of guarantee. His only hope was to ask Li Xiyuan, the general manager of China's Leasing Company. Du had sold a house to Li in the past, so they knew each other.

After returning to Shenzhen, Du paid a visit to Li. Du told Li that he had invited the Soviet State Circus to tour at 100 venues in China and could give the best advertising spots to his company. Li asked how much the advertising fee was. Du told Li he did not have to pay advertising fees, he only needed to provide him with an irrevocable guarantee of US$500,000. After thinking it over, Li agreed. During the conversation, Du learned that Li had also seen the Soviet State Circus perform in Beijing in 1957 and it had left a deep impression on him. In 1988, Li was once invited to the "Li Ning Sports Farewell Performance" which was planned and organized by Du. So, Li had some basic trust in Du's organizational ability.

With the US$500,000 guarantee, the Ministry of Culture was taken care of!

Where was the circus? Since 1957, Du had not seen the Soviet State Circus perform, nor had he been to the Soviet Union. He had to go to the Soviet Union to invite the Soviet State Circus, but at that time the Soviet Union was still a socialist planned economy. It could not possibly accept the invitation of a Chinese private entrepreneur. Only the involvement of the Ministry of Culture could solve the problem. The Ministry of Culture agreed to organize a delegation to the Soviet Union, but Du had to arrange for the foreign exchange expenses.

Du's only option was to approach Li again to tell him he was a member of the delegation to the Soviet Union, but unfortunately he had to cover the cost of international travel for the delegation. Li was happy to be a member of the delegation to the Soviet Union, and the cost was not too high, so he agreed.

After arriving in Moscow, the negotiation became a psychological war. There were about 80 large and small circuses among the best throughout the Soviet Union, but international performances were all arranged through one entity. The negotiation centered around the price per performance. The Soviet negotiator wanted US$5,000 for each performance and nothing less. Du counter-offered CNY10,000 per performance and nothing more. (At that time, the official exchange rate would have valued CNY10,000 at about US$2,100.) The first negotiation went nowhere. On the morning of the day the delegation was scheduled to return to China, the Soviet negotiator dropped the price to US$3,500, but Du insisted on CNY10,000. The deadlock continued.

On the flight back to China, everyone but Du was despondent. An official from the Ministry of Culture complained that he had not taken the reduced price, so the trip was a waste. Du was silent. He knew that without performances, the circus would not have wages to pay, so they would accept his offer. Before leaving Moscow, he left a message for his counterpart: They had one week to consider. If they accepted the CNY10,000 offer, send him a fax.

Would the counterpart accept his offer? Du had no idea.

After returning to Beijing, Du was restless. He went to the Ministry of Culture every day from 9:00 a.m to 5:00 p.m. to wait for the fax. The days passed with no updates. The deadline was on Friday at 5:00 p.m., but there was still no answer. Despaired, he returned to his hotel.

After a simple dinner, Du laid on his bed listless. Suddenly, he realized that Beijing is five hours ahead of Moscow. His counterpart had not gotten off work, so maybe there was still hope. He hurried back to the Ministry of Culture.

At 9:45 p.m. in Beijing, which was 4:45 p.m. in Moscow, the fax machine printed out a message. His counterpart accepted the CNY10,000 offer. Du was almost tearful with excitement.

After more than a month of preparation, the 83 handsome and beautiful performers, 12 beasts, and 10 large animals that composed the "Soviet State Circus" entered China at Manzhouli. The great circus spent three months in China and toured seven cities to give 97 performances. The last performance was held at the Beijing Worker's Stadium and all seats were occupied. To promote a friendly relationship between China and the Soviet Union, Jiang Zemin, Li Peng, Li Ruihuan, and other party and national leaders made an appearance to watch the performance. Du proudly mentions that the party and national leader's tickets were bought by the Central Affairs Office. Throughout all 97 performances, he never gave away a single ticket. It was not due to his reluctance, but instead it was his marketing strategy.

After the performances ended, Du calculated that after deducting all costs, he had profited CNY15 million. At that time, he had less than one month to repay his debts. He flew back to Shenzhen and repaid his debt. Then, he took his residual money back to Tianjin to restart his own real estate and retailing businesses.[8] He became a famous billionaire 10 years later.

I use this story to say: *Entrepreneurial decision making is not finding a solution with given constraints; it is changing the constraints themselves.*

According to the standard economic theories, so-called rational decision making refers to maximizing the objective function under specified constraints. From the firm's perspective, constraints include given resources, given technology, given consumer preferences (demand), and given institutions and policies, so profit is the objective function. Given these constraints, decision making is just a mathematical optimization problem. How large the profit objective an entrepreneur can achieve is entirely determined by constraints; totally unrelated to the entrepreneur's ability. The constraints are exogenous; entrepreneurs have no way to change them. Therefore, decision making is a computational program.

This type of rational-person decision-making model is a far cry from entrepreneurial decision making in the real world. From the perspective of entrepreneurial decision making in the real world, constraints are never given but can be changed. Resources, technology, and consumer preferences are not given and even the rules of the game can be changed. Of course, not all of the constraints can be changed, but entrepreneurs will never consider all constraints to be given and

---

[8] Du Sha's autobiography, Du (2018), was published by the Hong Kong Open Page Publishing Company Limited in 2018. In that Chinese-language edition, the details of his story inviting the Soviet State Circus to China can be found on pages 413–498.

unchangeable. The difference in entrepreneurial ability between individuals is to a large degree a reflection of differences in the ability to change constraints. A person that does not have the ability to change constraints cannot possibly become a successful entrepreneur. So-called innovation in essence is changing constraints to do what appears to be impossible.

Du's success came from changing the constraints he faced, not making selections under given constraints. Sino-foreign cultural exchanges were inter-governmental affairs, but he turned it into a private commercial activity. This is a change in the rules of the game. The Soviet State Circus was a state asset of the Soviet Union, but he turned it into a tool to make money by inviting it to tour China. This is a change in resources. He also changed the preferences of Chinese consumers. The Chinese audience originally did not have a "demand" for Soviet State Circus performances. By bringing the Soviet State Circus to China and implementing unique marketing strategies, Du created their demand for it.

We can use the phrase "you can't make bricks without straw" to explain the difference between entrepreneurs and others. For ordinary people, straw is a precondition for making bricks. If you asked them to make bricks, they would ask where the straw is. Without straw, they would be helpless. Entrepreneurs do not need "straw" to make "bricks." If they believe there are people that want bricks, and can make money from selling them, then they will think of a way to acquire straw. Even if straw is not readily available, they can convince people to produce it. Du did not have a circus before organizing a tour. He imagined that a tour can make money, so he went to Beijing and Moscow. He did something ordinary people perceived to be impossible.

People that want to change constraints are certainly confident in their own ideas. Pessimists do not have the impulse to change the *status quo*. Entrepreneurs are more optimistic than ordinary people. They believe "dreams" can come true and "assumptions" can become reality.

In fact, entrepreneurs are often excessively optimistic (Zitelmann, 2018, pp. 76–80). For example, a survey of 2,994 American start-up entrepreneurs found that 81% of respondents believed their individual success rate was above 70%, and 33% of respondents believed their own failure rate was zero, even though two-thirds of new businesses faced the problems of insolvency within four years (Cooper, Woo, and Dunkelberg, 1988).

It is precisely excessive optimism that makes entrepreneurs do many things (such as major innovation) that are impossible from the perspective of rational calculation. Venture capital and private equity investors tell us that having five out of 100 investments succeed is pretty good. If there was only a 5% chance of succeeding at something, I believe the vast majority of people would not be willing to do it. Entrepreneurs' confidence in success is much greater than the *ex-post* statistical probability. I often hear from successful entrepreneurs that if they had known how hard it would be, they would not have started. Underestimating challenges is common for entrepreneurs but it is also a major reason why entrepreneurs become entrepreneurs.

Further, entrepreneurs must often change more than one constraint. Multiple constraints are often inter-dependent. To get A, we must first get B; to get B, we must first get C; to get C, we must first get A. This is similar to building a tripod; the three poles must be put together at the same time.

A popular joke helps to explain this point. A man named Johnson told the head of the World Bank to nominate his son to be vice president. The World Bank chief asked him why. Johnson said his son was about to become Bill Gates' son-in-law. Johnson also proposed Bill Gates' daughter should marry his son because he was about to become vice president at the World Bank. If both the World Bank chief and Bill Gates believe Johnson, then his son will become the vice president of the World Bank and Bill Gates' son-in-law. After the fact, he did not lie to anyone!

For entrepreneurs to turn their imagination into reality, they must have the ability to change other's beliefs, to persuade others to do the things hoped for. In Steve Jobs' case, this ability was called a "reality distortion field."[9] In fact, according to my observation, all outstanding entrepreneurs must have this kind of reality distortion field ability, even if there is a difference in degrees. In my interactions with Du Sha, I felt his "reality distortion field." I remember that in 2004, I made a rule for myself not to be an independent director of any company. I did decline invitations from several large companies and financial institutions. But one day, Du burst into my office after we had not seen each other for several years. As soon as he sat down, he said he wanted me to join his board of directors. I told him it was

---

[9] See Isaacson (2011), chapter 11.

impossible. I could not break the rule I had set for myself. He then asked me not to refuse so quickly. He opened his laptop and talked to me about his company. After a while, I broke down and accepted his invitation. I have always felt like I was a person that dared to say "NO," but his reality distortion field was just too powerful.

Uncertainty means that better entrepreneurial ability cannot control all external factors. Even if entrepreneurial activity succeeds in changing constraints, it might fail. After success, people say the entrepreneur is a hero; after failure, he is a swindler! If Du could not make HK$14 million in 10 months to pay back his debt, the friends and banks that loaned him money would think he was a swindler. If he could not get the US$500,000 guarantee, the Ministry of Culture would think he was a swindler. If he could not bring the Soviet State Circus to China, the Ministry of Culture and his friend Li would think he was a swindler. Even if the Soviet State Circus toured China, but he did not make enough money to repay his debts, then he would still be thought of as a swindler! Luckily, his three poles came together at the same time. Of course, his success did not rely primarily on luck, but his entrepreneurship.

The difference between a swindler and an entrepreneur is entrepreneurs make a promise because they believe they will fulfill it. Swindlers want to steal other people's property from the beginning and know they will be discovered in the end. Success for swindlers means not being discovered until the end. Success for entrepreneurs means never betraying their identity.

Elon Musk is a living example. This entrepreneur, who immigrated from South Africa to the United States, became famous for Tesla's electric vehicles and SpaceX's successful launch of the Falcon Heavy rocket. Many people consider him a contemporary entrepreneur even greater than Steve Jobs. But Musk's Tesla and SpaceX have both been on the brink of bankruptcy multiple times. SpaceX's Falcon 9 rocket failed three times in a row. By the successful fourth launch, the company was struggling to pay its employees. Tesla had more than 1,200 orders, taking in tens of millions of dollars, but quickly ran out of money and was only able to deliver fewer than 50 vehicles. Musk risked jail time for misappropriating other people's property. In May 2008, thetruthaboutcars.com started a "Tesla Death Watch" column. One day there were even 50 articles about how Tesla would die. In October 2008, one of the company's employees even wrote an open letter condemning the company's deception of customers. Looking at the company's financial situation, Musk himself doubted that the car could go on. His wife began to see his life as a Shakespearean tragedy. At that time, the original investors also lost confidence and were unwilling to put more money into that bottomless pit. Some investors even wanted to remove Musk from Tesla. In order to convince investors to change their minds, Musk had to bluff that he could borrow another $40 million from SpaceX to complete a round of financing. In fact, SpaceX's financial situation was also perilous. After many twists and turns, SpaceX finally received a payment of $1.6 billion from the National Aeronautics and Space Administration (NASA) on December 23, 2008, bringing Musk to tears. The money was a pre-payment to SpaceX for 12 trips to the International Space Station. Without these funds, the company would have had to declare bankruptcy in a matter of hours. Musk would have gone down in history as a fraud, not the outstanding entrepreneur that people admire.[10]

Profit Is Not the Sole Objective of Entrepreneurial Decision Making

Cyrus West Field (1819–1892) was an outstanding American entrepreneur and financier in the nineteenth century, best known for laying the first trans-Atlantic telegraph cable.

Field was the son of a clergyman who made his money in paper manufacturing while still in his youth. At the age of 34, he sold his business and retired. For a man like him, having nothing to do made him feel empty. He came in contact with Frederick Newton Gisborne, an English-born Canadian engineer. Gisborne was attempting to lay an underwater telegraph cable between New York and Newfoundland in order to get information about the arrival of ships a few days in advance. When the project was halfway complete, the funds ran out. Gisborne went to New York to seek financial support.

Field knew nothing about cables and had never even seen one. However, he was attracted by Gisborne's project and decided to get involved. Field had bigger ideas than Gisborne. Field asked Gisborn why he was only laying the cable to Newfoundland and not continuing all the way to Ireland to connect the Americas and Europe.

---

[10] For the fascinating story of Elon Musk, see Vance (2015).

That was a crazy idea. The first underwater cable became operational between Dover, England, and Calais, France in November 1851. Within a few years, cables had been laid between Great Britain and Ireland, Denmark and Sweden, and Corsica and Mainland France. However, these cables were only a few dozen kilometers long. The difference between those cables and a trans-Atlantic cable is like the difference between a bungalow and a skyscraper.

More than 2,000 nautical miles separate Newfoundland and Ireland. How deep is the Atlantic? How much pressure is there at that depth? Can the cables withstand that pressure? Will the deep ocean's magnetic field cause the current to be lost? The answers were unclear. Although "gutta-percha" had been invented a few years prior, there were no reliable insulating materials or accurate measuring instruments. Even if these technical issues were resolved, that much cable made of copper and iron would weigh more than 9,000 tons. Where could they get a giant ship that can carry such cables? At that time, the largest ship had a carrying capacity of only 5,000 tons. Where can they get a high-power generator to transmit the current continuously over a distance that takes a ship two or three weeks to cross?

Therefore, when Field proposed his idea, engineers and other big figures opposed it. Western Union, America's largest telegraph company at the time, disregarded Field's plan. They planned to lay a cable from Alaska to Siberia through the Bering Sea, and then connect the Americas and Europe using above-ground telegraph wires. After all, the narrowest part of the Bering Strait is only 53 nautical miles wide. The technology for that short distance was mature and there were experiences to learn from.

However, Field was fascinated with the idea and the difficulties did not intimidate him. He devoted all his energy and wealth to operating the Atlantic Telegraph Company. He used his persistence and eloquence to persuade some wealthy people in the United States and Britain to join him. His list of shareholders included William Thackeray, the famous British novelist and author of the novel *Vanity Fair*, and Anne Byron, the widow of Lord Byron. These people invested in him out of moral zeal and had no objective to make money. Field sought out experts for technical support. Within the span of a few years, he crossed the Atlantic 31 times. He persuaded the US and British governments to lease him one warship each to help with construction. These were the largest ships they could get at the time.

After everything was ready, on August 5, 1857, Field personally led the warship USS *Niagara*, loaded with half of the cables and hundreds of sailors, and set out from Valentia, Ireland to begin laying the trans-Atlantic cable. HMS *Agamemnon* carried the other half of the cable. Before the departure, thousands of people came to the port to witness the historical moment. The British government sent a congratulatory message. A priest came to pray for the expedition.

The first few days were smooth. On the sixth day, after laying 335 nautical miles, the telegraph signal was still clear. But that night, just as Field was about to go to sleep, the familiar rattle of the winch suddenly stopped. The cable broke from the cable car. Finding that broken end would be impossible.

The first attempt had failed!

After close to a year of waiting and preparing, Field prepared a second attempt. In June 1858, two warships planned to depart from opposite coasts of the Atlantic to meet in the middle. They would then lay cable in opposite directions. However, not long after the HMS *Agamemnon* departed, it was hit by a severe storm. Although it arrived on schedule at the planned location, the equipment was damaged. After struggling to lay 200 nautical miles of cable, they had no choice but to go home in dismay.

The second attempt had also failed.

The two failures consumed half of the funds available and had nothing to show for either attempt. It was depressing. The stockholders wanted out. The chairman of the board advocated selling the remaining cable to reduce losses. The vice chairman concurred and resigned in writing to show that he did not want to have anything to do with the ridiculous project.

Field's firm faith did not waver. He explained that after such a test, the cable had proved itself to be good. There was enough cable on board for another experiment, so they had nothing to lose. His strong resolve overcame the shareholders' hesitation. At his insistence, the third attempt began.

On July 28, 1858, the two cable-laying ships met at the designated place in the middle of the Atlantic, then headed off in opposite directions. By August 5th, the west-bound USS *Niagara* reported it had laid 1,030 nautical miles of cable and could see the coast of Newfoundland. The east-bound HMS *Agamemnon* also reported it had laid over 1,000 nautical miles of cable and could see the coast of Ireland.

Success! On August 16, Queen Victoria of Britain sent a letter of congratulations to the US President, James Buchanan. For the first time in human history, information could pass instantaneously across the Atlantic. The New World and the Old World were connected! A global sensation! Everyone was excited! On August 17, newspaper headlines in New York and London hailed the victory. On August 31, New York City held a celebration. Field was a hero and sat in the first carriage in the parade while people called him "the Columbus of our time." President Buchanan also participated in the celebration but was in the third carriage of the parade.

Before the parade even began, Field got the word that the cable had suddenly stopped working properly. After September 1, the telegraph signal stopped completely. Wildman Whitehouse, the chief engineer hired by Field, was a medical doctor by training and an amateur engineer. The reason for failure was due to Whitehouse increasing the voltage when the telegraph signal became weak, which damaged the cable. In a few days, the bad news spread. Suddenly, public opinion took a 180-degree turn. Field became a criminal. People said he had "cheated a city, a country, and the whole world." There was a rumor that the Queen's message never actually crossed the Atlantic and was a hoax. Some people said that he knew the telegraph signal had gone out but hid the truth for his own self-interest and use the time to unload his stock at a high price.

Cyrus West Field was a national hero one day but had to escape his former friends and admirers like a criminal the next day.

However, Field was not a man easily defeated by failure. He carried that heavy cross for six years as he devoted himself to reviving his dream.

At that time, America was in a civil war, so it was impossible to raise funds and no one cared about the matter. Field went to England and raised £600,000 in Manchester, London, and Liverpool, as well as obtaining the original operation rights. Within two days, he had bought the largest ship in the world at the time, the SS *Great Eastern*, and began preparations. The *Great Eastern* was designed by Isambard Kingdom Brunel, the most outstanding British engineer. It had cost £250,000 to build and was launched in 1858. The original plan was to sail directly between London and Sydney, but there was insufficient traffic. The ship sailed between London and New York three times and bankrupted three entrepreneurs. The ship was idle, waiting to be sold. Field picked up a bargain when he bought the ship for £25,000, or one-tenth of the construction cost. The size of the ship allowed it to carry all the cables.

On July 23, 1865, the SS *Great Eastern* left the Thames with new cables weighing more than 9,000 tons. Unexpectedly, the first attempt also failed. Two days before reaching the destination, the cable broke, causing a loss of £600,000.

Field wanted to start over again, but financing was extremely difficult. Banks were no longer willing to lend. Fortunately, Sir John Pender, a Scottish textile entrepreneur, was optimistic about the business. He mortgaged his entire property to the bank to borrow £250,000 and invested in Field's business. Only then were manufacturers willing to make cables.

On July 13, 1866, the SS *Great Eastern* started a second attempt and finally succeeded! The telegraph signal from the other side of the Atlantic was very clear. On July 29, 1866, Queen Victoria and President Johnson exchanged official telegraphs. Coincidentally, a few days later, the missing old cable was also found. Both cables connected the Old World and the New World into one world. The cable service made £1,000 on its first day of operation. Field also cleared his own name and once again became a hero![11]

Investor John Pender also got rich and subsequently founded 32 underwater telegraph companies. These 32 companies eventually merged to form the Eastern Telegraph Company and laid most of the cables that linked Europe, Asia, and Africa. The Eastern Telegraph Company was later known as Imperial and International Communication Ltd, but changed its name again to Cable and Wireless Limited in 1934.

The point I want to explain with this story is: *Profit is not the sole objective of entrepreneurial decision making; entrepreneurs have objectives beyond profit.*

Instead of saying entrepreneurs pursue profits, it is better to say profit is a standard entrepreneurs use to measure their own success but for society it is a socially imposed constraint on entrepreneurial activity.

Setting profit maximization as the objective of the firm is a standard assumption in mainstream economics. From the perspective of

---

[11] For the story of Field's venture of the transatlantic cable, see Zweig (2015). In writing the above contents, I also incorporated materials from other sources.

mainstream economics, any behavior that deviates from profit maximization is an undesirable phenomenon caused by the agent's moral hazard, which could lead to efficiency loss and should be curbed. In many cases, this type of assumption has value for our understanding of firm behavior and market operations. However, this kind of assumption also misleads our understanding of the real world. In the real world, at least from the perspective of outstanding entrepreneurs, making money is not their sole objective, nor is it the end goal, even if they are the sole owner of the business, and, thus, an agency problem does not exist.

Joseph Schumpeter believed entrepreneurs pursued success, not profit. Specifically, entrepreneurs are driven by three non-monetary motives: (1) "the dream and the will to found a private kingdom, usually, though not necessarily, also a dynasty," (2) "the will to conquer," and (3) "the joy of creating." (Schumpeter, 1934, pp. 93–94.)

In this world, there are always some people who are ambitious; they want to do big things and stand out. In traditional societies, ambitious people that wanted to stand out could only build their own kingdom by conquering other people's territory, plundering other people's property, enslaving others, and finally making themselves king. They used the logic of power. In the market economy, individual rights are legally protected, so the logic of power does not work. The best way for ambitious people to stand out is to be an entrepreneur and establish a commercial kingdom. They can obtain control over more resources by providing valuable products and services to customers and by beating their competitors.

For an entrepreneur such as Jack Ma, Alibaba is the private kingdom he created. He sees hundreds of millions of customers use the services provided by his own company. There are tens of thousands of employees working under him. He travels with an entourage and meets with presidents and premiers in foreign countries. He is the center of all gatherings and is often profiled in the media. Everyone knows everything about him. It feels like being a king.

Wang Shi's choice was also typical. When he first started Vanke Property Company in the early 1990s, he recognized that under China's system, a person like him can either make money or become somebody, but not both. He focused more on making an impact, so he gave up his company shares to be a "professional manager." He did not really want to be a "professional manager." Instead, he wanted to build a commercial empire as the leader of the real estate industry. Vanke was the 'carrier' to realize his dreams. Vanke's success is his own success. He wanted to prove to others: "I can, and you can't!"

The joy of creation is the main reason many people choose to be entrepreneurs. Entrepreneurs act under uncertainty, which is always full of challenges. The challenge itself is a reward for those who like to work creatively. Every difficulty overcome is a victory!

It is hard to say that Cyrus West Field's underwater cable was profit driven. He wanted to be part of an earth-shattering event. He wanted to be the Christopher Columbus of his time. He wanted to change the world with his actions. While laying the underwater cable, he was always full of passion and joy, so he was able to face defeat over and over again until he finally succeeded. If he did not enjoy the process, he could not have lasted until the end.

Joel Mokyr, an eminent economic historian, studied entrepreneurs in the eighteenth century. He sees that many entrepreneurs in the Industrial Revolution were far less interested in making money than in technological success and taking on challenges. For example, a successful entrepreneur such as John Roebuck was more obsessed with technical matters than with making money once he was assured a decent life and respect from people (Mokyr, 2009, p. 367).

Entrepreneurs pursue not only profits, but also career success and the realization of their dreams. This is precisely the reason many entrepreneurial decisions cannot be justified by "expected profit maximization." According to standard economic models, if an investment project worth $10 million has a 10% probability of success, then only when profits exceed $100 million upon success, will entrepreneurs invest. However, in the real world, when entrepreneurs not only consider monetary compensation, but also non-monetary reward, they often "lose money" when doing things that shake the heavens and move the earth. As Schumpeter once said:

It is true that it must be borne in mind that even obviously disproportionate individual success has its function, because the possibility of attaining it works as a stronger incentive than is rationally justified by its magnitude multiplied by the coefficient of probability. Such prospects also belong, as it were, to the 'remuneration' of those entrepreneurs for whom they are not realized. (Schumpeter, 1934, p. 155)

A comparative study showed that employed professional managers cared more about money than entrepreneurs. They choose to be professional managers instead of starting a business because they believe the compensation is higher (Amit et al., 2000; Zitelmann, 2018, p. 66).

A large number of empirical studies found that the median income of American entrepreneurs is lower than that of professional managers. A very small number of entrepreneurs earning a very high income is the only reason the statistical average value for entrepreneurs as a group is higher than the median income (Astebro et al., 2014; Zitelmann, 2018, p. 77).

I am not negating the importance of profit in entrepreneurial decision making. Actually, on the contrary, I believe the profit system ensures the compatibility of entrepreneurs' personal goals and social interests. On the one hand, in the market economy, profit is a symbol of success for entrepreneurs. If entrepreneurs do not make money, it is difficult for them to prove their success, let alone establish their own kingdom. Therefore, even if they are not driven by profits, entrepreneurs must make money as a means to achieve their life goals. Ordinary people often ask: That guy has already made enough money to last lifetimes, why does he still want to make more money? The simple answer is: The sparrow cannot understand the ambition of a swan. For ordinary people, the point of making money is to take care of their family. For entrepreneurs, making money is a means to realize success.

On the other hand, from the social perspective, if a firm's revenue cannot exceed cost, then in most cases it means the entrepreneur wasted society's precious resources. The firm does not create added value for society, so it should be eliminated. Therefore, profit is the whip society uses to drive entrepreneurs to exert themselves. Profit is also a cage that constrains entrepreneurial behavior within a reasonable scope.

Traditional societies did not lack the type of ambitious people that are entrepreneurs in the market economy. However, on average, the bad things they did far exceeded the good things. Some people even brought about tremendous social disasters. The reason is they were not constrained by profit. Even if they made repeated mistakes, they could continue to acquire resources through violence. They could go further and further down the mistaken road. By comparison, under the market economy, because of profit constraints, entrepreneurs cannot keep making mistakes.

Challenges to Economics and Policy Implications

So far I have used a few stories to make conclusions about what entrepreneurship is NOT: Entrepreneurial decision making is not scientific decision making; entrepreneurial decisions are not making choices under given constraints; and profit is not the sole objective of entrepreneurial decision making.

As I said at the beginning, I believe these are universal conclusions. If my conclusions are basically correct, then mainstream economic theory faces a big challenge. Economics is theories about the market. The basic paradigm of mainstream economics is the rational decision-maker model. The rational decision-maker model means maximizing the objective function under the given restraints. Theories about "market failure" are derived from this paradigm. If entrepreneurs in the real world do not make decisions according to this kind of model, then market theory in mainstream economics is misleading and government intervention policies advocated by mainstream economists have no theoretical basis. Here, I give a very brief discussion of a few examples. Some detailed discussions will be done in later chapters.

The first example is about externality. According to mainstream economic theory, if positive externalities exist, then an entrepreneur's optimal decision making cannot fulfill the social efficiency requirement. In particular, entrepreneurs cannot have enough of an incentive to engage in major innovation because when the positive externalities of major innovation are too large, entrepreneurs only get a small portion of the total social income. However, regardless of whether it is due to "excessive optimism" or pursuit of goals that transcend profit, entrepreneurs often do things that are unthinkable from a rational calculation perspective (such as Field laying a trans-Atlantic cable). This means that so-called externalities do not necessarily weaken incentives for entrepreneurial innovation. This point applies to entrepreneurs during the Industrial Revolution as well as to entrepreneurs today. A recent study of inventions in contemporary America found that inventors earn, on average, only 2.2% of the total surplus from inventions (Nordhaus, 2004). Due to excessive optimism, many entrepreneurs fail. Even the most successful entrepreneurs experience failure. However, the small number of successful entrepreneurs bring about tremendous wealth to society, far exceeding what they get back themselves.

Non-profit objectives of the entrepreneur also apply to mitigating negative externalities. To be a socially respected "hero," many entrepreneurs seek to restrict socially harmful activities and improve the living environment in accordance with common social values. Historically, many environmental projects and anti-poverty projects have been initiated and sponsored by entrepreneurs. Most charities have been established by successful entrepreneurs. They do this either individually (like Bill Gates) or collectively (like The Nature Conservancy). International comparisons show that the more entrepreneur-dominated economies do much better in pollution control and imposing quality standards than the government-dominated economies, not the other way round (Djankov et al., 2002). Therefore, externalities do not constitute sufficient legitimacy for the government to interfere in the market.[12]

For another example, according to mainstream economic theory, monopolistic enterprises take advantage of their position to exclude competitors. Not only do they de-prioritize progress, but also use high prices to deprive consumers of surplus. However, if entrepreneurial decision making is not based on calculation, but is instead based on imagination and judgment, then competition will always appear in unexpected places from unexpected competitors. No enterprise can rely on existing products and technologies to maintain a monopoly position. They must judge correctly and produce better products for consumers. New ambitious entrepreneurs always attempt to use new ideas to subvert incumbent enterprises. Entrepreneurship is always more prominent in start-up enterprises than well-established enterprises. The large, old enterprises are always overwhelmed by new challengers due to a decline in entrepreneurship and the prevalence of internal bureaucracy. The reason is that as a company becomes larger and larger, strict rules and bureaucracy are necessities. Management must become professionalized and standardized, otherwise the company cannot operate efficiently and effectively. The essence of entrepreneurship dictates that the enlargement of the company and improvement of the management system will gradually dilute entrepreneurship. Also, entrepreneurs do not like their subordinates being

---

[12] Of course, I do not say all problems related to "externality" can be solved by the entrepreneur. It is critical to realize that "externality" is mis-conceptualized in mainstream economics. As Coase (1960) argued, externality is essentially the problem of defining property rights.

entrepreneurial. Thus, professional managers that succeed the founders are rarely entrepreneurial. Perhaps this is the main reason why it is difficult to build enterprises that last. Therefore, economists' so-called monopolies cannot constitute a legitimate reason for the government to interfere in the market. It is new entrepreneurs who beat down "monopolists," not the government's anti-monopoly bureau.

Industrial policy is another example. The premise of the effectiveness of industrial policy is that decision makers can come to a consensus about the direction of future industry and technological development. If entrepreneurs' judgment is unique, then innovation is non-consensus. Thus, industrial policy will not only be unsuccessful, but will also seriously restrain the role of entrepreneurship. Therefore, the best industrial policy is no industrial policy. In this way, numerous entrepreneurs will show their special prowess and innovation will continuously emerge. We do not need to worry about "the first person to eat crab" without the support of industrial policy. The nature of entrepreneurs is that they try new things. Industrial policy leads to the "herd effect" and always wastes resources, not to mention the negative consequences of rent-seeking behavior.

Our re-understanding of entrepreneurship also has important implications for the theory and practice of corporate governance. Traditional corporate governance theory not only ignores the positive significance of entrepreneurs' objectives unrelated to profit, but also ignores the conflict of cognition between entrepreneurs and investors. (Objectives unrelated to profit equate to "private benefits of control," which basically has a negative connotation in economics.) For example, mainstream corporate governance theory assumes minority shareholders are always correct and the controlling shareholder must be wrong. As a result, "improving corporate governance" equates to restraining entrepreneurs. The whole set of corporate governance law and policy turned corporations into quasi-bureaucratic organizations, which has seriously inhibited entrepreneurship. Those enterprises with the most "standardized" corporate governance often lack innovation. I believe that if Huawei were a listed company, it would be very difficult for it to exhibit the brilliance that it has today!

Corporate governance literature does not distinguish entrepreneurs from professional managers. Our re-understanding of entrepreneurship implies that professional managers and entrepreneurs are two different species. People that possess an entrepreneurial spirit not only have their own ideas but are also stubborn. They are unwilling to obey authority and often do not follow the rules. They like to order around other people, not be ordered around by other people. They break and reset the rules, not follow them. They are paranoid, not "Yes Men." When they were children, they were generally not well behaved (Zhen and Arvey, 2009).[13] These types of people often feel useless or intolerable within an enterprise because their creativity cannot be brought into full play.[14] At that point, they will leave their current employer to create their own enterprise and become an entrepreneur.

This is vividly exemplified in the article titled "The Dark Side of Entrepreneurship," published by the *Harvard Business Review* in the November 1985 issue (Kets de Vries, 1985). The author approvingly quotes an entrepreneur saying, "The entrepreneur who starts his own business generally does so because he is a difficult employee. He does not take kindly to suggestions or orders from other people and aspires most of all to run his own shop" (p. 161). In contrast with managers, entrepreneurs are suspicious of authority and are reluctant to integrate into existing organizations or bureaucracy. "Instead, they often experience structure as stifling. They find it very difficult to work with others in structured situations unless, of course, *they* created the structure and the work is done on *their* terms" (p. 161 Emphasis in original). The reason they become entrepreneurs is because they are incapable of bending to authority and are unwilling to follow the rules of existing companies.

Actually, a considerable number of entrepreneurs were once employees of other entrepreneurs.[15] For example, Andrew Carnegie, Henry Ford, Robert Noyce, Gordon Moore, and Andrew Grove were all employees before they started their own businesses. After Yahoo acquired Beijing 3721 Technology Co. Ltd., they hoped Zhou

[13] For a summary and more literature on the "nonconformism" nature of entrepreneurs, see Zitelmann (2018), pp. 81–85.

[14] Many people are currently keen to discuss ways to stimulate intrepreneurship within an enterprise. When an old company faces a decline in entrepreneurship and innovation, stimulating an internal entrepreneurial spirit is meaningful. Companies such as Cisco, Alibaba, Tencent, and Haier are working hard in this regard. However, doing so is not easy.

[15] A study of British entrepreneurs found that entrepreneurs had relatively modest pay before starting a business. This may indicate that when entrepreneurs are employees, they are indeed not good employees. See Evans and Jovanovic (1989).

Hongyi, the founder of the company, would stay on to manage Yahoo China. However, Zhou is an entrepreneur at heart, not a professional manager. In the end, his only choice was to leave and create his new company, Qihoo 360 (Zhou and Fan, 2017, Chapter 10).

Only by understanding what entrepreneurship is can we truly understand how the market operates and what the government should and should not do.

3 | Big Data Cannot Replace Entrepreneurs

Does economic development rely on government or entrepreneurs? This question has been debated in academic circles for more than 200 years.

Experience has proven it is better to rely on entrepreneurs. Since the Industrial Revolution, economies directed by entrepreneurs have developed very well, whereas economies directed by governments have performed poorly.

The perfect specimen of a government-directed economy is the planned economy system. Although central planning has failed world-wide, its theoretical foundation has not been totally eradicated. As a result, the ghost of central planning keeps reappearing in different forms, such as industrial policy, development planning, macro-control, and national innovation projects.

Especially over the last few years, with the emergence of big data and artificial intelligence, the feasibility of central planning has again become a popular topic. Jack Ma's statement during a speech was a single stone that stirred up a thousand waves. He said:

During an interaction yesterday, we discussed Marxism's views on whether the market economy was better than the planned economy. I believe over the last 100 years we thought the market economy has always been great. My personal view is a big change will happen over the next 30 years. The planned economy will get bigger and bigger. Why? Because we might obtain the data to discover the invisible hand of the market. Before the development of X-rays and CT machines, practitioners of Chinese medicine had no way to open a patient up and look. Therefore, Chinese medicine had a unique diagnostic system. However, after the X-ray and CT machine appeared, Earth-shaking changes took place. I believe clearly grasping national and world economic data will be like having an X-ray and CT machine, so in 30 years there will be new theories.[1]

[1] Jack Ma made these remarks on November 19, 2016, at a forum jointly hosted by the Zhejiang Chamber of Commerce and the Shanghai Zhejiang Chamber of Commerce. For the reader's convenience, the textual flow of Ma's speech was

Jack Ma's views could be generalized as a "big data-based planned economy." Jack Ma is an outstanding entrepreneur, not an economic theorist. Whether he seriously considered the consequences of his speech is not important, but we must take seriously the issue he presented. His views have been echoed by some people and might have some consequences that he did not want and even anticipate. However, more importantly, since the computer was developed, from time to time, some people have said that the rapid advancement of the computer's ability to store and process information has made the planned economy feasible, not only in theory but also in practice.

Can big data revive the planned economy? The essence of this question is: "Can big data displace entrepreneurship?"

The essential feature of the planned economy is the use of systematic and institutional force to negate entrepreneurship and deprive individuals the freedom to choose, especially the freedom to start a business and innovate. Under the planned economy, commercial speculation is a crime, so entrepreneurial activity is impossible.

Using data to make predictions is the core of big data. It is said that with the large scale, variety, and rapid updates that are the characteristics of big data, human behavior can be accurately predicted (Mayer-Schönberger and Cukier, 2013, chapter 1). Below, I will demonstrate, from five aspects, the impossibility of a big data-based planned economy. In other words, big data cannot replace entrepreneurs. These five aspects are not independent, but instead are interrelated.

From the View of the Essence of Knowledge

During the 1930s, a great debate on the feasibility of the planned economy occurred in Western academic circles.[2] One side, represented by Ludwig von Mises, F.A. Hayek, and Lionel Robbins, believed planned economies cannot resolve the economic calculation problem, and thus were unfeasible. The other side, represented by Oskar Lange, Abba P. Lerner, and others, believed planned economies could resolve the economic calculation problem, and thus were feasible.

grammatically revised but the meaning was preserved. For the original version of his speech, see http://tech.sina.com.cn/i/2016-11-20/doc-ifxxwrwk1500894.shtml

[2] For details of this great debate, see Jesús Huerta de Soto (2010).

Before the dispute was settled, Lange and other supporters of the planned economy unilaterally declared that they had won the great debate. This self-proclaimed victory was generally accepted by Western mainstream economists. Even the economist Joseph Schumpeter said, "As a matter of blueprint logic it is undeniable that the socialist blueprint is drawn at a higher level of rationality" (Schumpeter, 1942, p. 196).

However, this so-called victory was based on a misreading of Mises and Hayek's viewpoints. Lange and other mainstream economists did not truly understand what Mises and Hayek were saying.

The standard explanation of Mises and Hayek's reason for believing the planned economy is unfeasible is the limits of computing power. The planning authorities cannot solve thousands or even hundreds of millions of Walras equations. Lange believed the planning authorities did not need to solve massive equations according to specific knowledge related to technology, preferences, and endowments. They only needed a Walrasian auction (*tâtonnement*) mechanism to know the necessary equilibrium price for economic planning.

The truth, from Mises and Hayek's perspective, is that the planned economy's true (or at least primary) difficulty is not the limits of computational ability. Instead, the specific nature of the knowledge that economic activity depends on makes it impossible for the central planning organs to obtain this information. The market is primarily not a system that allocates scarce resources to a given competitive goal. Instead, it is a cognitive device that creates, discovers, and transmits tacit knowledge, that is, knowledge that does not seem to exist, is difficult to discover, and is difficult to transfer. Eliminating the market not only makes the transfer of knowledge impossible, but also eliminates knowledge itself.

Combining Chapter 1, we can use two dimensions, static and dynamic, to summarize Hayek's theory of knowledge.

From the static perspective, the knowledge required for human decision making can be put into two categories: Scientific knowledge (hard knowledge) and practical knowledge (soft knowledge). In Michael Polanyi's terminology, scientific knowledge is explicit knowledge that can be described, and tacit knowledge is practical knowledge that is difficult to describe. From the perspective of human decision making, both categories of knowledge are important, but for creative decision making, practical knowledge is more important.

In terms of scientific knowledge, a group of experts selected by appropriate methods may be able to best grasp all the best knowledge available. Practical knowledge, however, must be dispersed, local, subjective, and unspeakable, thus it can only be grasped and used by the people involved. It cannot be obtained by other people, especially the planning authorities. Hayek said: "It is with respect to this that practically every individual has some advantage over all others because he possesses unique information of which beneficial use might be made, but of which use can be made only if the decisions depending on it are left to him or are made with his active co-operation" (Hayek, 1948, p. 80). Because practical knowledge cannot be counted, it cannot be transmitted to any central authority in the form of statistics. Practical knowledge changes with time and place, so it can only be effectively transmitted through a flexible price mechanism. A planning organ attempting to collect this kind of information is like collecting water with a bamboo basket. "We need decentralization because only thus can we insure that the knowledge of the particular circumstances of time and place will be promptly used" (Ibid. p. 84).

This is the primary reason Hayek believed the planned economy was unfeasible, which is unrelated to computational ability.

Big data certainly allowed us to have more data. Even more data, however, is still just statistical data, which is far from unspeakable tacit knowledge. Tacit knowledge is the most important for facing contingencies and for imagination.

Imagine that Jack Ma, for example, kept a journal. Every day, he recorded every bit of information he received, the people he met, what decisions he made, and even why he made those decisions. Could other people use this to replicate Jack Ma's decisions? No! Most of Jack Ma's decisions are based on his intuitions and imagination, which he cannot clearly state himself. The "reasons" he wrote in a journal could not possibly include all of the reasons that led him to make the decision. The tacit knowledge that cannot be written down is the most important. If Jack Ma could use big data to tell the central planning organ his every word and action, could the planning organ plan an Alibaba? Impossible!

From the dynamic perspective, a large amount of knowledge is discovered and created during economic activity by the participants. It is the product of entrepreneurial practice. Without autonomous economic activity, the information itself does not exist. For example, if IBM could not autonomously develop the computer, but instead waited for the government's development directive, then most of the knowledge about computers would not have been created.

Obviously, collecting information that is yet to be created is impossible, regardless of the ability to communicate this type of knowledge. When the computer did not exist, how could we collect statistics on demand for the computer? Big data only collects information that already exists. It cannot possibly collect information that has not yet been created and discovered.

Hayek emphasized the dynamic nature of economic decisions. He said:

Economic problems arise always and only in consequence of change. As long as things continue as before, or at least as they were expected to, there arise no new problems requiring a decision, no need to form a new plan. The belief that changes, or at least day-to-day adjustments, have become less important in modern times implies the contention that economic problems also have become less important. (Ibid. p. 82)

Mises believed the role of entrepreneurial ability is to be a source of continuously created information in the market. It is connected to specific circumstances. Only the people acting in this environment can sense it. Mises said:

The entrepreneur's commercial attitude and activity arises from his position in the economic process and is lost with its disappearance. ...

The static state can dispense with economic calculation. For here the same events in economic life are ever recurring. ...

Under stationary conditions there no longer exists a problem for economic calculation to solve. The essential function of economic calculation has by hypothesis already been performed ... the problem of economic calculation is of economic dynamics: it is no problem of economic statics. (Jesús Huerta de Soto, 2010, pp. 105–107)

In 1921, Mises wrote:

It is the speculative capitalists who create the data to which he has to adjust his business and which therefore gives direction to his trading operations. (Ibid. pp. 178–179)

The computer did not exist in the 1930s, so neither did big data. However, Mises and Hayek's explanation of the unfeasibility of the planned economy already proved that even with the computer and big data, the planned economy could not succeed. The important tacit knowledge related to human behavior cannot be collected by a central planning organ. Big data cannot collect practical information that people have yet to discover or create. Planning regulations will cause the new knowledge that could be discovered and created by entrepreneurs in the market process to not exist.

If computers and big data can be utilized by not only government organs but also participants in the economic process, then the planned economy is even more unfeasible. Computers and big data cause people to continuously create difficult-to-quantify practical and unspeakable tacit knowledge, so the central planning organs have no way to centrally standardize economic activity. Therefore, just as Spanish economist Jesús Huerta de Soto pointed out, believing computers (and big data) can make the planned economy possible is just as laughable as believing that books and the invention of the printing press in an underdeveloped society will allow the government to obtain all of society's important practical and subjective knowledge. Books and the invention of the printing press brought about a result that was precisely the opposite: It gave society more variety and made it more difficult to centralize control (de Soto, 2010, p. 61).

The big data planned economy is a paradox. Big data is the result of countless spontaneous actions by people in the market economy. If the planned economy is implemented so that every person follows government decrees, then big data itself will disappear! Assuming the information created in the market also exists without the market is obviously ridiculous.

From the View of Entrepreneurial Decision Making

According to the views of Mises and Hayek, discovering, creating, and transmitting information through price and non-price means is the embodiment of entrepreneurship. This means that in the market economy, each person is an entrepreneur in some sense. Given the importance of entrepreneurs, however, it is necessary to explain the unfeasibility of the big data planned economy from the perspective of the significance of entrepreneurial decision making.

Within the framework of mainstream economics, the objectives and means of individual decision making are given. So-called decision making is selecting among given means those that maximize the given objective. Precisely as we already pointed out, however, this is quite far removed from true entrepreneurial decision making! In reality, entrepreneurship is not making decisions under given means and objectives, but instead is seeking, identifying, and selecting means and objectives themselves! An individual's level of entrepreneurship is to a large degree determined by intuition as well as the ability to seek out objectives and obtain means. If means and objectives are given and equivalent, then with the same data, all rational people will make equivalent selections. In reality, however, different entrepreneurs will make different choices even based on the same data and hard knowledge!

Why? Because entrepreneurial decision making is not only determined by data and hard knowledge. It is more dependent on soft knowledge. In terms of entrepreneurs, an individual's imagination, intuition, and judgment of market prospects, technological prospects, and resource availability are the most critical.

Of course, big data is useful to entrepreneurs because entrepreneurs need data when making decisions. True entrepreneurial decision making, however, certainly transcends data, and of course transcends big data. Decisions based only on big data are only scientific decisions, not entrepreneurial decisions. An entrepreneur that only makes decisions based on big data is not a true entrepreneur, but a manager only. An entrepreneur must think about and see the things big data cannot tell him.

Big data is a type of business. When big data did not exist, discovering and utilizing big data was the function of entrepreneurs. As soon as big data became prevalent, however, big data became "Columbus' egg" and was no longer the function of entrepreneurs. This is similar to when everyone began using electricity; electricity was no longer any enterprise's core competitive ability.

Schumpeter equated entrepreneurship with innovation.[3] Innovation is, to a large degree, a result of imagination. Big data is calculation, not imagination, and thus cannot tell entrepreneurs what to innovate. For example, data about the postal horse cart transportation industry could not tell Benz and Daimler to invent the automobile. Otherwise, horse cart drivers should have invented the automobile, not those two.

---

[3] Schumpeter (1934), chapter 2.

Data about the computer market also could not tell Bill Gates to create the software industry. Otherwise, IBM would have created the software industry, not Bill Gates. Similarly, data could not have told Pony Ma to create WeChat. Otherwise, China Mobile should have invented WeChat, not Tencent!

Let me use the movie industry as another example to further explain this point.

Imagine a movie production company could obtain data for all of the movies over the last few decades, including each movies' audience numbers, audience demographic structure, geographical distribution, showing times, box office sales, all media reviews, and even audience expressions (such as how much they laughed or how long they cried). Can this type of big data tell us which next movie will perform the best? No!

Each new movie is an invention. We do not have a way to predict which type of movie will be received well by the audience. As veteran Hollywood screenwriter William Goldman pointed out: "Why did Universal, the mightiest studio of all, pass on Star Wars? ... Because nobody, nobody – not now, not ever – knows the least goddam thing about what is or isn't going to work at the box office."[4]

Let me tell you a true story.[5] As the global leader in streaming, Netflix has data on viewing preferences of millions of users worldwide. It knows what actors, segments, and age settings its viewers like and converts these data into structured data that a computer can understand. These data provide a basis for decision making in film and television production. In 2012, the company applied the data from viewing selections of 30 million users, four million comments, and three million topic searches to the production of *House of Cards*. Netflix was convinced that those users who watched the British version of *House of Cards* also watched director David Finch's movie *The Social Network*. The American actor Kevin Spacey was also always popular with that audience. Thus, Netflix made them the director and protagonist of the American version of *House of Cards*. Jonathan Friedland, Chief Communications Officer at Netflix at the time, was quoted by *Wired Magazine* as saying: "We know what people watch

---

[4] Quoted from Easterly (2013), chapter 12.

[5] This story is drawn from Zhou Zhenghua's (2022) article "Qumei Da Shuju, Lijie Qiyejia" (pp. 96–98). Zhou's article is the review of the Chinese version of the current book.

on Netflix and we're able with a high degree of confidence to understand how big a likely audience is for a given show based on people's
viewing habits ... As time goes on, we get better at selecting what that
something for everybody is that gets high engagement" (Baldwin,
2012). In a company blog post in 2018, Chris Goss, Director of
Studio Technology, wrote: "Historically, the 'business' of filmmaking
is arduous, complex and layered with countless forms of
inefficiency ... We are focused on leveraging the power of technology
to enable our creative partners and strip away the tactical burdens of
managing productions at scale for the artists and the crew ...
We believe technology, paired with great creative talent, will help us
get there" (Goss, 2018).

Looking back ten years later, *House of Cards* has become an insurmountable peak for Netflix. Its record viewing data are like a monument or a long shadow cast behind a giant. The Netflix series *Hemlock
Grove, Arrested Development,* and *Orange is the New Black* were all
produced using big-data decision making but had mediocre performance. After trading as high as $691.69 in November 2021, Netflix's
share price dropped below $200 in April 2022.

Similarly, the book market went the same way. No doubt Amazon
has the book market's big data. It can recommend books based on
customers' past viewing and purchasing records. Amazon's big data,
however, cannot tell us which book will be a best seller in the future
and neither can it tell each writer what book to write next! If an author
wants to set a book-writing plan according to big data, then he
certainly will fail! If the planning organs set book publishing plans
based on Amazon or Dangdang.com's big data, it would be a disaster
for the book market!

I am not negating the significance of big data. Instead, I am saying
big data cannot replace the imagination and judgment of entrepreneurs. Allow me to use the transportation industry's intermodal containerization revolution to explain this point.[6]

Intermodal containerization was one of the most important innovations of the second half of the twentieth century. It had a tremendous
impact on international trade, economic globalization, and especially
the global distribution of supply chains. Before the 1950s, all goods –
whether they were transported via boat, rail, or automobile – were

---

[6] The following story is drawn from Smil (2006), pp. 220–226.

shipped loose. The same product shipped from the manufacturer to the retailer was re-packaged multiple times throughout the trip, wasting time and effort. The cost was high, a lot was stolen, and it was unreliable. On the pier, the mountains of merchandise left an impression on people.

Early on, in 1937, Malcolm Purcell McLean, a truck driver from North Carolina, had the idea for a shipping container. In 1955, he began to act. He sold his stake in the family's transportation company and borrowed money to buy seven old oil tankers. He converted them into platforms that could stack containers. Next, he converted his truck to be able to carry the containers. He installed steel frames on the deck that could quickly stack containers. He also modified the pier. On April 26, 1956, a modified World War II-era oil tanker departed from a pier in Newark, New Jersey, and headed toward Boston, Massachusetts, with 58 containers on board. He succeeded! Next, McLean modified the other old ships and opened a container shipping line between New Jersey and Texas. Other water transportation companies began to imitate McLean. By the end of the 1960s, the intermodal container era had arrived. Rail transportation also rapidly containerized. By the late 1990s, 60% of total international trade in goods by value was shipped via containers. Compared to loose transport, the transportation time from the manufacturer to the buyer declined by 95%. The unit cost of transportation declined greatly! Without the intermodal containerization revolution, it could be said the global division of labor linking industries that appeared after the 1970s could not have been possible.

Why did McLean – but not the original water transportation companies – "invent" container transportation? This cannot be explained using data. In terms of data, McLean started out as only a sole-proprietor truck driver, so the data he had was not on the same level as a traditional water transportation company. In terms of technical content, the shipping container does not count as a true "invention." Actually, in the early twentieth century, small containers of different dimensions were in use, but standardized and commercialized container transportation did not exist.

The basic reason is imagination. McLean had this type of imagination before others did. During an interview, he recalled that one day in 1937, when he was waiting anxiously on the traditional way of unloading, he suddenly had an idea:

I had to wait most of the day to deliver the bales, sitting there in my truck, watching stevedores load other cargo. It struck me that I was looking at a lot of wasted time and money ... The thought occurred to me, as I waited around that day that it would be easier to lift my trailer up and, without any of its contents being touched, put it on the ship. (quoted from Smil (2006), p. 222)

In summary, I want to emphasize that any data, no matter how big, cannot replace the alertness, imagination, and judgment of entrepreneurs. Alibaba's big data cannot replace Jack Ma. All of society's big data cannot replace entrepreneurs. If the government wants to establish a planned economy with a big data foundation (including industrial policy), not only will it eliminate big data itself, but it will also eliminate entrepreneurship and obstruct innovation and technological progress.

From the View of the Difference between Risk and Uncertainty

To understand the unfeasibility of the big-data-based planned economy as well as the nature of entrepreneurship, we must also recognize the difference between risk and uncertainty.

The reason entrepreneurial decision making cannot solely be based on data is because commercial operations and innovation primarily face uncertainty, not risk. Even though "the most certain thing is uncertainty" has become a catchphrase, when most economists and management scholars speak of uncertainty, they are referring to risk. Actually, uncertainty and risk are different. Frank Knight differentiated the two as early as in 1921. Unfortunately, his theories to this day have not changed the situation in economics where uncertainty and risk are considered equivalent. As pointed out by Rindova and Courtney (2020), Knight posed an epistemological question about "the nature and function of knowledge itself," whereas subsequent economic research emphasized choice under uncertainty, defined as how individuals make choices among well-defined options with uncertain outcomes. By identifying Knight's uncertainty with a subjective probability of outcomes, Arrow (1951) argued that "Knight's uncertainties seem to have surprisingly many of the properties of ordinary probability, and questioned the value of the distinction between risk and uncertainty." In arguing that business problems are similar to those solved through statistical methods, Arrow reduced uncertainty to risk. Arrow's misconception of uncertainty has been followed almost unanimously by mainstream economists (Kay and King, 2020).

Uncertainty cannot be reduced to risk. According to Knight's viewpoints, risk can be quantified, whereas uncertainty can only be qualitative. Risk has a probability distribution that is based on the law of large numbers, and thus it can be reduced and insured against. Uncertainty is unique. There are no *a priori* probabilities, statistical probabilities, or distribution functions, and thus it cannot be reduced or insured against. Risk is exogenous but uncertainty is endogenous (it depends on entrepreneurial actions).

The uniqueness of uncertainty means past data cannot provide all relevant information about the future. Parameter estimation, central limit theorem, least squares method, linear causality, Bayes' theorem, and other components of statistics are no help in resolving uncertainty.

Innovation is the function of entrepreneurs. The most basic characteristic of innovation is that it undergoes a process that is a series of uncertainties, not risk in the common meaning. No one can predict whether an innovation will succeed or not, nor can they calculate the probability of success.[7]

In an uncertain world, the most valuable predictions cannot solely be based on past data. This is the reason we need entrepreneurs: To deal with uncertainty by imagining the future! Precisely because the future is uncertain, entrepreneurs' imaginations about the future cannot be based on statistical models or calculations, but can only be based on their qualitative, subjective representations. Knight (1921) referred variously to these subjective representations as "image," "estimate," "judgments," "convictions," and "opinions." When entrepreneurs make entrepreneurial decisions, they are also making new knowledge, not just making use of existing knowledge. To generate new knowledge, they need to be forward looking, not backward looking (Fontana and Gerrard, 2004, pp. 626–627), overcoming constraints of thinking anchored in the past (Rindova and Martins, 2018). Any prediction that can be made through statistical models is not the work of entrepreneurs. It is no wonder the judgments of entrepreneurs are often incomprehensible to the average person. Zhou Hongyi, the founder of Qihoo 360, even said that when he got started with the Internet business, no matter what he did no one understood it, or they

---

[7] Chapter 10 of this book will provide detailed discussions of the four uncertainties of innovations.

even laughed at it in the beginning. Almost all great entrepreneurs have been laughed at.

No doubt big data can provide more information than sample or limited data of the past. It can help more accurately to calculate the probability distribution of risk incidents, and thus reduce risk. Therefore, big data is extremely valuable to insurance companies, commercial banks, and other institutions. However, big data is mostly unhelpful to venture capital or private equity investment decisions. No data can tell you the probability an innovation will succeed.

If the world we live in only had risk (such as the weather or natural disasters like earthquakes) but no uncertainty, perhaps the big-data-based planned economy would be possible. The real world, however, has both risk and uncertainty. Responding to uncertainty requires decision makers to be autonomous and entrepreneurial. If we mistakenly believe our world is only full of risk and attempt to respond to uncertainty with methods used for responding to risk, then the result will be the strangulation of human creativity!

From the View of People's Ideas Governing Their Behavior

For a long time, the basic viewpoint of mainstream economics has been that people's behaviors are completely governed by their interests. Rationality can explain everything. However, just as David Hume pointed out more than 200 years ago, people's behaviors are not only governed by interests, but also governed by their viewpoints. Additionally, people's understanding of interests is often perceived through viewpoints. In other words, what a person believes are his interests are often related to the views he holds. Therefore, even if people only act according to their own interests, behavior is influenced by viewpoints. John Maynard Keynes has a very famous quote:

The ideas of economists and political philosophers, both when they are right and when they are wrong, are more powerful than is commonly understood. Indeed the world is ruled by little else. Practical men, who believe themselves to be quite exempt from any intellectual influence, are usually the slaves of some defunct economist. Madmen in authority, who hear voices in the air, are distilling their frenzy from some academic scribbler of a few years back. I am sure that the power of vested interests is vastly exaggerated compared with the gradual encroachment of ideas ... But, soon or late, it is ideas, not vested interests, which are dangerous for good or evil." (Keynes, 1936, p. 400)

Viewpoints insert a wedge between cause and effect. Because viewpoints impact people's behavior, clearly distinguishing between reason and result is often not easy. The same phenomenon might lead to completely different consequences, depending on how people understand the phenomenon itself. For example, the 1930s depression brought the Social Democratic Party into power in Switzerland but in Germany the National Socialists (Nazis) took power (Berman, 1998). The 1997 Asian Financial Crisis led to a reduction in government power but the 2008 Global Financial Crisis led to an expansion of government power. What type of policy the government implements in the face of a financial crisis is determined by whether the authorities believe in Keynesianism or Hayek's business cycle theory.

Because people's behaviors are governed by ideas, we cannot accurately predict the future with past data. A "patriotic" movement can destroy a well-functioning company overnight and bring another company that is on the verge of bankruptcy back to life. No one could have predicted the collapse of the Soviet Union in 1991 based on past data because data cannot tell us how quickly people's views will change.

Big data cannot change this point. Big data did not predict Donald Trump's victory in the 2016 US presidential election. Similarly, big data did not predict the 2020 presidential election would end up like it did.

Therefore, grasping the future will always be an entrepreneurial affair. No one can solely use big data to successfully become the next Jack Ma, Pony Ma, or Elon Musk.

Ideas matter, implying that for the planned economy to succeed, the planning authorities must at the same time plan people's thoughts. People's thoughts, however, can never be planned, even if people could be brainwashed.

From the Perspective of Evolution Theory

The stability of a species comes from heredity. The evolution of a species comes from mutation. So-called mutation is just a mistake in the genetic replication process. If this mistake is a "good thing" that has a higher level of fitness, then nature or humanity will favor it. The new gene will continuously expand and replace old genes. This type of mutation causes species to evolve. Without genetic mutation, species would not evolve.

Heredity can be predicted, but mutation cannot.

This is the case for both species evolution and the progress of human society. Innovation is a mutation of social genetics. Without innovation there is no progress. Thinkers and entrepreneurs power mutation. Big data can tell us how people will act step by step but cannot predict what type of innovations will appear.

Innovation is the emergence and implementation of unique ideas and concepts. If this new concept is accepted by people, then it will slowly dominate society. If it is not accepted by people, but instead is choked to death immediately, then our concepts will not change and society will not progress.

The story of Yunnan tobacco might help us understand this point.

Tobacco came from the Americas and was introduced to China in 1575, but the history of tobacco in Yunnan spans a little over 100 years. The reason Yunnan could become the capital of Chinese tobacco – besides climate conditions – is related to the evolution of tobacco. The Nanyang Tobacco Company introduced a high-quality American tobacco species, called "jinyuan," to Yunnan. In 1962, a tobacco farmer in Lunan County found a distinctive "big jinyuan" in the tobacco field. The huge and magnificent flowers were a surprise, so he sent them to the Agricultural Science Institute of Yunnan Province. An expert determined it was a mutated jinyuan. The big jinyuan was cultivated and spread, so Yunnan tobacco surpassed others.[8] The big jinyuan was clearly not the result of a plan. If a plan had been strictly adhered to, it could not have survived.

For the same reason, innovation cannot possibly be the result of a plan made according to big data. Valuable innovations are necessarily created by entrepreneurs and screened by the market in the process of implementing them. Creations are often accidental, not consciously sought after, so they are a surprise. The planned economy, where everything is done according to already set methods, will necessarily strangle innovation and strangle the source of progress.

Expanding the "Lucas Critique"

Often, people recommend the government do this or that based on the phenomena they observe in the market. This way of thinking is incorrect.

[8] The story was drawn from Zhou Hua (2015), pp. 221–222.

Macroeconomics has a well-known "Lucas critique" that refers to economic models based on empirical data being unusable for policy making, because the implementation of policy will change that policy's underlying model.

I want to expand the Lucas critique as follows: Any empirical laws based on the market economy cannot be used for policy making because the implementation of policy will change the behavioral foundation of the observed empirical laws.

For example, assume we observe in the free market economy that enterprises in the steel industry with an annual output of 10 million tons are the most efficient. If the government decrees that enterprises with an annual output of less than 10 million tons cannot be invested in, then the enterprises with an annual output of 10 million tons will not be efficient because they are no longer the result of competition. Similarly, we observe that most of the Chinese entrepreneurs that appeared in the 1980s had not attended university. If a policy had been set, based on this observation, that only allowed people without a college education to start a business, many potential entrepreneurs would have missed the opportunity.

Many economists are keen on policy recommendations based on empirical relationships discovered by regression. The reason is they believe that the regressed result is the empirical rule. But progress in human beings is made possible by outliers, not by the regressed line. Outliers are black swans. Entrepreneurial decisions and innovations are outliers and should not be averaged out.

Big data is the product of market competition, and it cannot be put to service in the planned economy. If the government uses big data to make economic plans, the result will certainly be failure. The reason is the planned economy will eliminate big data.

Big data and artificial intelligence might replace a large number of non-creative jobs. It will never replace entrepreneurs, however, unless humanity truly enters a static equilibrium where nothing changes, there is no innovation, and there is no progress. As long as humanity still requires entrepreneurial creativity, we cannot implement the planned economy. Entrepreneurship is incompatible with the planned economy. Even if robots of the future can think like people, the planned economy still cannot be implemented, since different robots will have different ideas (otherwise it does not count as human-like thought), just as different people now have different entrepreneurial abilities.

At that point, there still will be unique entrepreneurial talents, even if they are robots.

Finally, I want to emphasize two points. First, I do not generally oppose planning. I oppose the planned economy, which is top-down, centralized planning implemented by government, regardless of the reason or the shape it takes. As Hayek pointed out, the debate is not whether planning should happen, but instead about who does the planning. Should many independent individuals with scattered and practical knowledge do the planning, or should a planning organ that lacks this type of knowledge but possesses power do the planning? (Hayek, 1978, chapter 14). In the market economy, each person and enterprise make their own plans, which is the embodiment of entrepreneurship. It is also the meaning of human action that Mises spoke of. From the perspective of this type of planning, of course big data is important. Enterprise planning in the big data era will certainly be different from enterprise planning of the past.

Second, my above criticisms of the big data-based planned economy theory are primarily based on my understanding of the essence of human knowledge and entrepreneurship. I did not mention the incentive mechanism issue. This is not to say the incentive mechanism is unimportant. On the contrary, distortion of the incentive mechanism is one of the primary reasons the planned economy failed. I only wanted to argue that even if incentives are not an issue, the big data planned economy is still unfeasible.

4 | *Prejudice and Hostility toward Entrepreneurs Is Common*

People's hostility toward entrepreneurs (business people) is a common phenomenon. In Roman times and the Middle Ages in the West, merchants could not engage in politics or become nobles. In the four occupations of traditional Chinese society, merchants were the lowest level. The phrase *"wushang bujian"* translates into English as "all businessmen are evil." In modern Western media, "greedy" is an adjective reserved for entrepreneurs. Most portrayals of entrepreneurs in movies and novels are negative. Entrepreneurs are often blamed for financial crises, environmental pollution, global warming, inequality, etc. Therefore, "hatred of the rich" is not a phenomenon in a specific culture. Chinese people "hate the rich" and so do Westerners. "Hating the rich" is also not a historical phenomenon. People in backward areas "hate the rich" and so do people in developed countries.[1]

Throughout human history, why was hatred for the rich, hatred for business activities, and hatred for entrepreneurs a common phenomenon? This question requires serious consideration. There is a deeper origin behind "hating the rich." Quite a few scholars have explored this issue. Let me list a few of them. The first is Ludwig von Mises, a representative of the Austrian School of economics. His book, titled *The Anti-Capitalistic Mentality*, is a study of the psychology behind people's hatred for the rich (Mises, 1972). The second is Friedrich von Hayek, a student of Mises and also a representative of the Austrian School of economics. Many of his writings touch on this issue, the most important of which is his 1988 book, titled *The Fatal Conceit*.

---

[1] Zitelmann (2020) provides a recent polling survey on the public opinions of the rich of four developed nations (Germany, America, France, and Great Britain). He finds that, although there are some differences between nations, it is the least risky and most politically correct to criticize the rich people in all four nations. Thus, the rich are an "admired but mistrusted minority." Part three of his book also surveyed common negative media representations of the rich, including newspapers, online, and Hollywood movies.

Chapter 6 is titled "The Mysterious World of Trade and Money." It explains why people disdain business activities. The third scholar is Thomas Sowell, an outstanding American economist. His book, titled *Intellectuals and Society*, analyzes intellectuals in a way that is extremely helpful for our understanding of the psychology and economics behind hatred for the rich (Sowell, 2012). To a large degree, hatred for the rich is instilled in modern society by certain intellectuals. The fourth scholar is German historian Rainer Zitelmann. He is a successful entrepreneur and prolific author, having written more than 20 books, of which three are especially valuable for our understanding of people's hatred for the rich. The first is titled *The Power of Capitalism*, the second is *The Rich in Public Opinion*, and the third is *In Defense of Capitalism*, published in 2019, 2020, and 2023, respectively.

Based on the opinions of the above four scholars and my own thinking over the years, I summarize people's prejudice and hostility toward entrepreneurs into two causes. One is psychological and the other is epistemological. Envy is the psychological cause. A misunderstanding of knowledge is the epistemological cause.

Envy: The Psychological Reason for Hostility toward Entrepreneurs

In China, envy is called "red eye disease." Envy is rooted in human nature. Everyone is jealous, although many are ashamed to admit they are. Envy transcends history, races, borders, and cultures. Ancient people were envious, and so are modern people. White people are envious, black people are envious, and so are yellow people. New Yorkers are envious and so are Beijingers. Interested readers can refer to German scholar Helmut Schoeck's classic book *Envy: A Theory of Social Behavior* (Schoeck, 1966). The difference between people is their degree of envy and ability to control it.

Envy can be defined as: An uncomfortable feeling, or even resentment, when a person sees something desirable that others have but he or she does not. Things that cause envy include wealth, fame, social status, beauty, talent, test scores, etc. It could be said that any difference between people can cause envy. For example, when other people's children go to a prestigious school, but your child does not have this opportunity, you will get envious.

Envy contrasts with admiration. Admiration means desiring some-thing that others have. Envy is wanting others to lose something, regardless of whether you can obtain it. If a person is very envious, he will gloat when he sees a wealthy person go bankrupt, a famous person have a scandal, or a beautiful woman become disfigured. Some scholars distinguish between benign envy and malicious envy. Using this definition, this text addresses malicious envy. Most scholars, how-ever, disagree with this distinction.[2]

Envy makes the people involved uncomfortable. According to Mises' theories, dissatisfaction with the current state is the reason people act. Therefore, to relieve this dissatisfaction, people take action. In general, there are about five ways to resolve envy.[3]

The first way is condemning society for its unfairness. When envious people see themselves at a disadvantage, the first thing they feel is a sense of injustice (Hoogland, Thielk, and Smith, 2017, p. 127). I am poorer than you, not because I do not work hard or have no ability, but instead because the social rules of the game are unfair. Why can't my children go to a good school? Why does your beauty attract attention? Thus, people think about ways to change the rules of the game and society's *status quo*. I must say that injustice does exist in reality, but it is different from the "injustice" condemned by envious people.

The second way is finding a scapegoat. A common psychological characteristic of human beings is the belief that one's own misfortunes are caused by others, with no personal responsibility for it.[4] This "other" is the "scapegoat" for the misfortune. The scapegoat must be a small number of people because it is easy to concentrate on them as a scapegoat and win the sympathy and support of the public. For example, Hitler made the Jews scapegoats for all the misfortunes of Germany. In any society, rich people are always a minority, so they easily become scapegoats for poverty. The reason I am poor is because those rich bosses (entrepreneurs) made all the money.

---

[2] For a brief review on literature of the distinction between benign envy and malicious envy, and its criticism, see Zitelmann (2020), chapter 4.

[3] In the terms of Alicke and Zell (2008), these kinds of methods are "the secondary control mechanism." Also see Zitelmann (2020), p. 56.

[4] For an interesting discussion and related literature on the psychology of scapegoating, see Zitelmann (2020), chapter 6.

The third way is occupying the moral high ground. There is a relatively objective standard for wealth because it is easy to measure. There is no objective standard for morality, however, because it is not easy to measure. Anyone can claim to be morally noble. For this reason, failure makes it easy to take the moral high ground (Mises, 1972). I am poor because I am virtuous, decent, kind-hearted, and affectionate. Those rich people are rich because they are venal, greedy, ruthless, selfish, immoral, deceitful, dishonest, and cruel for the sake of wealth. In short, wealth and morality are inversely proportional. We learned from Mencius that "he who seeks to be rich will not be benevolent" (*weifu buren*) (Legge, 1895. p. 240). Are the poor necessarily righteous? No. In my observations, there are inconsiderate rich people, but there are more inconsiderate poor people. Why do we not have the phrase "he who is poor will not be benevolent"? The answer is related to hatred for the rich.

The fourth way is changing the domain of comparison by emphasizing your own advantages and playing down your disadvantages. Because different domains are often difficult to compare, changing the domain of comparison helps in reducing psychological imbalances (Alicke and Zell, 2008, p. 87). For example, you are rich, so I will not compare our wealth, but instead compare our happiness. Money cannot necessarily buy happiness. You are more capable than me, so I will not compare our talents, instead I will compare our kindness. Kindness is more important than talents. You are better looking than me, so I will not compare our appearances, instead I will compare our intelligence. Beautiful women are usually dumber, and so on.

Fifth, it comes down to luck. There is nothing people can do about luck. When a person attributes other's success and their own failures to luck, it usually does not feel so bad. For example, when I lose money gambling or buying lottery tickets it is because of my bad luck. I feel relieved when thinking about it this way.

Of the five methods mentioned above, the first three are active, aggressive behaviors. They change social values or even lead to violent revolutions. The last two methods are passive and peaceful behaviors. They are personal self-cultivation and will not have a big impact on society.

Scholars do not pay enough attention to the impact of envy on human behavior and the social system. In fact, the egalitarian ideal is to a large degree the product of envy. The planned economy changes the traditional rules of the game to satisfy the psychology of averaging poverty and wealth, thus it is also a product of envy. Everyone eats the same, dresses the same, and has the same type of housing, so no one has a sense of superiority. But when you are wealthier than me, with more money, a bigger house, and higher status, I am happy to have our property confiscated because you have more to lose than I do.

Wealth and poverty are relative concepts. In this world, no matter how rich everyone's life is, the wealthy are always a minority. Therefore, envy is always there. Egalitarianism has a basis in the public opinion of any society. Egalitarian institutional arrangements, however, can only "kill wealth" but not "relieve poverty." The reason is that wealth is created, and changeable, not given and fixed. Existing wealth can be confiscated, but wealth that no one is willing to create cannot be. In fact, "relieving poverty" might not have been the goal in the first place. Killing the rich is!

Envy is also the psychological basis of various political movements. Seeing higher-ups pulled down, criticized, paraded through the streets, and thrown into prison gives many people a kind of psychological satisfaction (Feather, 1989).

There are also rich people in traditional societies, but they do not suffer common envy. In contrast, businesspeople and entrepreneurs suffer the most hostility. Why? To a large degree, this has to do with the operational characteristics of the market.

Envy is based on mutual comparison. Without comparison, there is no envy. Comparisons have a scope, referring to who is being compared. Generally speaking, people always tend to compare themselves with their peers, such as their classmates and neighbors. The more comparable the comparability, the greater the envy. Therefore, envy often occurs among the same types. For example, Chinese people will envy China's rich people, but are not very envious of America's Bill Gates or Warren Buffett. In China, during the planned economy era, rural people were not envious of urban people because they could only blame their own bad luck for being born in the countryside.

For people to be compared, there must be no insurmountable barriers between them. Traditional societies are hierarchical societies, identity societies. A person's rank and identity in that type of society is innate, not acquired, so people of different ranks are incomparable. The medieval nobility evolved over time. Nobles of the same rank were envious of each other, but commoners felt they were destined to be poor, so they did not envy nobles. Mises gives the example of a wife that asks her husband: "Why are you not a duke? If you were a duke, I would be a duchess." His reply would be: "If I had been born the son of a duke, I would not have married you, a slave girl, but the daughter of another duke." As Mises said, "the wealth of an aristocrat is not a market phenomenon," but the entrepreneur is. In the market economy, if other people make money but you do not, then you will feel ashamed in front of your wife (Mises, 1972, chapter 1). This is because in a market economy, everyone is equal, free, and has the opportunity to get rich.

Over time, money became a common unit of measurement for wealth, so the scope of comparison greatly expanded beyond the limitations of traditional society or a small village. In modern society, especially after the free movement of people, almost everyone believes they can be compared to anyone else. Even among strangers, comparisons can be made now that could not be made in the past. Thus, people will think: "I grew up in the same environment as that rich person, and even his family conditions were not as good as mine, so how did he become that rich?" If he inherited a fortune from his parents, then he is not self-made. If he made his wealth from scratch and I did not, then this annoyance will make me uncomfortable. Therefore, it is easier to envy entrepreneurs today.

In a market economy, anyone has the right to choose to be an entrepreneur. There are no institutional obstacles to being an entrepreneur. Successful entrepreneurs, however, are a minority at about 1% of the population. Outstanding entrepreneurs will only account for one in one thousand or one in ten thousands of the population. Therefore, entrepreneurs are the most suitable candidates to be the "scapegoats" of social problems. Scolding entrepreneurs, saying they are "greedy" or "have achieved wealth at the expense of others," might not be cheered on by the majority, but at least the majority will not be offended.

Zero-sum game thinking is the cognitive basis of envy. A zero-sum game is when society's wealth is fixed, so one person's gain is another person's loss. Some people becoming wealthy means that other people became poor. If society is a positive-sum game, then envy will lose most of its foundation, because the rich do not necessarily harm the interests of the poor. Everyone has the opportunity to become rich. You also have hope to obtain the things that other people obtain, as long as you work for it. Why do people keep a zero-sum game way of thinking?

This has to do with human cognitive evolution, as explained by American economist Paul Rubin in his article "Folk Economics" (Rubin, 2003). Briefly speaking, over millions of years of history, human society lacked technological progress and economic growth. Resources were very scarce. Land, as the most important or even the only resource, had a limited area. If you plant this land, I cannot. Over a long period of time human beings formed the zero-sum game way of thinking. Zero-sum game thinking, consisting of explicit beliefs about the economy, is still held by lay people, untrained in economics, even though the real world has become a positive-sum game of the market. Much of economic and social policy today is formed on folk economics (Boyer and Petersen, 2018).

The Epistemological Basis for Hostility toward Entrepreneurs: A Misunderstanding of Knowledge

The second reason for hostility toward entrepreneurs is related to people's (mis)understanding of knowledge. In other words, it is related to people's "ignorance."

Humans undertake many productive activities, some of which are very easy to understand. For example, farmers plant in spring and harvest in autumn. They plant melons to get melons and beans to get beans (i.e., "you reap what you sow"). Workers sweat from morning to night to turn raw materials into products. Everyone can see and feel their labor efforts. There is no mystery at all.

Yet, the average person does not understand how an entrepreneur can make money. Entrepreneurs do not work in the field like farmers or sweat like workers, so why are they rich? In particular, businessmen engaged in trade do not even change any material form of the product, so how can they make money? It seems as they did *ex nihilo*! The only answer is that they buy low and sell high, deceiving both the seller and the buyer.[5]

---

[5] Hayek (1988), chapter 6 provides a deep analysis of why profit made by business people seems mysterious for most people. "A neglected influence reinforcing such prejudices [toward business] has to do with physical effort, muscular activity and 'sweat of one's brows'. Physical strength, and the ordinary tools and weapons that often accompany its employment, are not only observable but tangible. There is nothing mysterious about them, even for most people who lack them themselves ... People could see how physical effort of the farmer or artisan added

One explanation is that people do not understand the role of "knowledge" in wealth creation. Some people are manual laborers while others are knowledge workers. If people can realize that entrepreneurs use knowledge to make money, some biases can be eliminated. The deep problem, however, is that there is an error in people's understanding of knowledge.

Throughout history and in all countries, intellectuals, learned people, and scholars are respected. Northern Song scholar Wang Zhu wrote in *Shentongshi*: "Everything is inferior, except for studying." People usually understand knowledge as knowledge learned from books, knowledge taught by teachers in a classroom, or knowledge that takes time to accumulate. Hayek calls this knowledge "scientific knowledge." Polanyi calls it "explicit knowledge." Sowell calls it "procedural knowledge." I call it "hard knowledge."

There is, however, another kind of knowledge. Hayek calls it "practical knowledge." Polanyi calls it "tacit knowledge." Sowell calls it "ordinary knowledge." I call it "soft knowledge." This knowledge does not come from books or teachers. There is no way it can be scientifically proven. It is unrelated to the amount of time spent studying. The biggest feature of this kind of knowledge is that it is not easy to encode and spread. It can only be used by the owner.

The success or failure of entrepreneurs is largely determined by practical knowledge, tacit knowledge, ordinary knowledge, or soft knowledge, not scientific knowledge, explicit knowledge, procedural knowledge, or hard knowledge. Although the latter knowledge is important, anyone can obtain it. Work related to it can even be delegated to professionals. Entrepreneurs' soft knowledge, to a large degree, is a unique entrepreneurial ability, including imagination, intuition, alertness, vision, judgment, subconsciousness, communication ability, persuasion, and organization. Most people do not have this ability. Even if they do, it is not outstanding.

Because most people do not understand the importance of soft knowledge, entrepreneurial money making appears to get "something

to the total of visible useful things – and account for differences of wealth and power in terms of recognizable causes ... But as soon as knowledge – which was not open or visible – was introduced as an element in competition, knowledge not possessed by other participants, and which must have seemed to many of them also to be beyond the possibility of possession, the familiarity and sense of fairness vanished" (p. 91).

from nothing." There must be magic, fraud, and immorality behind it. Thus, when we see those naughty classmates that dropped out of school but became millionaires or even billionaires, some people become recalcitrant: "I was a good student, and even went abroad to study for a doctorate, but he made much more money than me. Outrageous!"

Intellectuals' Prejudice toward Entrepreneurs

We can get a good understanding of intellectual prejudice toward entrepreneurs by combining psychological envy with epistemological ignorance. The "intellectuals" mentioned here refers to intellectuals as a whole, not all people called "intellectuals," let alone scholars in the general concept.

According to Thomas Sowell's definition, intellectuals are those who produce and disseminate ideas. Their final product is an idea (Sowell, 2012, chapter 1). University professors are intellectuals, but doctors and engineers are not, because the latter's final work product is a cured disease or some project, not ideas. A medical doctor like Doctor Zhang Wenhong, however, became an intellectual when he began to teach the public about preventing Covid-19. He was disseminating ideas. Of course, we could call him a public intellectual. People in the media are also included as public intellectuals. They primarily disseminate ideas to the masses.

Intellectuals dominate the market for ideas. The public opinion space in which we live is largely shaped by intellectuals. Most people admire intellectuals, thinking they are knowledgeable, but I want to throw some cold water on that point. British writer George Orwell, author of *1984*, once said: "Some ideas are so foolish only an intellectual could believe them, for no ordinary man could be so foolish" (Ibid. p. 4). That is the way it is. For example, when people's communes were established in China in the 1950s, the peasants thought that it was unfeasible and strongly opposed it, but those well-educated cadres thought it was feasible and vigorously advocated for it. As it turned out, on this matter, they were stupider than ordinary people.

This phenomenon can be well explained by Kahneman's concept of *"theory-induced blindness,"* which refers to:

once you have accepted a theory and used it as a tool in your thinking, it is extraordinarily difficult to notice its flaws. If you come upon an observation that does not seem to fit the model, you assume that there must be a perfectly good explanation that you are somehow missing. You give the theory the benefit of doubt, trusting the community of experts who have accepted it" (Kahneman, 2011, p. 277).

Mankind's biggest disasters in the twentieth century came from ideas that some intellectuals firmly believed in but were indeed very stupid. Sowell explained why intellectuals can cause such large catastrophes. First, the evaluation of ideas is mainly done among intellectuals, not by outsiders. Therefore, as long as a ridiculous idea has enough colleagues to justify it, accept it, and go along with it, it will become popular. Second, intellectuals are not responsible for the consequences of the implementation of their own ideas. Even when their ideas are proven wrong, their reputation within academia is not affected. For example, Jean-Paul Sartre returned to France in 1939 after studying philosophy in Germany, and he told the world that France is not much different from Hitler's Germany. Even after the fall of Nazi Germany, Sartre was still a leader in academia and was revered by intellectuals all over the world. Sartre is not an exception. Many famous intellectuals touted Hitler in the 1930s, but few have since apologized to the public (Sowell, 2012, pp. 8–12). Even fewer of the supporters of Joseph Stalin, Mao Zedong, and the Soviet System have expressed their regret.

This is in stark contrast to entrepreneurs. The product (or service) sold by entrepreneurs is not evaluated by the individual entrepreneur, or entrepreneurs as a group, but instead by their customers. If they cheat their customers, even if they do not serve jail time, they will be punished by the market. If they do not attract customers, then the entrepreneur goes bankrupt. He not only loses money and wealth, but also reputation!

The ideas of intellectuals might be incorrect, but this does not affect their influence in the slightest. To this day, most Western intellectuals are critics of the market economy. They do not have a favorable opinion of entrepreneurs. In other words, Western intellectuals are generally left leaning. Many of the negative portrayals of entrepreneurs in society are carefully crafted by leftist intellectuals. The idea of entrepreneurs and workers being in opposition was installed in workers by intellectuals such as Karl Marx and his followers, not the general public. In the words of Rainer Zitelmann, anti-capitalism is a "secular religion" for many Western intellectuals (Zitelmann, 2019, pp. 150–154).

Leftist intellectuals' hostility toward entrepreneurs is related to both human envy (Mises, 1972; Zitelmann, 2019), and intellectuals' misunderstanding of knowledge (Hayek, 1991; Sowell, 2012; Zitelmann, 2019).

Bookish people are conceited, so Sowell quotes Daniel Flynn: "Intellectuals tend to have an inflated sense of their own wisdom" (Sowell, 2012, p. 15). They consider themselves "intellectual elites" who deserve more wealth, higher social status, and more respect. That was the case historically. Many of China's bookish people passed the imperial examinations and entered the imperial court as officials. Some of them could become "only second to the emperor."

In the market economy, however, intellectuals have competitors: "Business elites." Business elites have not read as many books but have made more money, so intellectual elites have a type of instinctive envy and resentment toward business elites.

Intellectuals tend to think that the knowledge they have is the only true knowledge. Anything they do not know cannot be counted as knowledge. They look down upon the soft knowledge, practical knowledge that entrepreneurs have. In the market economy, many successful entrepreneurs have no formal education, no scientific training, and definitely do not have scientific methods to prove their own point of view. Even some entrepreneurs with formal education are unlikely to be top students in their class. The entrepreneurs without hard knowledge are wealthier, more expressive, and more influential than the intellectuals with hard knowledge, yet their social status is not lower. If entrepreneurs show off their wealth and make intellectuals feel like beggars, it will be even more difficult for intellectuals to have a balanced psychology. There must be a problem with society! Ironically, intellectuals who are skeptical of private property rights are enthusiastic supporters of copyrights (Hayek, 1991, p. 81).

Robert Nozick (1998) pointed out that the seeds of intellectuals' sense of superiority are planted in childhood. From kindergarten to university, test scores determine ranking, with awards given to top students. How is it that, upon entering society, accolades have nothing to do with test scores? How can the income of a famous philosophy professor not be higher than a grocery store owner's? Is selling snacks more important than developing guided missiles? For intellectuals, the world is upside-down. The market economy must be unfair. The prevalence of these opinions causes even entrepreneurs to be self-abased. Perhaps this is one of the reasons many entrepreneurs want to get another degree![6]

Further, as Hayek said, intellectuals have a "fatal conceit" that they have enough knowledge and ability to build an ideal society, and are also qualified to guide social progress. Intellectuals dislike spontaneous order because it makes them feel useless. The market economy evolved spontaneously; it was not designed by intellectuals. In contrast, the planned economy is designed by a small number of intellectuals, whose writings and speeches are disseminated to the masses and simultaneously imposed upon society by force. Therefore, unsurprisingly, intellectuals have a sense of alienation toward the market economy, but a sense of affinity toward the planned economy (Hayek, 1991, chapter 5). As Zitelmann (2019) pointed out, "Once we've grasped this essential difference between capitalism as a spontaneous evolving process and socialism as a theoretical construct, the reasons why many intellectuals have a greater affinity to the latter – in whatever form – suddenly becomes obvious" (p. 156).

The market economy always compares favorably to any existing system, so intellectuals are unwilling to compare the market economy with other actual systems. On the contrary, they always imagine an egalitarian ideal society, then compare the actual market economy with their ideal society. As a result, the actual market economy is always inferior to an ideal utopia. This becomes the basis for their criticisms of the market. As Sowell points out, leftist intellectuals are gifted in rhetorical skills and adept at language corruption (Sowell, 2012, p. 28). They use terms such as "caring for the poor," "caring for the disadvantaged," and "assuming social responsibility" to sanctify their ideas and show their moral nobility. Of course, we should not doubt the sincerity of even leftist intellectuals, and more often their mistakes come from ignorance. They are not responsible for the implementation of policy, nor are they accountable for the consequences of policy implementation. They create disasters that other people pay a dear price for, but they themselves remain unscathed.

---

[6] "Anti-capitalism in its various shapes and guises ... has succeeded in putting the business elite under enormous pressure ... [M]embers of this elite have surrendered to the anti-capitalist resentment espoused by career intellectuals" (Zitelmann, 2019, p. 168) . "No man or group of men can live indefinitely under the pressure of moral injustice: they have to rebel or give in. Most of the businessmen gave in" (Ayn Rand, 1961, p. 40).

According to my observation, contemporary Chinese intellectuals' hostility toward the market economy is not as common and strong as that of Western intellectuals. Why? Perhaps it is because the Chinese intellectuals have lived under the planned economy for more than two decades. Their memories of hunger and want under the planned economy are still fresh, whereas Western intellectuals have never experienced life under the socialist planned economy. That is why socialism is so attractive to them.

Will intellectualization of entrepreneurs change people's prejudices? This question is also worth thinking about. Today's entrepreneurs are very different from entrepreneurs 30 years ago, and even more so compared to entrepreneurs from 200 years ago. More and more entrepreneurs have attended university or even have doctorates. There are many outstanding entrepreneurs among graduates of Peking University and Tsinghua University. Will this change many intellectuals' prejudice and hostility toward entrepreneurs? Probably not. Because among those who have similarly gone to university, the ones who become entrepreneurs were usually the non-outstanding students in terms of their academic performances. The outstanding students become professors or engage in other work requiring procedural knowledge. For example, among physics doctorates, some people give up their studies to go into business because they believe they have no prospects in academia. The classmates with prospects in academia become scientists, but their income might be a fraction of those that succeed in business. Therefore, even if more entrepreneurs have academic degrees, it is difficult for professional intellectuals to change their prejudice toward entrepreneurs.

Economists' Contributions and Responsibilities

The biggest contribution of economists to people's correct understanding of entrepreneurs is the help in transitioning from the zero-sum game perception to the positive-sum game perception. Among economists, the contribution of Adam Smith, the father of economics, has never been surpassed. Before Adam Smith, the common perception was that self-interest harms others and making money is immoral. Adam Smith taught people to realize that, in the market economy, self-interest not only does not harm others, but also is the most effective way to benefit others. How much money is made has nothing to do with morality. People that became rich in business no longer bore moral shackles.

However, economists are also responsible for the hatred for the rich that is prevalent in society today. Mainstream economists assume that business decision making is resolved under given constraints, which is a computational problem. In turn, this interprets wealth as a fixed quantity determined by given technologies and resources. Further, according to the second principle of welfare economics, any desired redistribution of wealth will not influence resource allocation efficiency under the given distribution. This way, efficiency and equality can be dealt with separately. The ideal model is the market taking responsibility for efficiency and the government taking responsibility for equality. This type of model sounds very tempting!

Further, in the rational decision-making model of economics, all people have the same information and knowledge, all people can obtain similar technology, all people are similarly intelligent, practical knowledge is worthless, entrepreneurs are redundant, the work of entrepreneurs can be completed by a computer, and entrepreneurs are unrelated to economic growth. In the neoclassical market paradigm, capital hiring labor is equivalent to labor hiring capital, neither better nor worse (Samuelson, 1957). Neoclassical economics is unable to explain the existence of long-run profit. In fact, in neoclassical economics, profit is a manifestation of market disequilibrium and economic inefficiency. It is unrelated to entrepreneurship. Long-term profit is definitely caused by the existence of monopolies. Monopolies harm efficiency. Not only can countering monopolies improve efficiency, but it also helps income fairness.

Precisely for this reason, even though the proportion of economists that are anti-market and hostile to entrepreneurs is lower than that for other social sciences and humanities, understanding economics does not necessarily preclude people from prejudice and hostility toward entrepreneurs. Joseph Stiglitz, a 2001 Nobel laureate in economics, is a classic example. His writings are basically anti-market. In his view, giving the market free reign will inevitably lead to polarization between the rich and poor. Resolving the problem of income distribution requires government intervention. He repeatedly warns that China should not rely on the market-based system to solve its economic problems.[7]

---

[7] For representative arguments of Joseph Stiglitz against the market economy, see Joseph Stiglitz (1994, 2016).

Conclusion: How Can Hostility toward Entrepreneurs Be Reduced?

Human progress depends on the exertion of entrepreneurship, meaning the exertion of everyone's enthusiasm and creativity. To bring entrepreneurship effectively into play, people's envy must be restrained and resolved. An envious heart should not turn into envious action. The reason underdeveloped countries are underdeveloped is related to ineffective restraints on people's envy. If the cake made by one person is shared by all out of envy, no one wants to make a cake. If a person becomes an entrepreneur but success leads to everyone dividing the wealth and failure leads to everyone gloating, how many people are willing to be entrepreneurs?[8]

So, how can envy be restrained and resolved? We might as well work on two aspects.

The first is the systemic repression of envy. The private property system and the rule of law are the most effective and foundational restraints on envy. Being green with envy is okay, but plundering is not! If private property is not protected by the law, envy will turn into plunder. Entrepreneurship will be wiped out.

It is necessary to emphasize that even though envy often wears the guise of "social justice," this does not mean that "justice" itself is unimportant. On the contrary, justice is very important. Without justice, there is no market economy. The key issue is: What is true justice? In my view, true justice is legal equality and integrity equality. Justice defined in this way is the basic characteristic and requirement for the market economy. Legal equality is every person having equivalent rights and liberties. No one enjoys privileges that others cannot equally enjoy. Integrity equality is every person's integrity receiving equivalent respect. No one's integrity is discriminated against. Effective protections for private property are essential, both for ensuring legal equality or defending integrity equality. John Locke said: "Where there is no property there is no justice," and "I can as certainly know this proposition to be true as that a triangle has three angles equal to two

---

[8] In chapter 5, titled "The Envy-barrier of the Developing Countries," of his 1966 book *Envy: A Theory of Social Behavior*, Schoeck cited various sources on developing countries to show that "institutionalized envy" makes very few people dare to be successful businessmen and innovators, which inhibited development and technological progress.

right ones" (Locke, 1690, Book IV, chapter III). Violating property rights is the greatest injustice. Granting privileges to certain people is also injustice. These injustices are incompatible with a true market economy. While individual entrepreneurs might use privilege to make money, entrepreneurs – as a whole – are harmed by privileges. They should not be scapegoats for "injustice." The "justice" demanded by envy is true injustice.

The second is the suppression of envy through moral norms. The Bible lists envy as one of the seven deadly sins. It admonishes people to avoid envy as much as possible. Many different cultures have commandments to suppress envy. The Chinese sayings *"wu gong bu shou lu"* and *"junzi ai cai, qu zhi you dao"* translate as "refuse undeserved rewards" and "a virtuous man makes his fortune in the proper way." These are similar commandments.

We must acknowledge that egalitarianism is an expression of envy, not a solution to it. Using egalitarian redistribution to address envy is like adding fuel to a fire. Helmut Schoeck early on pointed out that as soon as the process of envy starts, it will not stop. The envious person can always find new reasons to be envious. The more egalitarian a society becomes, the stronger people's envy gets. The more you give, the more you prove your superiority, the more insignificant your loss becomes (Schoeck, 1966, p. 28; see also Zitelmann, 2020, pp. 75–77). The ancient Chinese phrase "one cup of rice nurtures gratitude, 10 cups of rice nurtures resentment" has the same reasoning. Observations show that in welfare states, a person always wants more than can be obtained. Failure is blamed on the paternalistic state, not the individual. Therefore, a welfare state is necessarily filled with discontent.

In order to reduce hostility toward entrepreneurs, in addition to restraining envy, we must also change cognitive limitations that cause ignorance. This can be done in two ways.

One way is to change people's perceptions. In my 1985 article "Entrepreneurs and Idea Modernization," I listed 10 big changes in concepts. Among them, I mentioned that changes in concepts of wealth and labor are extremely important for our understanding of entrepreneurs. If we believe that wealth is a fixed quantity (zero-sum game) instead of a quantity that can be created (positive-sum game), it is easy to see other people's fortunes as the reason for one's own poverty. It is easy to become green with envy, keen to engage in class struggle. If we believe that labor involves sweat, thus we do not consider the use of entrepreneurship to be a special form of labor, then we will have difficulty understanding why entrepreneurs make money. Regrettably, close to 40 years have passed, yet the concept transformation I spoke of is far from complete. So, I republished part of that article recently, but changed the title to "The Unfinished Conceptual Transformation."

The other way is to establish a correct market theory. Contemporary mainstream economics lacks entrepreneurs and cannot explain the existence of profit, so it has planted seeds of the anti-entrepreneur attitude. Economists have a responsibility to establish a correct market theory. To this end, economics must have a paradigm shift. Dispersed and subjective knowledge must be the starting point of economic research. The effective use of dispersed knowledge must be the foundational issue of the economy. Only in this way can we truly understand how entrepreneurs create wealth.

PART II

Entrepreneurs in Market Theories

5 | The Two Paradigms of the Market

Astronomy is the study of celestial movements. Economics is the study of market operations. There were two paradigms for celestial movements: Geocentric Theory and Heliocentric Theory. Even though ancient Greek astronomer Aristarchus proposed the Heliocentric Theory as early as 300 B.C., Ptolemy's Geocentric Theory dominated the world until Nicolaus Copernicus published *On the Revolutions of Heavenly Spheres* in 1543. Even after Copernicus, a very long time passed before the Heliocentric Theory was commonly accepted. Galileo Galilei and Giordano Bruno, early supporters of the Heliocentric Theory, were all persecuted by the religious authorities. Bruno was even found guilty of "heresy" by the Roman Inquisition and burned to death in Campo de' Fiori.

Similarly, with regard to market operations, there are also two major paradigms: The neoclassical static equilibrium theory and the Austrian School (and Schumpeterian) dynamic non-equilibrium theory.[1] Although the neoclassical paradigm's explanation of market operations is fatally flawed, it still rules the economics world. The non-equilibrium paradigm of the Austrian School and Joseph Schumpeter is on the fringes of economics, disregarded by mainstream economists. It is time for mainstream economics to have a fundamental transformation in its paradigm.

Part of this chapter is drawn from Zhang, Weiying. "A paradigmatic change is needed for understanding the real market." *China Economic Review* 66 (2021): 101602. Reproduced with permission from Elsevier.

[1] Kohn (2004) identifies the value program and exchange program as the two paradigms of the market. His value paradigm is identical to neoclassical economics. His exchange paradigm includes the Austrian School as well as new institutional economics, transaction cost economics, public choice theory, law and economics, and information economics. My own view is that the Austrian School is fundamentally different from all the others, which are essentially variants of neoclassical economics, of Kohn's exchange paradigm.

Differences between the Two Market Paradigms

Stated simply, the neoclassical economics paradigm is the static equilibrium paradigm, or designed paradigm, and the Austrian School or Schumpeterian economics is the dynamic non-equilibrium paradigm, or an evolutionary paradigm. The primary differences between the two paradigms revolve around the following aspects:

(1) *Understanding of market participants:* Are market participants all-knowing (have complete information), or is their knowledge limited? Are all people equally intelligent, or are there different degrees of intelligence?

(2) *Understanding of economic decisions:* Are economic decisions made under conditions of given objectives and means, or are objectives and means themselves changeable and to be discovered?

(3) *Basic functions of the market:* Is the market's basic function to allocate scarce resources or discover information and stimulate innovation?

(4) *Understanding of competition:* Is market competition a status, or a continuing discovery and creative process?

(5) *Understanding of the functions of prices:* Is price the sole coordinating mechanism, or is it only a signal that stimulates entrepreneurial action? Is price always in an equilibrium or non-equilibrium state?

(6) *Understanding of change:* Is change in the economy exogenous – totally determined by external factors – or endogenous – at least partially influenced by market players' choices?

(7) *Understanding of entrepreneurship:* Does the market need the entrepreneurial spirit? What is the primary function of the entrepreneur?

The neoclassical paradigm assumes that everyone is similarly all-knowing with equivalent unbounded rationality and decision-making ability.[2] Economic decisions are optimization calculations under given objectives and means. It understands the market and competition as a

---

[2] Modern information economics studies the implications of asymmetric information on resource allocation under the neoclassical paradigm and therefore concludes that asymmetric information leads to efficiency loss (market failure). For a representative argument, see Stiglitz (1994), Chapter 3.

type of status. It assumes that the basic function of the market is to efficiently allocate given resources under given technology and preferences. The basic characteristic of the market is equilibrium and stability. Price is the only coordinating mechanism, and it is always at an equilibrium level. It assumes that changes are exogenous. As soon as exogenous changes occur, the market automatically achieves a new equilibrium (comparative static analysis). In an equilibrium system, entrepreneurship is neither necessary nor possible.

The Austrian School of economics assumes that people are ignorant, with each person having limited, local, and compartmentalized information.[3] Not only do people have limited calculation and judgment abilities, but also these abilities differ from person to person (Mises, 1949, chapter 15). The market is understood to be a process. The basic characteristic of the market is continuous competition and the basic function of the market is to discover and transmit information and knowledge, as well as to coordinate people's actions to drive cooperation. As Hayek said:

The economic problem of society is thus not merely a problem of how to allocate "given" resources – if "given" is taken to mean given to a single mind which deliberately solves the problem set by these "data". It is rather a problem of how to secure the best use of resources known to any of the members of society, for ends whose relative importance only these individuals know. Or, to put it briefly, it is a problem of the utilization of knowledge which is not given to anyone in its totality. (Hayek, 1945, pp. 77–78)

The Austrian School acknowledges the value of equilibrium analysis but believes that the focus of economics is not equilibrium as a status, but instead is disequilibrium as a process. Changes that cause disequilibrium can be either exogenous or endogenous. The role of prices in resolving resource allocation is not the flawless transmission of relevant equilibrium price information to attain efficient resource allocation. Instead, non-equilibrium prices provide profitable opportunities that attract and expel the arbitrage behavior of entrepreneurs. Entrepreneurs are the driving force of market competition. They discover profitable opportunities that cause the market to trend from disequilibrium toward equilibrium. Without entrepreneurs, the market

---

[3] For the epistemological foundation of the market, see Hayek (1937, 1945, 1946, and 1978).

cannot possibly trend toward equilibrium.[4] In other words, the superiority of the market is not because it can attain optimum resource allocation at any time, everywhere. Instead, it provides a type of effective incentive that incentivizes entrepreneurs to continuously improve resource allocation by discovering opportunities and correcting mistakes.

A commonality between Schumpeter's theory and the Austrian theory is taking the market as a dynamic process.[5] The starting point of Schumpeterian economics is acknowledging that there are differences between market players. Some lead and some follow. Individuals are either an individual of action or a static person. Schumpeter believed that the basic function of the market is to drive technological progress and create new markets, new products, new production methods, and new resources. The basic characteristic of the market economy is disequilibrium and change, not equilibrium and stability. From Schumpeter's perspective, the neoclassical equilibrium model is a useful starting point for understanding the essence of capitalism, only because it explains how a system without innovation operates (equilibrium and stability). However, it is not an end point because change is a characteristic of the market economy. Change is primarily endogenous, not exogenous. As Schumpeter argued:

Capitalism, then, is by nature a form or method of economic change and not only never is but never can be stationary. And this evolutionary character of the capitalist process is not merely due to the fact that economic life goes on in a social and natural environment which changes and by its change alters the data of economic actions. This fact is important ... but they are not its prime mover ... The fundamental impulse that sets and keeps the capitalist engine in motion comes from the new consumers' goods, the new methods of production or transportation, the new markets, the new forms of industrial organization that capitalist enterprise creates. (Schumpeter, 1942, pp. 72–73)

---

[4] See Mises (1949), Chapters 15 and 16; Kirzner (1973) and (1992), Chapters 1 and 2. Kirzner (1992) provides a comprehensive review of the Austrian theory of the market.

[5] Schumpeter's theory of the market is mainly developed in his *Theory of Economic Development* (1934) and *Capitalism, Socialism and Democracy* (1942). His *Business Cycles* (1939) provides rich historical stories of capitalism and is very helpful for understanding his market theory.

Whereas a stationary feudal economy would still be a feudal economy, and a stationary socialist economy would still be a socialist economy, stationary capitalism is a contradiction in terms. (Schumpeter, 1943, p. 179)

For Schumpeter, entrepreneurial innovation is the prime source of changes in the market. Innovation is creative destruction. Entrepreneurs as innovators are the force that breaks equilibrium. Without them, there is no progress or development. In Schumpeter's view, market competition is not primarily price competition, but instead is competition in the aspects of product, technology, and service. Thus, competition and entrepreneurial spirit are inseparable.

Neoclassical Economics Is Not a Good Market Theory

A good market theory should be a theory that can explain what is happening in the real market and how the market operates in reality. The market in neoclassical economics is more of the economists' constructed market, rather than the real market. In Mises's words, the neoclassical market is "the imaginary construction of the evenly rotating economy" (Mises, 1949, p. 252). Therefore, neoclassical economics fails to tell us how the real market works. To prove the efficiency of the market, neoclassical economics made certain assumptions (certainty, complete information, perfect rationality, fixed endowments, etc.), both strong and impractical. These assumptions are critical to its conclusions, but the result is that our understanding of the market is distorted. According to neoclassical economics, the market's efficiency in theory is simultaneously the market's failure in practice, since not even one of the ideal conditions that support the market's efficiency is satisfied. For this reason, neoclassical economics is uglifying, instead of beautifying, the market.[6] The efficiency of the real market does not depend on the assumptions of neoclassical economics.

In contrast with neoclassical economics, the Austrian School of economics is a better market theory. The Austrian School of economics and Schumpeterian economics study the real market, not an imagined market. In the real market, the future is uncertain and indeterminate, and people are ignorant. People have incomplete information and

---

[6] Zhang (2015a) provides a vivid metaphor of how the market is uglified in neoclassical economics.

limited knowledge. Judgment and imagination are critical in decision making. The market is a discovery as well as a creative process. In this process, not all knowledge, resources, preferences, and technology are given. Instead, they depend on utilization and innovation by entrepreneurs. Because of people's ignorance, dis-coordination and misallocations are bound to occur in the market. However, these dis-coordination and misallocations are completely different from the market failure claimed in neoclassical economics. Resolving dis-coordination and misallocation relies on entrepreneurial activities, not government interference. The superiority of the market does not depend on disequilibrium never occurring. Instead, it depends on the market's ability to correct dis-coordination through entrepreneurial arbitrage and innovation, and thus to drive sustained economic growth. As a result, using the standards of neoclassical economics to judge whether or not the market is failing is a mistake.

"Perfect competition" is neoclassical economics' ideal template for the market. Any deviation from perfect competition is considered a "market failure." Specifically, neoclassical economics identifies three types of market failures: Market failures caused by monopolies; market failures caused by externalities and public goods; and market failures caused by asymmetric information.

The market failure theory is frequently used by government officials all over the world to support whatever interventions they want to make in the market. Let me present two stories from China to show this.

Story 1. In 2011, facing inflation pressure, the National Development and Reform Commission (NDRC) of China directed enterprise managers to not raise their prices. When asked by a journalist whether this requirement constituted intervention in enterprise autonomy, a senior official at NDRC answered: "No, this is not administrative intervention. The market coordinates resource allocation and improves efficiency. However, the effective functioning of markets presupposes full competition and symmetric information. Some enterprises with a dominant position and monopoly power are suspected of violating laws and rules. We made an appointment with them to re-affirm laws and regulations, directing them to better and legally exercise their pricing autonomy." [7]

---

[7] See the official website of the NDRC as of April 19, 2011, https://www.ndrc.gov.cn/xwdt/xwfb/xwfb/201104/t20110419_956798.html

Story 2. In the 2013 Summer Summit of the World Economic Forum in Tianjin, I happened to serve as a panelist on a panel with a vice president of China Mobile. One of the themes of the panel was about market liberalization. When I said that China should abolish the state monopoly in telecommunications, the vice president argued angrily: "No, we are not a monopoly. While we hold two thirds of market share that does not mean that we are a monopolist at all. There are three providers in our market, and competition is very fierce. Tencent is a real monopoly; everyone uses WeChat."

These two senior officials seem well trained in economics. The first one, at least, knows information economics and they both understand monopoly theory. Their arguments sound correct according to the neoclassical theory. Market share is everything in the neoclassical measure of monopoly power, and it is irrelevant whether the firm is private and operates in an open industry or is state-owned and operates in a closed industry. Tencent (private firm) does have a higher share than China Mobile (state-owned enterprise) in their respective markets, so the former is more monopolistic than the latter.

However, all three theories of market failure on which these two officials' arguments are based are wrong. I will discuss asymmetric information market failure in Chapter 6, monopoly market failure in Chapter 7, and market failure caused by externalities and public goods in Chapter 12.

Entrepreneurs' Status in the Market

Perhaps the most important difference between neoclassical economics and Austrian economics/Schumpeterian economics is their different understandings of the entrepreneur's status and function in the market. All the three market failure theories of neoclassical economics are natural consequences of ignoring entrepreneurship. The debate on industrial policy is related to whether we understand entrepreneurship.[8]

The market in neoclassical economics is a market without entrepreneurs. The neoclassical assumptions already excluded the possibility of an entrepreneur existing. If resources, technology, and preferences are all given and known by everyone, and the market is always in an equilibrium state, then how can there still be room for entrepreneurs?

[8] See Chapter 12 of this book.

However, entrepreneurs are central to the market in Austrian School economics and Schumpeterian economics. Because of the ignorance and disparity between the majority of players in the market, without entrepreneurs, resources could not possibly be utilized efficiently. New technologies and new products could not appear, so the economy could not possibly grow. Without entrepreneurs, there is no market economy as an economic system. Entrepreneurs are not only a force that drives the market toward equilibrium, but they are also a force that breaks old equilibriums and creates new potential ones. It is precisely the arbitrage behavior of entrepreneurs that discovers disequilibrium and efficiently allocates resources. It is precisely the innovation of entrepreneurs that leads to new products and new technologies. Only then can the economy maintain growth.

It should be pointed out that, while both Schumpeter and the Austrian School take entrepreneurs as the major driving force of the market process, Schumpeterian entrepreneurs differ from Mises–Hayek–Kirzner entrepreneurs. For Schumpeter, entrepreneurs are innovators. For Mises, Hayek, and Kirzner, entrepreneurs are arbitragers. Arbitrage entrepreneurs drive the market toward equilibrium (Kirzner, 1973, pp. 69–87), while innovation entrepreneurs break and disturb equilibrium (Schumpeter, 1934, p. 64). My own view is that arbitrage and innovation are two basic functions of entrepreneurs and that the market process can be better understood by a combination of these two functions. It is the interaction between arbitrage and innovation that drives sustained economic growth in a market economy. I shall discuss this point in detail in Chapter 10.

As Kirzner argued, the decision maker in neoclassical economics is a Robinsian *homo economicus* who makes optimal choices under given objectives and constraints (Kirzner, 1973, p. 38). For a Robinsian decision maker, consumer's preferences, production technology, and available resources are all given. The decision maker knows all relevant information, including the probability of all contingent states. Thus, decision making is a pure calculation of a mathematical problem. The solution is implied by assumptions. There is no need for alertness, imagination, and judgment.

In Austrian School economics and Schumpeterian economics, the most important decision maker is not a Robinsian *homo economicus*, but instead is the entrepreneur with a good intuition, rich imagination, smart judgment, and great creativity. The real market is full of uncertainty. It is uncertainty that makes entrepreneurship indispensable and the Robinsian decision model impractical and inessential. Entrepreneurs think "outside of the box," not "within the box." The entrepreneur must foresee something that most people cannot foresee, discover opportunities missed by others, and imagine a future which others think impossible. From entrepreneurs' perspective, objectives and constraints are not given, but instead they must be undetermined and changeable. In an uncertain and indeterminate world, preferences, technology, and resources are not already known, but instead must be discovered and even created. Entrepreneurs' decisions are not entirely implied by existing price data, but instead depends on intuition, imagination, and judgment. As Kirzner pointed out, entrepreneurship is not encapsulated in the mere possession of greater knowledge of market opportunities:

The aspect of knowledge which is crucially relevant to entrepreneurship is not so much the substantive knowledge of market data as alertness, the knowledge of where to find market data. Once one imagines knowledge of market data to be already processed with absolute certainty, one has...imagined away the opportunity for further entrepreneurial (as distinct from 'Robinsian') decision making. (Kirzner, 1973, p. 67)

The most entrepreneurial decision is to change, rather than to satisfy, constraints of resources, technology, and even consumers' preferences. As Schumpeter pointed out:

Yet innovations in the economic system do not as a rule take place in such a way that first new wants arise spontaneously in consumers and then the productive apparatus swings round through their pressure. We do not deny the presence of this nexus. It is, however, the producer who as a rule initiates economic change and consumers are educated by him if necessary; they are, as it were, taught to want new things, or things which differ in some respect or other from which they have been in the habit of using. (Schumpeter, 1934, p. 65)

In neoclassical economics, with given data, all rational people will make equivalent choices, such as the correct answer to an examination question is the same for all students. As I pointed out in Chapter 2, in the real world, even with the same data and hard knowledge, different entrepreneurs will make different judgments and choices, and we cannot tell who is right *ex ante*. Entrepreneurial decisions are not just determined by data and hard knowledge, they depend more on "practical knowledge" (or "tacit knowledge") that is difficult to express, codify, and circulate. In all these respects, individuals differ from one another. As pointed out by Hayek (1945), it is practical knowledge, not scientific knowledge and statistical data that play a decisive role in business decisions.

In simple terms, decision-making in neoclassical economics is a rational calculation which anyone can do, whereas entrepreneurial decision-making is an individual judgment. Mises (1949) wrote: "Entrepreneurial judgement cannot be bought on the market. The entrepreneurial idea that carries on and brings profit is precisely that idea which did not occur to the majority. It is not correct foresight as such that yields profits, but foresight better than that of the rest" (p. 871).

Schumpeter believed that innovation is the basic function of entrepreneurs. Entrepreneurial innovation is based on unique judgments, not rational calculation. Roebuck and Bolton funded the development of Watts' steam engine. The Stephensons developed the locomotive. Thomas Edison invented the electrical lighting system. Carl Benz invented the automobile. King C. Gillette invented the safety razor. The Wright brothers invented the airplane. Jobs and Wozniak invented the personal computer. Bill Gates created the software industry. Brin and Page founded Google. Jack Ma founded Taobao. Pony Ma developed WeChat. So many other innovations are based on the unique judgment of entrepreneurs, not data-based calculations that any person can do.

Another reason neoclassical economics is unable to understand entrepreneurs is because it assumes that producers' only goal is profit maximization. Certainly, pursuit of profit is a major goal of entrepreneurs, but, as Schumpeter pointed out and I quoted in Chapter 2, entrepreneurs have goals above and beyond (although related to) profit. These include: (1) the dream to found a commercial empire, (2) the will to conquer, and (3) the enjoyment of creating. By ignoring these non-profit goals, the expected-profit maximization model typically underestimates the entrepreneurial motivation to innovate. These non-profit motivations can more than offset the disincentives caused by "positive externality" as defined in mainstream economics. This will make the externality and even public good – based market failure theory invalid.

Let me exemplify this point using canal excavation in the history of England. Before 1759, England did not have a true canal or artificial waterway. The first true canal in England, the Worsley Canal, was promoted by Francis Egerton, 3rd Duke of Bridgewater. He owned major coal deposits near Manchester, but the high cost of transportation made coal mining almost impossible. In 1759, distinguished engineer James Brindley took on the task of building the Worsley Canal for the Duke of Bridgewater. The project was completed in two years. At the time, this canal was considered the "Eighth Wonder of the World." The excavation of this canal caused coal prices in Manchester to drop by half. It became the justification for a network of routes. From that point on, canal projects continued one after another. Within 30 years, water routes covered every corner of England. At one point in time, there was even an oversupply of canals.[9]

The construction of England's canal network was advocated entirely by private entrepreneurs. They also bore the costs and risks. The role of the monarch and Parliament was limited to sending people to investigate and approve. Two types of people played a major role in the construction, funding, and advocacy of canals. The first type were people such as the Duke of Bridgewater. They had mining resources to excavate and required inexpensive means of transportation. The second type were the emerging industrial giants such as ceramic entrepreneur Josiah Wedgwood, metallurgical entrepreneur Matthew Bolton, and others. Of note, Wedgwood is Charles Darwin's grandfather, and Bolton was an investor in the Watt steam engine. The motivation of these promoters cannot be attributed to profit only.

The Eight Paradoxes of the Mainstream Market Theory

It is commonly believed that mainstream neoclassical economics is a logically rigorous system. The reality is that there exist serious logical paradoxes within this system as a market theory. Below, I summarize eight paradoxes in mainstream neoclassical economics.

Paradox 1: The Precondition for Market Efficiency Is the Non-existence of the Market

According to the First Theorem of Welfare Economics, perfect competition, and only perfect competition, can achieve a Pareto optimum.

---

[9] See Mantoux (1928[1964]) for a detailed discussion of the construction of England's canal network.

Thus, perfect competition is the most efficient and desirable market structure. Any deviation from perfect competition will cause loss of efficiency in the allocation of resources. Preconditions for perfect competition are the absence of economies of scale and diminishing returns. In technical terms: The production set is convex. In other words, perfect competition is incompatible with an increasing return to scale.

However, preconditions for the existence of markets are division of labor and specialization. Without specialization and division of labor, markets cannot possibly exist. The precondition for division of labor and specialization is increasing returns to scale. Therefore, logically, market efficiency is preconditioned by the non-existence of a market. The factors that cause the market to appear – on the contrary – become the factors that cause market failure. This has been called the contradiction between the "invisible hand" and the "pin factory" (division of labor theory). The invisible hand and the division of labor theory cannot both be true. This conflict has been recognized by economists for a long time.[10] However, no one has explicitly pointed out that the absence of increasing returns to scale is equivalent to the non-existence of the market.

Paradox 2: Market Efficiency Is Incompatible with Innovation

Perfect competition is defined as an infinite number of small firms using identical technology to produce homogenous products at equivalent costs. Thus, each firm is too small to affect price. It faces a level demand curve with unlimited price elasticity.

Innovation is a basic means of market competition in reality. Innovation means doing something different from everyone else. It means using new production methods to produce differentiated products. Therefore, an innovator's demand curve certainly slopes downward. The more disruptive innovation is, the steeper the demand curve faced by the innovator.

Therefore, perfect competition is incompatible with innovation. In order to attain perfect competition, there cannot be innovation. Alternatively, as long as there is innovation, there cannot be perfect

---

[10] This is the reason Smith's theory of division of labor is ignored by neoclassical economists. See Young (1928), and Stigler (1951), among others. Also see Warsh (2007), chapter 4 for detailed discussions in a historical perspective of economics.

competition. According to the logic of orthodox economics, innovation inevitably leads to monopolies and causes loss of allocative efficiency. Efficient resource allocation and innovation are having our cake and eating it, too. This is the reason why innovation has long been absent from mainstream economics, and at best taken as exogenous, even in literature on economic growth.[11]

Paradox 3: The Efficient Market Is Incompatible with the Orderly Market

According to mainstream economic theory, the most efficient market is the atomized market. Each producer is nameless and insignificant. The consumer is unable to differentiate between the products of one firm from the products of another; no brands for products and no loyalty from consumers.

However, in a real market, brands are a commitment to the consumer. Brands are an important means that producers use to attract consumers and that consumers use to supervise producers. A market cannot effectively and orderly operate without brands. Without brands, fraudulent activity cannot be effectively exposed and restrained; and producers cannot possibly obtain the trust of consumers. Thus, market exchanges cannot exceed the scope of acquaintances.[12] In particular, a brand is related to the size of the firm. Only those firms who are big enough in a relevant market can have a brand. (Zhang, 2015a; 2015b, chapter 1) Therefore, according to the logic of orthodox economics, the most efficient market is necessarily the disorderly market. Alternatively, the orderly market is necessarily an inefficient market.

Paradox 4: Externality Theories Contradict Actual Technological Progress

According to mainstream economic theories, the existence of externalities will lead to misalignment between the individual optimum and the social optimum. This will bring about efficiency loss. Because the

---

[11] Schumpeter (1934, 1942) was the first economist to point out that perfect competition is incompatible with innovation. He therefore challenged mainstream economics.

[12] See Shearmur and Klein (1997), Kreps (1986), and Zhang (2018), chapter 8, among others.

spill-over effect exists in innovation and technological progress, individuals and firms in a competitive market cannot obtain the full social benefit brought about by innovation. Therefore, they cannot possibly have adequate incentive to engage in innovation. Technological progress in the market economy must necessarily be slow. Only when innovators obtain government subsidies can the speed of innovation be sufficiently rapid and optimal.

In reality, technological progress in the market economy has been the most rapid. Since the Industrial Revolution, technological change has been endless, with new products and new technologies continuously emerging. It has even caused some people to worry that technology has progressed too rapidly. Rapid technological progress in the market economy pulled humanity out of the Malthusian Trap. This point was acknowledged by Marx and Engels as early as 1848. In *The Communist Manifesto*, they stated that the bourgeoisie had created more in 100 years as the ruling class than all of human history before that. Mokyr (1990) gave a detailed description of technological progress in the history of humanity, and identifies the Industrial Revolution as "miracle years." He argues that the technological progress since the Industrial Revolution has provided society with what economists call a "free lunch."

In another aspect, according to mainstream economic theories, government is an effective means for resolving externalities. However, in those countries where the economy is dominated by the government, technological progress is the slowest, or even stagnant.

Paradox 5: Optimal Resource Allocation Is Incompatible with Economic Growth

The four previous paradoxes lead to the fifth paradox: Market efficiency is incompatible with economic growth. The reason for this is that optimum resource allocation requires perfect competition, meaning there cannot be increasing returns, innovation, or brands. The true source of economic growth is expanded division of labor and specialization, innovation and technological progress, and market scale. These all rely on increasing returns and brands. Therefore, according to orthodox economic theory, for the market to be efficient, there cannot be growth. Alternatively, for the economy to grow, the market cannot be efficient.

In the neoclassical theory of growth pioneered by Solow (1956), technological progress can be only taken as exogenous – an external shock – although various empirical studies show that technological progress was the major contribution to growth. The new growth model of Romer (1986, 1990) and others tried to endogenize the technological progress as an automatic side effect of production itself or the result of intentional investment in research and development, so it is called the "endogenous growth model." However, as Kohn (2004) pointed out, this endogenized technological progress is just like the Solow model's exogenous technological progress: It just happens. It is technological progress without innovation.

Paradox 6: *The Efficiency of Markets Is Equivalent to the Efficiency of Central Planning*

Neoclassical economics is believed to use stringent mathematics to prove the efficiency and superiority of markets. From this perspective, people that accept neoclassical economics would necessarily defend the market economy and oppose the planned economy. However, according to neoclassical economic theories, a series of assumptions (including given preferences, resources and technology, perfect competition, complete information, etc.) are the premise for market efficiency. On the one hand, this means that because reality cannot satisfy even one of these preconditions, the market is necessarily inefficient and failing. On the other hand, this means that if these assumptions can be satisfied, then the planned economy and the market economy are equally efficient.

Therefore, neoclassical economics cannot discriminate between a market system and a planning system, implying that if one truly believes neoclassical economics is a good theory of the market, then one cannot logically oppose the planned economy. At the very least, neoclassical economics cannot differentiate the merits and demerits of the planned economy and the market economy. Indeed, during the debate on the feasibility of the socialist economy in the 1930s, Polish economist Oskar Lange, a professor at the University of Chicago, used the neoclassical model to prove that the planned economy was workable. At the time, mainstream economists believed Lange's points were logically unassailable. What is curious is that the collapse of the Soviet Union and Eastern European planned economies has not yet made mainstream economists rethink the validity of the neoclassical model. For most of them, nothing seems to have happened!

Paradox 7: *There Is a Contradiction between Externality-based Market Failure and Monopoly-based Market Failure*

Neoclassical economics proves that externalities and monopolies both will cause market failure and invite government intervention. However, these two market failure theories are contradictory to each other.

According to the externality-based failure theory, if negative externalities (such as pollution) exist, then private profit maximization decisions will cause output to exceed the social optimum. However, according to the monopoly failure theory, if firms have price-setting power, then profit maximization output will be lower than the social optimum. Put in simple terms, it means that negative externality produces too much, and monopoly produces too little. This means that within an industry, if negative externalities exist, then a monopoly is good, because it can rectify the externality-led efficiency loss (excessive production). Similarly, if monopolies exist, negative externalities are also good, because they can rectify the monopoly-led efficiency loss (insufficient production).[13] Of course, at what degree they rectify each other, so that final output still exceeds, falls short, or precisely equates the social optimum, is an empirical issue. At least in theory, one cannot oppose externalities and monopolies at the same time!

Paradox 8: *There Is a Contradiction between Monopoly Theory and Agent Theory*

As described previously, according to neoclassical economic theory, monopolistic profit maximization output is lower than the equilibrium output under perfect competition conditions, thus causing efficiency loss (insufficient production). However, according to agency theory, because of asymmetric information, shareholders have no way of fully supervising managers, and thus the objective of managers cannot

---

[13] It is easy to demonstrate this by a conventional diagram of the monopoly demand and supply curves where the monopoly optimal output is smaller than the competitive output, which is larger than the social optimal output when the negative externality exists.

possibly be profit maximization as preferred by shareholders. Instead, it is more likely sales revenue maximization (or market share maximization). The gain from control rights is more closely related to sales revenue or market scale. The optimum output chosen by the manager will exceed profit maximization output.[14] This will lead to excess production. From this perspective, if monopoly profit maximization output is socially sub-optimal, then the moral hazard of managers can ease the efficiency loss caused by monopolies. Alternatively, if moral hazard is bad, then monopolies can ease the efficiency loss caused by moral hazard. Therefore, within an industry, simultaneously opposing monopolies and moral hazard is a contradiction.

The Paradigm Transformation in Economics Requires Scholars with Entrepreneurial Spirit

The theme of Adam Smith's *The Wealth of Nations*, published in 1776, is the ways market exchanges promote economic growth (national wealth). Smith proposed two core theorems: "the invisible hand" and "the pin factory." The "invisible hand" refers to market competition transforming the individual pursuit of self-interest into cooperation. The "pin factory" refers to increases in labor productivity and technological progress depending on the division of labor and specialization of labor. The division of labor and specialization of labor are constrained by market scale. In Adam Smith's view, these two theorems are not contradictory, but instead are mutually reinforcing. They both constitute the basis for large-scale human cooperation, or, in Hayek's (1988) terms, the "extended order." However, neoclassical economists argue that the invisible hand and pin factory are

---

[14] This result is shared by all managerial models, although different authors use different managerial objective functions. For example, in Baumol (1959) managers maximize revenue; in Marris (1964) managers maximize growth; and in Williamson (1964) managers maximize a managerial utility function (including staff or emoluments). The over-production problem can be mitigated by monopoly. Even if we assume that managers choose costly efforts instead of normal factor inputs (capital and labor), there is no certain answer that the manager's revenue-maximization effort will be smaller than the profit-maximization effort. Of course, not all agency problems can be mitigated by monopoly. The principal-agent theory suggests that an optimally designed incentive scheme can mitigate the moral hazard problem by aligning the agent's objective function with the principal's.

contradictory because the invisible hand is about diminishing returns to scale, whereas the pin factory is about increasing returns to scale. They cannot both be true at the same time. This means that we must choose between either having a market or having growth. If you want the market, you cannot develop. If you want to develop, you cannot rely on the market. As a result, the pin factory (division of labor) theorem has long been out of economists' sight.

According to the economic theories of the Austrian School and Schumpeter, Adam Smith is not wrong. Instead, the neoclassical economic paradigm is wrong. Adam Smith's market theory is a dynamic development theory, not a static equilibrium theory. The transition from the neoclassical static equilibrium paradigm to the Austrian School and Schumpeterian dynamic disequilibrium paradigm is actually the return to Adam Smith's basic proposition: How the market promotes economic development.

Of course, this paradigm shift will be very slow! Economists are already locked in a bad evolutionary stable equilibrium. Even though neoclassical economics is not a good market theory, from the perspective of each individual economist, it is still the theory with the greatest ability to survive. A scholar that wants to become famous in the world of economics, publish articles in the good journals, and have followers in the next generation will choose to follow the mainstream. It is the best "survival" strategy.

Even if we put aside vested interests, a paradigm shift in economics will not be easy. This is because the neoclassical static equilibrium paradigm is deeply rooted in the hearts of most economists. It has become their way of thinking. Therefore, when economists are not satisfied with any specific conclusions drawn from neoclassical economics, they are more likely to change some assumptions and modify existing theories rather than abandon the neoclassical paradigm completely. As a result, various "hybrid theories," similar to the "Tychonic system" in astronomy, have been developed.[15] New institutional economics, transaction cost economics, development economics, public

---

[15] The Tychonic system (or Tychonian system) is a model of the Solar System proposed by Tycho Brahe in the late 16th century. He combined the mathematical aspects of the Copernican system with the philosophical and "physical" aspects of the Ptolemaic system. In the Tychonic system, the Sun, Moon, and stars revolve around the Earth but the other five planets revolve around the Sun.

choice theory, government failure theory, information economics, new trade theory, endogenous growth theory, and so on, are all, in essence, hybrid theories.[16] It could be said that most "new" theories are nothing more than adding "epicycles" to the Ptolemaic system.

However, as Kohn pointed out, such hybrid theories are wrong and can only lead to chaos. Economics must replace the "geocentric model" with the "heliocentric model" instead of adding more "epicycles" or the "Tychonic system." At best, hybrid theories are only "technological progress without innovation" (Kohn, 2004, p. 331). Only innovation can lead to true development in economics.

Today's world of economics is not lacking followers and arbitrageurs of the mainstream system; it lacks disruptors and innovators. It needs disruptive macro-innovations more than continuous micro-innovations. The world of economics needs scholars with entrepreneurial spirit. Their research needs to be based on judgments, not calculations. They should dare to confront the mainstream and have an entrepreneurial adventurous spirit. Only then can economics become a good market theory.

---

[16] Probably the most ambitious economist in developing a hybrid theory is Xiaokai Yang. He tries to insert the division of labor and specialization into the neoclassical equilibrium framework by using "inframarginal analysis" (instead of the conventional marginal analysis). Yang self-defines his theory as "New Classical Economics." See Yang (1988), Yang and Ng (1993).

6 | *What Is a Good Market Theory?*

Recorded human history can be divided into two stages. The first stage is the period of history dominated by the logic of power.[1] The second stage is the period of history dominated by the logic of the market. The logic of power means that people cheat each other, conquer each other, and kill each other. History dominated by the logic of power is full of war, famine, and looting. Interactions were primarily zero-sum or even negative-sum games. As a result, human progress was extremely slow, and standards of living were stagnant for a very long time. When the logic of the market became dominant, people primarily spent energy and time on production, exchange, and creativity. Interactions were primarily positive-sum games. Technology greatly advanced and wealth significantly increased. Standards of living continuously increased and humanity achieved tremendous progress.

From the entire world-wide perspective, the period when the logic of power was dominant accounted for the larger portion of history. Even if we consider the last 5,000 years of human civilization, the logic of power was dominant in the first 4,800 years. The logic of the market was dominant only in the last 200 years.

Economics is the theory of how the market operates. Mainstream economics is the mainstream theories of how the market operates. It is simply called "neoclassical economics." I believe the mainstream economics we learn from textbooks does not provide good theories about the market economy. Therefore, there is a need to reflect on and criticize it.

This chapter is a revised version of Zhang, W. (2020). "What Is a Good Market Theory." *Ideas for China's Future*. Singapore: Palgrave Macmillan. https://doi.org/10.1007/978-981-15-4304-3_5 and is reproduced with permission of Springer Nature.
[1] I once used "the logic of theft" to refer to this stage (see Zhang, 2015b). Now I think "the logic of power" is a more proper phrase.

Of course, for a long time, there has been no shortage of critics of neoclassical economics. The primary criticism is that neoclassical economics embellishes the market. However, in my view, this criticism has not grasped the substantial defect of neoclassical economics. To the contrary, neoclassical economics defiles the market. To prove the market is efficient, neoclassical economics makes a series of unrealistic assumptions, as we have pointed out in the last chapter. This gives opponents of the market a voice, because none of these assumptions can be satisfied, so the market cannot be as efficient as argued by neoclassical economists. Many people who read economics textbooks are not left with a deep impression about how efficient the market is. Instead, their impression is that the market fails and government intervention is necessary. In the real world, the effective and efficient operation of the market does not require those assumptions. The rationale for government intervention in the market derived from these unrealistic and theoretical assumptions also does not stand!

In China, another criticism of the mainstream in economics is that it originated and developed in advanced countries, so it can only explain Western market economies, but not China or other developing countries. It especially cannot explain China's economic "miracle" over the last 40 years.[2] I believe this is scientific relativism.

I myself now am also a critic of neoclassical economics. Nevertheless, my criticism is fundamentally different from the above arguments. If a theory cannot explain the Chinese economy, then it is certainly not a good theory in general. China is not so special that we require a theory created specifically to suit China. A good market theory is certainly universal, meaning its explanation is as effective for the West as it is for China.

A good market theory, as I understand it, should include the six aspects below.

How Markets Advance Human Cooperation

All of humanity's superiority and progress come from cooperation. More than two thousand years ago, Xunzi, a Confucian scholar, said: Humans are not as strong as oxen or as fast as horses, but oxen and horses are used by them. How is this so? It is because humans are able

---

[2] Justin Lin is a representative figure of such criticism. See Lin (2010), pp. 243–269.

to form communities while the animals cannot. Why are humans able to form communities? It is because of social divisions (Hutton, 2014, chapter 9).

Human cooperation has existed since ancient times, but only in the market economy system did humanity's cooperation reach unprecedented breadth and depth. Stated simply, human cooperation in traditional societies was cooperation among acquaintances. It was cooperation among people that knew each other, and the scope of cooperation was limited. The market can expand interpersonal cooperation into cooperation among strangers. Local markets have turned into regional markets and regional markets have evolved into global markets. Today, human cooperation is global in scope among a few billion people. We have never heard of 99.99% of the people that are involved in production of goods and services we consume. We are even less likely to have even seen their face, yet we purchase the products they produce. Similarly, we produce products and provide services for people most of whom we do not know.

F. A. Hayek correctly conceptualized the market system as the "extended order" of human cooperation (Hayek, 1988, chapter 1). It is the extended order not only in the sense that cooperation transcends the blood and kin relation, but also in the sense that cooperation is not motivated by commonly perceived aims and altruism. In the extended order, different people have different goals but they can coordinate; and self-interested people can serve each other and make other people happy. It is through the extended order that human cooperation has reached a scope and level that ancient people thought was unimaginable, and that human living standards have progressed dramatically.

Cooperation is a positive-sum game. It benefits everyone involved. However, because humanity's long history was a period of zero-sum games dominated by the logic of power, from an evolutionary psychology perspective, humanity's current mentality is still a zero-sum game mentality (Rubin, 2003; Boyer and Petersen, 2018). Therefore, many people still understand the market economy from a zero-sum game perspective. When some people make money, we believe some other people have certainly been exploited, or someone else lost wealth. This is a classic zero-sum game way of thinking.

Economics has, from its origin, been concerned with how the extended order works. It should be said mainstream economics made an important contribution to getting rid of the zero-sum game mentality. Of course, the greatest credit goes to Adam Smith, the founder of classical economics. He proved that in a competitive market, one person's gain does not mean another person's loss. On the contrary, self-interest must first benefit others. That is the meaning of his metaphor "invisible hand."

Human cooperation in the market economy is not simply mutual aid in the traditional society or a few people cooperating to move stones or rowing boats. Instead, it is mutual dependence. This mutual dependence comes from cooperation in the market economy being based on the division of labor and specialization. Every person does different things. Because of specialization and division of labor, each person's potential can be maximized and each person's way of doing things can continuously improve. Division of labor and specialization also make innovation more likely. Innovation improves each person's labor productivity, so society's overall wealth can grow.

The benefits of division of labor and specialization come from economies of scale. However, according to textbook economic theories, economies of scale lead to imperfect competition and a small number of large firms (or even one firm) monopolizing the market. This will lead to inefficient resource allocation. Because there exists a "contradiction between the pin factory and the invisible hand" in theory, Adam Smith's theory of division of labor disappeared from neoclassical economics. Only by dropping the division of labor can the efficiency of the "invisible hand" be mathematically proven. The academic ambition of Xiaokai Yang was to resolve this contradiction. Unfortunately, his contribution has not yet been widely accepted!

Specialized division of labor is necessarily accompanied by information asymmetry. The reason for this is that division of labor is actually division of knowledge, as Hayek (1937 and 1945) pointed out. Specialized, local, and dispersed knowledge is the source of the division of labor's superiority. The exchange of different products is actually the exchange of different and specialized knowledge. In some sense, it is precisely because of "asymmetric" and "incomplete" information that the decentralized market system is superior to the centralized planned economy (Hayek, 1945 and 1988).[3] If we say that

---

[3] "It is with respect to this that practically every individual has some advantage over all others because he possesses unique information of which beneficial use

asymmetric information causes market failure and government intervention is required, the market cannot exist at all. If the theory that
asymmetric information leads to market failure is correct, how could
the traditional autarkic economy with perfectly symmetric information
possibly evolve into a market economy with asymmetric information?
As Hayek said: "Man has been able to develop that division of labor
on which our civilization is based because he happened to stumble
upon a method which made it possible" (Hayek, 1948, pp. 88–89).
This "method" is the market mechanism. Experimental economists,
such as Vernon Smith, have shown that market efficiency does not
require that agents have complete and perfect information, and Hayek
is right (Vernon Smith, 2008).[4]

Therefore, the mainstream in economics is not a correct or good
market theory.

How the Market's Reputation Mechanism Works

How can unacquainted people full of asymmetric information trust
each other? This is the function of the market's reputation mechanism.
As pointed out by Hayek, competition in the market is in a large
measure competition for reputation or goodwill (Hayek, 1946,
p. 97). Not only is the market an invisible hand, it is also a pair of
invisible eyes (Shearmur and Klein, 1997). The market remembers and
propagates information. It stores and disseminates the behavior of
entities. In a true market economy, any bad actions will be punished
(especially through lost reputation). Similarly, good actions will be
rewarded. In the market economy, "the millstones of the gods grind
late, but they grind fine." Precisely for this reason, honesty is

might be made, but of which use can be made only if the decisions depending on it
are left to him or are made with his active cooperation" (Hayek, 1945, p. 80).
[4] For an experiments-based criticism of the information asymmetry-led market
failure theory, see Vernon Smith (2008), chapter 5. Akerlof (1970) has been
widely regarded as the pioneering contributor to the asymmetrical information-
based market failure theory and was awarded the 2003 Nobel Prize in Economics
for this contribution. However, he does emphasize that numerous institutions
arise to counteract the effect of asymmetric information in the final section of his
paper, including guarantees, brand-names, certificates, and so on. His theory is
mistakenly understood as a market failure theory because for mainstream
economists, the market is not a complicated and sophisticated institution but an
abstract and impersonal price parameter. In fact, guarantees, brand names, and
certificates are all market solutions to asymmetric information problems.

considered the best commercial strategy. The countries where the market economy is most developed are the countries with the highest trust between people.

The reason mainstream economists believe asymmetric information leads to market failure, requiring government intervention, is because they ignore the market's reputation mechanism. They equate the market mechanism with price. They do not understand the entrepreneur.

In the formation process of the reputation mechanism, the firm, as an artificial construct by the entrepreneur, plays an extremely important role. It is the bearer of reputation for the entire market economy (Kreps, 1986). Why are we willing to purchase products from strangers or cooperate with them? Because their products are produced and sold to us under the name of some trademark. We remember these trademarks. These trademarks have owners. If they cheat us, the trademark's reputation will be damaged, which would injure the interests of the trademark owner. Therefore, trademark owners have an incentive to establish a good brand. The better the brand, the more customers favor them. I do not know the people that manufacture vehicles, but I know that the vehicle manufacturer has a set of systems to make someone accountable for workers' mistakes. This is the reason I trust the vehicle manufacturer.

In addition, a vehicle often has many component suppliers. The value added to a vehicle by the vehicle maker might not exceed 20% of the final retail price. The thousands of upstream vendors do not deal with the car buyer directly, so why should the car buyer trust them? Because the vehicle manufacturer supervises them for the car buyer. If any suppliers produce inferior components that are assembled into a vehicle, then the vehicle manufacturer must assume joint liability. In the market, a vehicle manufacturer is like a general contractor, because it takes responsibility for any component that has a problem. This is the value of branded firms.

Precisely for this reason, I say profit comes from responsibility.[5] The ability to assume liability determines firms' ability to make money (Zhang, 2015b, pp. 51–54). The reason big firms can make big money is because they must assume joint liability for a large number of employees and suppliers. If a firm does not want to assume this

---

[5] I will discuss this point more in Chapter 8.

liability, or does not have the ability to assume it, not only will it not become large, but also might go bankrupt.

However, neoclassical economics believes a firm that becomes large has price-setting power and monopolizes the market. This monopoly position reduces consumer surplus and brings about efficiency loss. Therefore, opposition to monopolies has become opposition to large firms. Nevertheless, a market without large firms or firms with a certain degree of scale cannot possibly effectively operate. In an atomized market with "perfect competition," trust cannot be built between customers and producers. Cooperation among strangers is impossible.

Government over-intervention can only lead to reputation mechanism failure. There are three reasons for this (Zhang, 2018, pp. 195–196). First, as government regulations become excessive, bureaucrats have greater discretion. With it, their behavior becomes more uncertain, so market players feel that the future is harder to predict, and they are more likely to pursue short-term interests. Second, the government's excessive regulation of market entry will perhaps create monopolies and monopoly rents. Enterprises that enjoy monopoly rents will no longer care about their own reputation. Further, because government-granted true monopolies exist, consumers are unable to punish enterprises. Finally, regulation itself leads to corruption and collusion between the regulator and the regulated (Stigler, 1971). Regulation entices enterprises to obtain quotas and privileges through bribery of government bureaucrats, instead of better servicing customers. When currying favor with bureaucrats is more profitable than with consumers, enterprises will not value their own market reputation.

Thus, government intervention cannot resolve the adverse selection problem caused by asymmetric information. Traditional theories tell us that the way to resolve adverse selection is to rely on government intervention. The reality we see is precisely the opposite. Worldwide, the countries with more government intervention have more severe adverse selection and a more chaotic market order. The World Bank commissioned Simeon Djankov, Rafael La Porta, Florencio Lopez-de-Silanes, and Andrei Shleifer to research market entry regulations in 85 countries. Their research found that when comparing the degree to which enterprises adhered to international quality standards, the more regulation a country had and the more examination and approval procedures there were, the less enterprises from those countries adhered to international quality standards (Djankov et al., 2002).

As economists, we should be amazed that in the market people are willing to purchase goods and services provided by strangers who are in far-away lands, and of whose goods and services our technical knowledge is limited. Yet, mainstream economists tell us that asymmetric information will lead to market failure. That is regrettable!

How the Market Brings about Change and Development

Markets have existed since ancient times. But as an economic system, referring to the dominant means people produce, exchange, and consume, the market only has about a 200-year history. In a traditional society, the producer and consumer of a product are the same person. Production is for direct consumption. If you want to consume something, you must produce it yourself. The market only plays a marginal role of "adjusting surpluses and shortages." In a market economy, producers and consumers are separate. Products must be sold on the market and consumption must be purchased from it.

In traditional society, both production methods and the types of products produced and consumed did not change for hundreds or even thousands of years. At most, there was a very slow change without an obvious difference between generations. In the 200 years since the Industrial Revolution, the greatest benefit the market economy brought about is the continuous growth and change in production methods and product types. The things we consume today are totally different from 200 years ago. Compared to 20 or even 5 years ago, there is a considerable difference. New products and new technologies appear all the time on the market. Product quality is continuously improving. Production and consumption structures are continuously changing. The market brought about all of this. Even resources themselves are endogenous. Petroleum was not a resource 200 years ago. Bauxite was not a resource 100 years ago. Silicon dioxide was not a resource 70 years ago. Thus, as argued strongly and repeatedly by Schumpeter, capitalism (the market economy) is essentially a process of endogenous economic change. In the absence of change, capitalism cannot exist. A good economic theory must explain this change, and in particular how and why new products and new technologies appear.

However, textbook mainstream economics is a theory of the circular economy. It assumes product types and production technologies are given. Its focal point is how an unchanging economy realizes "equilibrium" and "stability" through the price mechanism. It treats equilibrium and stability as the standard for measuring whether the market is efficient. Because technology, resources, and people's preferences are assumed to be given, traditional economics cannot explain development and change. Of course, mainstream economics also pays attention to economic growth. But economic growth in mainstream economics is only a change in gross national product aggregated in terms of prices. It is growth without innovation and structural changes, as though the entire economy only produces a singular product. So-called "development economics" arose in the 1950s. It was a response to defects in mainstream economics. However, development economics often became anti-market and pro-government interventionist economics. If we have a good market theory, development economics is unnecessary.

Mainstream economics cannot explain change and development because it ignores entrepreneurs.

Entrepreneurship Is the Soul of the Market

Entrepreneurship is the soul of the market economy. Without entrepreneurs, a true market economy is not possible, and neither is true progress. But entrepreneurs do not make an appearance in mainstream economic theories. The basic assumption of mainstream economics is that the world is certain and predetermined, which excludes entrepreneurs. In a world of certainty, every person is similarly intelligent and all-knowing. Every decision can be made with a calculation. The economy is in an equilibrium state without profit or loss. No one needs an imagination to make judgments about the future. Naturally, entrepreneurship is unnecessary (Mises, 2007 [1949], pp. 697–698).

The real world is not like this. The future is not only uncertain but also indeterminate. The consequences of a choice are unpredictable because they depend on various factors that cannot be controlled by the chooser. We do not know what consumers want. We do not know how technology will change. We do not know what other people will choose. To make a choice in such a situation, we need imagination, keen judgment, vision, and courage. This type of imagination, keen judgment, vision, and courage is entrepreneurship. Thus, as pointed out by Shackle:

The maker of such a choice has no ground to assign to it a unique, exactly specified sequel. For the course of history-to-come will include the unforeknowable choices-to-come and their effects of allowing or precluding sequels of their own. The present chooser must envisage history-to-come as a skein of endlessly many rival possible courses. (Shackle, 1979b, p. 21)

Economic choice does not consist in comparing the items in a list, known to be complete, of given fully specified rival and certainly attainable results. It consists in first creating, by conjecture and reasoned imagination on the basis of mere suggestion offered by visible or recorded circumstance, things on which hope can be fixed. These things, at the time when they are available for choice, are thoughts and even figments. (Shackle, 1972, p. 96)

Economic development either comes from improved resource allocation efficiency or technological progress. The resource allocation efficiency and the appearance of new products or new technologies are both the result of entrepreneurial activities. Without entrepreneurship, we would not even know the extent to which something should sell, so the market could not possibly trend toward efficient allocations. Without entrepreneurship, large-scale innovation and technological progress are economically impossible.

To appreciate the entrepreneur's essential contribution to technological progress, we must distinguish innovation from invention. As Schumpeter said: "The making of the invention and the carrying of the corresponding innovation are, economically and sociologically, two different things" (Schumpeter, 1939, pp. 84–85). Invention is a function of inventors, and innovation is a function of entrepreneurs. Innovations are usually more important than inventions. Schumpeter said:

As long as they are not carried into practice, inventions are economically irrelevant. And to carry any improvement into effect is a task entirely different from inventing of it, and a task, moreover, requiring entirely different kinds of aptitudes. (Schumpeter, 1934, p. 88)

Personal aptitudes – primarily intellectual in the case of the inventor, primarily volitional in the case of the businessman who turns invention into an innovation – and the methods by which the one and the other work, belong to different spheres. (Schumpeter, 1939, pp. 85–86)

Although entrepreneurs of course may be inventors just as they may be capitalists, they are inventors not by nature of their function but by coincidence and vice versa. (Schumpeter, 1934, pp. 88–89)

(W)ithout innovations, no entrepreneurs; without entrepreneurial achievement, no capitalist returns and no capitalist propulsion. (Schumpeter, 1939, p. 1033)

Innovation refers to the commercialization of new technologies and new products. Whether or not an innovation succeeds is determined by the innovation's degree of commercialization, meaning whether or not it brings value to consumers. Entrepreneurs turn inventions into commodities, making new products and technologies available to the public. Invention is necessary – but not sufficient – for technological innovation, not to mention that most inventions in the market economy are induced or triggered by entrepreneurial innovations. As Schumpeter said:

Inventions come about when the entrepreneur needs them. If the personality of the entrepreneur does not already wait in the wings in order to make use of each new invention, the inventions will never be implemented in practice. It is not inventions that have made capitalism, but capitalism that has created the inventions it needed. (Becker, Knudsen, and Swedberg, 2011, p. 167)

The entrepreneur has very different qualities from the inventor. For the inventor, the most important is curiosity but for the entrepreneur, the most important are alertness, imagination of the market, and perseverance. The inventor solves problems that have not been solved by others but the entrepreneur solves problems that the customer faces. The inventor is technology-driven, idea-focused, and detail-addicted but the entrepreneur is business-driven, action-focused, and strategic. For the inventor, invention is the end; for the entrepreneur, innovation is the means. The inventor works on his own but the entrepreneur organizes and motivates others to work. While the inventor is inclined to avoid risk and responsibility, the entrepreneur dares to bear risk and take responsibility. While the inventor is adept at dealing with things, the entrepreneur is good at dealing with people. The entrepreneur is more optimistic and ambitious than the inventor.

Paul Mantoux's comments on Richard Arkwright are still enlightening for our understanding of the entrepreneur's qualities:

His success, in fact, best illustrates what he really achieved, and what his place in economic history should be. He was no inventor. At the most he arranged, combined and used the inventions of others, which he never scrupled to appropriate to his own ends. ... He was the first who knew how to make something out of other men's inventions, and who built them up into an industrial system. In order to raise the necessary capital for his undertakings, in order to form and dissolve these partnerships which he used successively as instruments with which to make his fortune, he must have displayed remarkable business ability, together with a curious mixture of cleverness, perseverance and daring. In order to set up large factories, to engage labour, to train it to new kind of work and enforce strict disciplines in the workshops, he needed an energy and an activity not often met with. These were qualities which most inventors never had, and without which their inventions could not have resulted in the building up of a new industrial system. It was Arkwright who, after the inconclusive or unsuccessful attempts of the brothers Lombe, of Wyatt and of Lewis Paul, really created the modern factory. He personified the new type of the great manufacturer, neither an engineer nor a merchant, but adding to the main characteristics of both, qualifications peculiar to himself: those of a founder of great concerns, an organizer of production and a leader of men. Arkwright's career heralded a new social class and a new economic era." (Mantoux, 1928, pp. 238–239)

We know that new technologies occasionally appeared in traditional societies, but they rarely became a means for humanity to create value. It was even less likely for them to become products available for the masses. The reason is there was a shortage of innovative entrepreneurs. For example, the steam engine existed during the Roman Empire, but it did not become a part of Roman life. It did not bring about true economic growth for the Roman Empire. Bi Sheng, alive during the Song Dynasty, invented the movable printing press 400 years earlier than Johannes Gutenberg of Germany. While Gutenberg's printing technology spread over Europe within 50 years, Bi Sheng's invention was probably never put into use. One of the reasons is that Gutenberg himself was an entrepreneur but Bi Sheng was not.

Emphasis on entrepreneurship is not excessive under any situation. Our greatest mistake in emphasizing demand-side management in the past was ignoring entrepreneurship. We mistakenly believed we could rely on monetary and fiscal policy to adjust aggregate demand, investment, consumption, and foreign trade as a means to bring the economy out of recession or inhibit overheating. Now, the Chinese government is starting to emphasize supply-side policies, and this is good. However, if the focus points of supply-side policies are not on liberating the entrepreneurial spirit, allowing entrepreneurs to have more freedom to do business and innovate, or giving entrepreneurs more stable expectations about the future, these supply side policies cannot truly succeed.

Explaining How Economic Cycles and Fluctuations Happen

The theories about economic cycles and fluctuations we currently learn from textbooks are just the Keynesian theory of aggregate demand. This theory believes all economic fluctuations, both in times of prosperity and depression, come from changes in aggregate demand. Aggregate demand is either excessive or insufficient, so the way to resolve the issue is to adjust aggregate demand through monetary and fiscal policy. Experience has shown this theory is problematic. Any country that implements these theories will face many troubles.

During the Global Financial Crisis of 2009, China stimulated its economy according to this type of theory. China achieved 9.2% growth in 2009 and exceeded 10% in 2010. However, a careful study will find that many of the economic problems China faces today, especially overcapacity, were caused precisely by the aggregate demand stimulus policies implemented at that time.

The reason macroeconomic stimulus policies cause serious overcapacity is because, according to Keynesian theories, as long as investment is increased, then aggregate demand can be increased in the current year. Overcapacity turns into a self-reinforcing process. For example, how can excess steel capacity be resolved? One way is to build more steel plants because building new steel plants also requires steel as an input, thus increasing demand for steel. As soon as the new steel plant is operational, however, steel overcapacity will be more serious.

In Keynesian macroeconomic models, individual entrepreneurs vanish from the scene. Aggregated numbers, such as investment, consumption, and exports are all-important. Keynesianism only cares about the quantity of investment, not its quality and origin or who does the investing. Actually, who invests is more important than how much is invested. Entrepreneurs care about return when they invest. Whether they invest and how much they invest is determined by their judgment of the future return. When the government invests, however, it only cares about increasing aggregate demand, not return. This is the reason government investment is so wasteful and more likely to lead to overcapacity.

Within economics, there is a better theory, called the Austrian School's theory of the business cycle. This theory was originally proposed by Ludwig von Mises (1912 [1953]) and systematically developed by Hayek (1931). Roger W. Garrison (2001) provides a mathematical analysis of the Austrian business model.[6] According to this theory, any artificial prosperity created with monetary policy will certainly lead to a depression. The greater the degree of stimulus, the more serious the ultimate downturn will be. The reason is that artificially lowering interest rates, through credit expansion, will mislead entrepreneurs in making investment decisions and cause an unsustainable boom, which will eventually bust. If we understand and acknowledge this theory, I believe we will make fewer mistakes in our economic policies, especially macroeconomic policies.

It is worthwhile emphasizing Schumpeter's business cycle theory, which is totally ignored by economists today. After Keynes published his *General Theory* in 1936, Schumpeter published, in 1939, his *Business Cycles* in which he proposed his own explanation for economic fluctuations. Schumpeter's theory of business cycle and fluctuations is very different from Keynes' and also Hayek's. The key point of Schumpeter's idea is that business cycles and economic fluctuations are mainly consequences of entrepreneurial innovations and thus endogenous in capitalist society. The reason is that the distribution of innovations is uneven both in time and in space. First, innovations are not isolated events, and not evenly distributed in time. To the contrary, they tend to cluster and come about in bunches, simply because first some – and then most – firms follow in the wake of successful innovations. Second, innovations are not at any time distributed over the whole economic system at random but tend to concentrate in certain sectors and their adjacencies (Schumpeter, 1939, pp. 100–101).

The uneven distribution of innovations stems from the following three (realistic) assumptions. First, innovations entail construction of new plant and new equipment, or renovating old plants, requiring nonnegligible time and outlays. Second, almost every innovation is embodied in a new firm founded for that purpose, rarely in an old firm. New production functions intrude into the system through the action of new firms, while the existing or old firms for a time work on as before and then react adaptively to the state of things, under pressure of competition. Third, innovations are always associated with the rise of new entrepreneurs. Even in the world of giant firms, innovations still emerge primarily with "young" entrepreneurs, and "old"

---

[6] For a brief introduction to the Austrian business cycle theory, see Rothbard (1983), chapter 1. See also Skousen (2005), chapter 6.

ones display – as a rule – symptoms of conservatism. This explains why innovations are not carried into effect simultaneously by all firms (Ibid. pp. 93–98).

Because of the uneven distribution of innovations, business evolution is lopsided, discontinuous, and disharmonious by nature. It must be a disturbance of the existing structure and more like a series of explosions than a gentle, though incessant, transformation. Thus, the market economy necessarily experiences boom–bust fluctuations. Schumpeter demonstrates his points by detailed studies on the business systems in three countries (the United States, Britain, and Germany) and on the companies in five leading industries (textiles, railroads, steel, automobiles, and electric power). "In every span of historic time it is easy to locate the ignition of the process and associate it with certain industries and, within these industries, with certain firms, from which disturbances then spread over the system" (Ibid. p. 102). If we recognize the importance of entrepreneurs in markets, I believe that Schumpeter's business cycle theory is somewhat convincing. I even believe that a combination of Schumpeter's and Hayek's theories may provide us with a better explanation of economic fluctuations.

Here I shall also mention the so-called real business-cycle theory (RBC theory). RBC theory was introduced by Finn E. Kydland and Edward C. Prescott in their 1982 paper *Time to Build and Aggregate Fluctuations*. They envisioned that business cycles are caused by some external real (in contrast to nominal) shocks – i.e., random fluctuations in the productivity level that shifted the constant growth trend up or down. Examples of such shocks include innovations, bad weather, imported oil price increases, stricter environmental and safety regulations, etc. The general gist is that something occurs that directly changes the effectiveness of capital and/or labor. This in turn affects the decisions of workers and firms, who in turn change what they buy and produce and thus eventually affect output. According to RBC theory, business cycles are therefore "real" in that they do not represent a failure of markets to clear but rather reflect the most efficient possible operation of the economy, given the structure of the economy. Although innovations are treated as a factor affecting business cycles, however, they – like shocks – are exogenous in RBC theory and there is no role for entrepreneurs to play – very different from Schumpeter's theory.

Rights Take Precedence Over Utility

Mainstream economics is utilitarian economics. Jeremy Bentham, an English philosopher, jurist, and social reformer, was the originator of utilitarianism. Through the development of his student, economist John Mill, utilitarianism became the philosophical and moral foundation of economics as a whole.[7] Utilitarianism includes two aspects: individual utilitarianism and social utilitarianism. Individual utilitarianism refers to each person pursuing advantages and avoiding disadvantages, i.e., maximizing their own utility function. Social utilitarianism refers to maximizing so-called social welfare. The basic feature of social utilitarianism is the use of the legitimacy of ends to justify the legitimacy of means. In other words, as long as my goal is good, I can do anything to fulfill the goal. This goal can be "efficiency," "fairness," "economic growth," "national interest," "social welfare," or whatever else.

Another standard of justice, standing opposite to utilitarianism, is what I call "rights-priority." Rights-priority means that as individuals, we all have some basic innate rights. These basic rights cannot be taken away for any reason. The legitimacy of the goal cannot justify the legitimacy of the means. Rights-priority has a long historical tradition. It developed from the natural law theories of the Stoics in ancient Greece. German philosopher Immanuel Kant's theory of freedom from more than 200 years ago is a type of rights- priority. Among contemporary political philosophers, John Rawls' theories on liberty and equality, Robert Nozick's self-ownership theories, Murray Rothbard's natural rights theories, and F. A. Hayek's liberal evolutionism can all be classified as rights-priority philosophies, even though they disagreed widely.[8]

In many cases, utilitarian economics also champions the market economy, but it treats the market as an instrument. In other words, only when the market is considered to be conducive to efficiency, and to so-called maximization of social welfare, does utilitarian economics champion the market. As soon as the market is considered unfavorable to efficiency, such as situations where so-called monopolies, "externalities," "asymmetric information," and other "market failures" exist,

---

[7] For a critical review of Bentham and Mill's utilitarianism, see Murray N. Rothbard (1995), chapters 2 and 3. For a comprehensive review of utilitarianism, see Will Kymlicka (2002), chapter 2.

[8] Most rights-priority philosophers belonged to libertarianism. See Kymlicka (2002).

then utilitarian economics champions government intervention. Utilitarianism also treats support for private property rights and liberty as instruments. They are only means to achieve some social goal but have no ultimate value. It provides a moral basis for the violation of private property and the deprivation of individual liberty.

A good market theory should be of rights-priority (putting rights above interests) rather than utilitarian (putting interests above rights). Utilitarian economics is not conducive to establishing a real market economy because at any time some people can start with "good" ends to prove that market competition is bad. For example, the market can be negated under the pretext that it is not conducive to economic development or social stability. The market is not just a tool for gross domestic product growth. It is a way for humanity to realize self-worth and pursue excellence. As long as we respect people's basic rights and give each person equal liberty, then the market economy will come naturally. Conversely, if our systems and policies do not respect individuals' basic rights and freedoms, no amount of reform measures will be able to establish a true market economy system.

So far, China's reforms can be called utilitarian reforms. Economic development has been taken as society's greatest "good." Gross domestic product growth is the greatest "good." The standard to measure every policy is whether or not it is conducive to economic development and, in particular, the growth of gross domestic product. Whatever is conducive to GDP growth is good; whatever is not conducive to GDP growth is bad. For the sake of GDP growth, we can even ignore people's basic rights and dignity. If we consider issues according to the rights-priority perspective, we will have fewer policy errors. Policies like family planning, which have lasted for nearly 40 years, are justified by "increasing per capita income." Now, more and more people are starting to recognize the serious negative consequences of those policies, and therefore began to support a change in the family planning policy. Some scholars even suggest subsidies for having more children and imposing a penalty on those who do not have two or more children. This is typical of utilitarian economics thinking.[9] If we

---

[9] Aside from utilitarian economics, another reason for the emergence of family planning policies is that some conceited scientists, economists, and politicians believe they know what the optimal population size is. They think they can regulate the population in the same way they do the indoor temperature. Economists did not have the biggest influence on the original creation of the "one

adhere to rights-priority economics, the right to reproduce is a basic human right that cannot be deprived by anyone. "Increasing per capita income" cannot be a legitimate reason for restricting families from having children. Such a policy would not be possible, and China would not face such a rapid ageing problem.

In the past decade, since 2013, China's marketization process has been dramatically reversed back toward more and more government control. Entrepreneurs have become less and less confident in doing business. Utilitarian economics is partly responsible for this reverse. Doing business freely in China has never been recognized as a basic human right, either in the legal system or in culture. It is only an expedience. As a folk metaphor says: "Hold entrepreneurs in your arms when using them, and throw them into the fire when not using them." As long as founding and running a firm is not recognized as a human right, but only a means for whatever purpose the government has for it, then entrepreneurial potential cannot be fully realized. So, I think we economists have a responsibility to shift market theory from utilitarian to rights priority.

child" policy. Instead, three scientists from the Seventh Ministry of Machine Building used cybernetics and computers to make "future population forecasts" that persuaded the authorities. This might be the biggest "fatal conceit" committed by scientists in human history.

7 | Entrepreneurship Is the Best Anti-monopoly Law

Many people believe anti-monopoly policies face certain new challenges in the digital economy era. I want to emphasize, however, that the challenges faced in the implementation of anti-monopoly laws are not recent. They existed before the digital economy. The reason for the challenges is that the economic foundation of anti-monopoly laws is incorrect!

Introduction: The Village of Beautiful Women

First, let us discuss the conceptual issues of competition and monopoly. I previously wrote an article about corruption of language (Zhang, 2017, pp. 19–22).[1] Stated simply, corruption of language is putting an evil name on morality or putting a moral name on evil. In my view, the word "monopoly" in economics is a classic example.

What is the origin of this word in the English language? It originally referred to special licenses obtained from the monarchy, represented by the East India Company, chartered by Queen Elizabeth I of England in 1600. The company was granted exclusivity over trade between Britain and India and East Asia. Stated simply, a monopoly is a government-granted exclusive right to provide certain products and services. This is the original meaning of the word monopoly. In 1624, the British Parliament passed the *Statute of Monopolies* to prohibit these concessions (apart from patents).[2] In the English-speaking world, because "monopolies" had a negative connotation from the beginning, people

---

[1] The phrase "corruption of language" was first coined by George Orwell in an article in 1946. When attacking socialism, Hayek came close to Orwell in seeing that state socialism goes hand in hand with the corruption of language. See Scruton (2006), p. 221. In his 1988 book, Hayek used "poisoned language." See Hayek (1988), chapter 7.

[2] For a history of England's Monopoly Act of 1624, see Rosen (2010).

became accustomed to blaming the things they do not like on "monopolies." Schumpeter noted:

(T)he English-speaking public [was] so monopoly-conscious that it acquired a habit of attributing to that sinister power practically everything it disliked about business ... Economists, government agents, journalists and politicians in this country obviously love the word because it has come to be a term of opprobrium which is sure to rouse the public's hostility against any interest so labeled. (Schumpeter, 1942, p. 100)

The concept of monopoly gradually evolved into a technical concept in economics today. Monopolies are quantified according to the number of firms in an industry and their market share. Economists define monopoly in such a way that big companies cannot escape the blame.

To better explain the absurdity of this concept, let me tell a fable.

A villager found a picture of a beautiful woman and put it on his wall. The village chief saw the picture and admired the woman's beauty, and then felt the women in the village were all ugly. He discussed arranging plastic surgery for all the women in the village. The village chief established a "Plastic Surgery Committee" to set a "beauty standard" and identify which women needed which surgery. Once the standards were set, someone had to implement them, so a plastic surgery team was formed. Plastic surgery was performed one by one on the women that did not meet the standards. Afterwards, many women changed their appearance and were prettier than before, but they did not dare to laugh because of the effect on their face. Many other women lost features after the surgery while others were scared away. Some couples became unwilling to give birth to girls. After completing plastic surgery on the women in the village, the village chief did not stop. Women that passed through the village underwent surgery, so no women of other villages dared to pass through the village.

Although this is a fable, it explains well how anti-monopoly laws came about and the similar issues they face during implementation. Our anti-monopoly experts are like the village chief or committee members in the story. In anti-monopoly cases, their role is to determine the standards of "beauty" (competitiveness), determine which firms should undergo surgery, and tell the bureaucrats and judges which procedures to implement.

A basic challenge in economics currently is striking a balance between promoting competition and maintaining innovation vitality.

This is a reflection of the contradiction between economic theory and real economic observation. On the one hand, according to economic theory, competition is good and monopolies are bad, so competition should be promoted and monopolies eliminated to limit large firms. On the other hand, observing reality shows that the most innovative firms are often large firms that hold a certain "monopoly" status. These firms also have more resources to utilize for innovation. Therefore, to promote innovation, firms must be allowed to maintain a "monopoly." What is the source of this contradiction? There is a problem with concepts about monopoly and competition in economics. The definition of competition and monopoly in mainstream economics is wrong!

Therefore, the issues I discuss here not only occur in the current digital economy era, but also existed before the digital economy. This problem merely became more serious after entering the digital economy era.

The Economic Foundation of the Anti-monopoly Law Is Wrong

It must be noted that competition policy covers a wider range than anti-monopoly policy. Here, I will only discuss the problems with the anti-monopoly law. What is the economic foundation of anti-monopoly law? It is the neoclassical perfect competition model that we learned in economics textbooks. The perfect competition model is the previous fable's beautiful woman in the painting!

What is "perfect competition"? Each industry has multiple, or even countless, producers which are so small that not a single one has any impact on the industry as a whole. Each producer uses equivalent technology and has the same cost to produce the same products that are sold for the same price. This is the perfect competition model in mainstream economics. According to the logic of mainstream economics, only perfect competition will result in a Pareto optimum, and the market will be at its best. As soon as there is a deviation from the perfect competition model, monopolies form. Economists also categorize different forms of monopolies according to the number of producers in an industry, such as exclusive monopoly (only one producer), oligopolies (several large producers), and monopolistic competition (also known as "imperfect competition" between multiple small producers with certain differences in products). Regardless of the form monopoly takes, it causes an efficiency loss and makes a Pareto optimum impossible to achieve.

A simple demand–supply geometric diagram can be used to illustrate competition and the efficiency loss caused by competition in mainstream economics. Perfect competition means that a firm's demand curve is flat. The firm has no pricing power and can only accept a given price. The optimal production decision is reached when the price is equal to the marginal cost point, which is optimal from a social perspective. Alternatively, if any firm faces a downward-sloping demand curve, then it has market power to influence prices. Increasing prices will reduce demand and decreasing prices will increase demand. At this point, the individual optimal price (determined by the marginal revenue equal to the marginal cost) is higher than the marginal cost, thus there is a net social loss. Therefore, a nonperfectly competitive market cannot be efficient.

Mainstream economists argue that although perfect competition is not realistic, it is desirable as an ideal model. My argument is that perfect competition is not only unrealistic, but also undesirable and cannot be taken as the ideal model. It is undesirable because "the bulk of what we call economic progress is incompatible with [perfect competition]" (Schumpeter, 1942, p. 105). Anti-monopoly laws and policies based on this type of theory are of course also undesirable. As I have pointed out in Chapter 5: (1) "perfect competition" is incompatible with innovation because, according to the mainstream economics definition, innovation is necessarily monopolistic; (2) "perfect competition" is incompatible with the increasing returns to scale caused by the division of labor; and (3) "perfect competition" is incompatible with the reputation-based orderly market. If the market is really in a state of "perfect competition," I am afraid the market economy no longer exists.

As Friedrich Hayek (1948, chapter 5) pointed out, perfect competition in neoclassical economics is actually a lack of competition. Monopolistic measures in neoclassical economics are actually the means of competition in reality (Schumpeter, 1942, chapter 8). For example, innovation, which is the introduction of new production methods or producing different products, is the primary means of market competition. However, according to the neoclassical definition, innovation is equivalent to monopoly, since it allows the innovator to face a downward-sloping demand curve, thus granting price-setting power. According to the inference of neoclassical economics, the more successful innovation is, the more serious the monopoly and the greater the social efficiency loss is. Therefore, not surprisingly, firms that the government charges for anti-trust litigation are all the most innovative firms. Early examples were Standard Oil and the Aluminum Corporation of America. More recent examples are lawsuits against IBM, Microsoft, and Google.

Mechanically applying "perfect competition" to the market of economists would mean all economics professors write the same articles, teach the same courses, and are paid the same amount. Yet, every economics professor knows that to compete with other economists, they must have different theoretical viewpoints or policy views, write different articles, and even have different writing styles. However, according to the traditional understanding in economics, as soon as you do something different, a monopoly is created. Using this standard, almost every economist with outstanding contributions is a monopolist in the economics market. They have too many readers and account for too much of the market, so the government should intervene. Those economists that have obtained a Nobel prize should undergo an anti-monopoly review. Strangely, the economists who support the anti-monopoly law never point the anti-monopoly law at themselves.

The Difficulties in Enforcement of Anti-Monopoly Law

The problems anti-monopoly laws faced during implementation existed in the past but became more prominent in the digital economy era.

How to Define the Scope of the Market

Some economists claim the anti-monopoly law does not oppose monopolies themselves, but instead oppose the improper behavior of monopolists taking advantage of their market dominance. Regardless of what type of monopolistic behavior we want to oppose, however, we must first establish whether or not the subject of our allegation has a dominant market position. To determine whether a firm has a dominant position in its corresponding market, the scope of the market must first be determined. This is precisely the biggest problem. Different definitions of market scope will lead to completely different conclusions.

Economists use "elasticity of substitution" to define the market, but there is no objective standard to tell us how much elasticity of substitution counts as a market. The difficulty of measuring the elasticity of substitution is another issue. As a result, in the enforcement of anti-monopoly law, the definition of the relevant market is completely arbitrary and relies on the subjective judgment of the law enforcer. Different judges might have completely opposite judgments.

In the Internet and information economy era, market boundaries are becoming less clear. Market definition is more difficult. Enforcement will become more arbitrary.

For example, is Google a monopoly? This depends on how you view Google's market. If you point to the search engine market, where its share is over 90% in recent years (Tiago Bianchi, 2023), then it is undoubtedly a monopoly. If you view it as an advertising company, however, then its market share is much smaller (estimated to be 25% in digital advertising in 2022; Navarro, 2023). In the consumer technology products market, Google accounted for less than 0.24% of it in 2012 – a far cry from relevance, let alone monopoly. Therefore, whether Google abuses its dominant position in the market is related to how we define its market (Thiel and Masters, 2014, chapter 3).

A few years ago, there was a famous case in China between Qihoo 360 and Tencent, known as *360 v. Tencent*. In this case, Qihoo 360 accused Tencent of being a monopolist. Tencent denied the allegation and the focus of the dispute was on the definition of the market. Qihoo 360 advocated using a narrow market definition limited to instant messaging. Tencent, however, believed the services it provided and markets it participated in were much broader, so they should all be considered part of the relevant market. According to this definition, Tencent is not a monopoly. The court's decision utilized the concept that favored Tencent. If the market had been defined as Qihoo 360 advocated, then Tencent would have been in trouble.

How to Determine a Firm's Ability to Set Prices

Neoclassical economics says monopolies are bad because monopolists set monopoly prices above the competitive price level. They make profit by harming the interests of consumers and reducing the total social surplus. To determine whether a firm has a monopoly status, sometimes anti-monopoly authorities have to undertake a theoretical price test. For example, if the enterprise sets prices between 5% and 10% above the competitive price, how will demand change and what is the impact on the enterprise? If demand does not decline by much, then raising prices is profitable, so this enterprise has monopoly power. Obviously, this kind of theoretical price test is completely subjective and not scientific at all.

Ironically, most products and services provided by Internet platform "monopolists" are free. They do not collect what economists call "monopoly prices." This makes the price test impossible. When the European Union's anti-monopoly authority penalized Google, it had to define Google's monopoly status with a price test on Google's products. The price of Google's search service, however, is zero. How can the impact of a 5–10% increase in price on consumers be tested? It cannot. Of course, we can believe Google collects invisible prices by making consumers accept advertising and provide personal information, thus free is not really free. A 5–10% increase in advertising or data disclosures means what, exactly? In theory, experts could design a complex system of indicators and equations, then collect information on theoretical invisible price tests. This is not practical, however, and will not reflect the actual situation in the market.

How to Determine a Firm Is Implementing Monopoly Prices

According to existing theory and practice, enterprise behavior easily falls into the anti-monopoly trap. Regardless of how enterprises set prices, they can be scrutinized by the anti-monopoly entities. Ayn Rand, an American Objectivist writer, once said:

Under the Antitrust laws, a man becomes a criminal from the moment he goes into business, no matter what he does. For instance, if he charges prices which some bureaucrats judge as too high, he can be prosecuted for monopoly or for a successful "intent to monopolize"; if he charges prices lower than those of his competitors, he can be prosecuted for "unfair competition" or "restraint of trade"; and if he charges the same prices as his competitors, he can be prosecuted for "collusion" or 'conspiracy". There is only one difference in the legal treatment accorded a criminal or to a businessman: the criminal's rights are protected much more securely and objectively than the businessman's. (Rand, 1962, p. 1)

According to William Landes, a similar argument was made by Professor Ronald Coase of the University of Chicago: "he had gotten tired of antitrust because when the prices went up the judges said it was monopoly, when the prices went down they said it was predatory pricing, and when they stayed the same they said it was tacit collusion" (Kitch, 1983, pp. 163–234. Quotation is on p. 193). Therefore, any action is the wrong one. Whether an enterprise is monopolistic is entirely based on whether the enforcers believe it has monopoly status. This is ridiculous. Conceptual errors took root in our mainstream economics. What is the mistake? We get competition and monopoly completely backwards.

How to Differentiate between Appropriate Competition and Monopoly Behavior

Behavior defined as monopolistic in economics, such as bundling or resale-price maintenance, are common competitive methods in business. This behavior is not so-called monopolistic, but also, in many cases, protects the interests of consumers. A classic example of this is Microsoft providing its Internet browser for free, which was considered monopolistic behavior. According to this standard, almost every transaction can be considered "bundling." When I buy clothing, the seller always includes the buttons in the sale. Why can I not buy the clothing without the buttons? If the seller says the buttons are free, then can the makers of buttons accuse the clothing enterprise of bundling? How should the court decide? It is hard to believe the degrees provided by all universities are not "bundled."

We will find that behind these issues are layers of economic reasons. Mainstream economics understands the market as a state of affairs, but the true market is a process. Metaphorically, mainstream economists see the market as a picture, but the true market is a serialized drama. The difference between a state of affairs and a process is extremely important.

Mainstream economics' use of static equilibrium theory to observe the dynamic commercial world will bring about problems. For example, according to mainstream economic analysis, product pricing according to marginal costs is the most effective. This theory, however, does not consider how products come about. On the market, the vast majority of products are the result of a specific enterprise's innovation.

When prices are discussed in economics, we assume all products exist *ex-ante* and each enterprise only chooses to produce a certain quantity. Product innovation is lacking. The socially optimal price theory obtained under this assumption will be misleading. If in the year 2000 we had examined the Windows operating system, we would have viewed Microsoft as a detestable monopolist. The product already existed and its sales price was much higher than its marginal cost, so it necessarily would create a net loss for society. The Windows operating system was created by Microsoft under the leadership of Bill Gates. Before Microsoft, this product did not exist. If prices must be set according to marginal costs, then this product could not possibly exist. Prices set according to marginal cost could never recoup the research and development costs. Mainstream economics' optimal price theory has no criticisms for those who do not produce. Instead, it criticizes people who provide products that would otherwise not exist. The only reason is that they set a price higher than marginal costs.

If all products had to have prices set according to marginal costs, then the vast majority of products we now consume would not exist. Humanity would still be living in traditional, self-sufficient agricultural societies. Taking products from research and development to the market is a long and slow process that requires a large amount of inputs. Whether or not it will be successful is uncertain. No new products can be produced according to marginal cost prices. Our static equilibrium economic theories do not consider this, however. They simply treat the difference between price and cost as monopoly profit (which actually is entrepreneurial profit). We are misled to believe that without this monopoly profit, consumers could buy more products at lower prices. The fact is without this so-called monopoly profit, there would be hardly any new products available. Today's old products are nothing but yesterday's new products.

Let us take the steam engine as an example. James Watt began researching the steam engine in 1765 and applied for the patent in 1769. His first investor, John Roebuck, went bankrupt in 1773. In 1776, the Watt-Boulton Company produced the first steam engine, but did not make a profit until 1786. There was no profit over those 20 years, but there was a huge investment. If the British government at that time had required the steam engine to be priced according to marginal costs, then Watt's steam engine would never have existed!

Certainly, Watt and his partner were accused of "monopoly." Actually, the prices they charged were extremely fair. The buyer only needed to pay for the cost of manufacturing and installing the equipment, plus one-third of the savings from using an equivalent horsepower pneumatic machine. However, when paying the agreed royalties, the mine owners objected. In 1780, the mine owners in Cornwall petitioned Parliament to cancel the royalties. Watt's reply is worth a read by all economists and antitrust experts today:

> They charge us with establishing a monopoly, but, if a monopoly, it is one by means of which their mines are made more productive than ever they were before ... They say it is inconvenient for the mining interest to be burdened with the payment of engine dues, just as it is inconvenient for the person who wishes to get at my purse that I should keep my breeches pocket buttoned ... We have no power to compel anybody to erect our engines. What, then, will Parliament say to any man who comes there to complain of a grievance he can avoid?[3]

Economic growth comes primarily from entrepreneurs' innovation. Entrepreneurs open up new industries and markets through innovation and creativity to obtain entrepreneurial profit. If we expropriate enterprises' "monopoly profit" obtained through innovation, then the innovation function of entrepreneurs will disappear. Acknowledging the existence of "monopoly" profit is the premise of entrepreneurial innovation. This is another reason we should be mindful of the antimonopoly law.

Redefining Competition and Monopoly

Earlier in this chapter, I pointed out that traditional economics' concepts about competition and monopoly are wrong. How should we properly define competition and monopoly?

In my view, the essence of market competition is captured in two points: (1) Free entry, meaning no violent or forceful obstacles to entry (2) No governmental or otherwise protections or discriminations. Stated simply, free competition means policy or the law does not protect one group of people while at the same time prejudicing another

---

[3] Quoted from Mantoux (1928, p. 338. Referencing: Smiles, 1865, p. 281).

group. Alternatively, any forceful prohibition on entry into an industry or policy that prejudices producers or operators is monopolistic!

For example, Queen Elizabeth I granted a monopoly on British trade with India to the British East India Company. This protection was a type of prejudice against other people. Many of the industry entry restrictions we currently implement are also monopolistic.

Whether a market is competitive or monopolistic is unrelated to the number of enterprises. In reality, we see that even if an industry only consists of two firms, competition is fierce. This is similar to elections. In the 2016 US presidential election, Donald Trump and Hillary Clinton really clashed. Even if a market is dominated by one enterprise, as long as market entry is open, there is no monopoly. Although an enterprise like Microsoft has great market power, there are no limits on entry into the software industry, so we do not need to worry. Reality has proven this point.

True monopolies necessarily come from governmental – or related entities – limits on market entry or preferential treatment. When the government uses force (the law or policy) to reserve a part of the market or the entire market for one or a few enterprises, a monopoly is created. This is the original meaning of monopoly. For example, in China's telecommunication industry, the government only allows three state-owned enterprises to operate, but not other enterprises, so a monopoly is created. China's banking industry is similar. Although there are more than 200 commercial banks in China, it is still monopolized. As long as the government limits entry, a monopoly is created. Similar forceful means include licenses, franchises, preferential taxation, preferential lending, and subsidies. According to my previous definition of a monopoly, what is competition and what is monopoly is clear. When the courts judge cases, there should be no ambiguity. The previously discussed price test is unnecessary. You only need to check if there are entry limits and government protection. Without these things, there is no monopoly. With these things, there is a monopoly.[4]

The traditional definition of monopoly only looks at an enterprise's market share, but not how this share was formed. Confusing market

---

[4] Brian Simpson (2005, Chapter 2) distinguished between the economic and political concepts of monopoly. He believed that only the political concept of monopoly was correct. The political concept of monopoly is that the government uses force (laws and policies) to reserve all or part of the market for one or more companies.

advantage caused by entrepreneurship and innovation with monopoly position created by government protection will necessarily lead to ridiculous conclusions. As I mentioned in Chapter 5, at a forum in 2003, a China Mobile executive said China Mobile was not a monopoly, but Alibaba and Tencent were monopolies. According to the standard economics definition, he is not wrong! The problem arises from economics' definition of monopoly. According to my previous definition, Alibaba and Tencent are not monopolies because they came out of market competition. If you have the ability, you can also do it. No one prohibits you from making these products. However, China Mobile and then Industrial and Commercial Bank of China (ICBC) are monopolies. Without government permission, you cannot enter their industries.

Let me talk a little bit about the new market in the Internet era. Economists call it the two-sided market or multi-sided market.[5] The biggest characteristic of the two-sided market is its network effect. The more users there are, the greater the network's value for each user. The direct network effect existed in the past, such as in the traditional telecommunications industry. As more people used the telephone, the value each user obtained was greater. In two-sided markets, however, a platform with buyers and sellers has intersecting (indirect) network effects. The more sellers there are, the more valuable the platform is to buyers. Similarly, the more buyers there are, the more valuable the platform is to sellers. A ride-sharing platform like DiDi becomes more convenient with more drivers, so passengers obtain more value. The more people willing to use a ride-sharing platform, the more valuable the platform is to participating drivers. This is the so-called indirect network effect.

According to traditional economic theories, any market with direct and indirect network effects will form natural monopolies. What we originally called public utilities, such as gas and roads, are natural monopolies. High fixed cost inputs and low marginal costs are characteristics of industries with natural monopolies. From an efficiency perspective, in order to avoid duplicate construction and save on fixed costs, the product should be provided by one firm. Access restrictions are necessary. If a true natural monopoly exists, however, government

---

[5] For an overview of the two-sided market and its implications for antitrust law, see Evans (2003).

restrictions are not necessary because only one firm could survive profitably. An earlier mover will have lower costs and the second entrant will fail. Who is so stupid to run toward their own death? As such, the natural monopoly assumption and government entry restrictions are contradictory. If an industry is a natural monopoly, then the government does not need to implement entry restrictions. Alternatively, if entry restrictions are necessary, then the industry is not a natural monopoly. In China's telecommunications, the government only allows three state-owned enterprises, which proves it is not a natural monopoly.

Of course, one might also say that if the government does not limit entry into a natural monopoly industry, dumb firms might irrationally enter. If we assume that entrepreneurs are irrational, however, then entry should be limited in all markets, not just natural monopoly industries. Additionally, we have no way to prove that entrepreneurs are irrational but the government is rational. The government is also managed by people, not God!

In the digital economy era, many firms have the platform market characteristic that we just discussed. Chinese firms such as Alibaba, Tencent, and Baidu or American firms such as Google, Facebook, and Amazon are all multi-sided market platforms. If we do not change economics' definition of monopoly and competition, or if we continue to use misleading theories, then our current anti-monopoly policy can only be repaired superficially, but fundamental problems cannot be repaired.

If we utilize the free competition that I just defined, where no entry restrictions are enforced, then platform markets will not lead to so-called "monopolies." Borrowing from traditional concepts: It will not lead to sustained market monopoly. Here, "sustained" refers to being able to exist feeling no competition without the government's anti-monopoly measures. That will not happen!

Entrepreneurship Is the Best Anti-Monopoly Law

As Israel Kirzner pointed out, entrepreneurship and competition are two sides of the same coin. Entrepreneurial activities are always competitive, and at the same time competitive activities are always entrepreneurial (Kirzner, 1973, p. 94). If promoting competition is the goal of the anti-monopoly law, then I can say that entrepreneurship is the best anti-monopoly law. It is more helpful in breaking up a "monopoly" than any legal document or policy. Alternatively, any law and policy that hampers entrepreneurship is anti-competitive and will lead to true monopolies.

Freedom of entry is key. Kirzner even argued that the complete freedom of entry into all kinds of market activity is the necessary and sufficient condition for competition to exist without obstacles (Kirzner, 1973, p. 99). As long as freedom of entry exists, entrepreneurs will always attempt to find new opportunities. They will use these opportunities and innovative methods to overthrow the current market leader. They will find a way to end up on top. The inevitable bureaucratization of large enterprises also provides opportunities for new ones to replace old ones. Bureaucracy is incompatible with entrepreneurship. As argued by Schumpeter, innovations emerge primarily with young entrepreneurs, but established entrepreneurs often tend to be conservative. Nobody is ever an entrepreneur all the time. New firms' intrusion into an existing industry always entails "warring with an old sphere," which tries to prohibit, discredit, or otherwise restrict the advantages afforded the new firm by its innovation. Whatever may happen in a particular case, every entrepreneur's high profit is temporary, because competitors will copy innovation, causing market prices to fall. This sequence of cutting prices is observable in all industries except those protected by government monopoly. The challenges to the incumbents often come from the outsiders with completely new technological paradigms, making the incumbents' advantages completely obsolete (Schumpeter, 1939, pp. 105–108). Thus, "pure cases of long-run monopoly must be of the rarest occurrence and that even tolerable approximations to the requirements of the concept must be still rarer than are cases of perfect competition" (Schumpeter, 1942, p. 99).

Throughout history, this has been the case. Canals appear to be a classic natural monopoly. Who dug the majority of canals in eighteenth-century England? They were dug by private individuals. We say canals are public infrastructure, but private entrepreneurs were willing to dig them, so surely this is a good thing? The glory days of canals, however, lasted only a few decades, and then railways appeared in England. With competition from railways, we cannot say canals obtained monopoly profits, because even survival became an issue. In the end, they could only be used for sight-seeing. Competition was fierce from the beginning for railways. In 1840, the United States had

over 300 railroad companies. After reorganizations, only a few were
left that basically monopolized the industry. The glory days of railroads, however, was not very long. Who did it compete against?
Highways. With the development of automobile transportation, railroad transportation began to decline. Then came competition
from airplanes.

A more recent example is the computer industry. IBM produced its
first computer in 1945 but had no way to take it to market. The cost of
vacuum tubes was too high. Computers had commercial value only
after transistors and integrated circuits were invented. By the 1960s,
IBM was basically synonymous with computers. According to the
standard definition in economics, it absolutely was a monopolist.
A crisis occurred in less than 20 years as microcomputers began to
challenge IBM's monopoly status. A few microcomputer manufacturers even obtained monopoly status, but after Intel produced the microprocessor in 1971, personal computers (PCs) quickly appeared. None
of the companies that dominated the microcomputer market became
leading manufacturers of PCs.[6] When Apple's PC became all the rage,
IBM sought out Bill Gates to provide software. IBM and Microsoft's
agreement eliminated the possibility for anyone to monopolize the
market for PCs.[7] From that point, PCs could be produced by anybody,
and competition was fierce. Some well-known players in the PC market
are now out of business. IBM PC was taken over in 2004 by Lenovo, a
late-comer PC manufacture from China. After innovations like smartphones and iPads/tablets, PC firms even had difficulty surviving.

In the semiconductor industry, the dominant players have frequently
altered, not only between different firms, but also between different
countries. Intel was the inventor of the microprocessor, and has been a
major provider of PC chips for a long time. It missed the opportunity in
the smartphone market, however. It failed when it entered chip manufacturing in 2015 to compete with TSMC. Its market share in the
worldwide semiconductor industry dropped from 13.3% in 2008 to
9.7% in 2022, second to Samsung (10.9%). Samsung is a late-comer in
the semiconductor industry. With emerging AI, GPU may replace CPU

---

[6] Regarding the iterations of leading products and manufacturers in the computer
and hard disk industries (as well as similar examples from other industries), see
Christensen (1997), chapter 1.
[7] Regarding Microsoft's influence on the computer industry, see Walter Isaacson
(2014), chapter 9.

and Intel's leadership in CPU may be completely subverted. Nvidia is the inventor and a dominant player of GPU, but now faces challenges from Google, Microsoft, and others.[8]

In the smartphone market, Nokia was No. 1 and Blackberry was No. 2 in the global market in 2010, accounting respectively for nearly 40% and 20% of market share. They sounded like unshakable monopolists! Where are Nokia's smart phone and RIM (Blackberry) now? They both disappeared! They disappeared not because of the governmental anti-monopoly actions but because of competition from other entrepreneurs. Xiaomi was newly established in 2010 by Chinese entrepreneur Lei Jun, but its global market share reached 13.7% in the third quarter of 2023, making it the third largest producer of smartphones (Larocchis, 2023). The dominance of Nokia and Apple's iPhone did not stop Lei Jun from entering the smartphone market.

So, it is unfounded to worry that any enterprise will monopolize a market and then be able to maintain the monopoly without making progress. IBM's "monopoly status" was ended by market competition and innovation from a new generation of entrepreneurs, not an American anti-monopoly ruling. Even if the American government had not investigated IBM for monopolistic practices, and not spent that much money, how much worse would the computer market be today? Not at all worse off.

The anti-monopoly case against Microsoft at the turn of the millennium is a classic example. At the beginning of the 1990s, the US Justice Department (which was responsible for anti-trust enforcement) began to look at Microsoft as a "monopolist." Microsoft provided its own browser to its users for free, so it was accused of bundling, which violated the anti-monopoly law. A large number of legal scholars and economists participated in the case, with some supporting and some opposing. What was the final decision? Judge Thomas P. Jackson of the US District Court for the District of Columbia ruled that Microsoft violated the Sherman Antitrust Act and ordered Microsoft to split into two companies: One that produced operating systems and one that produced applied software. The D.C. Circuit

---

[8] Miller (2022) provides a detailed story of fierce competition in the semiconductor industry.

Court of Appeals overturned the ruling. The Department of Justice and Microsoft settled the case and the company was not required to split up.

What happened then? Google appeared in 1998, which was the same year the Department of Justice investigated Microsoft. Google quickly beat Microsoft. Many other companies, such as Amazon and Facebook, can now provide search. Now, even Google may be subverted by ChatGPT! What were we afraid of? The Department of Justice worried that Microsoft bundling a new product for free would inhibit new competitors, and thus harm the interests of consumers. The reality is that these were unwarranted worries.

Today many people in China worry that the same monopoly issue exists for Tencent and Alibaba. I think we do not need to worry. We do not need to judge the future according to economists' imagination or believe that things economists do not think of will not occur. Jack Ma of Alibaba, and Pony Ma of Tencent will not rule the world. The world changes in a way that exceeds our imagination. You might be dissatisfied with WeChat, but Zhifubao of Alibaba provides similar service as WeChat. Other competitors also appeared. WeChat could not halt the rise of Douyin (TikTok). Taobao could not hinder Pinduoduo. Remember that in 2008 when China's anti-monopoly law was enacted, a common concern in Chinese media was that GOME and Suning had monopolized China's household appliance sales. The media advocated initiating anti-monopoly investigations into these two companies. Within two years, however, these two companies faced pressure to survive. Of course, no one again pointed the sword of anti-trust at GOME and Suning.

In markets with free entry, competition always exists because competition is the essence of entrepreneurship. What keeps Pony Ma and Jack Ma busy? They will not feel that they are so big that they can sit back and relax, enjoying their large market share. That is not possible unless the government prohibits other people from creating exchange platforms. Innovation is unpredictable and unplanned, like the story of Cheng Yaojin in Chinese folklore.[9]

Because entrepreneurship is competitive, and the waves behind surge on those before, very few firms could stay in a leading position for very

---

[9] The stories related to Cheng Yaojin involve him showing up unexpectedly and either saving the day or disrupting a plan.

long unless they are more innovative than others. Even if they are hardworking and innovative, their dominant position is not guaranteed. Alibaba's market share in China's e-commerce dropped to 42.7% in 2022 from 61.2% in 2017. Pinduoduo, a late-comer, increased its market share to 15.5% in 2022 from 1.8% in 2017. Pinduoduo was founded in 2015 by Chinese entrepreneur Colin Huang. Jack Ma, the founder of Alibaba, may not have even known who Colin Huang was before Pingduoduo became a true competitor of Alibaba.[10]

Mark J. Perry, a senior fellow emeritus of AEI, compared the 1955 *Fortune 500* companies to the 2018 *Fortune 500* companies and found that there are *only 53 companies that appeared in both lists and have remained on the list since it started*. In other words, fewer than 11% of the *Fortune 500* companies in 1955 remained on the list over the next 63 years, and more than 89% of the companies from 1955 have either gone bankrupt, merged with (or were acquired by) another firm, or they still exist but fell out of the *Fortune 500* (ranked by total revenues) in one year or more. According to a 2016 report by *Innosight* (*Corporate Longevity: Turbulence Ahead for Large Organizations*), corporations in the S&P 500 Index in 1965 stayed in the index for an average of 33 years. By 1990, average tenure in the S&P 500 had narrowed to 20 years and is now forecast to shrink to 14 years by 2026. At the current churn rate, about half of today's S&P 500 firms will be replaced over the next 10 years as "we enter a period of heightened volatility for leading companies across a range of industries, with the next ten years shaping up to be *the most potentially turbulent in modern history*," according to *Innosight*.[11]

The above findings demonstrate that first, Schumpeter's creative destruction process indeed works in the market, and second, a firm can only survive and thrive by charging low prices, providing high-quality products and services, and great customer service, not as a result of a monopolistic status.

Anti-monopoly Law Protects Special Interests

Many examples show that anti-monopoly policies are done in the name of protecting the interests of consumers, but that actually protect

---

[10] Market share information was collected by the author from Chinese websites.
[11] The reader can find Perry's findings on the webpage (Perry, 2018).

the interests of producers. In many cases, anti-monopoly policies are trade protectionism in another form. The European Union's anti-monopoly agencies look for targets everywhere with a magnifying glass when they have nothing else to do. They investigated Microsoft for a while and then Google for a while, just like the village chief in the fable at the beginning of this chapter. This type of behavior is typical trade protectionism. What do that many people at the European Union do? They create work for themselves! We know that a trade union organizes strikes because otherwise the workers will think it is useless! Many anti-monopoly agencies are like this. Without initiating case after case, they cannot show their value, so they continue to find things to investigate.

Of course, we still have a lot to do now. In the digital economy era, what do we really need to do? For example, what is the problem with Baidu? If Google's entry was not restricted by Chinese authorities, could Baidu's search quality be in its current state? True anti-monopoly activities should be concerned with this issue. Why doesn't the government let Google in? Why doesn't it open up this market?

Of course, I previously discussed primarily economic issues, but many anti-monopoly activities are not economic issues. An important issue is that humans are inherently jealous. We get uncomfortable when we see other people succeed and are happy when we see celebrities embroiled in scandals. Another reason is we do not like to see individual firms throw their weight around. It is true that some companies are too capricious, and it is necessary to publicly criticize them. This is one of the reasons the anti-monopoly law is so popular. Politicians also worry that some people have too much money and might interfere in politics, so they should be beaten down from time to time.

The original motivation for the United States' anti-trust legislation might have been political. Legal history has shown that the US Congress did not design the Sherman Act to be a 'consumer welfare protection'. Senator John Sherman called the act "a bill of rights, a charter of liberty" and said:

If we will not endure a king as a political power, we should not endure a king over the production, transportation, and sale of any of the necessities of life. If we would not submit to an emperor, we should not submit to an autocrat of trade, with power to prevent competition and to fix the price of any commodity.[12]

[12] Quoted from Khan (2016).

In summary, we can see that the economic foundation of anti-monopoly law is wrong. Competition in neoclassical economics is not true competition. Most monopolistic behavior defined in neoclassical economics is precisely the means of competition. True free competition is free entry and a lack of forceful government protection or discrimination. It has nothing to do with the size and number of enterprises. As long as there is free entry, there is no need to worry about so-called monopoly, because entrepreneurship is always competitive.

Finally, a very important point is one I have made for a long time: The only monopoly to be opposed is a government-enforced monopoly, which is a privilege enjoyed by only certain enterprises, and includes restrictions on entry, franchise rights, fiscal subsidies, and financing concessions. That is the point made repeatedly by Schumpeter.

8 | Entrepreneurial Profit and Common Prosperity

Introduction

Income distribution is an important theme in economics. Many people worry that the market economy increases the gap between the rich and poor. This worry largely originates from a misunderstanding of profits and an ignorance of entrepreneurship.

In 2021, the Chinese Communist Party launched a campaign for "common prosperity." Particularly, it strongly emphasizes reducing the income gap through governmental redistribution policies and the so-called third distribution, referring to charity and donations.[1] While there is nothing wrong with common prosperity as an idea, and the idea of common prosperity is not new in China, a sharp escalation in official rhetoric combined with a crackdown on excesses in industries, such as Internet businesses and private education, has caused great anxiety among Chinese entrepreneurs and investors. The "third distribution" is a novel official slogan. It has put tremendous pressure on business people. Alibaba Holdings and Tencent Holdings, two leading Internet companies, announced contributions of CNY100 billion and 50 billion, respectively, to charitable funds immediately following the official call for common prosperity. Many other companies have followed suit. Some local governments have even begun to ask for charitable donations from the entrepreneurs who plan to make investments in their localities. Entrepreneurs' confidence has been shaken.

This chapter is a revised version of Weiying Zhang (2022) "Market economy and China's 'common prosperity' campaign," *Journal of Chinese Economic and Business Studies*, 20:4, 323–337, DOI: 10.1080/14765284.2021.2004350. Reprinted by permission of Taylor & Francis Ltd, http://www.tandfonline.com.
[1] For the Western media reports on this campaign, see e.g. www.thetimes.co.uk/article/xi-promises-third-distribution-of-wealth-in-billionaire-crackdown-c9xxl5hsc; https://www.reuters.com/world/china/what-is-chinas-common-prosperity-drive-why-does-it-matter-2021-09-02/

A senior party official tried to comfort anxious entrepreneurs by saying that "common prosperity" is not egalitarianism and does not mean "killing the rich to help the poor." Entrepreneurs' concerns are not entirely groundless, however, given China's current political, ideological, and public opinion climate. Downplaying the market and introducing more government interventions have been a dominant policy practice in China in the decade since 2013. This new campaign for common prosperity could be reasonably understood as a further step toward de-marketization in China.

The campaign for common prosperity, I believe, is based on common distrust of the market and common misconceptions about entrepreneurs and profit, although pursuing common prosperity has its own legitimacy. In my view, the market economy is the only system through which common prosperity can be achieved. Entrepreneurial profit is essential for the market to work toward common prosperity. In this chapter, I attempt to present a short theory of how the market economy generates common prosperity by arguing: (1) profit is a responsibility system under which everyone earns income only when he (she) creates values for others; (2) entre- preneurs are the major driver of wealth creation; (3) ordinary people are the biggest beneficiaries of the market economy; and (4) entrepre- neurship implies a high mobility of income distribution, not a deepening gap between the rich and poor. In so doing, I present both theoretical arguments and empirical evidence to show that our future development depends on our beliefs. If we lose our faith in the market and introduce more and more government intervention, we can only move toward common poverty, not common prosperity.

Seeing the Miracle of the Market Economy from History

To talk about the contribution of the market economy to mankind, one must look back at history. We can think of the period between 2.5 million years ago and 15,000 years ago as 99.4% of human history so far. According to Bradford DeLong, an economist at the University of California at Berkeley in the United States, it took that long for the world's per capita GDP to reach 90 international dollars (a measure of wealth using international purchasing power in 1990). Then, it took another 0.59% of the time, or until 1750, for the world's per capita

GDP to double to 180 international dollars. From 1750 to 2000, that is, within 0.01% of the time, the world's per capita GDP increased 37 times, reaching 6,600 international dollars. In other words, 97% of mankind's wealth was created in the past 250 years – that is, 0.01% of the time (cited from Beinhocker, 2006, pp. 9–10).

If you draw DeLong's data on XY coordinates, you can see that during 99.99% of the time from 2.5 million years ago to the present, the world's per capita GDP is basically a horizontal line. In the past 250 years, however, there has been a sudden – almost vertical – rise. Whether it is Western European countries, countries such as the United States, Canada, and Australia, or even Japan, economic growth has occurred in the past one or two hundred years. China's economic growth too has mainly occurred in the past 40 years.

The numbers alone cannot explain the full story. Our ancestors, that is, ordinary Chinese people more than 100 years ago, and even Chinese farmers 40 years ago, consumed things that were not much different from their ancestors alive during the Qin, Han, or Sui and Tang dynasties, but they were worse off than their ancestors alive during the Song Dynasty. It is the same in Europe. The ancient Romans could enjoy what an ordinary Englishman could consume in 1800, and even the Romans enjoyed more. What we can consume today is something that people could not imagine 100 years ago, or even 30 years ago.

The improvement of living standards has greatly extended the life span of people. In 1820, the world's average life expectancy was 26 years, which was about the same as in ancient Rome. However, by 2019, the United Nations estimated it had reached 72.6 years. Now, the average life expectancy in China has reached 77 years. Perhaps the biggest "drawback" of the market economy is the emergence of problems related to aging.

Some young people do not know history and may not know that China's food rations were abolished in 1993. Before the abolition of the rationing system, grocery stores required a food ration, an edible oil ration, a cloth ration, and so on. Forty years ago, the monthly salary of a division-level cadre in China was just over 60 yuan. At that time, a catty (500 grams) of eggs was more than 60 cents. In other words, a month's salary for a division-level cadre could only buy 100 catties of eggs. Now, the monthly wage of a babysitter in Beijing is about 5,500 yuan. That wage can buy 1,000 catties of eggs, which, if consumed at a rate of 10 eggs per day, is a two-year supply. When

I was in the countryside, the work points earned by farmers for a day's work were worth 20 cents, equivalent to half a catty of white flour. Now in my hometown, a part-time worker with limited skills and education can earn a daily wage of 150 yuan, equivalent to 100 catties of white flour.

Why did human miracles appear in the past 250 years? Why did China's economic growth in particular only appear in the past 40 years? Have people become smarter, wiser than in the past? Of course not. Human IQ and wisdom have not made much progress in recorded history. No matter how smart the Chinese are today, I believe that few can surpass Confucius, Mencius, and Laocius. The same is true in the West. Human intelligence has not changed much in the past few thousand years.

Could it be that the resources have increased? They have not. The Earth we live on is still the original Earth. Not only have resources not increased, on the contrary, the natural resources associated with the land are slowly decreasing. What has changed? The only answer I can provide is that mankind has developed a new economic system, the market economy. Britain began to implement the market economy more than 200 years ago, so the economy began to take off more than 200 years ago. China started to move toward a market economy 40 years ago, so China has made a huge leap in the past 40 years.

It is generally believed that the improvement of human living standards comes from technological progress. The questions are: What is driving technological progress? Why does technology advance under some systems, but not under other systems? The facts of historical development have proved that only a market economy can significantly promote technological progress and quickly commercialize new technologies to benefit the general public. Ancient society also had some technological inventions, but these inventions rarely created value for consumers and wealth for society. The reason was they were not produced under the pressure of market competition and were difficult to commercialize. What smart people imagine by inspiration may not really meet the needs of consumers.

Profit Is a Responsibility System

How and why does the market economy create economic miracles? The fundamental reason is that the market economy extends the scale and scope of human cooperation to a level that is not achievable under any other economic system. As we argued in Chapter 6, the market economy is cooperation between strangers. Hayek called this the "extended order" (Hayek, 1988). Cooperation between strangers makes everyone have better opportunities through specialization, which would be impossible if people only worked within a small group of acquaintances. The planned economy fails because it cannot provide necessary information and incentives for cooperation between strangers. But to achieve cooperation between strangers, there is a very important issue that must be resolved, and that is trust. If the buyer does not trust the seller, trade will not occur, so specialization will not be good for either. As a result, everyone has to produce for themselves, returning to a self-sufficient natural economy.

How is trust in the market established? I will focus on three concepts: Enterprise, profit, and entrepreneur. These three concepts are the key to understanding the market economy (Zhang, 2015b, pp. 9–12).

There are 1.4 billion people in China. If everyone produces their own products and sells them on the market, who can be trusted? Equivalently, if the trademarks of all commodities on the market were removed, what would you dare to buy? You may dare to buy the simplest commodities such as potatoes, rice, and fruits. Do you dare to buy things such as cars, computers, mineral water, and projectors that are difficult to distinguish in terms of quality and function? No! You would not dare to buy 99% of the goods on the market.

What is an alternative? One way is to divide 1.4 billion people into different groups, for example, into 30 groups, such as Henan people, Hebei people, Shandong people, Shaanxi people, Beijing people, and so on. After this grouping, despite not knowing everyone, we do know who is Shandongese, who is Cantonese, so we can make a certain kind of group responsibility. If someone cheats us, we know whether he is Cantonese or Shandongese, at least.

Enterprises are a kind of social grouping. Each company has its own name (trademark). Whoever cheated us, we can sue. Or, he cheated me this time, so I will not buy his things next time. In this way, when production activities appear through enterprises, each enterprise must be responsible for its own products so that we can build trust. If there is no enterprise, everyone is only engaged in individual production, and this cannot be done.

How does the enterprise enable us to trust each other? The answer is related to ownership allocation and the profit system. For example, assume that an enterprise is composed of 10,000 individuals. In theory, everyone can become the owner. The annual income of this enterprise is 100 million yuan, equally divided among 10,000 people, so each person gets 10,000 yuan. This sounds fair, but think about it: If something goes wrong, who will be responsible? If everyone is required to be responsible, the result may be that no one is responsible, so the company will have no revenue available for distribution.

In reality, companies use another way to allocate responsibility, that is, some people are held accountable for negligence, and others bear strict liability. The person held accountable for negligence receives contract income (salary), that is, if he does not arrive late or leave early, is not absent from work, does not violate the work regulations, and works for a month, then he must receive one month's salary by the end of the month. This is an employee. The other group of people, the bosses, takes profits and bears strict liability – or residual liability. Speaking in layman's terms, if others do not discover your mistakes, you are not responsible. You are called an employee. If you do not find other people's mistakes, then all the mistakes are yours. You are the boss. The boss does not have the right to demand sales revenue from consumers by claiming he has not made a mistake, nor can he take his employees to court because he has made a loss; while a worker can demand income from the boss if he has not made a mistake. If the boss refuses to pay him, he can take legal action against the boss. This is the difference between a boss and an employee.

Profit is the surplus of enterprise income after deducting costs such as wages. It may be positive or negative, very different from wages and other forms of earnings, which cannot be negative. Those who take profit must take risks, so it is an incentive mechanism. When any employee makes a mistake, the boss is the first to bear the responsibility. A restaurant provides a simple example. If the chef does not wash the dishes cleanly, causing the patrons to be hospitalized due to food poisoning, the owner must be responsible. Therefore, the boss must carefully supervise and regulate the behavior of the employees, so that customers can purchase the company's products with confidence.

Furthermore, the bosses of the company have to take responsibility not only when the employees of the company make mistakes, but also when the company's suppliers make mistakes. For example, if you bought a brand-name computer, but a certain part of the computer, such as the screen, chip, or fan, does not function, or the battery exploded, the computer manufacturer should be responsible first, not the supplier of the parts. In other words, a company uses its own brand to make a promise to consumers. It guarantees that if you buy the company's things, it will be responsible for all the problems. In this way, there will be a market that everyone can trust, orderly cooperation between strangers will take place, and the continuous increase of social wealth will be secured.

Therefore, I said that profit is a responsibility system and a way of assessment. To a large extent, profitability is determined by the entrepreneurial capacity to take responsibility for others. The market divides the accounting units through the organizational form of the enterprise and traces profit responsibilities, so that everyone is responsible for his actions, and there is trust in the market.

The Rich in the Market Economy Are Elected by Consumers with Monetary Votes

Why do some people become profit-taking entrepreneurs, while others become wage-earning employees? This is determined by the differences in entrepreneurial abilities between people (Zhang, 2018). In a market economy, everyone has the freedom to choose to be an entrepreneur or an employee. There is no discriminatory rule that Mr. A can be an entrepreneur and Mr. B can only be an employee. But the result of competition is that only those with high enough entrepreneurial ability will become entrepreneurs. Entrepreneurial ability is essentially the ability to take responsibility for consequences of others. On average, the size of the profit depends on the entrepreneur's ability. But because the market is full of uncertainty, no matter how capable entrepreneurs are, they may lose money! Behind a successful entrepreneur, there are usually multiple failed entrepreneurs. We cannot only see those entrepreneurs who have made a lot of money, but not those who have lost everything. If anyone is jealous of the money an entrepreneur has made, he can choose to be an entrepreneur on his own! One thing he must remember is that if he is not capable enough, he will definitely lose everything!

What is the market? The market is a system where others have the final say whether you have made something right, not yourself. What is valuable and what has no value must be evaluated in the market, and the buyer has the final say. Therefore, bragging is useless. If anyone does not create value for others, it is impossible to earn income. When two companies compete and we say that a particular one has more advantages, it means that this company can create more consumer surplus (that is, the difference between value and price) for consumers. The competition between enterprises is the competition to create surplus value for consumers.

There is a popular saying that entrepreneurs make money off consumers. It seems that consumers are being exploited by entrepreneurs. This statement is wrong. In a competitive market with no government-granted privilege, profits can only come from the value created by entrepreneurs for consumers. Consumers will not be willing to pay 10.01 dollars for something worth 10 dollars. In fact, the money an entrepreneur makes is only a small part of the wealth he creates, even a tiny part. Most of it becomes consumer surplus. No matter how much wealth Bill Gates has, it is a drop in the bucket when compared with the value that Microsoft has created for mankind!

In a market economy, on average, the money an entrepreneur makes is proportional to the number of customers he or she serves. An entrepreneur who only provides products and services to a few people cannot make big money. Only entrepreneurs who serve the mass market can make a lot of money (Mises, 1972, Chapter 1). Therefore, the rich (entrepreneurs) in the market economy are selected by consumers with monetary votes. Each of us is a consumer. If we are jealous of a certain entrepreneur making too much money, we can only blame ourselves for buying that person's products. If most consumers no longer use the products provided by Tencent, and no longer use WeChat, QQ, or online games, Mr. Pony Ma will immediately become a pauper. And all of us are unwilling to give up using Tencent's products, not because we are stupid or benevolent, but because they bring us greater benefits. We think it is worth the money. On the one hand, you willingly buy his products. On the other hand, you are angry at him for making so much money. This is a contradiction!

Ordinary People Are the Biggest Beneficiaries of the Market Economy

Who benefits the most from the market economy? The rich? No! The biggest beneficiaries of the market economy are ordinary people. To give a simple example, Thomas Edison invented the light bulb, which brought convenience to everyone. But the value of light bulbs is much smaller for the rich than the poor, because when there were no light bulbs, the rich could light a lot of candles, but the poor could not afford even one. For another example, now that television is available, everyone can watch the songs and plays performed by celebrities. In the past, only a few wealthy people and palace nobles could enjoy live performances. The same is true for cars. In the past, the rich could take a sedan, but the poor could only walk on foot. Now, ordinary people can have a car as a means of transportation. The difference between riding an Audi and a Xiali[2] is much smaller than the difference between sitting in a sedan and walking. This is true for all new products and new technologies. Takeout provides the greatest convenience to ordinary people. WeChat public accounts allow ordinary people to become "self-media" producers. Yes, some new products are only consumed by the rich at the beginning, and are considered luxury goods, but as the cost drops, they soon become a necessity for most people – this is the purpose of entrepreneurs creating this product. The rich are just paying for the research and development expenses of new products for ordinary people (Hayek, 2011[1960], pp. 97–98). Therefore, the biggest beneficiaries of the market economy are ordinary people, not the privileged class. At least from the perspective of consumption, the market economy has made people more equal.

How can consumers afford products produced by entrepreneurs? When entrepreneurs provide consumers with products in the product market, at the same time they create opportunities for consumers to earn income in the factor market. In a market economy, most people earn most of their income from wages. Wages come from work. Without work, there are no wages. Who created the job? Entrepreneurs! Job opportunities in a society are not given, but created by entrepreneurs. Without entrepreneurs, most people will have no job opportunities and therefore no income. Furthermore, the amount of wages workers can earn depends to a large extent on the ability of entrepreneurs, because the workers' productivity is positively related to the ability of entrepreneurs. The value created under entrepreneurs with high ability is greater than that under entrepreneurs with low ability. Therefore, the greater the number of entrepreneurs in a society and the higher their abilities, the higher the wages of workers. This is the reason why the standard of living of the ordinary working class in developed countries is even higher than that of some elites in

---

[2] A cheap car brand in China, produced by a manufacturer in Tianjin.

developing countries. It is also the main reason many ordinary people in developing countries are willing to immigrate to developed countries.

When I say this, of course, it does not mean that workers are fed by entrepreneurs. In a market economy, everyone supports himself. But, job opportunities for workers are indeed created by entrepreneurs. In this regard, China's experience can give a convincing explanation. In the planned economy era, China's urban population was less than 20% of the total population. Even with such low urbanization, urban-born people still could not find employment opportunities in the cities, and the government had to mobilize 20 million "educated youths" to the countryside. After Reform and Opening, hundreds of millions of rural people have been attracted to work in cities. Some companies have encountered difficulties in recruiting workers from time to time.

China's cross-regional data show that the more entrepreneurs there are in a region, the greater the number of employees, and the higher the average wage of workers. For example, in 2017, the average annual wage of an employee in the private sector is significantly positively correlated to the entrepreneur density (measured by the number of private firms per 10,000 residents) at the provincial level. The correlation coefficient is +0.79. On average, increasing one entrepreneur per thousand citizens will bring about an increase of 480 yuan in the annual wage (see Figure 8.1). The correlation holds consistently.

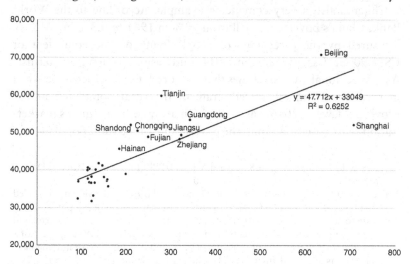

Figure 8.1 Density of Entrepreneurs and Average Wage of The Private Sector (2017).

Source: China Statistical Yearbook (2018).

Therefore, the best way to increase the income of workers is to make entrepreneurs freer and more competitive in the market, not the other way around! If entrepreneurs are eliminated, the vast majority of Chinese people will return to absolute poverty.

The Market Makes Income Distribution Fairer

It is understandable that many people are worried about poverty and uneven income distribution in society. However, some people attribute this phenomenon to market-oriented reform. Some even believe that the result of a market economy must be the widening of the gap between the rich and the poor. This is a misunderstanding.

In the pre-market economy society, whether in the East or the West, the vast majority of people struggled to survive. It was a common occurrence that people died of starvation due to famine. The market economy is the only effective way to solve the poverty problem. The more freedom there is in economic activities, the fewer the number of poor people. A study by the World Bank showed that in 2005, among developing countries, the extreme poverty rate of the most market-oriented countries was only 2.7%, while the extreme poverty rate of those countries without a free market was 41.5% (cited from Zitelmann, 2019, p. 129).

China is also a very convincing example. According to the World Bank, China's poverty rate fell from 88% in 1981 to 0.7% in 2015, as measured by the percentage of people living on the equivalent of US$1.90 or less per day in 2011 purchasing price parity terms.[3] A cross-regional analysis shows that the correlation coefficient between marketization and the poverty rate of the rural population at the provincial level in 2016 was –0.85.[4] On average, as a region's marketization score rose by 1 point, the poverty rate of the rural population in

---

[3] "Poverty headcount ratio at $1.90 a day (2011 PPP) (% of population) | Data," *data.worldbank.org*. Retrieved June 1, 2019.

[4] The marketization scores for both the national and provincial levels are compiled by the Beijing National Institute of Economic Research. The development of the private sector is one of the five components of the index and is strongly correlated with the four other components (government–market relation, development of product market, development of factor market, and development of intermediary organizations and legal environment). The marketization score in 2016 ranges between 1.29 and 15.98, which is the most recent data available. See Wang et al. (2017) for technical definitions and calculation of the marketization score.

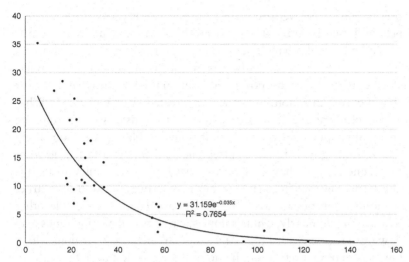

Figure 8.2 The Density of Entrepreneurs and Rural Poverty Rate (2012).
Source: China Statistical Yearbook (2013).

that region fell by 1.1 percentage points. Of the 12 regions with a marketization score lower than 8, only two regions had a rural population poverty rate of less than 5%; and of the 19 regions with a marketization score above 8, only two provinces have a rural poverty rate of more than 5%. Among the seven regions with a marketization score exceeding 10, no rural poverty rate exceeds 2%. We also find that the higher the entrepreneur density in a region, the higher the per capita disposable income and the lower the poverty rate (see Figure 8.2). Forty years after Reform and Opening, the absolute poverty problem in Chinese society was basically solved.

The market economy can solve the poverty problem more effectively because it provides ordinary people with opportunities to make a fortune. In a non-market economy, such opportunities are only available to a few privileged groups. The urban self-employed in China in the 1980s all came from the lower social groups. People with privileges could serve as soldiers or work in the government or state-owned enterprises, but what about those without privileges and connections? They had to start their own businesses! They picked up recyclable trash or set up street stalls to sell melon seeds, tea, and clothes. Thus, they became wealthy. This is impossible under a planned economy. By the way, China's garbage disposal and environmental protection have been greatly improved by people picking up recyclable trash! These people should be granted a big award for environmental protection!

It is undeniable that the government and charitable organizations can do something to solve the poverty problem. But we must understand that the money for poverty alleviation used by the government or charitable organizations in essence was created by entrepreneurs. What the government and charities could do is to transfer wealth from one group of people to another group. It is impossible to create something out of nothing. It is because entrepreneurs create wealth that governments and charities have money to be used for poverty alleviation. It is not surprising that international aid funds always flow from market economy countries to non-market economy countries, not the other way around. Similarly, China's domestic poverty alleviation funds also flow from regions with a high degree of marketization to regions with a low degree of marketization. If entrepreneurs do not have the enthusiasm to create wealth, the government will have no money to transfer, and charity will become like a river without a source. We must keep this in mind. We also need to remember that entrepreneurs are the largest philanthropists. Most charity foundations in the world are founded by entrepreneurs. John Rockefeller and Andrew Carnegie competed to be the richest man in America in their earlier life, but competed to be the biggest philanthropist in their later life.

Statistics on income distribution are very misleading, since the same income group in statistics can contain different people from year to year (Sowell, 2012, chapter 3; 2019, chapter 4). When discussing the income gap, people often ignore the vertical flow between the rich and the poor. A typical example is Piketty (2013), who argues that the rich have become richer and the poor have become poorer over the past century, assuming no change in the composition of the people in either group. In fact, one of the most significant characteristics of a market economy is that the rich and the poor are fluid. As Schumpeter said, in a market economy, the rich club is like a luxury hotel, always full of people, but the names of the guests are always changing (Schumpeter, 1980 [1934], p. 156). Similarly, the so-called low-income class, like an ordinary hotel, is always overcrowded, but from time to time some people move out, and new people move in, and the new residents may have been former VIPs (very important people) of luxury hotels.

According to the Hurun China Rich List, only 30 of the 100 richest people in 2010 are still on the list of 100 people after ten years. Among the top 20 in 2010, only three people are still on the top 20 list after ten years and six people are not even on the list of 100 people. A study by Professors Khor and Pencavel (2006) from Stanford University found that 50.4% of the people in China's lowest income group, one-fifth of the population, in 1990 had jumped out of the lowest group by 1995, and 2.1% of them had even entered the highest income group. Meanwhile, of the richest one-fifth of the population, only 43.9% still belonged to the highest income group by 1995, and nearly 5% had fallen into the lowest income group. This shows that Reform and Opening has greatly improved the vertical mobility of Chinese society. Most of the Chinese entrepreneurs who are now on the rich list were paupers decades ago, or some even just a decade ago. It can also be predicted that as long as China continues to adhere to market-oriented reforms, many of them will no longer be on the list within a few years. "Wealth cannot survive more than three generations" is the iron law of the market economy! Why? Because, as argued repeatedly by Schumpeter, the function of entrepreneurship itself cannot be inherited, and innovations are always associated with the rise of new entrepreneurs. Thus, entrepreneurs are not a social class like the nobility! (Schumpeter, 1934, pp. 78–79; 1939, p. 96)

Even if vertical mobility is not considered, and only the Gini coefficient is used to measure income disparity, I did a statistical analysis which shows a story different from the common belief. In 2001, for example, among the 30 provinces, municipalities, and autonomous regions in China, on average, the better market-developed regions, regions with fewer state-owned economic sectors, and regions with a lower proportion of fiscal expenditure in GDP, are the regions with the smaller income gap (Zhang, 2015b, chapter 13). The same signs of correlations hold consistently.[5] Given that government spending is commonly believed to be an important channel of redistribution from the rich to the poor, it seems surprising that the higher proportion of government spending in GDP brought about the higher income gap. But it is a fact! (Zhang, 2015b, p. 290)

---

[5] Marketization is related to economic freedom. The literature on the relationship between economic freedom and inequality across countries has found mixed results. Bennett and Nikolaev (2017) find that the results of previous studies are sensitive to the choice of country sample, time period, and/or inequality measure used. The detailed discussion of this literature is beyond the theme of this book.

What does this show? If the government is less involved in economic activities, people will have more freedom to engage in business activities, competition will be fierce, and the profits of business activities will be low relative to wages; if a region has only a few privileged and connected people who can do business, or only the most audacious dare to do business, profits from business activities will be very high. For example, there are more people in Zhejiang Province who do business, and there are more wealthy people, but the profitability relative to wages is very thin. In places like Northeast China, however, most people do not do business, but a few people who do business can make a lot of money. Why? Because their market environment is not good. Therefore, we see that the more open the market and the less the government intervenes, the smaller the income gap.

In addition, equality is not only reflected in monetary income, but also other aspects such as freedom, rights, and choice. What freedom did ordinary people have in the past? When I was in the countryside, the watermelons and apples produced on the farmers' private plots were sold only on the black market. Those who did this kind of business were considered criminals for speculation. They had to be criticized or even locked up. They did not even have the basic right to be a human being. At that time, the peasants could not afford to eat meat all year round, nor could they buy noodles, but as soon as the commune cadres came to the village, everyone rushed to host them with white flour and meat. Why? Only by establishing a relationship with the cadres could the children of peasants have hope to become soldiers or be recruited for public jobs, even though the chance was very small. Therefore, I do not think that Reform and Opening has made Chinese society more unequal, but instead more equal and fairer.

The Economists' Responsibility to Defend the Market

Over the past 40 years of reform and opening up, China's per capita GDP has doubled every ten years, and everyone's life has been greatly improved. This is a remarkable achievement.

China's achievements are largely made by the Chinese grassroots entrepreneurs following economic liberalization. The rise of entrepreneurs is largely related to changing ideas. In the early 1980s, with the emergence of self-employment and bonus systems, China had "red eye disease." Some people could not even accept "distribution according to work." If "distribution according to work" is not accepted, the economy will not develop, and everyone will live in poverty. Through the efforts of economists and other social scientists, "distribution according to work" has gradually been generally accepted. In this way, people have the enthusiasm to work. Later in the 1990s, the idea of capital and other factors of production participating in income distribution was accepted, and entrepreneurial profits were recognized. In this way, the entrepreneurial spirit of the Chinese people radiated. China has become a country of entrepreneurship, and everyone's life has improved.

Regrettably, in terms of ideas, we seem to be backtracking. "Red eye disease" is coming back. Entrepreneurs have become a target of criticism. Many people attribute the income inequality to the market-oriented reform and charge that entrepreneurs make too much profit. Given that the Chinese economy is still heavily regulated by the government and some "entrepreneurs" indeed make huge profits through their connections with government, it is easy to understand the popularity of criticisms toward entrepreneurs. China's recent campaign for "common prosperity" is somehow a response to the common hostility toward entrepreneurs.

This brings us back to the responsibility of economists. Why does society need economists? Because the market economy is too fragile and too vulnerable to damage, someone is needed to defend it. The planned economy was designed by a small number of intellectuals and then imposed on society from top to bottom with force, so there are always some powerful people defending it. The market economy is different. It was not designed by intellectuals or by anyone, but spontaneously emerged from bottom to top. This also means that the market economy is like a child without a mother. Anyone can mistreat it and stigmatize it without taking responsibility. People living in the planned economy system who criticize the planned economy inevitably take political and even legal risks, but no matter what system you live in, there is no risk in criticizing the market economy and entrepreneurs. In fact, countless people have been jailed and even paid the price of their lives for criticizing the socialist planned economy, but no one has ever gotten into any trouble for criticizing the market economy and entrepreneurs. In this sense, the market economy is really benevolent, and we should really cherish it.

People are easy to be misled by false ideas. Every Chinese is familiar with comedian Zhao Benshan's *Selling Crutches*. In that story, there was nothing wrong with the protagonist's legs, but the antagonist repeatedly said they had a problem. In the end, the protagonist felt that his leg really had a problem, so he could not wait to buy the antagonist's crutches. In fact, it is not the protagonist's legs that are faulty, but his brain. Many people are now "selling crutches." What are their "crutches"? Anti-market economy arguments. Many of the so-called failures of the market economy are fabricated by "crutch sellers."

When I say this, I have only one purpose: Let everyone better understand how a market economy works to strengthen our belief in entrepreneurship. What is the most worrying thing about China's future? It is not energy or environmental issues. These are of course very important, but not the most important. Technological progress driven by market competition and entrepreneurial innovations will surely find the answer for us. We do not have to be as pessimistic as Malthus was 200 years ago or the Club of Rome was 50 years ago. China's future development depends on our beliefs; what we believe and what we do not believe. As I have argued elsewhere, China's economic success of the past 40 years comes from marketization reforms and the rise of entrepreneurship (Zhang, 2019). China's future growth depends on innovative entrepreneurs (Zhang, 2017a). Common prosperity calls for restricting government and liberalizing entrepreneurship, not otherwise. If we strengthen our confidence in the market economy and continue to advance an entrepreneur-friendly institutional environment through market-oriented reform, China will move toward common prosperity. If we lose our faith in the market and introduce more and more government intervention in the name of common prosperity, the common prosperity would be a fool's paradise. Do not forget that the original intention of the socialist planned economy back then was to benefit the poor, but, as a result, more and more poor people were created, making the poor more miserable than before.

PART III

Uncertainty of Innovation and Industrial Policy

9 | Entrepreneurs in Economic Growth: Arbitrage and Innovation

Economic Growth Is a New and Uneven Phenomenon

From humanity's perspective, economic growth is totally a new phenomenon. Human history began 2.5 million years ago in the Paleolithic era, with *homo sapiens* having been around for about 200,000 years. The history of economic growth only stretches back 250 years, or one year for every 10,000 years of human history or 1.25 years for every 1,000 years of *homo sapiens* history, which is indeed very short. Before the Industrial Revolution, a lack of growth was normal and growth was abnormal. People did not talk about growth-related topics and economic stagnation did not cause anxiety.

Growth over the past 200 years, however, has not been a uniform phenomenon. The disparity in per capita income between nations has increased with the emergence of economic growth. In 1500, from a global perspective, the per capita gross domestic product (GDP) in the East was not much different from that in the West. From 1820 onward, the gap gradually widened. By 2000, the per capita GDP of the wealthiest countries was hundreds of times higher than the poorest countries. Per capita GDP is highest in Western European countries and countries with the same cultural systems, such as the United States, Canada, and Australia. China is far behind the world average. This is called the "Great Divergence."[1]

The correlation coefficient between population and GDP size can describe this great divergence. Before 1820, this correlation coefficient was basically close to 1, meaning a country with a large population was a country with a large economy. The correlation coefficient was still 0.9423 in 1820 but began to decline rapidly afterwards: 0.6393 in

---

[1] Kenneth Pomeranz used the term "Great Divergence" to refer to the historical period in which the Western world overcame growth constraints and surpassed China, India, and other Eastern countries in the nineteenth century. See Kenneth Pomeranz (2000).

1870, 0.3404 in 1913, 0.1554 in 1950, and 0.148 in 1973. In other words, by 1973, there was little relationship between population size and economic size, so a country with a large population might have a small economy and a country with a relatively small population might have a big economy. At the time, China had the world's largest population, accounting for 20% of the total, but its GDP ranked below thirteenth or fourteenth place. Within the two decades after the 1970s, most developing countries began to grow significantly faster than developed countries. Only by the end of the 1980s was the Great Divergence replaced by a small convergence. By 2003, the correlation coefficient between population and GDP size rose to 0.5185 (Zhang, 2015b, p. 340).[2]

Humans are curious, and – seeing this big growth and divergence – want to provide an explanation. The explanations provided by scholars can be roughly divided into four categories.

The first category is geographic determinism: A country's economic growth is determined by its geographic location and resources. French Enlightenment thinker Montesquieu is an early representative of this category. More recent representatives include the "California School" of history, bio-geographer Jared Mason Diamond, and economist Jeffrey Sachs, among others (Montesquieu, 1750; Diamond, 1997; Pomeranz, 2000; Sachs, 2000).

The second category is racial determinism: Economic growth is determined by human intelligence and differences in intelligence among different races leads to differences in economic growth. This is Social Darwinism's interpretation.[3]

The third category is cultural determinism: Economic growth is determined by cultural factors such as religious beliefs, values, and ethics. German sociologist Max Weber is this category's most famous founder and representative. He believed Protestant ethics shaped the spirit of capitalism and Confucian culture was not conducive to

---

[2] For the source of the data for my original calculations, see Maddison (2007), Statistics Appendix A.

[3] Social Darwinism, also known as social evolution theory, applies the idea of natural selection in Darwinian evolution theory to human society. This idea was first seen in the socio-cultural evolution theories of the English philosopher and writer Herbert Spencer (1892). Social Darwinism was popular from the nineteenth century until the end of World War II. Some argue that modern socio-biology can also be classified as a school of Social Darwinism.

economic growth.[4] More recently, some economic historians such as Gregory Clark (2007) and Joel Mokyr (2016), and economists such as Deirdre McCloskey (2006) and Edmund Phelps (2015, 2020) also favor a cultural explanation.

The fourth category is institutional determinism: Economic growth is determined by socio-economic systems. In particular, private property rights and the market system are conducive to economic development, whereas public ownership of property and the planning system are not. Most economists hold the institutional deterministic view, most notably Douglass North, Daron Acemoglu, and James Robinson, among others (North, 1990; Acemoglu and Robinson, 2012; Bernstein, 2004).[5] I myself hold this view. In particular, I believe that entrepreneurship in a market economy is the most important determinant of economic growth. The rise of entrepreneurs depends upon private rights-based institutions and free competition. Nevertheless, I also believe culture is an important determinant of the emergence of entrepreneurs (Zhang and Sheng, 2014 [1989]).

Driving Technological Progress Is the Market's Most Important Function

If we ask what the study of economics is, how will most economists answer? I believe they will say it is the study of the allocation of scarce resources. A follow-up question is: What kind of system can achieve optimal resource allocation? Most economists will say the market. Is there anything wrong with these responses? Of course not.

I want to emphasize, however, that the greatest benefit of the market is not achieving optimal resource allocation, which neoclassical economics or mainstream economics explain as equilibrium between the marginal value of each type of resource in different uses. Instead, the most important function of the market is to make the best use of everyone's enthusiasm and creativity, not efficient allocation of given

---

[4] Max Weber's *The Protestant Ethic and the Spirit of Capitalism* (1905).
[5] In *Power and Progress: Our Thousand-year Struggle over Technology and Prosperity*, Acemoglu and Johnson view government more favorable for picking up the best technologies from a "mixed bag." They argue that the government can perform better in selecting technologies and investing in these technologies for society than the market does. For a criticism of Acemoglu and Johnson's arguments, see McCloskey (2023).

resources. It is primarily manifested in the continuous improvement of labor productivity through technological progress.

Stated simply, the market drives economic growth through two channels: technological progress and allocation efficiency. Neoclassical economics' market theory focuses on resource allocation efficiency. In fact, the role of technological progress is primary and resource allocation comes second. The reason is simple. If resource allocation is all that matters, then as soon as equilibrium is reached, the economy will repeat day after day, year after year without any growth. This is the circular flow economy described by Joseph Schumpeter (1934, chapter 1) or the evenly rotating economy described by Ludwig von Mises (1949, chapter 14). Humanity's sustained and significant economic growth has only occurred over the past 200 years, and came primarily from the continuous creation of new technologies, new products, and new resources, not improvement in the efficiency of allocation of existing resources.

Resources Are Endogenous to Technology, Not an "Endowment"

Here, it is necessary to discuss the issue of resources. Neoclassical economists assume that resources are given and exogenous. Further, they believe resource "endowments" determine a country's comparative advantage. Economic development over the last 200 years or so, however, proves that resources are not endowed and fixed, but instead are endogenous and changeable. What is and is not a resource depends on the type of technology we have (Rosenberg, 1976, chapter 13; Mokyr, 2009, p. 102). The type of technology we have depends on entrepreneurial innovation. Peter Drucker (1985) said that innovative activities can endow resources with new capabilities and thereby create wealth. In fact, an innovative activity is itself the creative force of resources.

For example, crude oil is now considered the most important resource because it provides us with energy as well as materials. Before the middle of the nineteenth century, however, it was not a resource. Instead, it was considered a waste product. When people dug water wells or brine wells, they often encountered crude oil. It was a frustrating byproduct that could pollute water and salt, so the amount of labor required to deal with it caused problems. Crude oil is a dark, viscous liquid that, unlike coal, is practically useless in its natural state, so it requires refinement. People later discovered crude oil could be burned. After distillation, kerosene could be extracted, which originally was the most desirable product to meet the growing demand for lighting. Thus, crude oil became a resource. After refining kerosene, however, gasoline and heavy oil were the remaining waste products. Gasoline was dreadful; it easily evaporated and its low ignition point meant it also easily exploded. After the automobile was invented, people discovered that gasoline can be used as fuel for internal combustion engines. Thus, gasoline became a resource. Similarly, people's frustration with heavy oil gradually turned into fuel oil (for power generation). With the advancement of refining technology and development of the petrochemical industry, more than 300 chemical materials are extracted from crude oil. This turned crude oil into the modern economy's most important resource (Williams, 2000, pp. 223–226).

The Western Han people invented papermaking technology in the second century B.C. Chinese papermaking technology was introduced to the Islamic world in the eighteenth century, then introduced to Western Europe before the Renaissance. Until the beginning of the nineteenth century, however, the raw material used for papermaking was still shabby fabrics, such as cotton, linen, flax, hemp, and silk. Wood could not be used for papermaking because there was no way to artificially turn wood into pulp. In the middle of the nineteenth century, machine pulp technology appeared, so wood could be used for producing pulp. Due to the difficulty removing lignin (which accounts for 30–40% of the composition of wood), however, paper made from wood is only suitable for short-term uses (such as newspapers and toilet paper) (Smil, 2005, pp. 210–214).

Americans later invented the sulfite process, which removes lignin, resin, and other substances to produce pure cellulose for acceptable pulp. The U.S. papermaking industry relied primarily on the North's spruce and fir trees, whereas early technology could not utilize the South's faster-growing pine trees. Improvement in sulphate pulping technology in the 1920s made it possible for pine wood to become a raw material for pulp, making the world's most abundant tree useful. By the mid-twentieth century, more than half of US pulp production came from the South (Rosenberg, 2000, p. 32).

These examples illustrate that we cannot assume that resources are given, so-called endowments. Most of humanity's current resources were created by humans. Why does the Earth contain crude oil? Are crude oil reserves finite or infinite? This theory is debated. According to the mainstream explanation, plants and animals tens of millions or even hundreds of millions of years ago became deposits that turned into crude oil and coal, so crude oil reserves are limited. This explanation is not necessarily correct because crude oil should have been used up long ago, according to this theory. With the advancement of technology, however, new oil fields are constantly being discovered. Shale gas has now also become an energy resource.

Paul David and Gavin Wright provided documentation for the argument that America's position as the world's leading mineral-producing nation was not an exogenous fact of "Nature":

Minerals with economic value do indeed occur unevenly across the surface of the earth, but between 1850 and 1950, the United States exploited its resources potential to a far greater extent than other countries of the world. The abundance of American natural resources did not derive exclusively from geological endowment ... but reflected the intensity of search, technologies of extraction, refining, and utilization; market development and transportation costs; and legal, institutional and political structure after all of these. (David and Wright, 1996, pp. 1–2)[6]

In summary, human progress comes from new knowledge and technological progress. Resources themselves are a function of knowledge and technology. The type of resources we have and their value depends on the type of knowledge and technology we have. Technological progress is mainly brought about by the market economy. The true core of the market is entrepreneurship, which is the creativity of every person.

Two Growth Theories without Entrepreneurs

In recent decades, economists have also begun to pay attention to institutional issues. For a long time, when economists explained economic growth, they focused primarily on technical variables. These technical variables can be split into two categories. The first is stock, which includes capital, labor, and technology. The second is flow, which includes investment, consumption, and net exports.

[6] Quotation from Rosenberg (2000), p. 32.

These concepts come from mainstream economists' two ways of thinking: Supply-side thinking and demand-side thinking. The first is called neoclassical economic growth theory. The second belongs to Keynesian economics. The commonality is the absence of entrepreneurs.

The neoclassical growth theory was created by Robert Solow, an economist at the Massachusetts Institute of Technology, in his 1956 paper. In his 1957 paper, he performed an empirical study to determine the factors that contributed to the economic growth of the United States in the half century between 1900 and 1950 (Robert Solow, 1956, 1957). After some modifications and improvements by other economists, Solow's theory became the mainstream economic growth theory.

In the neoclassical growth theory, the entire economy is treated as a "production function." The production factor inputs are the independent variables and the output is the dependent variable (usually measured as gross domestic product). The stock of technology determines the production function. More advanced technology with the same factor inputs will result in higher total output. The simplest production function only includes two inputs: labor and capital. Following the neoclassical paradigm, Solow assumed the economy had constant returns to scale and that the respective contributions of labor and capital add up to 1. The portion of actual growth that exceeded 1 came from technological progress, so-called total factor productivity (TFP)". For example, if labor inputs and capital each increase by 1%, then growth caused by factor inputs is 1%. If actual output grows by 3%, then the excess 2% comes from TFP's contribution. Solow's research in 1957 found that close to 80% of the US' growth in the first 50 years of the twentieth century came from increased TFP and only 20% came from labor and capital contributions.

Here, it is necessary to discuss total factor productivity a little bit more. So-called total factor productivity cannot be explained by labor and capital. It is a surplus, i.e., the residual in regression analysis. If some other input variables (such as land or mineral resources) are added to the production function, then total factor productivity's contribution declines. Neoclassical economists assume the economy is always in the most efficient equilibrium state at that moment. Under this assumption, increases in total factor productivity must come from technological progress. This assumption, however, has problems. The economy is not always at equilibrium. The neoclassical growth model's estimates of total factor productivity increases might come from technological progress but also might come from improvements in resource allocation efficiency. This point is important for our understanding of China's economic growth over the last 40 years. After Reform and Opening, China's total factor productivity greatly improved.[7] Primarily, this came from improvements in allocation efficiency caused by entrepreneurial arbitrage activities. People's enthusiasm for work also improved.

The neoclassical growth model dominates explanations of growth. Economists use this model to measure economic growth in almost every country. Below, I will make reference to a few empirical studies on China's economic growth.[8]

Wang Xiaolu, Fan Gang, and Liu Peng (2009) of the Beijing National Institute of Economic Research studied China's economic growth using the neoclassical growth model. They found that during the planned economy period between 1953 and 1978, China's GDP grew 6.15% annually on average. Increases in capital inputs contributed 2.66% and increases in labor inputs contributed 1.71% but only 1.78% came from total factor productivity, representing less than 29% of the total. During any stage after Reform and Opening, however, total factor productivity's contribution improved sharply. Between 1999 and 2007, for example, China's GDP grew 9.72% annually on average and total factor productivity grew 4.1% annually on average, accounting for 42% of the growth.

Dwight Perkins, a professor of economics at Harvard University, and Thomas G. Rawski, a professor of economics at the University of Pittsburgh, also analyzed China's economic growth between 1952 and 2005. The result of their research was that between 1952 and 1978, total factor productivity's contribution only accounted for 11%. In the two decades between 1957 and 1978, total factor productivity's contribution was negative (−13%). In other words, output growth was

---

[7] Hsieh and Klenow (2009) estimate that if the allocation efficiency of China and India were adjusted to the level of the United States, China's manufacturing TFP would increase by 25–40%, and India's manufacturing TFP would increase by 50–60%.

[8] According to Wu's (2011) literature review, up to 2008 there were about 150 papers and articles estimating China's TFP growth, two thirds of which were published in international English-language journals or books.

much lower than input growth, meaning allocation efficiency decreased. After Reform and Opening, however, total factor productivity's contribution is positive and relatively high. In the period between 1990 and 1995, 57.3% of economic growth came from increased total factor productivity. This is tremendous progress (Perkins and Rawski, 2008).

Xiaodong Zhu (2012), an economics professor at the University of Toronto, found that between 1952 and 1978, China's total factor productivity contributed −72.03% to economic growth (according to per capita GDP calculations). Human capital's contribution reached 52.25%. Physical capital's contribution in terms of unit output was 116.15%. Labor participation's contribution was 3.63%. This means that although capital inputs were extremely large, production efficiency declined, so resources were seriously wasted and the appropriate economic growth did not occur. In contrast, during the 30 years after Reform and Opening, between 1978 and 2007, total factor productivity's contribution reached 77.89%.

Of course, as for how much total factor productivity contributes to economic growth is disputed among economists. This depends on the data and model used by the author. Total factor productivity's contribution, however, was significantly higher after reform than it was before, and this is not debated. I want to emphasize that this transformation was not primarily due to any technical innovation within China but was instead due to changes in the incentive mechanism. Both state-owned and private enterprises became more incentivized, which manifested in an increase in total factor productivity.

What problems exist in the neoclassical growth theory?

First, this theory assumes that technology is exogenous, like it fell from the sky, but does not consider which factors drove technological progress.

Second, the neoclassical growth model is only concerned with the quantity of capital, but not with who accumulates it or invests it. In the neoclassical growth model, regardless of who accumulates, the result is the same. Because technology is assumed to be exogenous and only capital can be controlled by people, the neoclassical growth theory objectively provides a theoretical basis for government-led capital accumulation. Many developing countries believe in this theory. Actually, who accumulates capital is more important than how much is accumulated in accounting books. The efficiency of government-accumulated capital and entrepreneur-accumulated capital is completely different.

This point is especially important for understanding Chinese economic growth. The magnitude of Chinese capital accumulation before Reform and Opening was not miniscule, but it did not bring about good economic growth. The reason is that capital accumulation was dominated by the government and state-owned enterprises, whereas there was zero capital accumulation from private entrepreneurs. This is key.

Even though the neoclassical model dominates economic thought, many economists have gradually come to recognize that technology is not exogenous. It is really a surprise that economists took this much time to be aware of such an obvious fact! Starting in the late 1980s and early 1990s, some economists proposed the "endogenous growth theory."[9] The founder of the endogenous growth theory, Paul Romer, was awarded the 2018 Nobel Prize in Economics. This theory modeled technological progress as a knowledge creation issue, believing that economic growth primarily comes from the accumulation of knowledge (including human capital). Because knowledge creation has increasing returns to scale and the knowledge created by one person can be used by anyone else, endogenous growth theory believes the government should focus inputs on education and scientific development while enterprises should increase research and development. Regrettably, endogenous growth theory also lacks a role for entrepreneurs. The technological progress it refers to is technological progress without innovation, thus it does not constitute a correct growth theory (Kohn, 2004).[10]

Keynesian economics is another mainstream economic growth theory. Keynesian theory was originally used to explain short-term economic fluctuations, not economic growth. However, it gradually evolved into currently the most fashionable economic model for explaining economic growth. Today, when discussing and forecasting the economic growth rate, economists, bureaucrats, commercial

---

[9] Paul Romer is the pioneer of the endogenous growth theory. See Romer (1986, 1990, and 1994). Other important contributors include Lucas (1988), Aghion and Howitt (1992), and Grossman and Helpman (1991), among others.

[10] Aghion and Howitt (1992), and Aghion et al. (2021) use Schumpeterian creative destruction to explain the puzzle of economic growth. However, their focus is still on technological changes, not the role of entrepreneurs.

leaders, media people, and even common people are all using Keynesian economics.

Stated simply, Keynesian economics is an aggregate demand theory. In contrast to the neoclassical growth model studying economic growth from the aggregate supply (production) aspect, Keynesian theory considers economic growth from the demand aspect. This theory is built upon the foundation of the statistical equation "aggregate demand = investment + consumption + net exports." Economic growth is thus determined by the three variables: Investment, consumption, and net exports. This is commonly called the "three chariots" growth theory. It is similar to how economic growth in the neoclassical model is determined by capital, labor, and total factor productivity.

What is the policy significance of this theory? Growth is equivalent to aggregate demand growth, so the government can intervene in, or even manipulate, economic growth. The primary means of doing so is using monetary and fiscal policy to stimulate investment, consumption, and net exports. China currently seeks to transform its means of economic growth. It is said that China has relied too much on "investment-push" and "export-driven" growth since 1978. Now it is time to transition to "consumption-push" and "domestic demand-driven" growth.

Many government bureaucrats especially like this theory because it provides legitimacy to the government obtaining and using power. Many economists also like this theory because it created a huge number of employment opportunities for economists. Each year, the official statistics show how much consumption, investment, and trade contributed to economic growth. However, it is often implausible. For example, the GDP growth rate of China in 2009 was 9.2%, of which 50% of the contribution came from final consumption and 87.6% came from investment. These two numbers add up to 137.4%, which exceeds 100%, so the only conclusion we can come to is that trade contributed –37.4%. What does this mean? After a year's worth of trade, the contribution to economic growth is negative? Does it mean that if we closed off international trade for a year – no exports and no imports – China's GDP growth rate would have increased by 3.5 points upwards to 12.7%? Therefore, my evaluation of this theory is that it is "excessively wrong."

First, why do people invest? We invest in order to increase productivity – to produce more in the future – and thus to live a better life. According to Keynesian theory, however, the goal of investment is not future-oriented, but is instead about increasing the current year's GDP. Whether or not investment is efficient and productive, therefore, is not important. If there is a surplus of steel but GDP (aggregate demand) is insufficient, what should be done? Build another steel plant, because that increases the current aggregate demand for steel and thus the growth rate will be higher. But what is the point? Why do we want to make such a wasteful investment? How much benefit does artificially created aggregate demand actually have for a country's future? Nobody cares.

Second, is consumption a means or an end? Everyone knows that consumption is an end. Everything humanity creates is ultimately for consumption. According to Keynesian theory, however, consumption is only a means to increase GDP. In 2009, the Chinese government set 8% GDP growth as a goal – and to "maintain the 8%." They encouraged the public to consume, including policies like Home Appliances Going to the Countryside. Consuming food and clothing were all part of achieving the goal of 8%. We put the cart before the horse!

Third, let us take another look at international trade. Trade makes international division of labor possible. Each country, region, and person can benefit from comparative advantage and specialization. According to Keynesian economics, however, only when exports exceed imports does trade make a positive contribution to GDP. If imports exceed exports, then trade makes a negative contribution to GDP. Because one country's surplus is another country's deficit, Keynesian economics changed trade from a positive-sum game into a zero-sum game. It provides a theoretical basis for trade protectionism and is not different from ancient mercantilism. After the Global Financial Crisis in 2008, the statistics show many years where trade made a negative contribution to China's economic growth. If this is so, would simply closing off imports and exports have made economic growth higher?

Some scholars even used aggregate demand theory to estimate how large the impact of the Sino-American trade war was on China. The conclusion was the "impact is not large." Even if trade between China and America was closed entirely, the impact on China's GDP would only be 2.4%. They came to their conclusion in this way: The products China exports to America equates to 3.6% of China's GDP. China's export value-added proportion is only 0.66, so 3.6% × 0.66 = 2.4%.

This logic is absurd! Imagine a house with four pillars and four people living in it. You ask how many people it can still house if one pillar collapses. They answer: "Three people."

Keynesian theory has misled national economic policy. Many governments manage the economy according to this set of theories, so there are more and more problems. Keynesian policies are like opium. Once you are addicted, it is hard to give it up.

The Entrepreneur-Centric "Smith–Schumpeterian Growth Model"

A common defect in neoclassical growth theory and Keynesian growth theory is they ignore the role of entrepreneurship in economic growth. This role is critical. Below, I briefly introduce an entrepreneur-centric growth theory, which I coined as the "Smith–Schumpeterian growth model" (Zhang, 2017a).

Adam Smith is called the "Father of Economics." The full title of his *magnum opus* is *An Inquiry into the Nature and Causes of the Wealth of Nations*. Unfortunately, his growth theory has been slowly forgotten by economists.

Smith believed that a country's economy and wealth grew primarily due to increases in the productivity of labor. An increase in the productivity of labor depends on technological progress, which we now refer to as innovation. Technological progress and innovation are determined by the division of labor and specialization. The division of labor and specialization are determined by market scale. The greater the market scale is, the more specific the division of labor is, the deeper specialization is, the more innovation there is, the higher labor productivity is, and the faster the economy grows. After the economy grows, people's incomes increase, so the market scale expands, forming a positive cycle (Yang and Borland, 1991). Within this positive cycle, market scale has a critical role and is extremely important for our understanding of trade and globalization's contribution to economic growth.[11] From the static perspective, market scale is not only determined by population but also by per capita income levels.

---

[11] The literature refers to trade-driven growth as *Smithian growth*. See Mokyr (2009), p. 5.

From the dynamic perspective, market scale determines per capita income levels and their growth.

According to Smith's growth theory, the essence of economic growth is not the GDP increasing 3%, 5%, or 8% like economists generally tell us about, but is instead the continuous appearance of new products, new technologies, and new industries. In other words, total growth and structural change cannot be separated. Total growth is not possible without structural change. This is what has happened over the past 200 years. The traditional society only had a few industries such as agriculture, metallurgy, ceramics, and handicrafts. Products were simple and agriculture was so dominant that the rest could basically be ignored. How many industries does humanity have now? According to international classifications, just among exported products, there are 97 two-digit industries, 1,222 four-digit industries, and 5,053 six-digit industries (Easterly, 2013, p. 262). These are constantly increasing, as well. According to Mintel's Global New Product Database, over 20,000 new products from 50 countries are added each month. That means 240,000 new products are introduced every year (Hauer, 2015). In terms of a retailer's measure of *stock keeping units* (SKUs), humanity only had between 100 and 1,000 types of products before the Industrial Revolution, but today there are between 100 million and 10 billion (Beinhocker, 2006, p. 9). As of March 21, 2021, there were 75,138,297 products sold on Amazon.com. If vendors are included, the number of products sold reaches 350 million.

But Adam Smith did not discuss the core driving force of economic growth's positive cycle. How does the market appear? How does the division of labor actually form? Where does innovation come from? These questions, in Smith's view, were a bit spontaneous.

More than 100 years ago, Joseph Schumpeter, the "Father of Innovation Theory," answered these questions in the book *The Theory of Economic Development*.[12] Schumpeter believed entrepreneurs were central to economic growth. Entrepreneurs are the kings of economic growth. No segment of economic growth can depart from entrepreneurs. In Schumpeter's view, economic growth = innovation = entrepreneurship. Entrepreneurs bring about "creative destruction" by

---

[12] The German-language version of *The Theory of Economic Development* was published in 1911. The first English-language translation was published in 1934. See also Schumpeter (1942), Chapter 2.

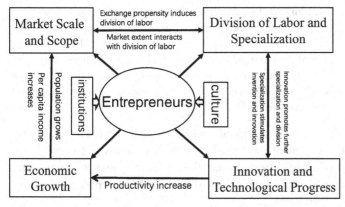

Figure 9.1 Smith–Schumpeterian Growth Model

continuously creating new products, new technologies, new markets, new raw materials, and new methods of organization. That is the core of economic growth.

Combining Smith's growth theory with Schumpeter's entrepreneur theory gives us the Smith–Schumpeterian economic growth model shown in Figure 9-1.

In the Smith–Schumpeterian economic growth model, entrepreneurs are at the center of Smith's growth positive cycle. The market does not naturally exist and is not viewable to everyone. Markets are to be discovered and created. An important role of entrepreneurs is discovering and creating markets. Schumpeter said:

Innovations in the economic system do not as a rule take place in such a way that first new wants arise spontaneously in consumers and then the productive apparatus swings round through their pressure. We do not deny the presence of this nexus. It is, however, the producer who as a rule initiates economic change, and consumers are educated by him if necessary; they are, as it were, taught to want new things, or things which differ in some respect or other from those which they have been in the habit of using. Therefore, while it is permissible and even necessary to consider consumers' wants as an independent and indeed the fundamental force in a theory of the circular flow, we must take a different attitude as soon as we analyze change. (Schumpeter, 1934, p. 65)

Schumpeter also said:

Railroads have not emerged because any consumers took the initiative in displaying an effective demand for their service in preference to the services of mail coaches. Nor did the consumers display any such initiative wish to have electric lamps or rayon stockings, or to travel by motorcar or airplane, or to listen to radios, or to chew gum. There is obviously no lack of realism in the proposition that the great majority of changes in commodities consumed has been forced by producers on consumers who, more often than not, have resisted the change and have had to be educated up by elaborate psychotechnics of advertising.[13]

Division of labor and specialization are also created by entrepreneurs. The creation of new markets and new industries depends on entrepreneurs' innovation. After the economy grows, converting increased wealth into new markets also relies on entrepreneurs' innovation of new products.

Here, it is necessary to emphasize the emergence of new industries as it relates to the division of labor and specialization. When mainstream economists discuss economic growth, they usually assume that each industry is "given." In fact, industries are not given, but instead are created by entrepreneurs. Since the eighteenth century, it is generally believed that the world has experienced three industrial revolutions. These three industrial revolutions were all initiated by entrepreneurs and every new industry was created by entrepreneurs. Even if a single entrepreneur did not create a new industry, we can point out representatives. For example, although the first industrial revolution began with the transformation of traditional industries (metallurgy and textiles), many new industries emerged. Abraham Darby developed the coke smelting industry; Thomas Newcomen, Matthew Boulton, and James Watt created the steam engine manufacturing industry; Henry Maudslay created the machine tool industry; George Stephenson and his son Robert created the railroad industry, etc. In the second industrial revolution, Thomas Edison created the electricity industry; George Westinghouse and Nikola Tesla created the electric motor industry; Alexander Graham Bell created the telecommunications industry; Gottlieb Daimler, Wilhelm Maybach, and Carl Benz created the automobile industry; the Wright brothers created the aviation industry; Guglielmo Marconi created the wireless telegram industry; Willis Carrier created the air conditioning industry, etc. In the third industrial revolution, Thomas Watson created the computer industry; Robert Noyce, Gordon Moore, and others created the integrated circuit

[13] Quoted by Rosenberg (1994), p. 57.

industry; Bill Gates created the software industry; Jerry Yang and others created the web portal industry; Larry Page and Sergey Brin invented the search engine industry; Elon Musk created the new energy vehicle industry; Sam Altman created the artificial intelligence industry, etc. And the world is about to enter or has already entered the fourth industrial revolution.

Not just big industries, small specialized sectors can also be traced to their entrepreneurial creators. The story of Mrs. Ida Rosenthal's creation of the brassiere industry is instructive. Ada was a New York seamstress. Dissatisfied with the way her dresses hung over her customers' corsets, chemises, and ferris waists, she attempted to make improvements and eventually invented the first bra. In the beginning, she gave away a custom-made brassiere with every dress she sold. She quickly realized that selling bras itself could be a more profitable business, so she gave up being a seamstress and began to make and sell bras. She found a partner and together they raised enough capital to open a workshop. By doing this, she also triggered other related businesses. A new division of labor was created. There were the tasks of designing of the brassieres, of making, packing, selling, advertising, and distributing them, and also the tasks of financing the work, printing labels, and providing hooks, eyes, elastic, and cloth. Once it became an economic activity in its own right, brassiere manufacturing multiplied into many divisions of labor; some of which had not existed before.[14]

Therefore, the point I want to emphasize is that when we discuss economic growth we must recognize that the behavior of entrepreneurs determines economic growth. This contrasts with saying there is an objective economic growth that determines what entrepreneurs should do. A history of economic growth is actually a history of entrepreneurial innovation and creation. This is the case for China over the last 40 years as well as the United States, Britain, Germany, Japan, and all other developed countries.

The Two Functions of Entrepreneurs: Arbitrage and Innovation

Arbitrage and innovation can be identified as the two functions of entrepreneurs. These two functions of entrepreneurs are my

---

[14] For the story of how Ida Rosenthal created the brassiere industry, see Jacobs (1970), pp. 11, 51, 56. Also see Warsh (2007), pp. 245–246.

generalizations based on combining Israel Kirzner's concept of the entrepreneur, which emphasized the arbitrage function, with Joseph Schumpeter's concept of the entrepreneur, which emphasized the innovation function. While it is commonly thought that the Kirznerian entrepreneur and the Schumpeterian entrepreneur are competing theories,[15] I believe their definitions are complementary. Kirzner argues that innovation is nothing but some kind of arbitrage. For example, he said: "In the course of this entrepreneurial process, new products may be introduced, new qualities of existing products may be developed, new methods of production may be ventured, new forms of industrial organization, financing, marketing, or tackling risk may be developed. All the ceaseless churning and agitation of the market is to be understood as the consequence of the never-ending discovering process of which the market consists" (Kirzner, 1985, pp. 30ff). However, as pointed out by Buchanan and Vanberg (1991), Kirzner's chosen theoretical framework and his attempt to incorporate the notion of innovation into his arbitrage process are disharmonious, because innovation in all its aspects cannot be understood as the discovery of errors or missed opportunities in the market. I believe separation of innovation from arbitrage is epistemologically and practically better for us to understand entrepreneurship and economic growth. The duality of arbitrage and innovation provides a complete concept of the entrepreneur. Correspondingly, the market is both a discovery process and a creative process. Without either of them, the market and economic growth cannot be well understood.

Arbitrage is the discovery of disequilibrium and exploitation of lucrative opportunities in markets under existing technological conditions and resources. Why do these opportunities exist in the market? It is simply because most people are ignorant and lack alertness.

[15] Kirzner himself makes it clear: "my description of the entrepreneur does differ from Schumpeter's and the entrepreneurial role in the Schumpeterian system is not identified with that which I have set forth. For me the important feature of entrepreneurship is not so much the ability to break away from routine as the ability to perceive new opportunities which others have not yet noted. Entrepreneurship for me is not so much introduction of new products or of new techniques of production as the ability to see where new products have become unsuspectedly valuable to consumers and where new methods of production have, unknown to others, become feasible. For me the function of the entrepreneur consists not of shifting the curves of cost or of revenue which face him, but of noticing that they have in fact shifted" (Kirzner, 1973, pp. 80–81).

Without realizing it, they may pay too much for inexpensive items or sell things at a low price that could fetch a high price. Some demand may be unrecognized and some resources may be misused. There may be some dis-coordinated activities in the production process. Entrepreneurs can recognize these types of opportunities. They trade or invest in pursuit of profit to correct mistakes in the market. Through entrepreneurial arbitrage, resources are more efficiently allocated, and profit opportunities gradually decline, so the market trends toward equilibrium. In this sense, as argued by Kirzner, the entrepreneur is an equilibrating force in the market (Kirzner, 1973).

Innovation creates or commercializes new things that did not exist, or breaks away from routines. In the technical terms of economics, if the market is at equilibrium, then all sales revenue is divided up by factor owners, net profit is zero, and there is no room for arbitrage. At that point, how can you make money? Innovate! Innovation breaks apart equilibrium by doing what Schumpeter talked about: Producing new products, introducing new production methods, discovering new raw materials, developing new markets, and creating new forms of organization.[16] In this sense, the entrepreneur is a dis-equilibrating force, a force for creating new opportunities and change (Schumpeter, 1934, chapter 2).

Two famous entrepreneurs in American history can clearly explain arbitrage and innovation. One is Armand Hammer (1898–1990), a twentieth century American entrepreneur, and the other is Frederic Tudor (1783–1864), a nineteenth century American entrepreneur. When Armand Hammer was a medical student at Columbia University in the 1920s, he participated in a humanitarian medical team that went to Russia. There, he found that Russians lacked grain and often had nothing to eat, but there were lots of precious animal fur and diamonds in the Ural Mountains that no one wanted. He knew America was the opposite. He thought this was an opportunity to make money, so he had his brother in the United States purchase wheat and ship it to St. Petersburg while he purchased fur and diamonds in Russia and shipped it to the United States. He made a lot of money from the trade. This is arbitrage. This turned Hammer into an

---

[16] While many innovations are involved in inventions, the innovation is different from the invention. Simply speaking, invention is creating new things and innovation is commercialization of new things. We have already discussed this distinction in Chapter 6.

entrepreneur. He also did other business in Russia, including the establishment of a pencil factory by importing the machines from Germany. Lenin called him "Comrade Armand Hammer." Later he founded Occidental Petroleum, a company he ran from 1957 until his death in 1990.[17]

Frederic Tudor's story, told in Chapter 1 of this book, of turning natural ice into a mass consumer product 200 years ago is an example of innovation. Schumpeter said that one aspect of innovation is creating a new market, which I understand as finding new uses for something. Tudor turned natural ice into a commodity, creating a new market.[18] Similarly, Westinghouse Co.'s introduction of the electric fan in 1889, the first electrical household gadget, and Texas Instrument's production of the first transistor radio are both innovations. These can be understood as either creating new products or as creating new markets for electric motors and transistors, respectively.

From this, we can separate entrepreneurs into two categories: arbitrage entrepreneurs and innovation entrepreneurs. For example, Silicon Valley entrepreneurs are almost all innovation entrepreneurs. Wall Street entrepreneurs are almost all arbitrage entrepreneurs. Bill Gates and Steve Jobs are innovation entrepreneurs. George Soros and Warren Buffett are arbitrage entrepreneurs. Ancient merchants were all arbitrage entrepreneurs. Sima Qian's *Biographies of Usurers* might be the first biography of entrepreneurs in human history. It wrote about 30 arbitrage entrepreneurs during the Western Han dynasty. Innovation entrepreneurs began to appear after the Industrial Revolution.

Of course, this is only a simplified classification. In reality, some entrepreneurs arbitrage as well as innovate. Some might arbitrage at first and then transition toward innovation – such as Ren Zhengfei, the founder of Huawei Company – or the opposite. In addition, many arbitrage activities cannot be profitably done without certain kinds of mini-innovations. Pure arbitrage entrepreneurs and pure innovation entrepreneurs are very rare in reality.

We can use a simple economic model to explain how the two functions of entrepreneurs drive economic growth. With given

[17] For Hammer's biography, see Cosidine (1975).
[18] Kirzner may say Tudor is an arbitrager, not innovator, because he did nothing more than found an unused opportunity for ice. This means that sometimes it is not easy to distinguish innovation from arbitrage, depending up the observer's perspective.

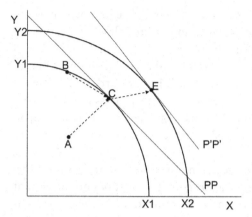

Figure 9.2 The Production Possibility Frontier Model of Economic Growth

resources and technologies, the maximum combination of products that any country can produce is limited. Economists call this the "production possibilities frontier." In Figure 9.2, we assume that only two types of products can be produced. The horizontal axis represents Product X and the vertical axis represents Product Y (the reader can understand X as corn and Y as soybeans). X1Y1 is the production possibility frontier under existing technology and resources. The production possibility frontier and consumer preferences together determine the marginal rate of substitution tangent point, which is the equilibrium point for resource allocation (such as Point C). At the equilibrium point, sales revenue equals cost, so there is no entrepreneurial profit or room for arbitrage. However, due to most people's ignorance or a distortion of the incentive mechanism, actual economic operations are within the production possibility frontier (such as Point A), meaning resources are not efficiently utilized. Alternatively, although production reaches the maximum possible frontier, mistakes have been made. There are too many soybeans but not enough corn, so at this point there is still a misallocation of resources (such as Point B).

When the economy is at Point A or Point B, arbitrage opportunities exist. Entrepreneurs discover disequilibrium (Points A or B), and then take the opportunity to engage in arbitrage. Resource allocation is improved through their arbitrage activity, causing the economy to trend toward equilibrium Point C. This brings about economic growth based on resource allocation improvement.

After the economy reaches Point C, arbitrage opportunities no longer exist. No further improvement in resource allocation can bring about economic growth. Where else can growth come from? It can only come from an outward movement of the production possibilities frontier, such as moving outward from X1Y1 toward X2Y2. This is the innovation function of entrepreneurs. In the process of innovation, entrepreneurs also create new arbitrage opportunities. This way, arbitrage and innovation continuously interact to allow the economy to sustainably grow.

Of course, in reality, arbitrage and innovation exist at the same time. Saying that "innovation breaks apart equilibrium" does not mean that entrepreneurs only have an incentive to innovate when the economy is at equilibrium. It is true that in most circumstances, less room for arbitrage means more pressure to innovate. Without innovation, the economy will eventually reach equilibrium through arbitrage. However, entrepreneurs may also "equilibrate" disequilibrium through innovation. Further, while innovation breaks apart equilibrium and brings about disequilibrium, it might bring about other innovations. For example, in the early stage of Britain's industrial revolution, when the introduction of the mechanical spinning machine broke apart the equilibrium between spinning and weaving, the shortage of weavers induced the innovation of the mechanical loom. This means that the production possibility frontier is continuously moving outward. This is the primary reason that the economy can never be at equilibrium.

Below, I use the development of the British steel and textile industries during the First Industrial Revolution to explain this point.[19] In the eighteenth century and first half of the nineteenth century, metallurgy and textiles were the two primary non-agricultural industries in Britain. In Figure 9-3, we use the horizontal axis to represent iron-steel output and the vertical axis to represent textile product output.[20]

---

[19] For the story of innovation during Great Britain's industrial revolution, see Mantoux (1928), chapter 2.

[20] There are two main processes in the textile industry: spinning and weaving. Because of the existence of trade, the output of British yarn did not equal the output of cloth. Here, I ignored this distinction. Also, in metallurgy, ironmaking and steelmaking are two difference processes. At that time, steel production was less than 1% of iron production. Therefore, the steel output mentioned here is actually iron output.

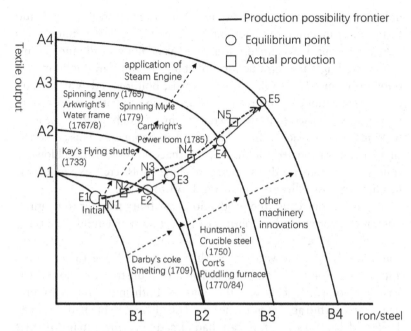

Figure 9.3 British Industrial Revolution in Iron/Steel and Textiles

Before 1710, Britain's production possibility frontier was B1A1, but Britain's actual output was within B1A1. Thus, room for arbitrage existed and not a small number of entrepreneurs pursued it, including importing Indian textile products and Northern European iron. In 1709, Abraham Darby's experiments using coke to make iron finally succeeded. This innovation enlarged the potential output of iron and changed Britain's production possibility frontier from B1A1 to B2A1. This provided other entrepreneurs with more space for arbitrage. Of course, some years had to pass for coke ironmaking technology to mature before this new space for arbitrage could truly appear. In the textile industry, John Kay's invention of the flying shuttle in 1733 increased the maximum possible production of textile products to A2. This way, Britain's production possibility frontier became B2A2. The mid-to-late eighteenth century was an era of endless innovation. In the textile industry, Richard Arkwright invented the water frame (1768), James Hargreaves invented the spinning jenny (1765), Samuel Crompton invented the spinning mule (1779), and Edmund Cartwright invented the power loom (1785). In the metallurgy industry, Benjamin Huntsman invented crucible steel (1750) and Henry Cort invented the puddling furnace (1784). These innovations were all revolutionary. In addition, there were many small innovations. This way, England's production possibility frontier gradually moved outward from B2A2 to B3A3. Afterwards, Boulton and Watt's steam engines transitioned from reciprocating motion to rotative operation, which could be used to power textile machines and be used in the iron-making industry (such as for blowers and air hammers). This and other smaller innovations (including blast furnace improvements, blowers, rollers, air hammers, drills, metal machine tools, etc.) expanded the production possibility frontier from B3A3 to B4A4.

As innovations cause the production possibility frontier to continuously move outward, the economy can never be at an equilibrium state. Entrepreneurs' arbitrage activity, however, causes the economy to continuously trend toward an equilibrium state. When the economy approached Point E5 equilibrium, Britain's industrial revolution was basically complete. This was the work of both innovation entrepreneurs and arbitrage entrepreneurs. This likely happened between 1830 and 1850. In 1830, Britain had already become a major textiles exporter, and textile exports accounted for 50% of total exports. In 1847, Britain's pig iron products exceeded two million tons, which was 71 times higher than in 1750 (Morgan, 2016).

The defect of Figures 9.2 and 9.3 is they are unable to present the change in product categories. Innovation often manifests as dimensional change in the production possibility frontier, meaning the appearance of new products, extension of the division of labor chain, and deepening of specialization. It also manifests as the continual upgrading of the demand structure and production structure.

Chinese Entrepreneurs: From Arbitrage to Innovation

The importance of the distinction between arbitrage entrepreneurs and innovation entrepreneurs can be exemplified by China's experience. From the perspective of entrepreneurship, stated simply, China's high economic growth over the past 40 years primarily came from improved resource allocation efficiency driven by entrepreneurs' arbitrage activity. This type of arbitrage not only includes China's grassroots entrepreneurs but also foreign entrepreneurs. A considerable part of China's economic growth was contributed by foreign entrepreneurs' arbitrage. Proof of this is that foreign enterprises' exports accounted for more than 40% of China's total exports.

Why can arbitrage bring about such rapid growth? It is simple. First, the long-term planning system seriously distorted resource allocation and the actual economy was far from the production possibility frontier, resulting in vast arbitrage opportunities within the Chinese economy after reform. In the early days of Reform and Opening, doing anything could make money. On the one hand, everything was in short supply in the product markets and, on the other hand, too many resources were idle. The household contract responsibility system in agriculture created huge redundancies in the labor force, given that more than 80% of the population lived in the countryside at the beginning of the reform. Land and capital were also not efficiently utilized. Thus, there were huge discrepancies between product prices and factor prices.

Second, opening up caused a gradual integration between the Chinese market and the international market, which brought about new disequilibrium and arbitrage opportunities (equivalent to moving the frontier outward). Many products that were inexpensive outside of China were expensive within China, whereas other items that were inexpensive in China and had low production costs were expensive outside of China. Importing the former and exporting the latter could earn a lot of money. This huge space for arbitrage not only attracted Chinese entrepreneurs, but also foreign entrepreneurs. China's town and village enterprises (TVEs) and private enterprises made a fortune on arbitrage. Foreign capital entered China on a large scale seeking arbitrage in the product market and factor market (especially the labor market). This is the reason that the growth in China's international trade was much higher than the growth in its gross domestic product.

Third, the big technological gap between China and the West also provided a big arbitrage opportunity. Some people have said that China spent 40 years doing what the West took 200 years to do, proving that the 'China model' is the world's best. This opinion overlooks a basic reality: China's success over the last 40 years was built upon the technological foundation accumulated by the West over the last 200 years. It is precisely the technology, products, thought, and management methods created by the West over the last few hundred years that made China's catch-up development and unconventional growth possible. For a long time, what Chinese entrepreneurs needed to do was just copy and imitate, not innovate. Chinese entrepreneurs did not need to do research and develop new products, nor did they need market tests. Most products that are liked by Western consumers are also liked by the Chinese. Imitation is always easier than innovation. There is nothing out of the ordinary about us walking faster on a road that another person had to build. On the actual market, almost every product and technology did not originate from China, but Chinese entrepreneurs can use them to make profits. Cell phones, computers, televisions, the Internet, automobiles, high-speed rail, tunnel excavators, and medical devices, even zippers, have all been taken from foreigners. The West's developed technology and innovative products plus China's huge market and the extremely low cost of labor provided both Chinese and foreign entrepreneurs with tremendous room for arbitrage.

However, the situation now is changing. Because of the reasons listed below, room for arbitrage is shrinking. First, in the mass consumer goods markets, anything that could be imitated or introduced has been introduced, and most traditional industries are in a state of overcapacity. Second, the labor cost advantage is slowly decreasing. China cannot compare with Southeast Asian nations, India, Bangladesh, or Brazil. Even compared to Western developed countries, China's labor cost advantage has declined significantly. Some have calculated China's manufacturing cost to only be 5% less than America's. By taking into account America's lower transportation and transaction costs, China's cost advantage almost disappears. A large quantity of foreign firms are leaving China, partly because of the increase in labor costs. Third, the environmental cost of rapid development in the past must be remedied. Fourth, other emerging economies such as India and Brazil are also implementing reform and opening, while at the same time developed countries have begun a return to manufacturing with a new technological revolution. These have all caused the room for arbitrage to become smaller and smaller.

As arbitrage opportunities are dramatically shrinking, it is difficult to sustain growth with arbitrage or make money from it. What will future growth depend on? It can only rely on innovation. Over the past 40 years, arbitrage entrepreneurs have driven China's transition from a planned economy to a more or less market economy. Even though this transition is still not complete, China's future growth requires innovation entrepreneurs to play an increasingly important role.[21]

This means that China's economic growth rate will decline substantially because innovation is a very slow process. The difference between innovation and arbitrage is the same as the difference between paving a path and walking on it. Worldwide, growth supported by innovation reaching 2–3% is impressive. Although China still has some room for arbitrage because there is still some foreign advanced technology that China has not used, the remaining arbitrage opportunities will not be easy to utilize. In the past, arbitrage was primarily in the consumer product market, but now China must transition toward arbitrage in the equipment market. It is easy to make knock off cell phones, but making knock off molds for the production of cell phones is relatively difficult, and making knock off equipment to make molds is even harder, let alone chips.

Innovation is more institutional- and culture-demanding. The reason is that compared to arbitrage, innovation takes much more time and faces much more uncertainty. Entrepreneurs will innovate only if they have a long time horizon and stable expectations about the future.

---

[21] For a detailed analysis of China's transition from arbitrage-driven growth to innovation-driven growth, see Zhang (2017a).

10 | *The Uncertainty of Innovation*

The Difference between Innovation and Arbitrage

In the previous chapter, I summarized the two functions of entrepreneurs. The first is arbitrage and the second is innovation. So-called arbitrage means using mature technology to find market opportunities and make a profit. So-called innovation refers to making products or technologies that did not originally exist and creating new markets.

Arbitrage can be further separated into three types: Cross-market arbitrage, intertemporal arbitrage, and production activity arbitrage (Kirzner, 1992, p. 50). So-called cross-market arbitrage means buying in one market and selling in another, something that pure merchants do. The profit they earn comes from the difference in prices between markets. Because prices in different markets are always changing, whether merchants can make money and how much they can make is determined by their judgments of price changes in different markets being correct. So-called intertemporal arbitrage refers to buying now and selling later, or selling now and buying later (i.e. short selling), based on forecasted price trends. Trading on futures markets and financial markets is classic intertemporal arbitrage. Whether money can be made is determined by the correctness of price trend forecasts. Production activity arbitrage refers to organizing factors of production to produce products. These types of arbitragers are producers. The profit they make is the difference between product price (sales revenue) and factor prices (cost). Of course, because all economic activities are a process that requires time, all judgments are judgments of the future. The significance of this is that all arbitrage is "speculation."

Innovation can be separated into subversive (macro) innovation and modification (micro) innovation.[1] So-called subversive (macro)

---

[1] Subversive innovation and modification innovation are common terms. Clayton Christensen (1997) distinguished between destructive technologies and sustaining technologies. Joel Mokyr distinguishes between macro-invention and micro-invention (Mokyr, 1990. p. 13).

innovation is zero-to-one innovation, innovation that completely replaces existing products and technologies. This type of innovation might create a new industry or redefine an industry. Schumpeterian creative destruction normally refers to this type of innovation (Schumpeter, 1942, chapter 7). Modification innovation means improving the quality and performance of a product or reducing its production cost. The automobile industry provides examples. Benz and Daimler invented the automobile around 1886. This was subversive innovation because it would subvert the traditional postal horse carriage transportation industry and create the automobile industry. Later, Henry Ford introduced the assembly line, which was also subversive because it completely transformed the automobile's production methods. The automobile basically lacked further subversive innovation until recently with the appearance of electric vehicles and autonomous driving. However, the American automobile industry had more than 600 modification innovations between 1900 and 1981 alone (Abernathy et al., 1984).

Another example comes from the computer industry. After IBM introduced the first commercial computer in 1945, there was an evolution from large-scale machines to micro-machines, to personal computers, to notebooks, to tablets, and to smartphones. Each one was subversive innovation to the previous one. However, each category of computer also had many micro-innovations and modification innovations. Features continuously improved and costs dropped dramatically for large-scale machines, micro-machines, personal computers, as well as today's smart phones.

What is the difference between arbitrage and innovation? Two dimensions are the most important: time horizon and the degree of uncertainty.

Arbitrage is short term and innovation is long term. Intertemporal arbitrage in financial markets can be completed in seconds. Production activity arbitrage requires a relatively longer time, but building a factory only takes one or two years, which can be planned. Innovation, however, requires between three and 10 years or longer to see the outcome. The steam engine, for example, was drawn up by Watt in 1764, patented five years later, and truly entered the market in 1776, meaning it took 12 years. The Boulton & Watt Company did not turn a profit until 1786 (Mantoux, 1928, p. 336). The Wright brothers invented the airplane in 1903, but the first passenger airplane

(DC-3) entered commercial use in 1936, so there were 33 years in between (Rosenberg, 2000, p. 61). The Xerox copy machine is another example. Chester Floyd Carlson spent three years inventing a xerographic copier. Another six years passed before he found a sponsor (a non-profit organization). Another 15 years passed until the first copier for commercial use, the Xerox 914, entered the market in March 1960. A total of 24 years (Tellis and Golder, 2002, pp. 117–120)! It took 30 years for ASML Holding of Holland to develop and introduce EUV lithography into the market (Miller, 2022, Chapter 39). Even some simple innovations can be very time-consuming. For instance, baby diapers took Procter & Gamble a full 10 years from research and development to market entry (Ibid. p. 110). Today, some new technology companies can quickly obtain funds, but it is investors' money, not customers' payments. It also does not mean the market has acknowledged them, but instead means investors are making a bet. There is still a great distance until true success.

Many people mistakenly believe obtaining patents is innovation. Actually, patents are just innovation's first step. It could even be said that it is the first step in a long march of 10,000 miles. Innovation is different from inventions. Obtaining a patent proves that an invention succeeded. Innovation makes patents have commercial value. A series of obstacles must be overcome between obtaining a patent and realizing commercial value. For example, improving functionality, increasing quality, and reducing costs until market acceptance requires overcoming traditional forces that obstruct innovation. Many companies do not die during the invention process, but they die in the process of realizing commercialization after obtaining the invention.

John Enos collected information on 46 major innovations, of which 11 were in the field of petroleum refining. He found that the average interval between invention and innovation was 11 years in petroleum refining and 13.6 years in other fields. Different innovations vary greatly; the fluorescent lamp took 79 years, the gyro-compass took 56 years, and the cotton picker took 53 years, but DDT, the long-playing record, lucite Plexiglas, and shell molding took three years. The shortest period was one year, for freon refrigerants. The mechanical sector has the shortest innovation time lag, followed by the chemical and pharmaceutical sectors. The electronics sector has the longest innovation time lag (quoted from Rosenberg, 1976, pp. 69–70).

In terms of uncertainty, innovation's uncertainty is much greater than arbitrage's. We can even refer to arbitrage's low uncertainty as risk. It has a certain predictability. Innovation's uncertainty is true uncertainty. It cannot be predicted. Soon, we will use a large number of examples to explain this point. Of course, differences exist in the time period and uncertainty of modification innovation and subversive innovation. The time period and uncertainty of modification innovation is between that of arbitrage and subversive innovation, as shown in Figure 10.1.

The differences between arbitrage and innovation in time horizon and uncertainty lead to different profit curves, as shown in Figure 10.2. Simply put, arbitrage makes money in the beginning, but as time goes

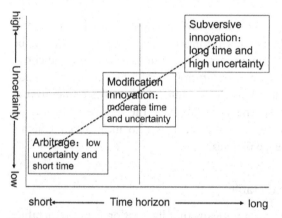

Figure 10.1 Difference between Arbitrage and Innovation

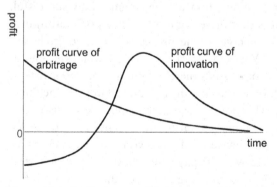

Figure 10.2 Profit Curves of Arbitrage and Innovation

by, profit becomes lower and lower until there is nothing left. Economists call this state "equilibrium," where no profit exists. Innovation loses money in the beginning and might sustain losses for many years. At some point in time, a few lucky entrepreneurs will make money. After the breakeven point, profit increases slowly at first and then may increase dramatically for some years. As soon as innovators make a lot of money, however, other entrepreneurs can arbitrage the same or similar technology so that there will be less and less profit until there is no more money left to be made. Thus, as argued by Schumpeter, every innovation's high profit is temporary, because competition eventually drives down market prices (Schumpeter, 1939, pp. 105–108). This means that entrepreneurial profit can only be sustained by successively successful innovations, not one-off innovations.

This difference has a very important implication for investors and entrepreneurs alike. It means that innovation entrepreneurs must be more patient and have longer-term expectations than arbitrage entrepreneurs. At the same time, institutions and policies must provide relatively greater predictability and stability to investors and entrepreneurs. Otherwise, entrepreneurs might have the motive to arbitrage, but not a strong motive to innovate. This also means that China's system faces enormous challenges.

Innovation Is Unpredictable

The uncertainty of innovation means that innovation is unpredictable, referring to our inability to predict, using existing scientific knowledge and statistics, whether an innovation will be commercially successful. The underlying reason is that there are innumerable potential futures of which only one will emerge as the process of competing choices unfolds (Buchanan and Vanberg, 1991, p. 171). As Shackle puts it: "the content of time-to-come is not merely unknown but nonexistent, and the notion of foreknowledge of human affairs is vacuous" (Shackle, 1983, p. 33). This point is especially applicable to disruptive innovations, which are imaginary creations of the entrepreneur. Some of the new products and new technologies we use now, such as an online ride-hailing service, WeChat payment, facial recognition, artificial intelligence, and cloud computing, were predicted by very few people 10 years ago, let alone 20 years ago. Even fewer people believed they would succeed. Similarly, we now have no way to predict which technologies and industries will be dominant in 10 or 20 years.

Saying that innovation is unpredictable does not mean that no one wants to predict it. In fact, many people want to predict the future, especially experts. They are more than happy to do so. However, as Clayton Christensen pointed out: "the only thing we may know for sure when we read experts' forecasts about how large emerging markets will become is that they are wrong" (Christensen, 1997, p. 15). His words not only apply to experts, but also most entrepreneurs. Even the greatest entrepreneurs have difficulty predicting the future.

Allow me to provide a few examples to exemplify this point.

The story of the steam engine. The contribution of the steam engine to the Industrial Revolution is second to none. When steam engines are mentioned today, people naturally think of James Watt. He turned the steam engine into power. When Watt devoted himself to the invention of the steam engine, however, very few people were optimistic about it. Very few people were willing to invest and his invention work was interrupted several times due to a lack of funds. He relied on surveying work to feed his family. British iron entrepreneur John Roebuck was the first entrepreneur/investor to look favorably on the steam engine. Roebuck, however, went bankrupt in 1773. He owed a lot of money to dozens of creditors. The only asset he held was one-third of the steam engine patent. (Watt owned one-third and the other one-third had been previously transferred to Matthew Boulton.) The creditors thought the patent was worthless, so they refused to accept it. Boulton made a proposal: He was willing to pay £630 for that one-third of the equity held by Roebuck. If they agreed, then they should not bother Roebuck again. As soon as he said it, dozens of creditors quickly agreed to the deal, fearing he would change his mind. They split the £630 and Boulton obtained all of Roebuck's share in the steam engine. This incident shows that at the time, most people were not optimistic about the prospects of the steam engine. Boulton wrote in a letter to Watt that "The thing is now a shadow, it is merely ideal, and it will cost money to realize it" (Mantoux, 1928, p. 332).

The fight between the direct current and alternating current. Most people know of Thomas Edison as a genius inventor. In fact, Edison was also an outstanding entrepreneur. He established the first electric lighting system in history (1882) and ushered in mankind's electrification era. In the early days of the electrical system, there was a debate as to whether direct current or alternating current would be the dominant technology. Edison insisted that direct current would dominate, but his rivals George Westinghouse and Nikola Tesla held diametrically opposed views. Edison launched a movement against alternating current. To justify his beliefs, he even used some unethical tactics, including electrocuting horses and dogs to prove that alternating current was the "electricity of death." It turns out, however, that Edison's prediction was wrong. Alternating current, not direct current, later dominated the electricity supply system (Smil, 2005, pp. 83–89).

The conflict between gasoline and electric vehicles. Scientific *American,* a magazine showcasing technological progress, covered the tiny improvements in steam engine technology in the 1890s, but paid little attention to nascent automobile manufacturing. Edward Byrne, the magazine's editor-in-chief, in 1900 wrote a 467-page systematic review of nineteenth-century inventions. He only wrote seven pages on the automobile, the same as the bicycle (Smil, 2005, p. 121).

Edison's mistaken prediction also occurred in the automobile industry. In 1900, the United States had 8,000 automobiles, of which 50% were steam-powered, 30% were electric-powered, and 20% were gasoline-powered. Steam-powered vehicles soon went out of favor but electric vehicles looked especially promising. In 1896, Riker's electric vehicle beat Duryea's gasoline-powered vehicle during a race at Narragansett, Rhode Island.[2] Three years later, during a race in France, a bullet-shaped electric vehicle surpassed a speed of 100 kilometers per hour. Electric vehicles are clean and low noise. They do not require high-pressure steam boilers, squeaking hot steam, dangerous cranking, or flammable gasoline. Edison believed that fuel vehicles had no future, whereas electric vehicles were the future. As late as 1910, he was still tirelessly looking for high-power-density batteries, believing that the cost of electric vehicles would come down. As it turned out, electric vehicles failed and gasoline vehicles dominated the market. Of course, more than 100 years later, electric vehicles have made a comeback and have the potential to replace gasoline vehicles.

---

[2] Charles Edgar Duryea (1861–1938) was an American engineer and created the first gasoline-powered vehicle. He also co-founded the Duryea Motor Wagon Company.

However, for just over the last one hundred years, Edison's prediction was obviously wrong (Smil, 2005, pp. 123–124).

Airships and airplanes. Humans took to the sky in two different ways: Airships and airplanes. In 1899, *Scientific American* predicted that airships, not airplanes, would dominate the sky in the future. The airship was invented in 1900, three years earlier than the airplane. Before World War I, airships were already in commercial operation, whereas airplanes were just hobbyist toys. Ferdinand von Zeppelin, inventor of the airship, even thought that the airplane would be nothing more than a 'footnote' in the history of aviation. After World War I, the contest between airships and airplanes was absolute. Hugo Eckener, a German aeronautical engineer and pilot of the first circumnavigation flight in 1929, was adamant that airships would overcome airplanes. A report by the US Department of Commerce said that Eckener's circumnavigation and Atlantic triangle flights proved the airship was superior to the airplane for transoceanic flights. Juan Trippe, an American aeronautical entrepreneur, had the opposite opinion. He believed the airplane would be the protagonist of future aviation. Finally, shortly before World War II, after an airship crash, the airplane won. The airship became a 'footnote' in the history of aviation.[3]

Cloud computing. On March 28, 2011, an annual meeting of Chinese IT leaders was held at the Wuzhou Guest House in Shenzhen. Three people sat on the stage and debated the future of cloud computing. Two of them were pessimistic about the technology and only one was optimistic. The pessimistic ones were Pony Ma, the founder of Tencent Technology Co., and Robin Li, the founder of Baidu, both of whom are technology giants. Pony Ma said that cloud computing is a good concept, and a phenomenon like Avatar might appear in hundreds or thousands of years, but it is too early to do it now. Robin Li believed that cloud computing is "old wine in a new bottle," not a new technology. He said that more and more Internet applications based on cloud computing will appear in the future, so cloud computing is not a good way to make money. Jack Ma was the only one of the three to be optimistic about cloud computing. He believed that cloud computing is a mechanism for processing,

[3] For a detailed discussion of the dual between airships and airplanes, see Chapter 11 of this book.

storing, and sharing data, so his Alibaba had cloud computing to meet the needs of users. If they did not do cloud computing now, later they would go under. Reality proved Jack Ma's judgment correct. Compared to Pony Ma and Robin Li, however, Jack Ma did not really understand the technology. Of course, Pony Ma and Robin Li quickly changed their views. It could even be said that without cloud computing, Tencent would not be what it is today.[4]

Examples are too numerous to enumerate. Innovation is unpredictable because, as was already mentioned, the future is uncertain and indeterminate. Nathan Rosenberg, once an economist at Stanford University who specializes in technological progress, said:

The essential feature of technological innovation is that it is an activity that is fraught with many uncertainties. This uncertainty, by which we mean an inability to predict the outcome of the search process, or to predetermine the most efficient path to some particular goal, has a very important implication: the activity cannot be planned. No person, or group of persons, is clever enough to plan the outcome of the search process, in the sense of identifying a particular innovation target and moving in a predetermined way to its realization – as one might read a road map and plan the most efficient route to a historical monument. (Rosenberg, 1994, pp. 92–93)

The uncertainty of innovation can be summarized as four aspects: (1) technological feasibility uncertainty; (2) commercial value uncertainty; (3) complementary technology uncertainty; and (4) political, cultural, and policy uncertainty. In contrast, arbitrage only has the second and fourth types of uncertainty.

Four Uncertainties of Innovations

Uncertainty of Technological Feasibility

So-called technological uncertainty refers to whether a certain innovation is technically possible under the level of scientific knowledge and technical means at the time is unknown in advance. This point is particularly emphasized by Rosenberg (2000, p. 59).

Before the success of Abraham Darby's coke ironmaking experiments, whether coke could make iron was technologically uncertain.

---

[4] See NetEase Tech (2010).

After this uncertainty was resolved, the popularization of the coke ironmaking process, especially after Henry Cort's puddling process, turned Britain's disadvantaged position in the iron industry into the commonly recognized dominant position in Europe within just a few years. In the past, iron was precious and only used to make knives and farm tools. Iron became abundant, so it could not all be used up making these traditional products. What else could iron be used for? Nobody knew. In 1776, John Wilkinson proposed using iron to build bridges. The idea was technologically feasible. Traditionally, bridges were constructed of stone, brick, or wood. Iron was at least as hard as stone, brick, and wood. The first iron bridge was shortly thereafter erected over the River Severn. Then Wilkinson suggested using iron to build ships. This time, everyone thought he was crazy. Traditionally, ships were made of wood that is lighter than water. Iron is heavier than water. At the level of knowledge at the time, it was unknown whether something heavier than water could float. When Wilkinson came up with the idea of using iron to build ships, no one believed it. Of course, we know that Wilkinson succeeded in the end. At the end of his life, Wilkinson liked to say that iron was destined to replace most of the building materials used at the time so that one day people would see houses made of iron, avenues made of iron, and bridges made of iron (Mantoux, 1928, p. 316). British insurance companies, however, were not willing to provide insurance services for iron ships until a hundred years after Wilkinson proposed the concept.

Similarly, *Scientific American* in 1899 was not optimistic about the airplane's prospects because it was technologically uncertain whether something heavier-than-air could float in the air until the Wright brothers succeeded in 1903.

In the 1850s, Cyrus West Field wanted to lay an undersea cable across the Atlantic. Even Samuel Morse, the inventor of the telegraph, was not optimistic. Western Union, the largest telegraph company in the United States, even scoffed at the idea. At the time, even though undersea cables existed, they only spanned less than 100 kilometers, such as the narrowest point between England and France. The narrowest part of the Atlantic Ocean is 2,300 miles. How deep the sea is, how much pressure is on the seabed, whether the quality of the insulator was reliable, and whether electrical signal can travel more than 2,300 miles were all unknown. Was the transatlantic cable technologically feasible? It was not known in advance. Because of this,

Western Union preferred the route through Siberia and the Bering Strait rather than investing in a transatlantic undersea cable.

When Edison invented the light bulb, which type of material was feasible as a filament was technologically uncertain. Edison's laboratory experimented with more than 6,000 types of plant fibers, ranging from rare woods to common grasses. In the end, a type of Japanese bamboo was selected because its core has a perfect cellulose structure, which produces a solid and high resistance carbonized filament that lasts for 600 hours (Smil, 2005, p. 43).

Gillette safety razors are prevalent today and are a must-have for almost all men. When King C. Gillette proposed an ultra-thin, low-cost, disposable blade more than 100 years ago, however, all the metal experts and knife-makers that he knew believed this was not possible. Industry insiders believed razors should be made of expensive, hard metal and last a lifetime. His friends laughed at his idea, but this did not affect Gillette's judgment. He led a team through tireless research and after a few years, succeeded (Tellis and Golder, 2002, pp. 84–90, 106–110).

In the early 2000s, when Steve Jobs proposed making the iPhone, Microsoft was developing the tablet with a stylus. Blackberry and Nokia mobile phones had keyboards. At that time, developers were already working on the multi-touch for computers, but Jobs decided to apply the technology to mobile phones first. He was not sure whether it would succeed on a phone. Jobs said to his engineers, "I want to make a tablet, and it can't have a keyboard or a stylus. So could you guys come up with a multi-touch, touch-sensitive display for me?" Apple's technical staff thought it was impossible. Given the popularity of BlackBerry phones at that time, many team members advocated for a keyboard, but Jobs rejected it. "Think of all the innovations we'd be able to adapt if we did the keyboard onscreen with software. Let's bet on it, and then we'll find a way to make it work." At the insistence of Jobs, this entirely new technology was born, allowing us to enter today's smartphone era, led by the iPhone. It is conceivable that if the current mobile phone were still a keyboard input type that requires two hands or a stylus, as Bill Gates imagined, then it would be impossible for smart phones to spread so fast or be so successful (Isaacson, 2011, pp. 467–469).

In semiconductor device fabrication, visible light lithography was used in the 1960s for IC-production, with wavelengths as small as

435 nm. Later, ultraviolet (UV) light was used, with a wavelength of 365 nm at first, then excimer wavelengths of 248 nm and then 193 nm, which was called deep UV. The next step, going even smaller, was dubbed Extreme UV, or EUV, with wavelengths near 13.5 nm. For many years, the EUV technology was considered impossible by many people. EUV is absorbed by glass and even air, so instead of using lenses, as before, mirrors in a vacuum would be needed to focus the beams of light. Reliable production of EUV was also problematic. Then the leading producers of steppers, Canon and Nikon, stopped development, and some predicted the end of Moore's law. By 2018, Dutch company ASML succeeded in deploying the EUV-LLC IP after several decades of developmental research with a total investment of $40 billion. This led *MIT Technology Review* to name it "the machine that saved Moore's law" (Miller, 2022, chapter 39).

Today, we see many new technologies, such as new energy vehicles or driverless technology, and we still do not know how many branches they have. For example, there are six or seven types of battery technology, as well as hydrogen fuel technology. Some of these innovations have been proven to be technologically feasible. Whether some of the other ideas are technologically feasible is still a question waiting an accurate answer.

Uncertainty of Commercial Value

Even if an innovation is technologically feasible, whether the market accepts it is not knowable beforehand. Although consumers do not really know exactly what they want (as Schumpeter pointed out), they have the final say. This is the meaning of "consumer sovereignty." Therefore, when entrepreneurs innovate, they must first conject possible consumer preferences. The conjecture might be correct or wrong. Consumer preferences are changeable and unstable. Consumers are often very conservative and suspicious of new products. This creates the uncertainty of commercial value. Pony Ma and Robin Li were not optimistic about cloud computing at the time, not because it was technologically unfeasible, but because its commercial value was uncertain.

In the story of American entrepreneur Frederic Tudor, told in Chapter 2, there was no technological problem transporting natural ice from Boston to Martinique in the Caribbean, or anywhere else, within a certain period of time. There was also no technological problem preserving ice. In the first ten years or so, however, local consumers did not accept it or know what to do with it. Tudor could not avoid being jailed for debt.

Steve Jobs founded Apple in 1975. Apple's annual sales had already reached $1.5 billion by 1984. Jobs had made a name for himself. In May 1985, however, the board of directors fired him. Why? The major reason was that his Macintosh computer continued to disappoint, selling only 10% of the forecast (Isaacson, 2011, p. 195). The Macintosh was the first successful mass-market personal computer. It had a graphical interface with a built-in screen and mouse. It was launched in January 1984 as Apple's flagship product. In the first few months after its launch, sales were great. Jobs became more well known and the Apple Lisa and Macintosh were merged under his leadership. In the second half of 1984, however, Macintosh sales rapidly declined. Despite their attractive appearance, Macintosh computers were slow, underpowered, and had no built-in hard drive. When people realized the limitations, interest waned. By the end of 1984, Macintosh sales fell below 10,000 a month. This became Jobs' Waterloo!

Yidao Yongche was the first online ride-hailing service platform in China. Zhou Hang founded it in May 2010, about the same time as Uber in the United States. Zhou had a keen insight into Internet applications. As early as 2007, he thought of doing mobile payments, ebooks, mobile car washes, and real-name social media. When he founded Yidao, he did not know about Uber, so he was doing something original. Yidao positioned itself to provide high-end car services for business people to get around anytime, anywhere. Zhou once described his vision: Whether a person was in Beijing's central business district or Xinjiang or Tibet, as long as they hailed a ride, Yidao could provide it. After Yidao received its first round of funding in August 2011, it began to market itself, but the number of rides hailed did not meet expectations. In 2012, Zhou adjusted the strategy, leading to a breakthrough related to credit cards. With a steady source of customers, Yidao maintained a market share of 80% in 2013. A year later, the online ride-hailing platforms fought an unprecedented subsidy war. At first, Yidao did not join the subsidy war and even passed on a substantial financing opportunity. Zhou believed that online ride-hailing is a niche market where Yidao should provide a high-quality and differentiated service. He also believed that the government would not allow the subsidy war to continue. Things did not go the way he imagined, however. Soon, Yidao was overtaken by Didi and Yidao's market share fell sharply. In October 2015, Leshi Holdings obtained 70% of Yidao's equity, becoming Yidao's controlling shareholder. Zhou had no choice. Four months later, he left Yidao. The company went from the leader of ride-hailing platforms to a nobody.[5]

Certain products are technologically successful, even perfect, but fail commercially. For example, Concorde was the first supersonic aircraft in human history, with a speed of 2,200 kilometers per hour. It was jointly manufactured by Britain and France in 1969 and formally put into commercial operation in 1976. Due to high fuel consumption, high operating costs, loud noise, and potential safety hazards, however, it was completely withdrawn from operation in October 2003 after a major crash. Airbus developed and produced the A380 as the world's largest passenger aircraft, regarding it as the "flagship" product of the twenty-first century, known as "superjumbo." The A380 made its maiden flight on April 27, 2005. The first commercial flight was on October 25, 2007. After the A380 entered service, it broke the Boeing 747's 35-year record in the field of long-range, super-large, wide-body aircraft and ended its 30-year monopoly in that market. On February 14, 2019, however, Airbus announced it would stop the production of the A380 in 2021. The reason was that it was not commercially viable for both the manufacturer and the operators.

During visits to some companies, I have often found that there are many new products in their exhibition halls, but few new products in the market, because most of their new products are not accepted by the market.

Uncertainty of Related Technology

A very important reason innovations are uncertain in terms of commercial value is that almost all innovations are not perfect in the beginning. They are often inferior to the original product but cost more. The performance and efficiency of the original internal combustion engine, for example, was inferior to that of the technologically mature steam engine. When the automobile first appeared, it was not

---

[5] For Yidao's story, see Zhou Hang (2018), pp. xxiii–xxvii.

as comfortable as a horse carriage and not much faster but with more pollution and noise. When frozen food first appeared, the taste and nutritional value were substantially inferior to fresh food, so few people were willing to buy it. The original personal computer did not compare in function to the microcomputer, but the price was not lower. The initial resolution of cameras on mobile phones was so low it was impossible to take nice photographs. The eventual value of an innovation depends on the emergence of other related technological innovations.

Related technological innovations might be complementary or competitive. Complementary technological innovation will improve the original innovation and make it commercially successful. Rosenberg called this "technological complementarities" (2000, p. 62). Competitive technological innovation will reduce the value of the original innovation completely. What are the related innovations? Will they appear? When will they appear? These answers are unknown. We do not even know what the related technology is in advance. This is the uncertainty of related technologies.

Watt invented the steam engine in 1765 and patented it in 1769, but had not been able to produce a steam engine that could be put into use. Why? Because he was unable to produce a qualified cylinder. The production of the qualified cylinder needed a new machining tool. The chance came only when John Wilkinson invented new boring machines. Wilkinson was a manufacturer of cannons. To improve his cannons, he continuously researched and improved the performance of boring machines, eventually inventing a new one. Wilkinson's new boring machine could produce suitable cylinders, so the first steam engine was put into use in 1776. Over the next two decades, Watt's steam engine cylinders were all basically produced in Wilkinson's factories (Rosen, 2010, chapter 8).

A combination of seemingly unrelated technologies can have unexpected significant effects. The "birth" of laser technology is a famous case. Now lasers are ubiquitous. We even use laser pointers when teaching a course. Medical examinations and operations in hospitals are inseparable from laser technology. However, when Bell Telephone Laboratories scientists discovered the laser in 1960, their patent attorney advocated against applying for a patent because it was useless for telecommunications at the time. A decade later, Corning produced a super-clear glass that, even if it is as thick as a bus, can transmit light like window glass. Engineers at Bell Labs tested lasers with this glass to great effect, leading to fiber optics. With fiber optics, we have the combination of information technology and communication technology, thus leading to the Internet. Information technology became information and communication technology (Rosenberg, 2000, pp. 63–65).

I mentioned the competition between electric vehicles and gasoline vehicles over 100 years ago. Why did gasoline vehicles overcome electric vehicles? The main reason is the endless technological innovations related to gasoline vehicles, including improvements in gasoline quality, engine improvements, the invention of gear transmissions, and the invention of the carburetor nozzle. The most important is the increase in engine efficiency. The engine weight to power ratio (weight per watt) was 270g/W for the Otto engine in 1880, 40g/W for the Daimler-Maybach engine in 1890, 8.5g/W for the Mercedes engine produced by Maybach in 1901, and 5g/W for the Ford Model T in 1908. After World War I, the engine continued to improve, finally reaching 1g/W. In other words, 98% of the weight-per-watt efficiency gains between 1880 and 1960 were achieved before World War I (Smil, 2005, p. 128). Whether electric vehicles can replace gasoline vehicles in the future mainly depends on breakthroughs in battery technology. Battery technology breakthroughs are uncertain.

In the war of the currents, why did AC beat DC? Because complementary technologies related to alternating current appeared, such as induction motors, inexpensive alternating current meters, rotary converters (converting high voltage alternating current to low voltage direct current), and the invention of transformers. Nikola Tesla's induction motor turned alternating current from pure lighting into power. The transformer made it possible to transmit electricity over long distances with ultra-high voltage (Smil, 2005, pp. 84–89).

Before the year 2000, the television market was dominated by cathode picture tubes. Several different types of new television technologies then emerged. Among them, rear-projection television and plasma television were the most promising, but by 2010, LCD televisions dominated the market.[6] The success of LCD televisions is largely due to the "fusion-formed glass" produced by Corning. The British

[6] "Organic light-emitting diode" (OLED) is the latest display screen technology. LED television is actually still an LCD screen, but the backlight is changed from the original CCFL fluorescent lamp to white LED lighting, thus it is also called WLED (white light-emitting diode).

developed liquid crystals for display electronics as early as 1973, which
were used in the displays for portable calculators and electronic
watches. The display screen's material is the application bottleneck.
Traditional materials (ordinary glass) cannot produce qualified large-
screen television displays. Corning engineers believed that the way to
break through this bottleneck was to use fusion-formed glass. Between
2000 and 2010, Corning's continuous and substantial improvement in
the quality of fusion glass broke through this technical barrier. In fact,
Corning produced a car windshield using this process as early as the
1960s, but the results were disappointing. The product never came to
market until it unexpectedly found a use as an LCD screen (Marsh,
2012, p. 96).

Uncertainty Caused by Politics, Culture, and Policy

Schumpeter said that innovation is "creative destruction." What did he
mean by destruction? It means that some people's interests will be
harmed because new technologies and products will replace old technologies and products. Those harmed by innovation might resort to a
variety of means to resist innovation, including political and legislative
means or public opinion, even violence.

In addition to vested interests, traditional culture and customs can
also become obstacles to innovation. Schumpeter said:

This reaction may manifest itself first of all in the existence of legal or
political impediments. But neglecting this, any deviating conduct by a
member of a social group is condemned, though in greatly varying degrees
according as the social group is used to such conduct or not. Even a deviation
from social custom in such things as dress or manners arouses opposition,
and of course all the more so in the graver case. This opposition is stronger in
primitive stages of culture than others, but it is never absent. Even mere
astonishment at the deviation, even merely noticing it, exercises a pressure on
the individual ... this resistance manifests itself first of all in the groups
threatened by innovation, then in the difficulty finding necessary cooperation, finally in the difficulty in winning over consumers. (Schumpeter,
1934, pp. 86–87)

In fact, as pointed out by economic historian Joel Mokyr, 'innovation' was originally a term of abuse because innovators invariably
disrespected the ideas, institutions, thinkers, and rulers revered by
most. Only after the Enlightenment did innovation become a term of

praise (Mokyr, 2009, p. 33).[7] Even if innovation came to be commended today, however, it did not protect innovative practices from hostility and resistance. Cyril Smith, a historian of technology, said: "every innovation is born into an uncongenial society, has few friends and many enemies, and only the hardest and luckiest survive."[8]

At best, uncertainty induced by political, cultural, and policy considerations slows the diffusion of innovation. At worst, it leads to a complete failure of innovation or even the destruction of the innovators themselves.[9]

William Lee was a graduate of Cambridge University and invented the stocking frame in 1598. The equipment was too expensive for an individual to own, so workers had to go to Mr. Lee's residence, leading to the the beginnings of a factory. His machine, however, was considered a harmful innovation because it threatened the workers that knitted manually. With people out to harm him, Lee was forced to find refuge in France with a few workers. Thanks to the protection of Henri IV, Lee set up a factory in Rouen. Lee died in Paris (Mantoux, 1928, pp. 191–192).

John Kay was a weaver from Bury, England. In 1733, he invented the flying shuttle, which not only could weave faster, but also weave wider cloth. This angered the other weavers, who accused him of trying to deprive them of their livelihood. In 1738, he went to Leeds and was met with horrific hostility. Manufacturers were eager to use his invention but refused to pay the royalties he wanted. Lengthy litigation resulted, which caused Kay to go bankrupt. In 1745, he returned to his hometown, Bury, but his opponents followed him there. A riot occurred in 1753, with a mob sacking his house. The wretched inventor hid in a sack of wool to flee to Manchester, then took a boat to France (Ibid. pp. 206–208).

James Hargreaves invented the spinning jenny in 1765. In 1767, he produced a few machines for sale "and at once fell a victim to that unpopularity which inventors in those days seldom escaped." Workers in the city of Blackburn broke into his house and destroyed his machines. He moved to Nottingham, but certain dishonest merchants

---

[7] Mokyr attributes this observation to Peter Gay who noted innovation's meaning changed from a negative to a positive. See Gay (1969), p. 3.

[8] Quoted from Taylor (2016), p. 213.

[9] For various examples of people resisting innovation, see Mokyr (2002), chapter 6; Juma (2016), Chapter 2.

refused to pay him. He sued them, but because the spinning jenny was sold before the patent, his patent rights were declared invalid (Ibid. pp. 216–219).

The steam coach appeared early on in England. On July 27, 1829, Goldsworthy Gurney (1793–1875), an English inventor and entrepreneur, tested the first steam coach on the road, reaching speeds of 14 miles per hour. This was two months earlier than the Rainhill Trials. After successful tests, in 1831 he began providing a passenger service between Cheltenham and Gloucester. He obtained financing. Later, dozens of steam coach companies appeared in England. The speed of steam coaches continuously increased as technology improved. Some observers estimated they could reach speeds of 50 miles per hour. The commercial operation of steam carriages, however, came to anger too many people, including traditional passenger horse-drawn carriage operators, sellers of oats, stable owners, road trustees, horse breeders, road-adjacent farmers, and new railroad operators. These people petitioned Parliament, alleging that steam coaches were unsafe, boilers were prone to explosions, wheels damaged roads, the noise frightened pedestrians and horses, sparks ignited crops on the side of the road, and so on. As a result, Parliament and local governments imposed heavy taxes and various regulations on steam coaches. The most notorious of them was the Red Flag Act, which required a person to precede any steam coach in motion by 60 yards with a red flag to warn pedestrians and other carriages. This made steam coaches slower than humans, so steam coach companies went bankrupt (Taylor, 2016, pp. 183–186).

We generally associate tea with Chinese culture and coffee with Western culture. In fact, tea entered Europe no later than coffee, which is native to East Africa and first became popular in Turkey. When coffee was introduced to Europe, it was met with strong resistance. England's first coffeehouse was established at Oxford University in 1650 by Lebanese merchants from the Ottoman Empire. Whose cheese did coffee move? To borrow a phrase from Spencer Johnson, coffee "moved the cheese" of beer halls, dealers of tea and other beverages, as well as the guardians of traditional culture. Their efforts prompted the authorities to impose strict regulations on coffeehouse operating hours and banned takeouts. The University of Cambridge stipulated that students must obtain professor approval to go to coffeehouses, otherwise they will be punished. An Englishman wrote a pamphlet proclaiming that if British people drink coffee, they will degenerate into Turks. In the eyes of the British, the Turks were barbarians and only they drank coffee. Citing "national security," Charles II in December 1675 declared that all cafes in the country must close down by January 10 of the following year. The popularity of coffee in continental Europe was also fraught with ups and downs. The Swedish Parliament repeatedly considered imposing a heavy tax on coffee in the period between 1870 and 1914, with the debate only ending after World War I (Juma, 2016, Chapter 2).

Bi Sheng invented movable-type printing around 1040, but it did not catch on. In 1445, Gutenberg invented the printing press, which soon became popular in Europe. In the Islamic world, the printing press was subject to persistent and strong resistance. In 1485, Sultan Bayezid II issued a decree prohibiting the printing of books in Arabic script. In 1508, the Shaykh al-Islam issued a *fatwa* allowing non-Islamic communities to use movable-type printing, but the Islamic community could not. In 1515, Sultan Selim I reinforced the edict, making it punishable by death. Why? There were hundreds of thousands of scribes for the Koran. They had high status but risked losing their jobs once printed books became available. This inevitably led to their resolute resistance. They said that the Koran is sacred and must be copied by hand, whereas printing it by machine defiles it. Under this thinking, printed scriptures could not be sold locally. The first printed version of the Koran appeared in Egypt in 1832, nearly 400 years after Gutenberg invented the printing press (Ibid. chapter 3).

Today, in the 21st century, 'innovation' has become a trendy word and a symbol of the spirit of the times. A few people oppose "innovation" abstractly, but innovation is always specific and there will always be people who resist specific innovations. Some people boycott online ride-hailing. Some people boycott Internet finance. Some people boycott group buying. Some people boycott Bitcoin, and so on. Many boycotts often come under the guise of public interest, national security, human health, or cultural identity, when in fact there are vested interests behind them. The government's regulation of online ride-hailing in China is a typical example. The profits made by traditional taxi companies actually come from license rent. If there are no restrictions on online ride-hailing, taxi companies' license rent will disappear. The price of a taxi license will drop to zero. Therefore, both taxi companies and taxi drivers who bought their licenses are motivated to prevent the emergence of online ride-hailing.[10] The rationale for the introduction of strict regulatory policies (especially the "Beijing citizens and Beijing cars" policy in Beijing) is the safety of consumers. One passenger incident can be a reason for stopping all operations. In fact, everyone knows that online ride-hailing is much safer than traditional taxis.

For Chinese entrepreneurs, policy uncertainty is perhaps the biggest uncertainty. What is legal today may not be legal tomorrow. What can be done today cannot be done tomorrow. Policies change between day and night. Implementation can be strict or lenient.

I would like to stress one point in particular. The uncertainty of international politics is closely related to the conflict of values. Whether it is Sino-US relations or Sino-European relations, conflicts to a large degree originate from values, not commercial interests. The conflict of values causes many innovations to encounter resistance from the government and the market. We can see this from the boy-cotts of Huawei, TikTok, and WeChat in the United States and Tesla in China. All of these are related to the conflict of values, which is a big challenge for entrepreneurs. I discuss this point in Chapter 16.

The Market as an Error Correction Mechanism

The uncertainty of innovation means that we have no way to innovate according to prior plans. Innovation can only rely on entrepreneurs "crossing the sea with Eight Immortals, each showing their magical powers." Innovation can only be decentralized decisions, with each entrepreneur making his own judgment. Therefore, the planned economy and innovation are incompatible. The basic feature of a planned economy is centralized decision-making, a mechanism in which a small group of people have the final say. Industrial policy is also incompatible with innovation because industrial policy assumes that innovation is predictable.

Policymakers make mistakes under any mechanism. In fact, entre-preneurs often make mistakes. Almost all entrepreneurs have made

---

[10] I myself openly criticized at a forum the imposition of restrictions on online ride-hailing in 2015. Shortly after the forum, a letter jointly signed by more than 30 taxi companies and government regulation offices was sent to Peking University leaders, asking the university to punish me. I was charged of defaming the taxi drivers.

mistakes. The difference is that in a market economy, the market itself is an error correction mechanism. Any entrepreneur who makes a mistake, and puts himself in financial trouble, provides other entrepreneurs with the opportunity to make money. Therefore, entrepreneurs are the most motivated to not only correct their own mistakes but also to discover other people's mistakes. Under the planned economy, however, it is not a rational choice. Instead, concealing mistakes is a rational choice. Therefore, small errors will accumulate into large ones.

Everyone knows about Elon Musk trying to take humanity to Mars. Should we worry about this type of person being an entrepreneur? No, because his resources are limited. He obtains resources based on other people's consent. If consumers do not buy products or investors do not invest money, then Musk can only stop.

However, it is not hard to imagine that if Musk took hold of government resources, and the allocation of these resources was not restrained, then disasters would occur. For example, imagine Musk decided to initiate human immigration to Mars and send one million people there. If the first attempt fails, then the people on the spaceship will die. As an entrepreneur, he would have to stop another attempt until a safer solution is found. He has no way to force other passengers to join the second attempt. However, if he was a dictator of the political regime, he might consider it the cost of the lesson. He will continue to make one attempt after another. In the end, he might successfully send one million people to Mars, but millions of people become guinea pigs.

Therefore, we should thank the market economy. It can encourage the most creative and ambitious people to create wealth for society, but also guarantees that these people (entrepreneurs) do not bring about fatal disasters. The concept of China's 'whole nation force' system might be advantageous for dealing with unexpected, external crises, but it is unable to encourage innovation and even might lead to disaster.

11 | *The Airship and Airplane Duel*

Today, people take an airplane for basically all long-distance domestic travel, not to mention international travel. No means of transportation is faster, more convenient, or safer than an airplane. However, in the decades before the end of the 1930s, airplanes had a strong competitor: Airships. At the time, it was not clear who would be the winner.

In the end, airships lost out to airplanes due to a series of reasons related to technology, economics, politics, and war, but especially to the entrepreneurs involved. However, this is an after-the-fact assessment. From the beforehand perspective, airships were not destined to be unsuccessful. This example best exemplifies that the future is uncertain and indeterminate and the consequences of innovations are unpredictable. It also shows the essential role of imagination in entrepreneurial decisions.[1]

Humanity's Two Paths to the Sky

Airplanes and airships are both flying machines, but their operating principles are different. Airplanes are heavier than air. Airships are lighter than air. Simply put, an airship is lifted by gas that is lighter than air (hydrogen, helium, or hot air) whereas an airplane is lifted by movement that creates a difference in air pressure above and below the wings.

Humanity dreamed of flying like a bird for a long time. It is said that in about 400 B.C., the Greek Archytas designed and created the first flying machine. It was shaped like a bird, possibly propelled by steam, and flew about 200 meters. Some people suspect this flying machine was hung in the air from a wire.

---

[1] The materials of this chapter are drawn from the following references, of which Alexander Rose's book is the main one: Hammack (2017); Hiam (2014); Rose (2020); Vaz and Hill (2019).

Due to limitations of knowledge, technology, and raw materials over a long period of history, the dream of flying was unrealistic. However, the Industrial Revolution made flying more and more possible, so some inventors were eager to try.

The earliest flying machines to be tested were lighter than air. For example, in 1784, French inventor Jean-Pierre Blanchard attached a hand-driven propeller to a hot air balloon. The next year, he successfully flew over the English Channel. In 1852, French engineer Henri Giffard created an airship driven by steam and flew 27 kilometers.

In addition to lighter-than-air flying machines, people also tried to make heavier-than-air flying machines. In 1799, the British scientist George Cayley was the first to propose design concepts that used fixed wings to create lift and propulsion and to control an aircraft. To prove the effectiveness of his theory, he built and tested a glider in 1849. For this reason, he is called "the father of aviation." Between 1867 and 1896, German inventor Otto Lilienthal made many gliders based on Cayley's theories and experiments. He used his glider in over 2,000 flights until he died on August 9, 1896 after falling 17 meters.

Did airships or airplanes have the most hope of allowing humanity to fly?

Until the end of the nineteenth century, many observers appeared to be more optimistic about airships than airplanes. Airships were like clouds and could float in the air, whereas airplanes were like birds and relied on their own power to take off and land.

Engineers and scientists generally believed heavier-than-air flight was impossible. *Scientific American* bet on airships. In December of 1899, *Scientific American* referred to heavier-than-air flying machines as "a very hazardous and fatal form of recreation" and "nothing more than a wonderfully ingenious toy." It argued that unless pilots could think like birds and respond immediately to a continuously changing environment, the airplane would never become "a machine of commercial or military utility."[2]

Zeppelin and the Wright Brothers: The War of the Cloud and Birds

Scientific American appeared correct. Seven months after it made the judgment described above, German inventor Count Ferdinand von

---

[2] *Scientific American*, "Airship or Aeroplane – Which," December 9, 1899.

Zeppelin's airship LZ-1 successfully flew on July 2, 1900. The LZ-1 was the first rigid-framed, controllable airship with passengers. Thus, it is considered to be the first true airship.

Ferdinand von Zeppelin was an aristocrat that rose to the rank of general in the German army. Zeppelin steadfastly believed that airships not only had military uses, but also had immeasurable commercial value. At the age of 52, he was discharged from the army, so he turned his attention entirely to airships. He petitioned the German government for funding to develop airships, but a military commission determined the idea was "practically useless." He then created a joint stock company to raise funds. After more than a decade of effort, he finally succeeded. His name became synonymous with airships.

However, reality quickly proved *Scientific American*'s judgment was very incorrect.

Three years after the successful test flight of the LZ-1, the American Wright brothers flew the *Flyer* I at Kitty Hawk, North Carolina on December 17, 1903. The *Flyer* I was the first true airplane. It relied on its own power to take off and was controlled by the pilot. It proved that humans do not need to think like a bird but can fly like a bird.

At that point, from a technological perspective, lighter-than-air airships and heavier-than-air airplanes were both feasible.

However, in terms of performance, Zeppelin's LZ-1 was far better than the Wright brothers' *Flyer* I. During the test flight, the LZ-1 carried a crew of five, reached an altitude of 410 meters, flew for 17 minutes, and covered 6.3 kilometers (or a speed of 27 kilometers per hour). The first flight of the *Flyer* I only carried one pilot, reached an altitude of three meters, covered 37 meters, and only flew for 12 seconds (or a speed of 10.9 kilometers per hour). In later test flights, the *Flyer* I could not come close to the LZ-1 in terms of flying time, altitude, distance, or speed.

From that point on, Count Zeppelin and the Wright brothers continued to improve their products. Between 1905 and 1909, Luftschiffbau Zeppelin GmbH produced the LZ-2, LZ-3, LZ-4, and LZ-5. The company received financial support from the government and the military acquired the LZ-3. German Emperor Wilhelm II inspected the company's facilities. An accident that destroyed the LZ-4 turned out to be a blessing in disguise for Count Zeppelin because the company received 6.5 million marks worth of public donations. The reason was Germans regarded the multiple successful flights of the LZ-4, especially the 12-hour flight over Switzerland, as the pride of the nation. The business of Count Zeppelin was the business of the German nation!

In sharp contrast to this, the Wright brothers' airplane did not receive much attention from the American government and public. Certain people in the media, including the editor of the *Scientific American*, even doubted the authenticity of their invention. In 1905, the brothers wrote letters to the governments of the United States, Britain, France, and Germany hoping to sell their airplane, but there was no interest. For a long time, the European media accused the Wright brothers of fraud. In August of 1908, Wilbur Wright made multiple successful flights in France. Only then did they make a name for themselves and instantly become "World Heroes." A French company quickly established a purchase contract. At the same time, Orville Wright lost control of the aircraft during a test flight from Fort Myer, near Washington, D.C. Orville broke his leg in the crash and Lieutenant Thomas Selfridge, the passenger, died. In July of 1909, with the help of Wilbur, Orville performed a flight that fulfilled the Army's requirements (carry a passenger, fly for one hour at an average speed of 40 miles or 64 km per hour, and land safely). The US Army paid $30,000 for the plane.

The "war of the cloud and birds" between the airship and the airplane became a rivalry between Count Zeppelin and the Wright brothers. Neither side was willing to recognize the other as a true competitor, but at the same time was jealous of the public attention the other side received. In an interview in 1908, Count Zeppelin said the airship was superior to the airplane as a means of transportation because the airplane's altitude and range of movement were limited.

In August of 1909, Orville Wright met Count Zeppelin for the first time at a party hosted by the German Emperor. They both congratulated each other on their success, but during an interview a few days later, Orville Wright commented that the airship had already reached the limit of its capabilities. The airship was like the steam engine whereas the airplane was like the internal combustion engine. The airship was the past and the airplane represented the future. Count Zeppelin commented privately that the Wright brothers' machine was nothing more than a sports toy. It was suitable for performing in front of an audience, but in the end would be nothing more than a footnote in the history of aviation. Wilbur Wright wrote in an article that the airship would quickly become a thing of the past and Count Zeppelin had wasted all his money in spending it all on airships.

After the Wright brothers, a number of airplane companies quickly sprang up. In 1911, just in the United States there were 146 airplane manufacturers and 114 different airplane engines. However, before World War I, in terms of altitude, speed, flying time, load, or safety, airplanes could not compete with airships.

When the airplane could still only do air shows, airships already began commercial operations. In light of Luftschiffbau Zeppelin's difficulty obtaining military orders, in 1909 the company decided to use airships for inter-city commercial passenger service and founded the German Airship Travel Corporation (abbreviated in German as DELAG). The Hamburg America Line was the largest investor in DELAG, which obtained the exclusive right to sell airship passenger tickets.

Between June 22, 1910 and July 14, 1914, DELAG made 1,588 commercial flights, accumulated 3,176 flight hours, traveled 172,535 kilometers, and carried 34,028 passengers. Although there were a few accidents, no deaths occurred, which can be considered a miracle in the history of aviation.

After the start of World War I, airships and airplanes were both used in battle. The German military converted all nine of DELAG's airships into weapons of war. During the war, Luftschiffbau Zeppelin built 91 new airships for the military. Airships were primarily used for reconnaissance and pelting London and Paris with bombs.

However, despite the German military's hype about the threat of the airship, the damages caused by airships on the enemy was limited. During the war, property damage in Britain caused by airship bombing was £1.5 million. An estimate in early 1918 of Germany's total expenditures on airship manufacturing, maintenance, manpower, hanger construction, gas production, and fuel reached £13.25 million. Germany put 100 airships into the war but only had 16 left when the war ended in November 1918. The number of enemy fatalities caused by all airship bombings was less than half the number of people that died in the torpedoing of the ocean liner RMS *Lusitania* by a German U-20 submarine in May 1915 (557:1,198). Actually, the number of airship crew fatalities was close to the number of casualties inflicted on the Allies.

In addition to airships' weaknesses as a weapon of war (such as the impact of the changing climate and low accuracy), a major reason for the limited effect of airship bombing was great improvements made to airplanes during the war. Airships were easily attacked by airplanes. For example, Britain's B.E.2c fighter produced in 1915 had a maximum speed of 72 miles per hour and a maximum altitude of 10,000 feet. The Sopwith Camel produced in 1918 had a speed of 113 miles per hour and could reach 19,000 feet. A typical fighter in 1915 took 45 minutes to reach an altitude of 10,000 feet but newer models only needed less than eight minutes to reach 15,000 feet. By 1917, airships could perform bombing missions between 16,000 and 18,000 feet but new models of British fighters could fly to an altitude of 17,300 feet.

Of course, during World War I, airships also improved by leaps and bounds. A typical airship engine in 1914 was 630 horsepower. By 1918, it was 1,820 horsepower, three times higher than in 1914. Over the same period, airships' maximum flight radius increased from 2,000 miles to 7,500 miles, useful lift increased from 9.2 tons to 44.5 tons, maximum altitude increased from 6,000 feet to 21,000 feet, continuous flight time increased from 22 hours to 177.5 hours (calculated using a stable speed of 45 miles per hour), and maximum flying speed increased from 47 miles per hour to 77 miles per hour.

The Eckener–Trippe Duel

In the early 1920s, airships and airplanes were considered parallel technology. Neither side had an impact on the other. The common view was that airships were suitable for long distances and airplanes were suitable for short and medium distances.

However, two people held views on the opposite extremes of each other. One was the German entrepreneur Hugo Eckener and the other was the American entrepreneur Juan Trippe. Eckener was fanatically in the "airship faction," believing the airship was the only feasible and effective means of air transport. Trippe was steadfastly in the "airplane faction," believing that even in transoceanic flights airplanes would certainly beat airships. Competition between airships and airplanes in the 1920s and 1930s was to a large degree a duel between Eckener and Trippe.

Eckener was born in 1868 and was 30 years younger than Count Zeppelin. He studied experimental psychology at university and was a local newspaper journalist and editor. He was assigned to cover the first flights of the LZ-1 and LZ-2. His report on the problems that occurred during the airship flights included some criticisms that caught the attention of Count Zeppelin. The Zeppelin Airship Company hired Eckener as a part-time publicist. Eckener was moved by Count Zeppelin's perseverance and quickly became an airship fan. He joined the company full time and assumed important positions.

After Count Zeppelin passed away in 1917, Eckener became his successor. Eckener wanted to resume airship production and passenger transportation plans after the end of World War I. However, because the Treaty of Versailles gave the remaining airships to Britain, France, and the United States as war reparations and prohibited Germany from producing airships larger than one million cubic feet, his plan was frustrated. The company almost began to produce consumer goods.

Coincidentally, two airships awarded to the United States were intentionally destroyed by the company's workers so they would not become war trophies. Eckener used this opportunity to bring the company back to life, maintain airship production capacity and technology, and retain technical personnel. He proposed using Zeppelin's company to produce the new airships that would compensate the United States. The American and German governments did not oppose the plan, and the British government could only reluctantly agree with the added condition that military airships could not be produced.

Zeppelin's company produced the ZR-3 (later renamed the USS *Los Angeles*) for the United States. Eckener personally flew it from Friedrichshafen, Germany directly to the U.S. Naval Air Station at Lakehurst, New Jersey. The flight covered 4,867 miles and lasted 81 hours. The ZR-3 had a crew of 43 and could carry more than 20 passengers. It had the longest service length among all US Navy rigid airships.

After piloting the airship to the United States, Eckener was warmly welcomed in New York with a parade. He became a hero in the hearts of Americans. Eckener made a special trip to a training school for airplane pilots. He told the trainees that after graduation, none of them would find a job.

Eckener's judgment that airships would beat out airplanes seemed to be based on sufficient facts. That same year, the US Army Air Service used five Douglas World Cruisers (a single-engine, two-seat biplane) to circumnavigate the world. The trip took 175 days and they made 69 stops. Even the Boeing 40A, introduced in 1927, could only carry two passengers.

How could the airplane outcompete the airship?

In 1925, the Allies ended the prohibition on Germany's production of large airships. Eckener and his Zeppelin company had a tremendous opportunity. After the Weimar government refused to provide support, Eckener traveled the country to raise funds to manufacture *Graf Zeppelin*. The new airship could reach speeds of 128 kilometers per hour, had a flight radius of 10,000 kilometers (calculated using an average speed of 117 kilometers per hour), could carry a crew of 36 and 24 passengers, and had an effective load of 8.7 tons.

Eckener personally piloted *Graf Zeppelin* on a flight that departed Friedrichshafen, Germany on October 11, 1928 and arrived in Lakehurst, New Jersey on October 15 with a crew of 40 and 20 passengers (among them were four paying passengers at a cost of $3,000 per person). The trip lasted 111 hours and 38 minutes and the return trip lasted 71 hours and 51 minutes. The flight time was much shorter than the sailing time of any steamship.

Eckener became "Columbus of the Sky."

American pilot Charles Lindbergh had already completed the first solo, non-stop flight across the Atlantic when he flew a single-engine plane from New York to Paris in 1927. However, in Eckener's view, this was just Lindbergh's personal adventure to win applause, but did not mean that airplanes could provide profitable and sustainable transatlantic travel. In order to fly continuously for 3,600 miles, Lindbergh's plane was filled with fuel, a few life-sustaining sandwiches, and nothing much else. He also did not dare to fly the plane back to New York.

To further demonstrate the powerful flying capabilities of the airship, Eckener departed in August 1929 from Lakehurst, New Jersey for the first flight to circumnavigate the world. *Graf Zeppelin* made stops in Friedrichshafen, Tokyo, and Los Angeles before returning to Lakehurst. The return trip to Friedrichshafen brought the entire trip to 41,268 kilometers and a total flight time of 345 hours and 42 minutes. The longest portion, from Friedrichshafen to Tokyo, was 11,247 kilometers and took 101 hours and 49 minutes. The trip from Tokyo to Los Angeles was 9,653 miles long and took 79 hours and three minutes. It was the first non-stop transpacific flight.

Eckener changed from "Columbus of the Sky" to "Magellan of the Sky."

After circumnavigating the globe, the *Graf Zeppelin* began scheduled flights forming a transatlantic triangle between Germany, Brazil,
and the United States.

Juan Trippe was 31 years younger than Eckener. He was born in
1899 in New Jersey to Northern European immigrants. While studying
at Yale University, he became fascinated with airplanes. During World
War I, he joined the US Navy Reserve. In 1920, he joined the National
Intercollegiate Flying Association and served as treasurer. After gradu-
ating from Yale University, he found a job on Wall Street but got tired
of it and founded Long Island Airways. In 1927, he founded the
Aviation Corporation of the Americas, which later became Pan
American Airways (Pan Am). Investors in the company were his
friends and Yale classmates.

Airplanes at that time were primarily operated for the US Postal
Service. Competition was already fierce for domestic routes, so Trippe
wanted to make more money on international routes. He used various
methods to obtain local flying privileges from Caribbean and South
American governments. Establishing many international routes from
North America to the Caribbean and South America turned Pan
Am into the first airline to operate intercontinental flights.

Trippe also expanded the aviation business from purely mail delivery to passenger transport. Under his leadership, Pan Am continuously
ordered new planes, recruited excellent pilots, and established new
routes. It quickly became the flagship carrier of the American aviation
industry and made an important contribution to promoting the development of aircraft transportation.

Trippe's greater ambition was to open transatlantic flights. At that
time, only a dozen or so large-scale steamboat companies were providing transatlantic passenger and cargo transportation. A one-way trip
took six or seven days. Eckener's triangular transatlantic airship flights
not only competed with Trippe's Pan Am flights between the United
States and South America but also might have made Trippe's plans for
transatlantic flights just a dream. When Frederick Rentschler, Trippe's
former partner and co-founder of United Aircraft and Transport
Corporation, formed a partnership with Eckener to throw millions of
dollars at airships, Trippe felt particularly attacked.

Actually, after Eckener successfully completed triangular transatlantic flights, everyone knew Trippe was hopeless! However, Trippe
believed people were praying to the wrong god. They mistakenly

believed the current state would sustain, but he saw the future. He firmly believed the rapid advancement of aircraft technology would make the airship's advantages disappear.

Trippe decided to go head-to-head with Eckener. He needed new airplanes, ones that were bigger and could fly longer distances. The most advanced airplane at the time, the Sikorsky S-40 with 38 passenger seats, did not satisfy his needs.

It must be said here that new, more advanced airplanes were requirements proposed by the airlines themselves. Airplane manufacturers did not take the initiative to produce them. In this sense, Trippe's contribution to the advancement of the airplane manufacturing industry was enormous.

On June 26, 1931, Trippe wrote a letter to the six largest airplane manufacturers, inviting them to produce a new generation of airplanes for Pan Am. The specific requirements were: A multi-engine flying boat with a flying radius no less than 2,500 miles facing 30 miles per hour headwinds.

Four manufacturers quickly responded saying that kind of airplane was technologically impossible. The other two companies were Sikorsky Aircraft and Glenn L. Martin Company. Sikorsky Aircraft was a long-term partner of Pan Am. After extensive, in-depth technical consultations, Trippe decided to purchase three S-42 airplanes from Sikorsky Aircraft for a unit price of $242,000. At the same time, Trippe also ordered three M-130 airplanes from the Glenn L. Martin Company for a unit price of $417,000. He paid sky-high prices for new airplanes at a time when the airplanes used in US domestic routes cost about $78,000.

Sikorsky and Martin were both outstanding inventors and entrepreneurs. Martin was known for innovative designs. The M-130 airplane he planned to produce was 91 feet long, had a wingspan of 130 feet, was powered by four engines each with 830 horsepower, had a range of 3,200 miles (more than Trippe's specification), could carry 36 passengers, had a maximum speed of 180 miles per hour, and could reach an altitude of 10,000 feet.

The S-42 and M-130 were both delivered in 1934. The original plan was to use them for transatlantic flights. However, according to a previous aviation rights agreement with British Imperial Airways (primarily related to traffic rights in Newfoundland), both parties had to start Atlantic routes at the same time. Because Imperial Airways still

· had not produced a suitable airplane, Trippe could not establish transatlantic routes. Given the situation, Trippe decided to first establish transpacific routes.

However, the Pacific is wider than the Atlantic. More stops are required along the way. In order to establish Pacific routes, Pan Am first built the hotels and basic infrastructure required for flights on Midway Atoll, Wake Island, and Guam. Among them, Wake Island was originally uninhabited and an unknown coral island that Trippe himself found out about in a library book.

On April 16, 1935, the S-42 took off from San Francisco, California toward Hawaii on its first survey route to China. On November 22, 1935, the M-130 (later renamed *China Clipper*) departed from San Francisco and made layovers in Midway, Wake Island, and Guam before landing in Manila on November 29. The entire trip was 7,517 miles and flight time was 59 hours and 48 minutes.

In October 1936, Pan Am formally established scheduled weekly passenger flights between San Francisco and Manila, Philippines. In 1937, an S-42 flew from Manila to Hong Kong. Trippe also purchased shares in China National Aviation Corporation and provided aviation services within China.

On July 5, 1937, Pan Am's S-42 and Imperial Airways' *Caledonia* took off at the same time in opposite directions and successfully flew across the Atlantic, then returned. Two years later, Pan Am established successive transatlantic passenger flights to Portugal, Britain, France, and other countries.

The Hindenburg Disaster and the End of the Airship Era

As airplane aviation advanced by leaps and bounds, Eckener and his airship business faced new challenges. These challenges were primarily related to politics, not technological or commercial aspects.

In the Weimar Republic's 1932 presidential election, Eckener was considered by the Social Democratic Party and others as the candidate with the best chance of beating Adolf Hitler. Eckener had domestic and international prestige and anti-Nazi beliefs. In the end, because President Hindenburg decided to seek another term, Eckener did not pursue it further. However, his status as a potential presidential candidate angered Hitler and the Nazi Party. After Hitler came to power in January 1933, Eckener did not conceal his criticisms of the Nazi Party.

Hitler wanted to arrest him but was blocked by President Hindenburg. Joseph Goebbels, the Nazi Propaganda Minister, wanted to use airships for Nazi propaganda. Eckener disapproved, so the Nazis blacklisted and marginalized him. Nominally, Eckener was the chairman of his two companies, but the real power was controlled by Ernst August Lehmann, a pro-Nazi internal rival.

Eckener's enthusiasm for airships, however, was not diminished by Nazi suppression. His professional talent was also indispensable for the company. He still had the opportunity to participate in the design and manufacture of airships. After *Graf Zeppelin* entered commercial operations, Eckener began manufacturing the LZ-129 airship. The LZ-129 was larger than *Graf Zeppelin* and was designed especially for transatlantic transport. Some people proposed naming the LZ-129 after Hitler, but Eckener proposed *Hindenburg*. Even Hitler could not oppose the name because Paul von Hindenburg was Germany's most respected politician. Not only was he the former president, he was also a hero of World War I.

The first test flight of the *Hindenburg* was in March 1936. It was piloted by Eckener himself with a crew of 47 and carried 87 passengers. During the opening ceremony of the 1936 Summer Olympics, the *Hindenberg* was displayed over the Berlin Olympic Stadium. In 1936, the *Hindenberg* undertook 17 transatlantic roundtrip flights in total. Ten trips were made to America and seven were made to Brazil. During one stop in New York, Eckener made a "Millionaires Flight" with wealthy and famous passengers. Juan Trippe was invited and rode in the airship.

Lehmann, the general manager of Zeppelin Company, announced that the company would have no less than four airships by 1940 operating between Europe and the Americas. The company was also considering providing airship passenger transportation to India and Asia.

In March 1937, the *Hindenberg* began its first triangular transatlantic flight. At that time, Trippe was traveling around the world with his wife and was in Europe. He suddenly decided to take the *Hindenburg* from Frankfurt, Germany to Rio de Janeiro, Brazil instead of taking a scheduled steamship. To avoid explosive media reports such as "Pan Am Boss Takes Airship across the Atlantic," they used fake names: Mr. and Mrs. Brown.

After a smooth arrival in Rio de Janeiro, Trippe told his wife the final days of the airship was coming soon and airships would not exist in five years.

Even Trippe did not think the final days of the airship would come so quickly!

On May 6, 1937, the *Hindenburg* arrived above New York. At 7:25pm, the rear of the airship suddenly ignited while landing in Lakehurst, New Jersey. The flame turned into a complete burn in only 37 seconds. Of the 97 people on board, 35 people died and many of the rest were seriously injured. Captain Lehmann died the day after the disaster. Eckener was not in the airship.

The disaster marked the end of the era of airships. The *Graf Zeppelin* was quickly grounded. Later, Hermann Goering ordered it scrapped. The upcoming LZ-130 (*Graf Zeppelin* II) was never put into use.

After the crash, even the US government was criticized because it did not sell Eckener helium. Airships of the past used hydrogen gas, which was highly flammable. Helium is a substitute for hydrogen because it provides similar lifting power but does not ignite. While manufacturing the *Hindenburg*, Eckener decided to use helium to avoid a possible disaster caused by flammable hydrogen. However, at the time, only the United States had the ability to produce helium and the cost was high. To buy helium, Eckener even wrote a letter to President Roosevelt requesting assistance. Due to Nazi aggression, the American government worried helium would be used for military purposes, so in the end it refused Eckener's request. People have said that if the *Hindenburg* had been filled with helium, the disaster might not have happened.

Here, it is necessary to review the development of airships in other countries.

After World War I, the passion to develop airships ran through France, Britain, the United States, and other countries. The Allies awarded Germany's L-72 airship to France as war reparations. France renamed it *Dixmude*. Because there was no operating manual, the French had no choice but to learn on their own. After a few successful flights, in December 1923 the airship and its 53 crewmembers went missing over the Mediterranean. France's passion for airships ended.

In early 1919, England produced its own airship and completed the first round-trip flight across the Atlantic. The R-34 was actually a "knock-off" of Germany's L-33, which the British captured during the war. After deciding long-distance passenger flights were not possible with airplanes, in 1923 the British government, led by the Conservative Party, launched the "Imperial Airship Scheme." They wanted to use airships to link different parts of the British Empire together. The British government decided to form a fleet of large airships and the manufacturer, Vickers, prepared to accept £4.8 million in government funds to satisfy the need. However, the Conservative Party did not have enough time to implement the plan before the Labour Party took power. The Labour Party's Secretary of State for Air, Lord Christopher Thomson, was a staunch airship advocate. The Labour government leaned toward giving the Air Ministry a choice between an airship by the privately owned Vickers and one by the state-owned Royal Airship Works. The better performing operation would produce more airships. The R-100 was manufactured by Vickers and was labeled the "Capitalist" airship. The R-101 was manufactured by the Royal Airship Works and was labeled the "Socialist" airship.

To demonstrate the superiority of socialism, the funding for the R-101 was almost unlimited. In the end, the cost of the R-100 was £337,000 whereas the R-101 was £527,000. The R-100 was completed first but was only allowed to be unveiled after the R-101 was finished. These two airships were the largest in the world at that time. The R-100's flight speed was 81 miles per hour and had a flight radius of 6,338 miles. If it entered commercial operations, it could carry 140 passengers. On July 29, 1930, the R-100 departed for Montreal, Canada. The trip took 79 hours and the airship returned safely.

On October 4, 1930, the R-101 began its first flight toward India. After flying 397 miles over seven and a half hours, the airship crashed near Paris, France. Of the 54 people on board, 48 died. The most prominent person among the dead was Lord Thomson, Secretary of State for Air. Much of the blame for the crash lays with Lord Thomson. He rushed the R-101 through the required test flight and ordered the flight toward India for his own political achievement and to show the superiority of the "socialist airship." As a result, his own life was taken.

After the R-101 crash, the British government decided to sell the R-100 as scrap metal for less than £600. Britain never again developed airships.

William Adger Moffett's passion for airships was even greater than that of Lord Thomson's. Moffett was a rear admiral in the United

States Navy and was the architect of American naval aviation. Through his efforts, America not only accepted the German-built USS *Los Angeles* (as war reparations), but also produced the USS *Shenandoah*, *Akron*, and *Macon* airships.

USS *Shenandoah* (ZR-1) was the first airship to use helium. Its first flight was in September 1923 and later it successfully crossed North America, giving the US Navy experience with rigid airships. In September 1925, during the *Shenandoah*'s 57th flight, the airship was destroyed in a storm over Ohio.

USS *Akron* (ZRS-4) was an airship that also used helium and entered service in September 1931. It was the first airship aircraft carrier because it could launch and recover fighter planes while in flight. In the early morning of April 4, 1933, the *Akron* was caught in a storm off the coast of New Jersey. Only three of the 76 people on board survived the wreck. Rear Admiral Moffett was among the casualties.

USS *Macon* (ZRS-4) was the *Akron*'s sister ship and entered service in 1933. During maintenance off the coast of California, the *Macon* ran into a storm and hit the water. The airship sank and two crew members were lost.

After the *Akron* and *Macon* accidents, the US government lacked heavyweights such as Rear Admiral Moffett to advocate for airships. America never produced another airship. The workers producing airships at the Goodyear factory were let go.

From the accidents described above, people easily get the impression that airships lost out to airplanes to a large degree because airships had too many accidents. Actually, there were not fewer airplane accidents than there were for airships. From 1908 until the outbreak of World War I, the United States alone had more than 500 people die in airplane wrecks, whereas 40 people died in airship accidents. During the 16 months between January 1, 1936 and May 1, 1937, domestic aviation accidents killed an average of six people every month in the United States and there were no less than 10 serious airplane crashes during the period. In just the two-week period between December 15 and December 30, 1936 there were five airplane wrecks causing 41 deaths. Between January 25 and March 2, 1937, another 29 people died in airplane crashes. (These statistics are limited to scheduled flights. Confirmed deaths in 1936 and 1937 for private airplanes had reached a total of 541.)

By comparison, the *Graf Zeppelin* did not have one passenger or crew member die between its first flight in 1928 and its last flight in 1937. Over nearly a decade, that airship flew 144 transoceanic flights (143 over the Atlantic and one over the Pacific) covering 1.70 million kilometers and lasting 17,177 hours (716 days). It transported 13,110 passengers and carried 106,700 kilograms of mail and material.

Perhaps the main reason for the airship's final defeat was the difference in technological innovation, especially the invention and continuous improvement of jet engines. Jet engines made airplanes fly higher, faster, and further with more passengers. Airplane travel was safer and more comfortable, eroding the airship's traditional advantage.

However, the emergence of jet engines was not predicted. Frank Whittle invented the gas turbine when he was a pilot officer of the U.K. Royal Air Force (RAF) and applied for the patent in 1930. The Air Ministry even refused to pay the £5 renewal fee for his patent, because it was thought valueless either in military or commercial applications.[3]

Will Airships Make a Comeback?

During World War II, the Zeppelin Company transitioned to producing airplane components. Eckener lived in seclusion, occasionally making an appearance to earn a living. After the Royal Air Force bombed the airship manufacturing facility and his home, Eckener and his wife had to move in with their daughter. After the war, Eckener was invited to visit the United States for a few months by a few American friends passionate about airships. That was the first time he traveled to and from the United States on an airplane. When he previously visited the United States, he always piloted an airship himself.

During his 85th birthday party in 1953, he told his followers and admirers that the airplane had beat out the airship; and expecting the airship to still have a chance was like thinking the automobile might give the road back to horse carriages.

Eckener passed away on August 14, 1954.

Except for a short dispute with large shareholders in 1939 and 1940, Trippe controlled Pan Am until he retired in 1968. During World War

---

[3] For the story of Whittle's invention of the jet engine, see Smil (2006), pp. 66–70; and Jewkes et al. (1969), pp. 262–266.

II, Pan Am cooperated closely with the US government and military. The company made a tremendous contribution to transporting Allied military supplies and personnel. Many of the pilots that flew "The Hump" to support China in its war against Japan came from Pan Am.

Fourteen months after Eckener passed away, Trippe ordered the first 707 from Boeing. In October 1958, Pan Am's first Boeing 707 began scheduled flights from New York to Paris. The airplane's speed was 600 miles per hour and could carry 135 passengers with a flying altitude of 32,000 feet. The flight radius was 4,000 miles and the maximum takeoff weight was 168 tons.

In 1965, Trippe asked his old friend William M. Allen, the president of Boeing, to design and build an aircraft "much larger than" the 707. The end result was the Boeing 747. Even though the Boeing 747's length was less than one-third of the *Hindenburg*, its passenger capacity and flight speed were six times higher with an equivalent flight radius.

Trippe predicted the Boeing 747 would in the end be replaced by the supersonic airplanes under development at the time and would be relegated to cargo transportation. However, after entering use in 1969, the 747 quickly became the symbol of transoceanic travel and is still the flagship aircraft of passenger aviation. Supersonic airplanes were not as successful as Trippe predicted. As mentioned in Chapter 9 of this book, the Concorde was successfully manufactured in 1969 and formally entered commercial operations in 1976 but ended operations in October 2003.

Over 100 years ago, Count Zeppelin, the inventor of the airship, predicted that the airplane would just be a footnote in the history of aviation. Looking back more than 100 years later, contrary to his prediction, the airship became a footnote in aviation history.

Will airships return? It is hard to say. After all, more than 100 years ago, petroleum vehicles defeated electric vehicles, but today electric vehicles have the potential to replace petroleum vehicles. In fact, there are indeed occasional calls for the revival of airships and some people put those calls into action. Due to new and improved materials and technologies, they say future airships will be very energy efficient, especially for long-distance freight. At the very least, airships have unique advantages in humanitarian rescue, tourism, climate and environmental monitoring, and wireless communication in remote areas.

From the long historical perspective, it is difficult to determine what innovation has a future and what does not. Perhaps the best way is to leave it to entrepreneurs to judge, and the market will make the final assessment!

12 | Entrepreneurship and Industrial Policy

Industrial policy refers to selective intervention and discriminatory treatment in different industries by the government, either for economic development or for other purposes (such as national security), within the production of private goods. It is intended to support some sectors and restrain others. Measures include market access restrictions, investment scale controls, credit and funding rationing, tax incentives and fiscal subsidies, import and export tariffs, non-tariff barriers, land price concessions, etc.

The key words here are "private goods" and "selective intervention." Government investment in public goods is not part of industrial policy, although differences of opinion exist between economists on what are public goods. General policies are also not part of industrial policy.[1] A unified corporate income tax is not an industrial policy, but supportive income tax relief is. Patent protection is an intellectual property issue but is not part of industrial policy. Regional policy is also not an industrial policy, although it is often accompanied by industrial policy.[2]

The role of industrial policy in economic development has been disputed in economics and policy fields for a long time.[3] In China, the debate between advocates and opponents has recently boiled over as the government increasingly takes industrial policy as the national

---

[1] Although economists have different definitions of industrial policy, "selective intervention" is a basic feature of industrial policy. See Pack and Saggi (2006).

[2] In the debate on industrial policy, Justin Lin, a strong advocate of industrial policy, gives an overly broad definition of industrial policy (Lin, 2016). According to his definition, almost everything the government does is industrial policy. He includes such things as the government's investments in public goods, infrastructure, education, and scientific research, as well as patent protection and establishing the rule of law, within industrial policy. See Lin (2016). In this way, criticisms of industrial policy are tantamount to an anarchist denying the role of government. This is not conductive to discussions of the issue.

[3] For a review on different arguments up to 1999, see Kosacoff and Ramos (1999).

strategy of development. Justin Lin and I are the representatives of each side.[4] Partly in response to China's industrial policies, the American government has also introduced industrial policy in past decades in one way or another. Examples include the legislative passage of the CHIPS and Science Act and the Inflation Reduction Act overseen by President Biden. The United States' response further provokes the Chinese government to be more stubborn in its industrial policy. So, the industrial policy of different countries can re-accelerate each other.

Below, I will discuss four points. The first is the paradigmatic differences between supporters and opponents of industrial policy. The second is the two reasons for industrial policy to fail. The third is externalities and coordination failures not constituting justifiable reasons for industrial policy. The fourth is "the theory of comparative advantage strategy" being logically and historically inconsistent. My main viewpoint is that true understanding of entrepreneurship will undermine the foundation of industrial policy.

The Disagreement between the Two Market Paradigms

The disagreement between advocates and opponents of industrial policy is actually a disagreement between the two different market theory paradigms. One is the "neoclassical economics paradigm" and the other is the "Mises–Hayek paradigm." The neoclassical paradigm is a "design paradigm" whereas the Mises–Hayek paradigm is an "evolution paradigm" (Mises, 2007[1949], Hayek, 1991[1988], Smith, 2008).[5]

Neoclassical economics understands the market as a resource allocation tool. To prove the allocative efficiency of markets, certain strong, but unrealistic, assumptions are necessary. When these assumptions are not satisfied, a so-called market failure occurs, including market failures caused by externalities, imperfect competition, or information asymmetry.

---

[4] A widely reported open debate between Justin Lin and Weiying Zhang took place at Peking University on 19 November 2016. See, e.g., Issaku Harada, "China's great industrial policy debate rages on," https://asia.nikkei.com/Economy/China-s-great-industrial-policy-debate-rages-on. This chapter is largely the revised version of my arguments presented at that debate.
[5] The Mises–Hayek paradigm is also called the Austrian paradigm. See Chapter 5 of the current book.

The neoclassical economics' concept of market failure is the theoretical foundation for most supporters of industrial policy. Justin Lin (2012) states so clearly. In response to Ha-Joon Chang's criticism of him for being "too faithful to neoclassical economics" and unable to liberate "himself from the shackles of neoclassical economics," Lin defended himself by saying:

Neoclassical economics is simply a useful tool in all this, not a constraint. It is flexible enough to model the externalities, dynamics, and co-ordination failures that give the government a role to play, while also providing the metrics to judge whether government is supporting industries that take the economy too far from its areas of comparative advantage. Without the former, developing countries may lack the wisdom to seize opportunities to develop competitive industries and lay the foundation for sustainable industrial upgrading and development. But without the latter, as the historical record emphasizes, governments can make any number of costly mistakes. (Lin, 2012, pp. 133, 137)[6]

My evaluation of neoclassical economics is not as high as Lin's. I argued earlier that neoclassical economics is not a good market theory. As pointed out by Buchanan and Vanberg (1991), neoclassical economics is a misconception of the market. It treats the market only as an allocation process of given resources, rather than a discovery process of knowledge and a creative process of imagination. So-called market failure is actually a failure of (neoclassical) market theory, not a failure of the market itself. The market theory developed by Mises and Hayek is a better analytical paradigm.

The difference between the neoclassical paradigm and the Mises–Hayek paradigm is prominently manifested in the acknowledgement of the role of entrepreneurs, as we discussed in Chapter 5. The market in neoclassical economics is a market without entrepreneurs. Neoclassical assumptions make the existence of entrepreneurs have no value. If preferences, resources, and technologies are given and information

---

[6] It is interesting that, on the one hand, Lin builds his own arguments on a foundation of market failure theory in Western mainstream economics but, incomprehensibly, on the other hand, he launches high-profile criticisms of other people for "unfeasible imitation of mainstream Western economics" in China. See Lin (2016). Why is neoclassical theory an invincible "artifact" in his hands but a vulnerable "myth" in the hands of others? I do not understand what Lin means when he says "imitation," but in my view, if anyone is "imitating," then he is definitely one of them.

is perfect, then there is no uncertainty and each person is equally intelligent, so of course there is no use for entrepreneurs.

In the Mises–Hayek paradigm as well as Schumpeterian framework, the entrepreneur is the protagonist of the market. Discovering and creating opportunities for transactions are the basic functions of the entrepreneur. Entrepreneurial discovery and arbitrage of disequilibrium leads the market toward equilibrium. Entrepreneurial innovation causes the market to continuously create new products and new technologies that drive the continuous upgrading of the consumption structure and industry structure.

Economists who believe in the neoclassical paradigm sometimes use the term "entrepreneur." However, their version of an "entrepreneur" is nothing more than a calculator: Given ends and means, calculate the optimal input and output according to the "marginal revenue equals marginal cost" rule. Such a decision does not require imagination, tact, or judgment. From a true entrepreneur's perspective, however, imagination, tact, and judgment are essential. As we will see, industrial policy debate is strongly related to the different understandings of entrepreneurship.

I should be fair to neoclassical economics. Although neoclassical economics is not a good market theory and can easily mislead our understanding of the real market, it is still a useful tool for analysis of some policies. In particular, in the 1970s, the Public Choice School used the neoclassical economic paradigm to develop the government failure theory. To a certain extent, this corrected the fallacy of market failure theory, which no longer constituted a sufficient justification for the government to intervene in the economy. The supporters of industrial policy emphasize market failure, but barely touch upon government failure. In their theories, government officials are omniscient, omnipotent, and fully dedicated to others over their own interests! They hardly tell us why government officials are more capable and proactive than entrepreneurs in judging the future.

Why Is Industrial Policy Destined to Fail?

I have pondered industrial policy for a long time. In the mid-1980s, Japan's industrial policy was highly praised by certain Chinese economists and government officials. During the summer of 1987, I was part of a delegation from the Economic System Reform Institute of China for a half-month visit to Japan. After this visit, I came to the conclusion that the popular views in China on Japanese industrial policy were unrealistic for two reasons. The first was the overestimation of the role of Japan's industrial policy. The second was the incorrect assessment of the method. The reason Japan's early industrial policies did not lead to disastrous consequences was that mistaken industrial policies were always resisted by entrepreneurs.[7] The automobile industry is a typical example. Without the resistance of Soichiro Honda and others, the Japanese automobile industry would not be what it is today.

Although many early studies portrayed Japan's industrial policy as a model of success, after the 1990s, numerous more comprehensive studies came to a different conclusion: Japan's industrial policy was generally a failure. For instance, Michael Porter and his co-authors used detailed information to show that in Japan's 20 most successful industries, industrial policy played no role, or was very minimal. Conversely, in Japan's seven least successful industries, industrial policy had a major impact (Porter, Takeuchi, and Sakakibara, 2000). After the 1980s, mistakes abounded in Japan's industrial policy, including fifth-generation computing research and development, analog technology, mobile communications, and others that were led astray by industrial policies.[8] The mythical Ministry of International Trade and Industry was shattered.

Pre-reform China implemented a planned economy. After reforms, industrial policy replaced planning targets. Scholar-officials Liu He and Yang Weimin had this to say in their book *China's Industrial Policy: Theory and Practice*:

Planning is industrial policy and industrial policy is planning. Both embody the government's intervention in economic life and resource allocation." (Liu and Yang, 1999, p. 31)

Since the 1980s, China has experienced many examples of industrial policy failures, but very few successes. Even Justin Lin does not deny this. Which structural imbalances and overcapacity in China's economy are not the result of industrial policy guidance?

[7] See Zhang Weiying (2006[2014]).
[8] See Takashi Yunogami's 2013 book published in Japanese by Bungeishunjū Ltd. A Chinese-language version was made available by the China Machine Press in 2015 (Yunogami, 2015).

I have tried to find the theoretical reasons that industrial policies fail. I discovered that the reason industrial policies fail is the same reason the planned economy failed. In short, the failure of industrial policy is due to, first, the limitation of human cognitive ability and, second, incentive mechanism distortion.[9] In more general terms, one reason is people's ignorance and the other is due to their shamelessness. The limitation of cognitive ability is more fundamental than the incentive mechanism.

Cognitive Limitations

One basic assumption of industrial policy supporters is: Technological progress and new industries are predictable, and therefore can be planned. This assumption is completely wrong. New industries always come from innovation. History has shown that innovation and new industries are unpredictable. The reason is the process of innovation contains a series of uncertainty. There is no statistical law for innovation to follow. The uncertainty of innovation makes it impossible to foresee the results of experimentation and from there formulate a path to a specific goal in advance. We do not know the destination of the journey, so we can only continuously correct mistakes as we go. Objectives can be misleading, since we do not actually know the steps required to reach distant goals, as argued convincingly by Stanley and Lehman (2015). "Hindsight is 20/20" for economist's analysis of innovation and industrial development. If innovation can be predicted, then it is not innovation! No one from 30 years ago predicted the dominant industries of today (new energy, biopharma, AI, etc.) and the events of 30 years from now cannot be predicted.[10]

The unpredictability of innovation means that the freedom of economic experimentation is the only way to achieve innovation. Vacuum tubes and transistors were invented with no inkling of their potential use in computation, but proved crucial in creating and commercializing the

---

[9] I systematically expressed my views in the keynote speech titled "Why Is Industrial Policy Destined to Fail?" given to the Yabuli China Entrepreneur Forum Summer Summit on August 25, 2016. The full text of the speech can be found on the webpage: www.yicai.com/news/5153303.html.

[10] For questions about the government's difficulty in obtaining the information needed to formulate industrial policy, see Sanjaya Lall (2004). Also see Pack and Saggi (2006); Easterly (2013), chapter 12; and Rosenberg (1994), chapter 5.

computers successfully. The computer became possible only because it was not planned. That is what Hayek meant when he talked about the "independent efforts of all people" with different knowledge and different opinions, instead of locking oneself on a predetermined path.[11]

This is the advantage of decentralized decision making. Each entrepreneur decides to do or not do something based on his or her own alertness, imagination, and judgment. He may be right or wrong. Market competition determines success and failure. Successful innovation brings about profit and is continuously applied and spread, becoming a point for new growth. Failed experiments are stopped.

Industrial policy is centralized decision-making, which means society's resources are concentrated on the goals selected by the government. This is a big gamble! There is a negligible chance of success but the cost of failure is great and certain. If each person has a 90% chance of making a mistake, when 10 individuals separately make decisions, then the probability of them all making a mistake at the same time is only 34.9%, so the probability of at least one person succeeding is 65.1%. As long as one person succeeds, then the product is available for society. Alternatively, if a collective decision is made, the probability of success is only 10%.

Government officials do not have the alertness and judgment of entrepreneurs. This is an indisputable fact. Even if they did, they do not have the same incentives as entrepreneurs. Experts are also incapable of formulating industrial policies. Experts are not entrepreneurs. In regard to innovation, they might have the necessary hard knowledge but they lack the required soft knowledge. Relying on entrepreneurs to formulate industrial policy also cannot succeed because success of the past is not a guiding light for the future. Innovations that have a major impact on economic development usually come from unknown entrepreneurs rather than already successful business leaders. Many glorious enterprises went out of business due to the disruptive innovation of new and more innovative entrepreneurs. In addition, entrepreneurs differ over what industries and technologies will be promising and

---

[11] Limitation on the government's ability to make industrial policy is an application of Hayek (1937) and his theory of knowledge. See Hayek (1948), chapters 2, 4, 7–9.

the majority are very likely wrong, as we saw in the cloud computing debate in Chapter 10.

Allow me to cite a study by Jiang Xiaojuan in the 1990s to illustrate the problem of expert decision-making. In the early 1980s, electric fan production was in "catch up" mode at the time, so the Ministry of Machine-Building and Electronics Industry invited a number of well-known domestic experts in production technology, market analysis, and economic management to discuss countermeasures. Based on extensive research and analysis, these experts believed that China's annual electric fan production capacity should be maintained at about 10 million units over the next few years. They advocated selecting a few strong enterprises as "designated producers." The supervisory departments formulated corresponding policies. In practice, however, there was a big gap between the experts' forecast and reality. The market for electric fans and their production scale expanded rapidly. The actual production and sales of electric fans in the early and mid-1980s were twice as high as the forecast. By the late 1980s, annual output and sales of electric fans reached 50 million units, of which exports alone reached 10 million units. After a few years of fierce competition and survival of the fittest, the structure of the electric fan industry became more reasonable. Production is concentrated among a few brand-name enterprises, but not according to the original model envisioned. Jiang Xiaojuan concluded that the use of "scientific" procedures and methods in the formulation of many industrial policies has not led to their "scientific conclusion" occurring (Jiang, 1993, pp. 3–18).

Some people argue that although innovations and new industries are unpredictable, so industrial policy might fail, industrial policy may work well for mature industries to be developed in developing countries, given that developed countries have shown the way for these industries. My answer to this argument is that there is no need for industrial policy in mature industries. While government officials may have better judgment on mature industries than new industries, they cannot be better than entrepreneurs themselves. There is no reason to say that the importance of some mature industries is recognized by the government but not by entrepreneurs. The opposite is more likely true. China's automobile industry is an example. Mr. Li Shufu, a grassroots entrepreneur of Zhejiang Province, foresaw very early the industry would boom, so he applied for a license to make cars in 1992. But his application was rejected by the State Planning Commission simply because "China has enough car makers." Mr. Li started his automobile business about 10 years after his first application.

Incentive Distortions

Industrial policies create power rent through discriminatory market entry requirements, taxes and subsidies, financing and loans, land concessions, import and export licenses, and other methods for different industries and firms. This necessarily leads to rent-seeking behavior from entrepreneurs and government officials.[12] From a practical point of view, both the formulation and implementation of industrial policy is full of a series of rent-seeking activities. The promulgation of a specific industrial policy is not so much the result of sciences and cognition as it is the result of interest games. As a consequence, the entrepreneurs who receive policy support are often not true innovation entrepreneurs, but instead are policy arbitrageurs and rent-seekers. Fraudulent payments for new energy vehicles is a typical example.[13] It is not difficult to understand that the firms taking money from the government have no respectable innovation to show for it!

The unpredictability of innovation means that industrial policies are bound to make mistakes. Government officials and experts, however, are generally unwilling to acknowledge their own mistakes because mistakes expose their own ignorance. One way to conceal mistakes is to provide more support to failed projects. The result is one mistake after another! On the contrary, entrepreneurs in the free market are unable to conceal their own mistakes. They also have no power to prohibit others from proving they are wrong!

Let me explain this point using the telecommunications industry as an example. There are three international standards for 3G telecommunications: CDMA2000, WCDMA, and TD-SCMDA. TD-SCDMA was claimed as China's "proprietary" technology. Before it was officially adopted as the applied standard for 3G in China, the CEOs of the three major telecom operators and two successive Ministers of

---

[12] For rent-seeking theory, see Krueger (1974). For cases of rent-seeking in developing countries, see Jomo (1990). For China's rent-seeking in industrial policy, see Yang (2013), pp. 1–9.

[13] A government survey shows that many so-called new energy car makers get government subsidies by faking sales numbers. See Zhang, Jie (2016).

Information and Industry (Wu Jichuan and Wang Xudong) all opposed it because the technology was thought to be very immature. It should be said that their judgment was correct. In 2006, however, a dozen or so distinguished fellows of the China Academy of Sciences (CAS) jointly signed a letter in support of TD. The CAS fellows enjoy a very prestigious position in China. With their joint letter, then-President Hu Jintao endorsed it. In the end, China Mobile was required by the government to adopt the TD standard. After TD became the model for the "innovation country," all objections were eliminated. It was not until 2014, when *Caixin Weekly* published a series of articles about "TD-style innovation," did the truth begin to come out. The way to conceal the mistaken decisions about TD was to speed up 4G. In fact, China Telecom's CDMA2000 and China Unicom's WCDMA had just been put into use and were far from saturation. There was no need to replace them with 4G immediately. The TD mistakes and premature phase-out of 3G wasted trillions of yuan, but no one has been held responsible.[14]

The incentives of government officials and entrepreneurs are very different. For entrepreneurs, losses from failures and gains from successes are their own. When government officials act, successes do not have a similar monetary gain, whereas failures might come with a certain career risk (even though this is not always the case). Therefore, government officials consider ways to avoid individual responsibility.

One way to avoid personal responsibility is to listen to the opinions of experts. In this way, after any problems with policies occur, they can say that they solicited the opinions of experts beforehand. Of course, the officials themselves are not responsible, or at least have an excuse. It could be said that listening to expert opinion has become an important excuse for government officials to shirk their responsibilities. Another way is to faithfully implement the policies of the higher-level government. Whatever the central government calls for, I will do. Or people "follow the trend." Whatever other people (or other regions) do, I will do. For example, if someone else makes anime, then I will make anime. If someone else makes solar energy, I will also make solar energy. This way, even if it fails in the end, everyone has failed, but I have not failed alone. Of course, I am not personally responsible.

[14] See Kan Kaili (2014).

We see, therefore, that once the central government encourages any industry, that industry necessarily experiences overcapacity and becomes crisis ridden. No government-supported industry will give up until it is totally broken.

In short, due to human cognition limitations and incentive mechanism distortions, industrial policies are doomed to fail. Actually, industrial policies will obstruct innovation because industrial policies mislead entrepreneurs, causing them to put resources into areas and projects that should not get them. The development of China's photovoltaic industry is a typical example. Japanese enterprises' investments in analog technology is another example. If entrepreneurs proceed with the government's industrial policy, there cannot be true innovation. To innovate, Chinese entrepreneurs require a rule of law environment for liberty and fair competition rather than the support of industrial policy.

Therefore, I advocate abolishing industrial policy in any form. The government should not give any industry or enterprise special privileges!

The advocates of industrial policy argue that even though many industrial policies have failed, we cannot conclude from this that the government cannot formulate the correct industrial policy. So, the issue is not whether industrial policy is needed, but rather the type of industrial policy that should be formulated. This viewpoint is similar to the viewpoint some people had in the 1980s about the planned economy. They believed the planned economy itself was not bad, but instead the planned economy had not been implemented properly! As long as the law of value and science were respected, the planned economy could work well. I hope that my two reasons for the failure of industrial policy prove that the "correct industrial policy" hoped for by its supporters has not existed in the past, does not exist today, and will not exist tomorrow.

It is necessary to say a few more words about government officials' incentive mechanism. Some people seem to believe that government officials' rent-seeking behavior can be resolved through incentive mechanism design. If this belief is not naïve, it is at least a misunderstanding of the incentive theory.

Government officials are agents with multiple roles and many goals. If we can obtain information about the consequences of all behaviors, then of course we can design an incentive mechanism that removes any room for rent seeking. In theory and in reality, however, it is impossible to obtain such information. No effective measurements of a government official's inputs and outputs are available, so there is no way to effectively motivate them. We can only implement procedural supervision and control of government officials, such as have them manage fewer things or clarify what they can and cannot do. This is the meaning of "limited government."

As far as industrial policies are concerned, there is a special difficulty for designing incentive mechanisms. The consequences of a policy take a long time to appear. A policy that looks good in the short term might be bad in the long term. The outcome of a policy depends not only on its formulation, but also on its implementation. Government officials, however, often change their positions from time to time, and it is impossible to define the personal responsibility of each official. Every official has sufficient reason to defend his or her decisions. It is difficult to distinguish whether the "holy text" is wrong or the monk reads it wrong. Who should be responsible for the mistakes of 3G? What about the photovoltaic industry policies?

The only effective incentive mechanism I can think of is: If a certain industrial policy is to be implemented, government officials and experts in favor of it should be asked to invest part of their property or use it as collateral. If they think this investment is good, here is a good chance to make a lot of money! Investing with taxpayer money will always involve serious adverse selection and moral hazard.

The best incentive mechanism can only alleviate people's incentive problem but cannot solve people's ignorance.

Externalities and Coordination Failure Do Not Constitute Reasons for Industrial Policy

The primary reasons for the defense of industrial policy are "externalities" and the market's "coordination failure." These two reasons, however, are untenable.

Some people believe that due to the positive externalities of technology, without government funding, entrepreneurs do not have an incentive to innovate. This statement is not valid in theory and is inconsistent with experience. From the theoretical perspective, it results from misunderstanding of how entrepreneurs make decisions, which is related to the neoclassical paradigm. In the neoclassical paradigm, all decisions are based on marginal analysis. Marginal analysis is important for daily management decisions, but in the real market, innovation is not a marginal issue, but an issue of life and death. Xiaokai Yang (1988) called it "inframarginal." Entrepreneurial decisions related to innovation are not primarily based on a comparison of marginal revenue and marginal cost, but instead are based on judgments of market and technology prospects or the pressure of competition and the temptation of "monopoly" profits. When Bill Gates foresaw "every family and every desk with a computer," did he calculate that using marginal revenue and marginal cost? No!

The greater the technological innovation, the less likely the decision is marginal. An innovation that brings about an expected return of one billion yuan to an entrepreneur but ¥10 billion for society does not mean the entrepreneur will not pursue this innovation. As long as the expected cost does not exceed one billion yuan, then the entrepreneur will pursue this type of innovation. Besides, and probably more importantly, as we argued in Chapter 2, the goal of entrepreneurs is not just making money. Their decisions are not just based on calculation of expected profits. Building a commercial kingdom, surpassing rivals, and the joy of creation, all play an important role in innovations, a role even bigger than pure profit. Assuming that neoclassical economists assume profit is the only concern of the entrepreneur does not mean that in reality entrepreneurs are motivated only by profit. When Matthew Boulton invested in James Watt's invention of the steam engine, he wanted to sell steam engines to the entire world, not obtain the entirety of the positive externalities brought about by the steam engine. When Bill Gates created the software industry, he sought to have his software on every person's computer, not to have all of the benefits brought about by software.

The externality argument is inconsistent with the facts. According to the neoclassical theory that externalities lead to market failure, technological progress is necessarily slowest in the free market, if it is not entirely impossible. However, the experience of the last 200 years has proven technological progress is fastest under the free market.

Without government funding, Watt and Bolton still invented and produced the steam engine, George Stephenson and his son Robert invented and produced the first steam locomotive, Carl Benz and Gottlieb Daimler invented the automobile, the Wright brothers invented the airplane, Thomas Edison invented electric light, Alexander Graham

Bell invented the telephone, IBM invented the computer, Bill Gates produced Microsoft Windows, Pony Ma provided us with a free micro-messaging system (WeChat), and Jack Ma provided the Taobao trading platform. The list goes on and on. Nobody can deny that all these innovations have large social externalities. Entrepreneurs are willing to undertake these types of innovations, so I do not know what other innovations would not be done without government subsidies.

One shall not underestimate the adventurous spirit of entrepreneurs. Entrepreneurs take risks based on convictions and vision, not calculation. Anyone who is only willing to innovate with government subsidies is a rent-seeker at best, but not a true entrepreneur at all! Subsidizing this type of person will lead to people like Mr. Nanguo, the man who pretended to play a wind instrument in the Kingdom of Qi's royal orchestra during the Warring States period. He was revealed incompetent by the new king when the orchestra members were asked to do solo performances. To incentivize innovation, we need a patent system and effective protections for intellectual property, not government subsidies!

Furthermore, the unpredictability of innovation means the government does not know "who is the first person to eat crab" because they do not even know what "crab" looks like.[15] The government should not obstruct "crab eating" but there is also no need to pay the bill for "crab eating." That will induce people to pretend to "eat crab" when in fact they are eating steamed buns in the shape of crab. The experience gained from eating steamed buns is meaningless for eating crabs!

Coordination failure is another reason for industrial policy. This is also a misunderstanding of the market mechanism and entrepreneurship. Coordination is a function of entrepreneurs (Kirzner, 1992, chapter 1). The so-called coordination failure is nothing more than a manifestation of market disequilibrium. Disequilibrium means arbitrage opportunities exist, so the greater the coordination failure, the bigger the profit from correcting it. One of the major functions of entrepreneurs is finding disequilibrium in the market, then engaging in arbitrage so that the market trends move toward equilibrium. In reality, countless entrepreneurs coordinate supply and demand. The ability to coordinate determines an entrepreneur's ability to make money and succeed! Let me provide a few examples.

---

[15] Lin (2016) vividly compares innovators to "the first person to eat crab" and believes the government should subsidize that type of person.

Jack Ma's Alibaba coordinates hundreds of millions of buyers and sellers, so it earns a lot of money. When I buy watermelons from a street stall, I can pay with WeChat thanks to Pony Ma. Frederick Smith founded FedEx because a coordination failure existed in postal delivery. Despite obstacles from the US Postal Service, he achieved success and created a new logistics model. SF Express is also an example of entrepreneurs resolving coordination problems.

The history of the planned economy proves that government coordination is not more effective than market coordination. Under the planned economy, the State Planning Commission and State Economic Commission were busy all day and the production enterprises hustled, but consumer goods were in short supply everywhere. Under the market economy, we have what we want. Given such a sharp comparison, I do not understand why some people still believe the government is more capable than the market in coordinating economic activity. In my observation, the markets where entrepreneurship is suppressed – by the system or policies – are markets with serious coordination failures!

The Paradox of "Comparative Advantage Strategy Theory"

It is necessary to discuss the so-called comparative advantage strategy theory. In the industrial policy debate in China, Professor Justin Lin uses "comparative advantage strategy" to defend industrial policy. He argues that industrial policy based on comparative advantages is the only correct industrial policy. This theory is logically contradictive, however, and does not conform to the experienced facts.

Dani Rodrik, a professor of international political economy at Harvard University, is right when he commented: "Lin wants to argue both for and against comparative advantage at the same time, and I cannot quite see how this can be done" (quoted from Lin, 2012, p. 54). In my view, Lin is trying to use Ricardo's free trade theory to prove Friedrich List's nationalism.

In Adam Smith and Ricardo's time, the British government implemented mercantilist trade protectionist policies. The goal of both Smith's absolute advantage theory and Ricardo's comparative advantage theory was to prove that free trade will make each country's advantage play a role without interference from the state. This will benefit both parties to the transaction, whereas trade protection

policies are detrimental. Since that time, the theory of comparative
advantage has become the theoretical cornerstone of free trade.

One consequence of Ricardo's use of the nation as a unit of analysis
is that it seems that comparative advantage is a matter of the nation.
Actually, comparative advantage is an individual or firm matter, not
the nation's. The essence of international trade is trade between individuals or firms. Countries cannot exchange with each other unless
they are planned economies. Therefore, there is no need to include the
state in analysis of the benefits of comparative advantage (Mises,
1949, chapter 8).

Comparative advantage is actually just "core competitiveness" in
management studies. Abiding by comparative advantage is a basic
behavioral principle for market participants, which does not require
a national strategy. As Adam Smith said, the meaning of market
competition is each person engaging in the work they do best for the
greatest gain while at the same time allowing others to complete the
work they do best. Any entrepreneur that does not produce or
exchange according to comparative advantage will fail. Even the average person knows to utilize his or her comparative advantage. Blind
storytellers and masseuses are classic examples. Only idiots will violate
comparative advantage.

In the traditional trade theory, comparative advantages are determined by factor endowments. The import and export structure of
various countries, however, shows that the majority of industries with
comparative advantages are unrelated to factor endowments. Factor
endowment determination theory assumes that capital and labor
(including talent) do not flow between countries. When capital and
talent are mobile, the importance of factor endowments will decrease
significantly, if not disappear.

Further and more importantly, the reason factor endowments are
not essential is that comparative advantages, in reality, are dynamic
and endogenous. They are a process of learning and practice. Dynamic
comparative advantages are primarily created by entrepreneurs, not
endowments. Alternatively, entrepreneurs are the most important,
most precious resource. Lin, however, completely ignores the importance of entrepreneurs in determining comparative advantage. Allow
me to use two examples to explain this point.

The first example is the British textile industry. Britain did not have
resource endowments for the textile industry, because its soil is not

suitable for growing cotton and the quality of cotton grown in the country is very poor, but textiles became the leading industry of the British Industrial Revolution. The industry was created from scratch by British entrepreneurs through numerous innovations, including John Kay's flying shuttle, John Wyatt's spinning machine, James Hargreaves' spinning jenny, Samuel Crompton's spinning mule, and Sir Richard Arkwright's spinning frame and modern industrial factory. Of course, the British government made a "contribution." In 1700, the British government banned the import of cotton fabrics from India, China, and Persia. Two decades later, "all persons resident in England were forbidden to sell or to buy these fabrics, or to wear them or to have them in their possession, under penalty of a £5 fine for private persons and £20 for merchants" (Mantoux, 1928, p. 205). The goal of the prohibition was to protect the wool industry, not develop the cotton industry! Unintentionally, it protected a strong cotton textile industry!

The second example is the automotive industry in the United States and South Korea. Americans did not invent the automobile. Until 1904, France was the world's largest automobile manufacturer. Starting from that year, the US' production output exceeded France's. The gap quickly expanded from there. By 1933, 73% of global automobile output came from the United States. Germany and France accounted for 4% and 8%, respectively (Easterly, 2013, p. 302). The reason the United States surpassed Germany and France was, to a large degree, due to the success of Henry Ford's assembly line innovation. It had nothing to do with the United States' factor endowment.

South Korea's automobile industry competitive advantage was created by entrepreneurs like Chung Ju-yung, the founder of Hyundai Motor Group. Mr. Chung originally worked in the automobile repair business, and later shifted to car making. It is interesting to note that Lin once thought that South Korea's development of automobiles violated its comparative advantage because South Korea's factor endowment structure at that time was not suitable for the development of the automobile industry. He concluded that South Korea had failed in this regard.[16] He wrote on the topic in 2001, a difficult period for South Korea's automotive industry after the East

---

[16] Lin expressed this point of view in a lecture at the University of Chicago on May 14, 2001. Chapter 6 of his book *New Structural Economics* (Lin, 2012) was adapted from this speech.

Asian Financial Crisis. By the 2010s, however, South Korea had become the world's fourth-largest automotive exporter. Automotive exports account for 8% of total export revenue.[17] I wonder how Lin can explain that? His basic method of argument is: If it succeeds, it is because comparative advantage was utilized; if it fails, it is because it ran counter to comparative advantage. He did not expect the examples that appear to be failures – at the time of his writings – to later succeed.

Similar to the automobile industry, South Korean comparative advantage in the semiconductor industry today comes from the entrepreneurship of Lee Byung-chul, the founder of Samsung Group, and his son Lee Kun-hee, but has nothing to do with South Korea's factor endowments (Miller, 2022, chapter 23). Because comparative advantages are created by entrepreneurs, a country can have different comparative advantages from time to time, depending on its entrepreneurs' choices.

Lin believes that China's economic success over the last 40 years or so was the result of China transitioning from a catch-up strategy to a "comparative advantage strategy." This is not in line with the facts.

China's development over the past 40 years is indeed related to the utilization of comparative advantages, but this is the result of spontaneous actions of entrepreneurs during the process of economic liberalization, marketization, privatization, and globalization. It has nothing to do with the government's development strategy. Lin does not seem to approve of liberalization, marketization, and privatization. In an article published in 2016, he said: "The secret to the success of the Chinese path was breaking the myth of neoliberalism's so-called liberalization, privatization, and marketization" (Lin, 2016).

As far as I know, the Chinese government has formulated many industrial policies since the 1980s, but it has not formulated any "comparative advantage strategies." Town and village enterprises (TVEs) are a typical example of utilizing comparative advantages. But they emerged spontaneously, not as a result of the government-designed strategy. By the early 1990s, labor-intensive products produced by TVEs had become important export products. Before 1992, however, the central government repeatedly suppressed TVEs because of their "high energy consumption, high pollution, and low efficiency."

---

[17] For Chung and development of the South Korean automobile industry, see Easterly (2013), pp. 261–274.

The State Planning Commission explicitly banned the sale of important means of production and the granting of loans to TVEs. The economic adjustment that began in 1989 also focused on a TVE crackdown.

Half of China's exports come from foreign investment. Foreign investment comes to China to utilize comparative advantages. This only requires opening up, not industrial policies.

The examples listed above, and many others, prove that comparative advantage is created by entrepreneurs in the market. Natural comparative advantage is almost negligible, because only geography is immutable and everything else changes with development. If we want to utilize comparative advantage, free markets plus entrepreneurs are sufficient. A national strategy is not required to utilize comparative advantages, unless everyone is an idiot. If everyone is an idiot, how can bureaucrats be smart enough to establish a strategy? The fact of the matter is anything the government can see clearly has already been seen by entrepreneurs in the free market. Anything entrepreneurs in the free market do not see clearly, the government will see even less clearly. Industrial policy blurs the vision of entrepreneurs and entices them to be rent-seekers. It does more harm than good.

If you want to counter comparative advantage, you need a national strategy. Looking back on history, most industrial policies formulated by governments were intended to counter the existing comparative advantage. Japan's industrial policy was once highly applauded, but the Japanese government targeted higher income elasticity industries, such as machinery, electronics, and automobiles, rather than the industries Japan had a comparative advantage in, such as textiles. In the 1970s, the Japanese government began to target the high technology industries in order to assure Japan was at the forefront of technological development, which had nothing to do with Japan's factor endowments (Porter, Takeuchi, and Sakakibara, 2000).

The comparative advantage Lin talks about is not a comparative advantage that appears in the market, but is instead a comparative advantage based on his own judgment. This is the only way to resolve the logical contradiction of the "comparative advantage strategy theory." Comparative advantage in his theory is determined by factor endowments. He also says, however, that factor endowments and comparative advantages are expressed through market prices. If the comparative advantage is not based on his own judgment, but instead appears in the market, then his strategy is only to follow the market.

He not only wants the government to lead the market, but also to follow the market. Lin's original words were: "For [firms] spontaneously to enter industries and choose technologies consistent with the economy's comparative advantage, the price system must reflect the relative scarcity of factors in the country's endowment. This only happens in an economy with competitive markets" (Lin, 2012, p. 24). Besides the government having the power to distort prices, who else has the ability to distort prices? If the price system, determined by the competitive market, can reflect comparative advantage, why does the government still have to tell entrepreneurs what the comparative advantages are? Does Lin believe entrepreneurs in the market cannot comprehend market price signals, but government bureaucrats and specialists can?

In fact, there are great differences between regions in a country as big as China. A certain region's comparative advantage might be meaningful, but it does not make much sense to talk about a comparative advantage of the entire country. The difference between China's regions are even greater than the difference between some regions and other countries. Even within provinces, there are big differences between areas. For example, in Shaanxi Province, the southern, central, and northern portions differ. Is land scarce in China? Take a look at the western region, which is desolate. Is there a labor surplus in China? In the most densely populated southeast coastal areas, the supply of labor is insufficient, so it is recruited from the interior. This highlights the importance of entrepreneurs. Talk of competitive advantage removed from entrepreneurs is meaningless.

Furthermore, a country's factor endowments that determine its comparative advantage cannot tell that country which industries to embrace. What can a country having a comparative advantage in "labor-intensive industries" tell us? Nothing, because there are too many labor-intensive industries. What should and should not be done must be judged by entrepreneurs. Perhaps the most labor-intensive industry is the government. According to the theory of factor endowment-determined comparative advantage, should countries with large populations enlarge government departments? In fact, in the same country and same region, both labor- and capital-intensive industries can succeed. The textile industry is labor intensive, but in the 1980s, the six large state-owned textile enterprises in Xianyang, Shaanxi were put out of business by textile township enterprises in coastal areas. What does this have to do with factor endowments? Nothing! The only relationship is with entrepreneurship.

Globalization and technological progress have made industrial development non-linear. Which industries develop in a country, at any point in time, depends on the judgment of entrepreneurs. Even some industries in underdeveloped regions are worthy of study for advanced regions. When Columbus discovered the Americas, for example, the continent as a whole lagged Eurasia, but corn and potato cultivation was still introduced from the Americas to Eurasia.

Beware of Industrial Policy's "Self-Justification"

We must beware of industrial policy's "self-justification." A type of policy might appear to succeed but is actually wrong. Imagine, for example, the government wants to develop fox raising. Owners of foxes get financial subsidies, tax reductions, cheap land, preferential credit, and even preferential admissions for their children to go to prestigious schools. All fox-related businesses get fiscal subsidies and exemptions for taxes and fees. People who eat fox meat and wear fox furs get price subsidies. Anyone who wants to raise or eat other animals (such as pigs, sheep, and cattle) must also raise or consume a certain amount of fox. The fox industry would be very prosperous. Further, if the government passes a law stating that anyone who raises non-fox animals will be severely punished, then the fox industry will definitely become the country's largest breeding industry. However, this does not prove that the fox industrial policy is correct. This is what I mean by saying industrial policy's self-justification cannot prove it is correct.

My use of this analogy is purposeful. Currently, electric vehicles receive preferential treatment and subsidies, so they have developed rapidly. If the government uses legislation to prohibit the use of gasoline-powered vehicles and only allows electric vehicles by 2030, for example, then the elimination of gasoline-powered vehicles will be a decisive victory for electric vehicles. However, this does not prove that an industrial policy to encourage electric vehicles is correct. Using industrial policy to eliminate other options is extremely dangerous.

Looking back on the competition between gasoline-powered vehicles and electric vehicles, it was gasoline-powered cars that relied on the market to succeed. Over the last century, gasoline-powered vehicles are many times more efficient overall. In 1885, engines weighed 270 grams per watt of power (for the Otto engine), but by 2002 the weight was reduced to one gram. By comparison, the increase in electric vehicle efficiency was much slower. Changes in new technologies today or tomorrow might cause electric vehicles to completely replace gasoline-powered vehicles, but this must be determined by the market, not the government. Government policy might eliminate a technology with more potential. The potential for progress in gasoline-powered vehicles is still tremendous. We can only leave it to the market to reward and punish, not the government.

PART IV

Institutional Ecology of Entrepreneurship

13 | *What Determines the Allocation of Entrepreneurial Talents?*

The Rareness of Entrepreneurial Talents

International experiences have shown that the primary difference between poor countries and rich countries is not resource endowments, but is instead the difference in resource allocation methods. Certain relatively resource-rich countries are relatively backwards, whereas certain countries that lack resources are relatively advanced. The most typical example is a comparison between Japan and Argentina. Argentina has much more resources than Japan, but Japan's economy is much more developed than Argentina's. Russia is another example. It is the most resource-rich country in the modern world, especially in regard to natural resources, but economically it is a relatively backward country. Within a country, there is a similar dynamic. China's western region is the more resource-rich region but it is also economically backward. The coastal region does not have many natural resources, and arable land is especially scarce, but yet it is the economically developed region. Why do these countries and regions with abundant resources grow relatively slower economically? This is a case worth researching.

I want to discuss specifically the issue of talent allocation. Talent in an individual refers not only to attributes that are useful for creating value, such as education level but also innate human characteristics such as work ability and health. In any country, what is the scarcest and most valuable talent? Entrepreneurial ability. Even though in certain respects there is some entrepreneurial ability in everyone, only a small amount of the population can be called and truly become entrepreneurs. Therefore, entrepreneurs are a special category. Joseph Schumpeter used singing as a metaphor to explain the scarcity of entrepreneurial ability. He said that although any healthy person can sing – if willing – but the number of singers that can truly move us is extremely small.[1]

We can also use intelligence quotient (IQ) distribution to explain the scarcity of entrepreneurial ability within a population, although we cannot equate IQ with entrepreneurial ability. Actually, for entrepreneurs, perhaps emotional quotient (EQ) is more important than IQ. The average IQ is 100 with a standard deviation (mean square deviation) of 15. This means that 68% of people's IQ falls within one standard deviation of the average (100), or between 85 (100 – 15) and 115 (100 + 15); 95% of people's IQ is within two standard deviations, or between 70 (100 – 30) and 130 (100 + 30). In other words, only 2.5% of people have an IQ above 130. People with an IQ above 140 account for 0.4% of the population. In a country with a population of one million people, only 4,000 people have an IQ above 140. In my judgment, the number of people that can be called entrepreneurial within a population probably does not exceed the number of people with an IQ above 130.

Entrepreneurial talents are not the same as certain other special natural talents for particular activities (such as singing, painting, and sports), because they can be used in many aspects (Shleifer and Vishny, 2002, pp. 53–54). People with entrepreneurial talents can be politicians, bureaucrats, lawyers, generals, or religious leaders. They can also be entrepreneurs, engaging in industrial and commercial activities. Regardless of whether they get into politics, religion, or business, they have greater opportunities to succeed than other people.[2] The primary

[1] "Perhaps half the individuals in an ethically homogeneous group have the capacity for it to an average degree, a quarter in progressively diminishing measure, and, let us say, a quarter in a measure above the average, and within this quarter, through a series of continually increasing singing ability and continually diminishing number of people who possess it, we come finally to the Carusos. Only in this quarter are we struck in general by the singing ability, and only in the supreme instances can it become the characterizing mark of the person. Although practically all men can sing, singing ability does not cease to be a distinguishable characteristic and attribute of a minority, indeed not exactly of a type, because this characteristic – unlike ours – affects the total personality relatively little" (Schumpeter, 1934, pp. 81–82, footnote 2).

[2] A well-known example in Chinese history of a statesman-turned-merchant is Fan Li (536 – 448 B.C.) during the Spring and Autumn period. He was from the state of Chu and helped King Goujian guide the Kingdom of Yue in its struggle against the Kingdom of Wu. Later, he amassed tremendous wealth as a merchant and is now remembered as one of the Gods of Wealth. Another example is Talleyrand of France, who was a bishop with large tax income despite his prodigious

difference between poor countries and rich countries is not actually the abundance of entrepreneurial talents. Instead, it is the allocation of entrepreneurial talents, that is, where are entrepreneurial talents used in a country. China's high rate of economic growth over the last few decades primarily came from the reallocation of entrepreneurial talents. They transitioned from politics to industrial and commercial activity. This was a historic change in China over the last two thousand years.

The Impact of Different Entrepreneurial Talent Allocations on the Economy and Society

What impacts do different allocations of entrepreneurial talents have on a country's economy and society? From the perspective of economic growth and social development, the best allocation is to have all the entrepreneurial people engaged in industrial and commercial activities, i.e. being an entrepreneur. The worst allocation is to have them all work in government, i.e. being engaged in non-productive activities, especially rent seeking. I am not saying that the government is not important. It is very important. A characteristic of the government, however, is that a large number of government personnel are engaged in re-distribution of wealth, not wealth creation. In theory, re-distribution of the national income is primarily through the government. In reality, many of the activities the government is engaged in are rent-seeking activities, whereas the business world is engaged in value-creating activities. This way, whether the most capable people in society are allocated to government or business, meaning the most capable people are creating value or distributing value, or even rent seeking, will have a series of influences on a nation.

The capabilities of those who engage in business activities determine the economic growth of a country (Shleifer and Vishny, 2002, chapter 3; Baumol, 1994, chapter 2). If the most capable people are within the government – engaged in rent-seeking and redistribution activities rather than value-creating activities – then the abilities of the people engaged in business activities will be the same as, or even lower than, the general population. That country's economic growth will be

entrepreneurial skills (demonstrated when he escaped to the United States after the French Revolution) (Shleifer and Vishny, 2002, p. 55).

extremely slow or even stagnant (Olson, 1982). Why? Because, in the long run, the speed of technological progress determines the economic growth of a country. The things we enjoy today are different from the things our ancestors enjoyed 200 years ago. This is the result of technological progress. The speed of technological progress is primarily determined by the abilities of the most capable people engaged in business activities (Lucas, 1978; Shleifer and Vishny, 2002, chapter 3). For example, the speed of technological progress in the software industry during the 1980s and 1990s was to a large degree determined by the ability of people such as Bill Gates, not by the people whose abilities were weaker. Therefore, if the most capable people are not engaged in entrepreneurial activities, but only the less capable people are, technological progress of a country would be very slow. Landes (1969) argues that the different allocation of entrepreneurial talents is one of the reasons why the Industrial Revolution took place in England in the eighteenth century but not in France.

The different allocation of ability also has an impact on the size of the enterprise. The size of an enterprise is represented by how much capital you employ, how much labor you employ, and how big a market you serve. I believe that every entrepreneur has the ambition to make the enterprise larger. The size of an enterprise is largely determined by the competence of business leaders. As demonstrated by Professor Robert Lucas (1978), a Nobel laureate, highly competent entrepreneurs lead large businesses and entrepreneurs with lesser abilities lead smaller businesses. Of course, there are other factors that affect the size of a business, including the influence of unforeseen incidents, and the size of actual enterprises varies from business to business. For a country and a region as a whole, however, it can be said that highly capable people lead larger businesses and people with lesser abilities lead smaller businesses, so the ability of entrepreneurs determines the average size of enterprises. If the portion of the population with the highest abilities are engaged in business activities, the average size of enterprises in a country will be relatively large. Alternatively, if only the people with lower or the lowest ability are engaged in business activities, the average size of enterprises in a country will be relatively small.

One reason for this is that people are often reluctant to accept being led by people who are less capable than themselves. If an entrepreneur is highly capable, slightly less capable people are willing to work in the enterprise and accept being led by the entrepreneur. Thus, the scale of the enterprise can expand. Therefore, as we can see in the United States, very high-quality people are willing to join large companies as department managers or to work their way up from the bottom to become a department manager. Conversely, if the person in the highest position in the enterprise has a relatively low ability, many people will not follow that person. Instead, the others will start their own businesses. In the end, there will be many stunted enterprises, but no big ones. Therefore, from a macro comparison between countries, the countries that have large enterprises and the countries that lack them is largely related to the allocation of entrepreneurial talent. Of course, I am referring to private enterprises under free competition, not enterprises maintained through government funding. The size of state-owned enterprises has little relationship to the ability of their leaders. It mainly depends on the resources and exclusive operational rights granted by the government.

What effect does entrepreneurial ability have on workers' wages? We know that in a competitive labor market, the wage level of workers is determined by their marginal productivity. If a firm pays workers a wage higher than their marginal productivity, the firm will go bankrupt sooner or later. If a firm pays workers less than their marginal productivity, the firm will have difficulty attracting employees. Therefore, a firm must compensate employees according to their marginal contributions. Of course, there are other factors that determine wages, including social fairness, but marginal productivity is fundamental.

In simple terms, so-called marginal productivity is: How different would the enterprise's output be with you or without you? The bigger the difference, the higher your marginal productivity. An employee's marginal productivity is largely determined by the entrepreneurial ability of the firm. It is not entirely determined by the employee's own ability. In other words, how much value the same person can create depends on the entrepreneur he is working for. The more capable the entrepreneur is, the higher the employees' marginal productivity. As the saying goes: "An incompetent soldier is one incompetent soldier, but an incompetent general creates many incompetent soldiers." Why is it that some people can go from making a few hundred yuan a month at a loss-making firm to making tens of thousands of yuan a month at profitable companies? Because the value they create is different in different companies. Therefore, there is a relationship between the level of workers' wages and the allocation of entrepreneurial talents in society. If the most entrepreneurial people in society are engaged in industry and commerce, the wages of the working class in that society will be high. If only people with lesser abilities are engaged in industry and commerce, the wages of the working class in that society will be lower.

A related question is: What effect does the allocation of entrepreneurial talents have on the income distribution gaps? Some people might believe that while placing the most entrepreneurial people in the business sector increases total national wealth, it also widens the gaps in income distribution. But that does not have to be the case. There is no evidence that countries where the most capable people are engaged in entrepreneurial activities have greater income distribution gaps than countries where the most capable people are working in government. In addition, when discussing income distribution, we should not ignore the distribution of power. Income in monetary form is one of the factors that determine people's standard of living, but not the only one. We should not only be concerned about the monetary Gini coefficient, but also the power Gini coefficient. When the most entrepreneurial people work in government, the monetary Gini coefficient might be small, but the power allocation Gini coefficient might be large, it is just that no one has calculated it. Some years ago, a municipal party committee secretary told me that he had offered lower-level cadres severance of one million yuan to leave the government, but he had no takers. What does this mean? It means the power they have is worth more than one million yuan! Did we count this implicit compensation in the income statistics? No! Therefore, in an economy where government officials have a lot of power, the gaps in living standards are far greater than the gaps in monetary income.

People tend to be more biased toward observable gaps than unobservable ones, which I call "observability bias." For example, one company might have high wages but a terrible corporate culture, whereas another company might have lower wages but offer a friendly working environment, better learning opportunities, the potential for promotion, etc. When choosing a job, many people might be attracted to the first company, but regret joining the company later. The same is true of dating. How much influence does another person's beauty have on your happiness? It might not have a big influence, but most people consider looks first when finding a partner, because appearance is easier to observe than other traits. Society is the same way. In traditional societies, an extreme inequality of power distribution exists, but people seem to be able to tolerate it. Once that turns into an uneven distribution of money, people cannot tolerate it. Further, when the most capable people are allocated to work in the government, corruption will be relatively serious. Power will be monetized to a high degree and even the income gaps will be high. This is the situation most developing countries are in. Compared to the developed countries where the most capable people are engaged in commerce, the income gaps in these developing countries are much larger. When a society's most outstanding people are allocated to commerce, they can create wealth that makes everybody better off, although the degree of "better" varies. However, if society's most outstanding people are not allocated to commerce, but instead are allocated to the government, as in developing countries, they will be only redistributing wealth. They take wealth from the hands of some and transfer it to the hands of others. Society's overall wealth will not increase. Even if the income gaps are small, there will be common poverty.

The things the most successful people are doing will guide the activities of everyone else in society. As was stated previously, in the market, a person's compensation is determined by marginal productivity. In non-marketized organizations, however, the compensation a person receives is often not related to the amount of wealth he creates.

I distinguish between two types of organizations (societies): A productivity-oriented organization and a destructivity-oriented organization. In a productivity-oriented organization, the status and compensation a person has within the organization is determined by his productive contribution to the organization: I worked better than you, so my treatment is better. I have a higher position and the boss appreciates me. Alternatively, I perform poorly, so I have nothing better than you. Therefore, in this type of organization, people engage in productive competition. The contest is to contribute to the organization. Each person has an incentive to improve their own ability to create value. This is favorable, healthy competition.

In contrast, in destructivity-oriented organizations, the compensation and status of a person is not determined by contribution to the organization. Instead, it is determined by a person's lethality and destructive power to the other members.[3]

As Wu Si explained in his 2003 book, in the past Chinese society was destructive. It was a contest to harm others, because your ability to harm others determined your status and wealth. For example, the person with a gun would get more than the person with a knife. The person with a cannon would get more than the person with the gun. In other words, it is better to not work than to work, and it is better to make trouble than to not work. Whoever has the means to cause harm to other people will be promoted. In this type of organization, people's efforts are spent on activities to destroy others. Instead of competing to improve productivity, they are competing to increase destructive power. In my view, many state-owned enterprises in China are more like destructivity-oriented organizations.

If society's most capable people are allocated to industrial and commercial fields, there will be productive competition. On the contrary, if the most capable people are allocated to the government, then there will be destructive competition. This can explain the reason most people in traditional Chinese society could create value but did not. Chen Zhongshi, author of *Bai Lu Yuan* [*White Deer Plain*], provides an example: After the Xinhai Revolution (of 1911), the peasants of Central Shaanxi wondered whether they still had to pay imperial grain taxes now that the emperor had gone. As it turned out, not only did they have to pay grain taxes, they had to pay the tax over and over again. When a warlord came, the tax was levied. When that warlord was driven away, another one came and levied the tax again. People finally realized that it was better to collect taxes from others than to pay taxes to others, so they all took up arms to collect taxes from others.[4] It is a very unfortunate thing to have society's most capable people allocated to the government, but it is not the most unfortunate. It is most unfortunate when the most capable people are spending all their energy on civil conflicts. The most outstanding people competing for power is common in the history of China.

The allocation of entrepreneurial talents also determines society's moral level. If the most capable people are engaged in industry and commerce, people are more likely to be honest and trustworthy,

---

[3] Wu Si (2003). Wu is a non-traditional historian in China.
[4] Chen Zhongshi (1993). Chen is one of the most famous fiction writers.

forming a good market order. Conversely, if the most capable people are engaged in politics, it is more likely that there will be a fraudulent, dishonest social ethos. Even an honest person by nature may lose many of the virtues inherent in human nature and adopt many dishonest behaviors once he or she becomes a politician. In contrast, in commercial fields, your competitiveness determines your ability to create value. As a business person, unless you have monopoly privileges granted by the government, you cannot impose on others. You will be recognized and respected only when you create value for others.

What Determines Entrepreneurial Talent Allocation?

What factors determine human resource allocation? How come in some countries, highly capable people are entrepreneurs but in others they are politicians or government bureaucrats? Here, the two basic assumptions about people's career choices in economics are important.

The first assumption is that each person will choose the career that brings about the best composite compensation. Here, "composite compensation" is not only pure monetary income, but also includes non-monetary compensation such as power and social status. Because each person has different preferences, the substitution relationship between monetary income and non-monetary compensation is different. For example, some people prefer power (commanding others). Regardless of personal preference, people always prefer the occupation with the highest "composite compensation": For a given monetary compensation, more power is better; for a given power, more monetary compensation is better.

The second assumption is that the most capable people will always choose the careers with increasing marginal returns to ability, as argued by Shleifer and Vishny (2002, chapter 3). An example of so-called "increasing marginal returns" is me having 10% more ability than you, so when I do the same work, my return is 20%, 30%, or even higher than yours. Which sectors are characterized by having increased marginal returns? Entertainment and sports are typical industries with increasing marginal returns to ability. The appearance fee for celebrity singers is dozens of times higher than for ordinary singers. Is there such a big difference in ability? Obviously not. The sports world is the same. The difference between first and second place in the hundred-meter dash is very small, but the advertising revenue for the champion is many times higher than the runner-up. This is the case of the increasing marginal returns to ability.

In terms of entrepreneurs, there are two sectors with increasing returns: Government and commerce. In government, ability growth and returns growth differ. Returns grow much higher than ability. For example, how different are the capabilities of deputy minister and minister compared to their compensation? Assume society is healthy and that the promotion of government officials can be truly merito-cratic. The people that are ministers might be 2% or 3% more capable than the people that are deputy ministers. After becoming ministers, though, in China the mandatory retirement age is 65, whereas it is 60 for deputy ministers. This five-year gap represents the best five years in terms of remuneration, so the composite compensation is very different. The difference between bureau heads and deputy bureau heads is similar. Bureau heads have much more power than deputy bureau heads. Generally speaking, the capability gaps between section members (*keyuan*), section heads (*kezhang*), division heads (*chuzhang*), bureau heads (*juzhang*), and ministers (*buzhang*) is smaller than their compensation gaps. This is why it is said that government is a classic sector of increasing marginal returns to ability.

The situation is similar in industrial and commercial spheres. The gap in profit earned between two people that are involved in similar businesses will be much larger than the gap in their ability. Their capabilities might be 5% different, for example, but one person suc-ceeds and the other person goes bankrupt. Similarly, within a firm, a vice president and the president might differ in capabilities by a few percentage points, but their compensation will be different by more than just a few percentage points. Within an enterprise, compensation increases are much steeper than increases in position. Compared to promotions, compensation increases at a faster rate. Economics has some empirical research and theoretical models to explain this (Rosen, 1982).

Because the government sector and the business sector both are industries with increasing returns to ability, both are attractive to highly capable people. If the government is open and commercial activity is free, whether the most-capable people decide to go into business or the government is determined by their relative compen-sation level. If a society's compensation system is such that the com-posite compensation of the most capable people is higher in the government than in commerce, the most-capable people will move into the government and only people with inferior abilities will go into business. Alternatively, if the compensation is higher in commerce than in the government, the most-capable people will move toward commerce and only people with inferior abilities will work in the government. Of course, if the government is closed for some particular ethnic groups, but commercial activity is free, then the most entrepreneurial people of the excluded groups can only engage in commercial activities, as in the case of Jews in Europe, the Chinese in Malaysia, and the Indians and Lebanese in Africa. Alternatively, if the government is open but commercial activity is restricted, the most outstanding people will be attracted to the government. Such was the situation in China from the end of the Sui and Tang dynasties to the Ming and Qing dynasties.

Property rights protections have a lot to do with the relative gap between business and government pay. Property rights protections are very different for the commercial world and the government. The government has force and power, whereas the business community does not. Government bureaucrats are much more able to protect their own interests than business entrepreneurs. Also, entrepreneurs' rights are easily harmed by government bureaucrats. Therefore, if the most capable people can either be engaged in the high-risk commercial sector or the low-risk government sector, they will prefer the safety of the government sector when a society's property rights protections are weak. The weaker property rights protections are, the more attractive the government is to the most capable people. In particular, if politicians and government bureaucrats can arbitrarily extort the commercial world, outstanding talent will hardly choose to be entrepreneurs.

One important reason the rights of entrepreneurs are difficult to protect is that entrepreneurs obtain profits, not wages. Government encroachment of profit income is much easier than of wage income. Not only is this so because the working class is the majority and entrepreneur class is a minority, but also because profits and wages are completely different forms of income. Wages are relatively fixed and generally protected by contracts. Wage earners also need to pay taxes which are relatively transparent. The government cannot change it overnight. In contrast, profit is a residual income, something that cannot be protected by contracts. It is very sensitive to government policies. Even if the government does not change the tax rate, there are many ways to make profit disappear, such as through restricting business entry and price regulations, which are confiscations of entre-preneur property in disguise.

It should also be pointed out that, due to the difficulty of protecting property rights in different industries, the attractiveness of industries is different for outstanding talent. Property rights protection in the hard-ware industry, for example, is easier and more effective than in the software industry. This point had a major impact on the development of China's economy. If protection for intellectual property rights cannot effectively improve, China's best entrepreneurs will avoid the software industry but be more interested in industries such as real estate. There are institutional reasons why people like Bill Gates appeared in America.

The political system is last but not least. The greater the discretion-ary power of the government and the higher the degree of centraliza-tion, the easier corruption becomes, so the most capable people will be more willing to work in the government rather than in enterprises (Shleifer and Vishny, 2002, pp. 69–71). In contrast, the more the law restricts bureaucrats and the less power the government has, the harder corruption becomes, so the business world becomes more attractive to outstanding talent. Strengthening the rule of law construct is critical to the efficient allocation of entrepreneurial resources.

Of course, whether an individual chooses to engage in commercial activity or be a bureaucrat is related to that individual's preferences. People have the desire to obtain both wealth and power. Even though there is a certain substitutability between wealth and power, generally speaking, people with a stronger desire for wealth will choose entre-preneurial activities whereas people with a stronger desire for power will choose rent-seeking activities.

The Evolutionary Stable Equilibrium of Entrepreneurial Talent Allocation

An entrepreneurial person's expected reward from choosing to be an entrepreneur or a rent-seeker engaged in unproductive activities is not only determined by entrepreneurial ability, it is also determined by the number of entrepreneurs and rent-seekers in society, as well as their relative proportions.

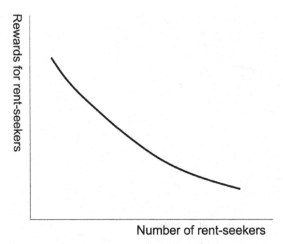

Figure 13.1 The Expected Return and Number of Rent-Seekers

The expected return of rent-seekers decreases as their numbers increase, as shown in Figure 13.1. (The horizontal axis represents the number of rent-seekers and the vertical axis represents rent-seekers' expected reward.) There are two reasons for this. First, rent seeking is a zero-sum game. Given society's total wealth, the more rent-seekers there are, the lower the reward each rent-seeker can obtain. Second, given entrepreneurial resources, the more people are engaged in rent seeking, the fewer people there are to engage in productive activities and thus create wealth. Thus, there is less total social wealth available to seize.

What is the relationship between an entrepreneur's expected reward and the number of entrepreneurs? You might think that the entrepreneur's expected reward also decreases as their numbers increase because the fiercer competition is, the harder it is to make money. This intuition is wrong for two reasons. First, a positive-sum game exists between entrepreneurs. They create opportunities for entrepreneurs to make money. Second, an increase in social wealth will enlarge the scope of the market and create new market demand, thus providing new opportunities to entrepreneurs. For example, when an entrepreneur hires workers to open an automobile factory, this creates demand for components, catering, housing, cultural facilities, and other aspects that are opportunities for other entrepreneurs. As local employment increases and residents' incomes continue to rise, demand for high-end

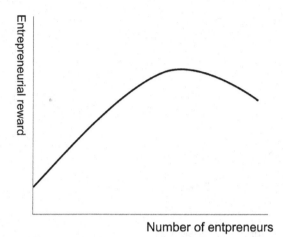

Figure 13.2 The Expected Reward and Number of Entrepreneurs

consumer goods will emerge. In turn, this provides opportunities for entrepreneurs who produce high-end consumer goods, and so on. Thus, the expected return of entrepreneurs increases with the number of entrepreneurs. In reality, we do see that it is easier to make money in places with a high density of entrepreneurs. On the contrary, it is difficult to make money where the density of entrepreneurs is low. Of course, when the density of entrepreneurs exceeds a certain level, competition among entrepreneurs will create a crowding-out effect. At that point, the expected return of entrepreneurs will decrease as the number of entrepreneurs increases. Therefore, the expected reward curve for entrepreneurs resembles an inverted U-shaped curve that rises and then falls, as shown in Figure 13.2.

Figure 13.3 shows the relationship between the number of private and foreign enterprises per 10,000 people and the rate of return on assets for all industrial enterprises among China's 31 provinces, municipalities, and autonomous regions in 2016. The figure shows that the rate of return on assets first increases with the per capita number of entrepreneurs, but then declines. It only declines in areas with extremely high entrepreneur density and the degree of decline is small.

Further, entrepreneurs' expected reward and the number of entrepreneurs is not independent from the number of rent-seekers. First, from the static perspective, an increase in the number of rent-seekers reduces entrepreneurial rewards, as demonstrated in Daron

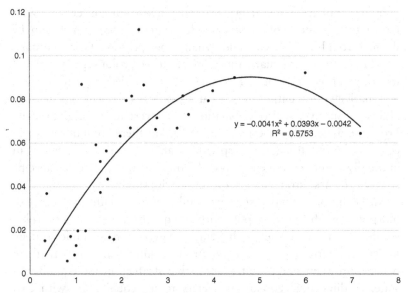

Figure 13.3 The Density of Entrepreneurs and the Profit Rate on Assets (2016)

Acemoglu's (1995) paper. As the number of rent-seekers increases, the more interference there is in industrial and commercial activities. This makes it more difficult for entrepreneurs to make money. Second, from the dynamic perspective, the activities of rent-seekers not only affect the current reward structure but also the future reward structure, thus they influence future career choices. There are three reasons for this: (1) Rent-seeking activities have a negative impact on entrepreneurial innovation, slowing or even stagnating future economic growth and resulting in fewer future entrepreneurial opportunities; (2) Rent-seekers usually become rent setters by using their own political power to create new rent-seeking opportunities. They increase entry thresholds and risks for industrial and commercial activities; (3) Rent-seekers change the non-monetary rewards of the two occupations. For example, in a society with more rent-seekers, the social status of rent-seekers increases relative to entrepreneurs. As the "official standard (*guanbenwei*)" becomes more pervasive, industrial and commercial activities become despised, thus reducing the attractiveness of being the entrepreneur. Below, I will use the evolutionary game method to analyze dynamic evolutionary equilibrium of entrepreneurial talent allocation.

In evolutionary game theory, the most important concept and analytical tool is the evolutionary stable strategy (ESS), which can be defined from both the static and dynamic perspectives. From the static point of view, a particular strategy is said to be evolutionarily stable if its population cannot be successfully invaded by mutations. Alternatively, any entity that deviates from this strategy has a lower ability to survive, so the population will revert to its original state. From the dynamic perspective, assuming that there are multiple strategies in the initial state, if a specific strategy or some strategies can gradually dominate the entire population over time, then this specific strategy or these strategies are evolutionarily stable.[5]

An evolutionary stable strategy equilibrium can either be a monomorphic equilibrium or a polymorphic equilibrium. A monomorphic equilibrium refers to there only being one evolutionary stable strategy in the equilibrium state. A polymorphic equilibrium refers to there being more than one evolutionary stable strategy in the equilibrium state. A dimorphic equilibrium refers to an equilibrium with two coexisting evolutionary stable strategies.

Whether a behavior can become the dominant behavior of a group, and thus become the evolutionary stable behavior, is determined by its fitness. In this text's example, there are two possible behaviors (strategies): either be an entrepreneur or be a rent-seeker. The fitness of each one is its relative reward. If the expected reward of being an entrepreneur is higher than that of being a rent-seeker, then the fitness of entrepreneurs will be higher than for rent-seekers. With the passage of time, the number of entrepreneurs will gradually increase, and the number of rent-seekers will gradually decrease. Conversely, if the expected reward of being an entrepreneur is lower than that of being a rent-seeker, then the number of entrepreneurs will gradually decrease and the number of rent-seekers will gradually increase. Here, the increase or decrease in the number of people in an occupation might either be the result of the new generation's choices or a change in the old generation's occupation.

For simplicity, we assume that the total quantity of entrepreneurial talents is fixed. Additionally, we assume the capabilities of entrepreneurs are the same. Therefore, there is a trade-off between the scale of

---

[5] The evolutionary stable strategy was defined by John Maynard Smith in his 1982 book titled *Evolution and the Theory of Games*.

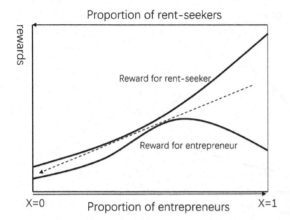

Figure 13.4 The Rent-Seeker-Dominated Monomorphic Equilibrium

entrepreneurs and the scale of rent-seekers. If we use X to represent the proportion of entrepreneurs in a population, then $1 - X$ is the proportion of rent-seekers. $X = 0$ means all entrepreneurial talents are engaged in rent-seeking activities, and $X = 1$ means all entrepreneurial talents are engaged in entrepreneurial activities. This way, in a graph with X as the horizontal axis, the expected reward of rent-seekers is an upward sloping curve because the larger X is, the fewer rent-seekers there are. Entrepreneurs' expected reward curve is similar to the one shown in Figure 13.2.

To summarize, there are four possible evolutionary stable equilibrium states.

Equilibrium I: The Rent-Seeker-Dominated Monomorphic Equilibrium. In Figure 13.4, regardless of the relative scale of entrepreneurs and rent-seekers, the expected reward of rent-seekers is everywhere higher than that of entrepreneurs, so rent-seekers have a higher fitness than entrepreneurs. A highly authoritarian and corrupt society is most likely to be this way. The result is that, regardless of how many entrepreneurs there were in the initial state, as time passes, there will be fewer entrepreneurs and more rent-seekers. All entrepreneurial talents will become rent-seekers, meaning $X = 0$. $X = 0$ is an evolutionarily stable equilibrium because even if a small number of entrepreneurs appear as a "variation," they will disappear over time and the system will revert to $X = 0$.

Equilibrium II: The Entrepreneur-Dominated Monomorphic Equilibrium. In Figure 13.5, regardless of the relative scale of

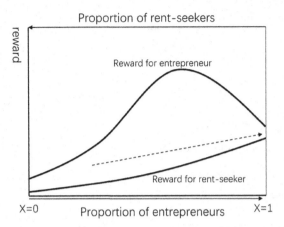

Figure 13.5 The Entrepreneur-Dominated Monomorphic Equilibrium

entrepreneurs and rent-seekers, the expected reward of entrepreneurs is everywhere higher than that of rent-seekers, so entrepreneurs have higher fitness than rent-seekers. A highly democratic and rule-of-law society is most likely to be this way. The result is that, regardless of how many rent-seekers there were in the initial state, as time passes, there will be fewer rent-seekers and more entrepreneurs. All entrepreneurial people will become entrepreneurs, meaning $X = 1$. $X = 1$ is an evolutionarily stable equilibrium because even if a small number of rent-seekers appear as a "variation," they will disappear over time and the system will revert to $X = 1$.

Equilibrium III: The Entrepreneur-Dominated Dimorphic Equilibrium. In Figure 13.6, when the scale of entrepreneurs is less than X^*, entrepreneurs' expected reward is greater than rent-seekers' expected reward, thus entrepreneurs have higher fitness. When the scale of entrepreneurs is greater than X^*, rent-seekers' expected reward is higher than entrepreneurs and their fitness is higher. Therefore, if $X < X^*$ in the initial state, the number of entrepreneurs will gradually increase and the number of rent-seekers will gradually decrease as time passes until $X = X^*$. If $X > X^*$ in the initial state, the number of entrepreneurs will gradually decrease and the number of rent-seekers will gradually increase as time passes until $X = X^*$. Here, $X = X^*$ is an evolutionary stable equilibrium. Any deviation caused by any "variation" will be corrected and the system will revert to $X = X^*$, meaning the proportion of entrepreneurs will be X^* and the proportion of rent-

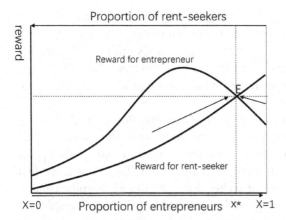

Figure 13.6 The Entrepreneur-Dominated Dimorphic Equilibrium

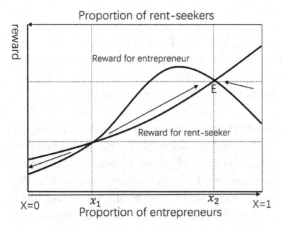

Figure 13.7 Rent-Seeker-Dominated Monomorphic or Entrepreneur-Dominated Dimorphic Equilibrium

seekers will be $1 - X^*$. I call this a "entrepreneur-dominated dimorphic equilibrium" because there are more entrepreneurs than rent-seekers in this type of equilibrium state.

Equilibrium IV: Rent-Seeker-Dominated Monomorphic or Entrepreneur- Dominated Dimorphic Equilibrium. In Figure 13.7, at $X = x_1$ or $X = x_2$, entrepreneurs' expected reward is equivalent to rent-seekers' expected reward. However, $X = x_1$ is not an evolutionary stable equilibrium, but $X = x_2$ is. This is because any variation that slightly deviates from $X = x_1$ will cause the system to move toward $X = 0$ or $X = x_2$, depending on the variation's direction. Even if the initial state has a certain proportion of entrepreneurs, they will be eliminated if the scale of entrepreneurs does not reach x_1, leaving only rent-seekers. Only when the scale of entrepreneurs exceeds x_1 will the system converge on the evolutionary equilibrium state $X = x_2$, similar to the situation in Figure 13.6.

Among the four evolutionary equilibriums, the most ideal is the second type of equilibrium, the entrepreneur-dominated monomorphic equilibrium. Next would be the third type of equilibrium, the entrepreneur-dominated dimorphic equilibrium. The worst is the first type of equilibrium, the rent-seeker dominated monomorphic equilibrium. If there is a big enough variation in the fourth type of equilibrium when $X < x_1$, such as a sufficiently large group of entrepreneurs is introduced from the outside, then it can move to $X = x_2$, similar to the third type of equilibrium.

How do these four situations correspond to reality? Roughly speaking, underdeveloped countries, including Latin American countries and some African countries, are close to the first equilibrium. Traditional Chinese society was also similar to the first situation. Every person with entrepreneurial abilities wanted to enter the government. Only when quotas made it impossible to enter the government did they choose to engage in industrial and commercial activities. Developed countries are close to the second equilibrium. People with entrepreneurial abilities go into business and only those without entrepreneurial abilities work in the government. Perhaps Singapore is similar to the third situation. Both the business sector and public sector are filled with elites. Japan after the Meiji Restoration probably belongs to the fourth situation. When the Meiji government sold state-owned enterprises at a low price to the samurai class, the scale of entrepreneurs crossed the critical point x_1. The result was an evolution toward x_2 where most elites were engaged in industrial and commercial activity, but some elites worked in the government.

The Rise of China's Grassroots Entrepreneurs

Now we will take a look back on China's situation. What was China like for more than two thousand years before the reform and openness? Stated simply, it was an open public square and a closed marketplace. Beginning with the First Emperor of Qin, the system of commanderies and counties lasted from one dynasty to another. Besides the emperor, all positions in the government were open to the public. As long as you had ability and were lucky, you could enter the government. In the Han Dynasty, those with virtue and filial piety were selected from areas according to the proportion of the population and sent to the central government for training. After the Sui and Tang Dynasties, there was a formal imperial examination system. As long as a commoner's child studied hard and took the exam, there was hope of becoming an official up to the level of minister or chancellor. In contrast, after the Emperor Wu of Han, major industrial and commercial activities were monopolized by the government, disallowing private operations. Even if it was allowed, there were many restrictions and merchants were preyed on by officialdom. This is different from Western countries. The West has had an aristocracy for a long time. Political power was monopolized by the nobility, closed off to the common people. Nobility was only passed on to the eldest son. Younger siblings had to make it on their own. Thus, the West developed industrial and commercial cities while China did not have commercial cities. All cities in Chinese history were political centers, not commercial centers. In China, being an official is the best option, not a merchant. Government officials have high status, wide discretion, and opportunities for corruption. In terms of social status, among the four occupations of scholar-official, peasant, craftsman, and merchant, the merchants' status was the lowest, even lower than a peasant. Their commercial interests were not effectively protected and their property was easily expropriated. Generally speaking, the composite compensation of government officials was higher than for merchants. The result was the belief that "the student, having completed his learning, should apply himself to be an officer" (*xue er you ze shi*).

Under this type of incentive mechanism, the ablest people were attracted into the government for more than 2,000 years. This is one of the major reasons Chinese society has been able to maintain unity for a long time. Of course, it is also a major reason modern China became backward. Beginning in the seventeenth and eighteenth centuries, the road to officialdom was opened in England and some other European countries, but industrial and commercial activities opened up even more. Especially in England after the Glorious Revolution established constitutional monarchy, the actions of the king and government were restrained by the legislature and judiciary. Private property was effectively protected, patent law was implemented, and industrial and commercial activities became the most attractive option. From this, England became the world's factory.[6] At the same time, in China, officialdom was open but commerce was closed. It was much more attractive to study for imperial examinations than do business. As a result, Westerners made big enterprises while Chinese made big government. More than 30 years ago, when I was writing *Entrepreneurs: Kings of Economic Growth*, I mistakenly believed China lacked entrepreneurial talent. Now, looking back, China did not lack entrepreneurial talent. Instead, China's problem was a mis-allocation of entrepreneurial talent. Everybody that could run an enterprise were all officials. We know that many Southeast Asian countries' economies are dominated by Chinese-run enterprises. When many Chinese immigrate to other countries, they engage in commerce. They are willing to take risks. There is entrepreneurship in their bones.

Why do Chinese people become good entrepreneurs after leaving the country, but within the country they can only be bureaucrats? The reason is simple. Those countries' politics are not open to the Chinese, but industrial and commercial activity is. The people that drifted to Southeast Asia could not possibly be officials in the government. The only way for them to improve their own status is to do business. They make money and then buy off the local high officials to protect them-selves, thus becoming successful entrepreneurs. Similarly, why are Jewish people so talented at business? Because Jews were discriminated

---

[6] In Britain, before 1829, Nonconformists were excluded from Parliament, the military, and the civil service. They were excluded from Oxford and Cambridge, so they had to seek an education in Scotland or their own schools. Therefore, they were an important source of entrepreneurs. They accounted for 7% of the population but half of manufacturing entrepreneurs during the Industrial Revolution. Unitarians played a major role in economic progress. James Watt (mechanical engineer and chemist), Josiah Wedgwood (pottery entrepreneur), Thomas Beddoes (physician and popular science writer), and James McConnel (Manchester textile manufacturer) in the eighteenth century and the Stephensons (the father and son) that invented the locomotive in the nineteenth century were all Unitarians. There were fewer than 2,500 Quakers at the time. A study of Birmingham estimated that they accounted for 1% of the city's population but 66% of business owners in the iron-making and leather industries. In the early eighteenth century, Quakers owned and operated half of England's ironworks. Perhaps Abraham Darby is the most famous of them all. See Joel Mokyr (2009, pp. 361–362).

against and did not have political status in any country. They could neither hold office nor buy land, so all they could do was business. They became the most business-minded group in the world. If Jews had high political status in any country, the ablest Jews might not do business, but instead go into government.

The Reform and Opening started by Deng Xiaoping turned China from the first type of equilibrium (entirely dominated by rent-seekers) to the third type (entrepreneur-dominated dimorphic equilibrium). The internal and external opening up increased entrepreneurs' expected reward, making more and more entrepreneurial people willing to be entrepreneurs.

What changes have occurred in China over the last 40 plus years of Reform and Opening? The most important is the change in the allocation of human resources. In particular, the allocation of China's entrepreneurial talents has undergone a historical change. Why do I say it is historical? Because in more than 2,000 years of history, the most outstanding people were concentrated in the government, serving as officials. In the last 40 plus years, more and more outstanding talents have turned to the business world, to industrial and commercial activity. Problems that had not been solved for more than 2,000 years have now been solved. Sima Qian once said: "A family with a thousand catties of gold may stand side by side with the lord of a city; the man with a hundred million cash may enjoy the pleasures of a king" (Watson, 1961, p. 499) If we can achieve that, then there is no need for people with entrepreneurial talent to be officials.

Specifically, before 1978, China's most outstanding talents, those with entrepreneurial qualities, were allocated to two sectors. The first was the government sector. The second was outside the government in rural areas (under the planned economy, China's industrial sector was subordinate to the government). Within the government, talented people were distributing and even destroying wealth. What were the talented people doing in the rural areas? They could not engage in the activities they were best at: industry and commerce. They also had no hope of becoming government officials. Except for farming like a common peasant, the best they could do was "speculative" activities. At that time, those activities were defined as criminal. Many of the entrepreneurial peasants who engaged in these activities were arrested and sent to prison.

Reform and Opening unleashed the market, providing a new arena for people with entrepreneurial qualities that had traditionally been suppressed. Generally speaking, over the past 40 plus years, the rise of China's entrepreneurs experienced the following four waves.[7]

The first wave was the rise of peasant entrepreneurs in the 1980s. We know that town and village enterprises were the driving force of China's economic growth in the 1980s. What type of people ran town and village enterprises? They were the capable people clustered in rural areas, such as village party secretaries, revolutionary committee chairmen, or even "speculators" recently released from labor camps. Regardless, they were entrepreneurial people. They had more business wisdom, had a better sense of market trends, were more able to grasp opportunities, were more risk-taking, and more willing to endure hardships than the average person. Under the planned system, these people could not do what they should, but now could. This pushed forward China's economic development. If we measured the intelligence of two groups of people, one from among the people that were in prison at the time or had been to prison and the other from random people selected on the street, which group, on average, would be more entrepreneurial? I dare to say the prisoners were more entrepreneurial! Why? If the most talented person's talents are not allowed to create wealth, then he will turn into a force for destruction. In other words, if he cannot be a loyalist, he is likely to become a revolutionary.

The second wave occurred in the 1990s. This was the wave of intellectuals and party cadres "jumping into the sea." The elites that originally worked in government departments or state-run institutions left their original workplaces one after another to transition toward running a business. Many of the contemporary superstars of Chinese business circles are from this group. Of course, people like Liu Chuanzhi, the founder of Lenovo Company, were prophetic when they jumped into the sea (*xia hai*) in 1984, but the next real wave formed in the 1990s. Deng Xiaoping's Southern Tour in 1992 gave people the freedom to start a business. "Jumping into the sea" became these people's optimal choice. It could be said that the rapid economic development of the 1990s was to a large degree pushed forward by these people.[8] They dominate the real estate sector and new financial sector.

---

[7] In an article titled "Property Rights Reform, the Rise of Entrepreneurs, and China's Economic Development," I analyzed the rise of China's entrepreneurs in the first three waves. See Weiying Zhang (2015b, chapter 10).

[8] Chen Dongsheng, the founder of Taikang Life Insurance, referred to these entrepreneurs as "Ninety-twoer" entrepreneurs. See Chen Hai (2012).

The third wave occurred at the turn of the century. This wave of entrepreneurs was dominated by people returning from overseas study and people with engineering backgrounds. Internet and high-technology companies such as Baidu, Alibaba, Tencent, Sina, Sohu, NetEase, AsiaInfo, Dangdang, and Neusoft were founded by these type of entrepreneurs and all appeared at this time.

The fourth wave came after 2010. It is the wave of entrepreneurs born in the 1980s and 1990s. This generation of entrepreneurs created new emerging industries such as online ride hailing, online gaming, online education, take-out, short-form videos, online payments, and artificial intelligence.

China's current contingent of entrepreneurs in general emerged from these four entrepreneurial waves. Now, these four generations of entrepreneurs are gradually integrating. From finance to manufacturing, both online and offline, they are becoming a source of innovation for China's sustained economic growth. This is the impact on China of the historical change in the re-allocation of entrepreneur talents.

This is one basic judgment of mine about 40 plus years of development in China. Of course, the potential of China's entrepreneurial resources is far from being exhausted. The Chinese government still hoards too many outstanding talents and controls too many resources. The energy of the entrepreneurs already engaged in industrial and commercial activities has yet to be fully utilized. Some people might disagree with me. They believe the government also needs high quality talent. I agree with this point, especially during a period of economic transition. High quality officials are critical for setting correct policies. I mean to say that, at least over the long term, a large portion of the most capable people should be engaged in business activities – creating wealth – instead of concentrated in the government – redistributing wealth. In a normal rule-of-law country, the government should be dominated by second-rate talent on the straight and narrow. Too many first-rate talents concentrated in the government is not only a waste of human resources but is also not conducive to the stability and unity of society.

The final point to make is that, strictly speaking, the statement that entrepreneurs create wealth and government officials redistribute wealth only holds in a rule-of-law country. In an economy with a very imperfect rule of law or one without it, government officials have a lot of discretionary power, and business activities often require permission

from the government to proceed. In this type of economy, even entrepreneurs are not always creating wealth. They are likely to collude
with government officials in rent seeking and make money from connections with power. In China, the value-creating activities of entrepreneurs are often mixed with rent-seeking activities. This is the
institutional problem, a problem that must be resolved through reform.
The next step China must take is reducing the space for rent-seeking
activities until we finally eliminate them. At that point, the only way
for entrepreneurs to make money is to create value for society.

14 | *Entrepreneurs and Capitalists*

The relationship between the entrepreneur and the capitalist is a very important issue, and also highly debated. There are two extreme views. On the one extreme, Marxists identify entrepreneurs as capitalists. They think capitalist-entrepreneurs are pure exploiters; appropriating surplus value created by workers but with no productive contributions. On the other extreme, Schumpeter separated entrepreneurs entirely from capitalists. For Schumpeter, the entrepreneurial function is not connected with the possession of capital. Although the accidental fact of possession of capital constitutes a practical advantage, capitalists are necessary for entrepreneurship only in the sense that they provide purchasing power to entrepreneurs so as to make innovation possible. Thus, the relationship between capitalists and entrepreneurs is nothing more than that between creditors and debtors (Schumpeter, 1934, chapter 3). He also argued that risk-bearing is not part of the entrepreneurial function; it is the capitalist who bears the risk. The entrepreneur bears the risk only when he also happens to be a capitalist (Schumpeter, 1939, p. 104).

During the planned economy regime, China adopted the Marxist doctrine, and entrepreneurs were persecuted as capitalists. During the past four decades since the reform, China has practically taken the Schumpeterian view, but ideologically still holds the Marxist doctrine. As a result, while the importance of entrepreneurs is more or less acknowledged, the legitimacy of capitalists is yet to be recognized. Which view one holds depends upon a person's attitude toward the market. This constitutes a big obstacle for further marketization. Given that the Marxist doctrine is still the official ideology, the legitimacy of entrepreneurs is vulnerable. Entrepreneurs are often criticized as

Part of this chapter is drawn from Zhang, W. (2020). Entrepreneurs and Capitalists in the Market. In: *Ideas for China's Future*. Palgrave Macmillan, Singapore. https://doi.org/10.1007/978-981-15-4304-3_8. Reproduced with permission of Springer Nature.

capitalists and blamed for income inequality by some anti-market voices, which frustrates entrepreneurs and makes them less confident in doing business.

My basic arguments are as follows. First, no capitalists, no entrepreneurs. Second, the government can substitute for neither entrepreneurs nor capitalists. State-owned enterprises (SOEs) cannot produce entrepreneurs. And third, for entrepreneurs to function effectively, the corporate governance structure of the firm must be entrepreneur-centric.

The Role of Capitalists Is Selection of Entrepreneurs

What kind of ownership system can produce true entrepreneurs? For a long time and even today in China, a popular viewpoint is that entrepreneurs are important, but the ownership system is irrelevant. Entrepreneurs are necessary, but capitalists are not. I disagree.

As early as in 1986, I wrote the paper titled "Entrepreneurs and the Ownership System" to address this issue.[1] The core viewpoint of this paper is that entrepreneurs are the product of the private property system. Without the private property system, entrepreneurs cannot truly exist. Later, in my doctoral thesis submitted to Oxford University in 1994, I developed a theory called "an entrepreneurial/contractual theory of the firm" attempting to provide a logical foundation for why capital hires labor, meaning the reasons the owners of capital have such an important status and their relationship to entrepreneurship in the market economy (see Zhang, 2018a). My theory had two major conclusions.

First, entrepreneurs are the most critical to the firm but also can slack off most easily. When they perform their role by making a strategic decision, we lack a certain and hard indicator to supervise and restrain them. The only way to make them accountable for their own behavior is to make them assume risk. This means letting them

---

[1] The Chinese title of the paper is "Qiyejia yu Suoyouzhi – Jingji Tizhi Gaige Zhong de Zhongda Lilun Wenti," first published in *Jingji Tizhi Gaige Yanjiu Baogao* (1986, Issue 30), an internal publication of the Chinese Economic System Reform Institute. A first part of the paper was made public as "Gufenzhi yu Qiyejia Zhineng de Fenjie" (Shareholding System and Separation of Entrepreneurial Functions) in *Jingji Yanjiu* (*Economic Research Journal*, 1987, Issue 1). See Zhang Weiying (1999).

receive the residual, rather than a fixed contractual income. Common workers have a contractual wage. Regardless how much money the firm makes, as long as common workers get to work on time and are not obviously negligent, they have a right to a pre-determined wage. Entrepreneurs cannot take a salary. Only after everyone else takes what they should, does the residual belong to the entrepreneur. This is the reason an entrepreneur's income is called profit. Only in this way do entrepreneurs have an incentive to make good decisions and work hard.

Second, in any society only a small proportion of people truly have sufficient entrepreneurial talent. But as for who has entrepreneurial talents, we do not have a firm indicator, such as a test or a certification of entrepreneurial talents, to determine this. To ensure people with true entrepreneurial talents run firms, there must be a system that makes sure non-entrepreneurial people do not dare pretend they are entrepreneurial. At the same time, it must motivate truly entrepreneurial people to dare to start a business and innovate. I proved this system is capital-hiring-labor.

When an entrepreneur has an idea, whether he can successfully start a business depends on whether he can acquire enough capital. Only with capital can entrepreneurs shift resources to their entrepreneurial purposes. Given the world's uncertainty and the difficulty observing entrepreneurial talents, providers of capital must take risks. If a person must take risks with his own capital, the question will be: Should I run the business, or have someone else do it? If that person's entrepreneurial ability is insufficient, he will not pretend to have great abilities. Of course, many entrepreneurial people have insufficient capital. If any person could start a business with other people's money without obligations to the capital-providers, meaning that if I gain from success but you lose from failure, then too many non-entrepreneurial people will pretend to be entrepreneurial. This gives owners of capital the authority to select entrepreneurs. Capitalists have an incentive to select entrepreneurial people to run the firm precisely because they must assume risk. If they choose the wrong person and give capital to a non-entrepreneurial person that screws up the firm, then the capitalists will lose money. Therefore, the capitalist functions as a type of owner. The owner holds the residual rights (formal authority) (Grossman and Hart, 1986). This function further evolved into joint-stock companies of today. In other words, capital-hiring-labor is a mechanism of selecting entrepreneurs. This is the origin of the capitalist firm.

So-called venture capital is the evaluation and selection of entrepreneurs by deciding whether a requirement for funding is met. Naturally, investors supervise and constrain the entrepreneurs they invest in.

The implication of my theory is: When a country eliminates private capitalists, it actually also eliminates the mechanism for selecting qualified entrepreneurs and eliminates the environment in which entrepreneurs are born. We see in countries without capitalists that there are no rules to guarantee the most entrepreneurial people run a company. The people that do run companies cannot possibly be entrepreneurial. This is the circumstance in every country with a centrally planned economy.

The Government Can Substitute neither for Entrepreneurs nor for Capitalists

When decisions are made in centrally planned economies, they are made by the government, that is, by some officials in the government. Whether a firm should be established, what firms produce, how they produce it, and who they produce it for are all determined by government officials. All production materials are owned by the state, and the state determines how to allocate them. The government replaces both the entrepreneur and the capitalist. Stated simply, the essence of the planned economy is replacing the entrepreneur and capitalist at the same time.

We have watched every experiment with central economic planning fail. Every country that has replaced entrepreneurs and capitalists with the government has failed. This is the cause of the failures of the Soviet Union and was the reason China and India had to reform. Here, I want to point out many people mistakenly believe India has been a market economy since it became independent in 1947. Actually, after India gained independence, the government followed the planned economy of the Soviet Union, but the degree of planning was not as high as in Eastern Europe or China. Some activity was left to private firms, but state planning was still dominant. By 1990, India had already completed eight five-year plans. In the beginning of the 1990s, India started market-oriented reforms.[2]

---

[2] For a brief history of the Indian economy and its recent economic reform, see Aiyar (2016).

How come the government can replace neither entrepreneurs nor capitalists? The reasons are very simple. First, government officials do not have business talent like entrepreneurs. Even those who are innately entrepreneurial would lose their entrepreneurship once they worked in the government. Entrepreneurs have special talents and need decision autonomy. They must find things to do and make independent judgments about the future. The government needs people that can follow orders. Entrepreneurs do not fear making mistakes, whereas the government officials try to play safe. Entrepreneurs do the right thing, whereas government officials do things the right way. Government officials focus on procedures, not whether the substance is correct or worthwhile.

This point becomes clear upon observing government officials' actual performance. Any person that goes into the government and acts according to the methods set by the government is very unlikely to be entrepreneurial.

Second, even if government officials are entrepreneurial, they do not have the same type of incentive mechanism as entrepreneurs do. When an entrepreneur makes a mistake, he might go bankrupt or even commit suicide. As long as a government official respects procedure, no cost will be personally borne for poor decisions. Government officials are also not accountable for selecting wrong candidates like capitalists are. When a capitalist selects the wrong person, the capitalist assumes the risk. Giving your own money to a non-entrepreneurial person to run your firm or invest your money might leave you with nothing. When a government official gives public money to a non-entrepreneurial person, does the government official have any liability for losses? No! This is the reason nepotism is a serious problem for the selection of SOE managers. Many people still have an illusion that the government can imitate the market. It is assumed stock ownership by government departments can imitate capitalist ownership. This will never succeed because there will never be a way to make government officials take the risks for their own decisions like private capital owners do.

The government's inability to replace entrepreneurs and capitalists is particularly exposed in imitating entrepreneurs' innovation function. Some people believe that the government can substitute for entrepreneurs and capitalists partly because they misperceive that the most important economic problem is allocation of *given* resources under *given* technologies. Actually, entrepreneurship is more essential for innovation than for allocation.

As we argued earlier, innovation is unforeseeable. Letting the government decide the fate of innovations would be dangerous. Let us take a few examples. When Frenchman Philippe Lebon invented gas lighting in 1799 and applied for a patent, Emperor Napoleon, who had always been an enthusiastic supporter of technological progress, did not see the potential and called gas lighting "a folly." As a result, the British were the first to use gas lighting. The French did not put it into use until after 1815 (Mokyr, 2002, p. 239). When George Stephenson invented the steam locomotive, no one thought the locomotive was of much importance. The British government mandated locomotives could not exceed the speed of horse carts. When Carl Benz invented the automobile in 1886, very few people thought much of automobiles. A local government in Germany mandated automobiles could not exceed walking pace. As a result, before the start of World War I, France had 2.3 vehicles and Britain had 2.6 vehicles for every 1,000 people, but as the country that invented vehicles, Germany only had 0.9 vehicles for every 1,000 people. Its automobile production was only one-third of France's (Ibid. p. 272). These examples are endless.

Innovation being unforeseeable means the government cannot plan for innovation. It can only be left to the trial and error of entrepreneurs in the market. It cannot rely on government funding. Only investors in the market can make judgments, and investors must be dispersed, not centralized. When governments want to play the role of entrepreneurs and investors, they must act according to a unified procedure, but there is no unified standard for innovation.

I will give two examples. The world-famous Cisco is the first example. The company was started by Leonard Bosack and Sandy Lerner, husband and wife alumni of Stanford University. After they founded the company, they sought out funding. They went to 72 investors, but none of them was willing to invest. The 73rd investor they met with was willing to invest.

Another example is Mr. Pony Ma of China. When he first started Tencent, it was difficult to find investors. I once met a famous venture capitalist that said he is filled with remorse whenever he thinks about Ma. The reason is Ma once asked him for US$500,000, but the venture capitalist was not optimistic about the technology and turned it down. Eventually, Ma found a South African venture capital firm called

Naspers. Today, Tencent's biggest shareholder is not Ma, but instead is this South African investor. Allegedly, Naspers invested in a dozen Chinese companies, but all of them failed except Tencent!

These two stories tell us that diversified financing sources are essential for innovations. If I have an idea I want to turn into a product, I can keep going to the next person until I find someone to invest. Once I get funding, I may do something to change humanity's destiny. If the government established a committee to manage investments, then projects would be scored, and only the qualified ones would get investment. No matter what kind of people (officials, experts, or entrepreneurs) are sitting on the investment committee and regardless of what kind of rule the committee follows, the committee's decision is the final decision, and the missed chances are missed forever.

The lack of innovation in Chinese enterprises is related to the government's attempt to replace entrepreneurs and capitalists. To this day, most investment funds are still controlled by the government and state-owned banks. Among those famous Internet companies, which one did the Chinese government invest in? None of them. China has the highest savings rate and highest reserves of any country, but China invested in very few new technology companies using its own capital. Instead, it was foreign capital that was invested in companies such as Baidu, Alibaba, Tencent, and HC360. The government and state-owned banks cannot truly provide funding for innovation. At best, they can only maintain a circular economy.

The State-Owned Enterprise System Cannot Produce Entrepreneurs

It is necessary to discuss the problem of SOEs. Some people argue that SOEs can be as efficient as private enterprises as long as the government appoints entrepreneurial people to manage them. This argument implicitly assumes that the SOE system can produce entrepreneurs. This assumption is problematic.

In my 1986 paper, I proposed the "impossibility theorem of entrepreneurs under the state ownership system." At that time, many people were under the illusion that if we turned SOEs into joint-stock companies, established holding companies, and implemented interlocking shareholding, then we could have the same market economy as Western capitalism. If we separated operation from ownership, we would have entrepreneurial managers running the state-owned enterprises. I said this was impossible. Why is this impossible? There are five reasons.

The first reason is the impossibility of separating the government and enterprises. If SOEs exist, do not even think about having true separation of government and enterprises. The basic reason is that, as the legal owner, the government must hold residual rights (authority) over SOEs. These residual rights are discretionary rights, cannot be contractually defined, and have to be executed by some government agents. Otherwise, SOEs would become ownerless. As early as in the 1980s, the direction of SOE reform was toward separation from government, but even today we have not accomplished the separation of government and enterprises. Relatively speaking, the separation of party and enterprises should be easier, yet we have still not accomplished it. The party committees of SOEs are very powerful and intervene in business decisions.

The second reason is the impossibility of effective ownership constraints. The reason entrepreneurs in the market economy want to work industriously and innovate is because there is the ownership right constraint in the background. Entrepreneurs themselves hold a considerable stake of the firm and outside shareholders' interests are sensitive to the entrepreneur's performance. The government officials represent ownership rights, but they are not real shareholders. You can never expect pseudo shareholders to perform according to the principle of the true shareholder. They hold owner's rights but bear no responsibility of the owner. Their interests are little related to the SOE's true value. They have very different incentives from true owners.

The third reason is the impossibility of resolving the short-term behavior of operators. The problem of short-term behavior exists in all state-owned enterprises. The leaders of SOEs only consider short-term issues. They can hardly consider matters further than three years away. However, we know an entrepreneur without long-term considerations cannot truly create an outstanding or innovative enterprise. Why? Innovation is a sustained long-term process. Three to five years might pass between new product inception and market acceptance. Ten or 20 years might be needed for a major technological breakthrough. If an entrepreneur does not consider the long run, he cannot actually create a truly innovative enterprise in the market economy.

How come leaders of SOEs cannot consider the long run? Because their positions are political appointments. The political standard for appointment cannot be entrepreneurship-based, nor can it be long-term performance-based. The officials with the power to appoint someone will not allow them to continue just because of good performance, nor will they remove them just for bad performance. Whether or not a position is secure depends more on political factors and personal relationships. This is just the way leaders of SOEs are selected.

Observations suggest that, if the leaders of SOEs want job security, they should pursue mediocrity. Why? If they perform too well, someone with better relationships will take over the position. Of course, if they perform too poorly, that is also a problem. I know of a large state-owned conglomerate with five subsidiaries. One very capable leader turned the fifth-ranked subsidiary into the first-ranked subsidiary. In the end, the head of the conglomerate appointed his secretary to replace the very capable person. The former secretary then turned the first-ranked subsidiary back into the fifth-ranked subsidiary. This type of example is prevalent. This is the reason I say managers of SOEs cannot be made to truly consider the long-term.

The fourth reason is the impossibility of hard budget constraints. We know that SOEs have a systematic default, which is Hungarian economist Janos Kornai's concept of the "soft budget constraint" (Kornai, 1980). Under the private ownership system, budget constraints are tight. If your earnings cannot offset your costs, you will go bankrupt. What does a soft budget constraint mean? Even if your earnings are smaller than your costs, you can still survive and even thrive because the government continues to provide support. With this expectation, managers of SOEs have little pressure to work industriously. Starting in the 1980s, the Chinese government attempted to continuously harden SOE budgets, but this issue is still not resolved. As soon as a SOE has a financial problem, the government saves them in most cases. The larger the enterprise, the greater the government help. Currently, the fiscal budget still includes subsidies for SOE losses. Even certain very profitable SOEs still receive billions of yuan in "policy subsidies" every year.

The fifth reason is the impossibility of checks and balances between managers and workers. While the government is the legal owner of SOEs, ideologically workers are the "master" of SOEs. This implies the managers of the SOEs have two principals. Because these two principals have conflicts of interests, the managers, as agents, can play a game between them. In practice, the managers are more likely to favor the "master" (workers) against the "owner" (government). The reason is workers are close companions, while the government is like an absentee landlord. Starting in the 1980s, many managers and workers of SOEs partnered to continuously increase their wages and bonuses. In today's terms, they colluded to carve up state assets. This problem has yet to be resolved. Therefore, we see that whenever a SOE relies on a monopoly to make money, employee wages will always be much higher than the market wage. Part of that wage should be understood as capital gains or consumer surplus, not labor's marginal contribution to the firm.

In addition to the five points from above, I want to emphasize that SOEs cannot become innovative firms, nor the vectors of innovation. The reason this is impossible is related to both the previously mentioned short-term behavior of SOE leaders and the required supervision of state-owned assets.

As was previously mentioned, innovation cannot be foreseen. It might succeed, but it might fail also. Imagine a SOE leader that attempts innovation and fails. What should happen? Could we assume the government will forgive the person, because it is natural that innovation might fail? If this were the case, then many SOE leaders would attempt meaningless innovation (including buying useless patents from individuals), and thus embezzle state-owned assets.

On the other hand, if the innovation fails and people are held personally liable, will truly innovative people then innovate? They will not. If 100 attempts are successful, but one is a failure, SOE leaders might not just face disciplinary action, but also prison time. There have been examples of this. If this is the way it is, then truly innovative SOE leaders will not innovate. Maintaining the *status quo*, as opposed to innovating, is the rational choice for SOE leaders!

Corporate Governance Must Be Entrepreneur-centric

Corporate governance is a hot topic both in academia and policy circles. It is mainly concerned with motivating and monitoring management of the corporation through incentive schemes and regulatory rules. However, in my view, a serious problem exists in contemporary corporate governance theories and practices (Zhang, 2018c). Its biggest issue is ignoring entrepreneurship.

Mainstream corporate governance theories assume that everyone is equally smart and rational, and there is a unique best solution to any business issue. Under this assumption, the problem faced in corporate governance is only the conflict of interest between investors and managers. The way to resolve this problem is to design an optimal incentive and restraint mechanism according to the principal-agent theory in economics that resolves the agent's "moral hazard." A so-called perfect corporate governance structure, established through the law or norms on the basis of such a theory, actually turns enterprises into quasi-bureaucratic institutions. "Perfect corporate governance" constrains professional managers, but it does not stimulate entrepreneurship. As a result, entrepreneurship is severely inhibited. Some excellent companies, such as Huawei, have chosen not to go public. Ren Zhengfei, the founder and the CEO of Huawei, knows that if the company went public, according to the rules of listed companies, his entrepreneurial role in the company would be difficult to play.

Corporate governance theories focus exclusively on conflicts of interests between investors or shareholders and operators (Hart, 1995; La Porta et al., 1997). In fact, there are two types of conflicts – not one – between shareholders or investors and operators or entrepreneurs. One is the conflict of interest, and the other is the conflict of cognition. Given that the future is uncertain and indeterminate, and that different people have different imaginations and judgments, the conflict of cognition is more challenging than the conflict of interest.

As I mentioned before, the reason an entrepreneur is an entrepreneur is because he can see what others cannot see. The essence of entrepreneurship is that it is very personal. The entrepreneur's judgments are often incomprehensible and unacceptable to ordinary people. As Israel Kirzner said, "entrepreneurship reveals to the market what the market did not realize was available, or indeed, needed at all" (Kirzner, 1979, p. 181). Mark Casson said: "The entrepreneur believes he is right, while everyone else is wrong. Thus the essence of entrepreneurship is being different because one has a different perception of the situation" (Casson, 1982, p. 14). Where most people do not see opportunity, an entrepreneur sees opportunity. Where most people mistakenly believe an opportunity exists, the entrepreneur disagrees. Most people (including shareholders) do not have such prediction and judgment abilities.

Therefore, entrepreneur's judgments might not gain the approval of investors (this is especially the case for small stockholders). Conflicts of cognition between investors and entrepreneurs are inevitable.

Traditional corporate governance theory has a basic assumption that shareholders are always right. It is assumed all rational people have the same judgments of the future, so perspectives are aligned on "good projects" and "bad projects." Thus, anything the entrepreneur does to displease the investor must be because the former gains at the expense of the latter. If something goes wrong, the operator must be blamed. This assumption is incorrect.

The shareholders are not always correct because many shareholders are not entrepreneurial. Even if they are entrepreneurial, there will still be conflicts because different entrepreneurs have different judgments about the same issue, or at least their judgment cannot be entirely the same as the operator. This is the reason many partners or even brothers that start a business together part ways in the end. Werner Siemens and Johann Halske at Siemens, Herbert Dow and his financial backers at the Midland Chemical Company, Henry Ford and Alexander Malcomson at Ford's second company, Bill Gates and Paul Allen at Microsoft, Steve Jobs and Steve Wozniak at Apple, the "Six Gentlemen" of Vantone Real Estate Group of China, the four Liu brothers of Hope Group, and the three classmate-founders of New Oriental, to name just a few, are all examples.[3] The main reason for their separation was a conflict of cognition, not a conflict of interests. The conflict of cognition is similar to a quarrel between a husband and

---

[3] For Werner Siemens and Johann Halske at Siemens, see Bahr (2017), chapter 8; for Hernert Dow and his financial backers, see Levenstein (1998), chapter 3; for Henry Ford and Alexander Young Malcomson, see Gleason (2016); for Bill Gates and Paul Allen at Microsoft, and Steve Jobs and Steve Wozniak at Apple, see Issacson (2014), chapters 8 and 9. Vantone Real Estate Group of China was established in 1990 by Feng Lun, Pan Shiyi and four friends. The six founders separated in 1994, with Feng staying with the original company and each of the other five starting up new companies. The Hope Group was founded in 1982 by the four brothers of the Liu family from Xinjin County, Sichuan Province and in 1995 was divided into four different companies, two of which are now on the list of the top 500 private firms in China. New Oriental Education was founded in 1993 by Yu Minhong and two years later Wang Qiang and Xu Xiaoping, two of Yu's classmates of the English Department of Peking University, joined the company with a common vision to build the best education business. In 2010, Wang and Xu left the company to start an investment business. Based on their stories, a film titled *Partners* was made and well received in China.

wife while decorating their home. The couple disagree not because they have different interests, but because they have different ideas as to what is the best design, material, color, and so on. I am willing to make a bold prediction: Most start-up business partners will split up in the end. Moreover, the more entrepreneurial the partners are, the more likely they are to split up. They are unable to convince others, so doing their own thing is for the best. People who are prone to compromise are unlikely to be great entrepreneurs!

Shareholders are not always correct. I want especially to emphasize that in most situations, small shareholders are incorrect. In corporate governance, I believe giving small outside shareholders a particularly large veto power is dangerous. It is not conducive to the development of the enterprise, nor is it beneficial to the small shareholders themselves. This is particularly true in the case of innovations, because innovations are often too entrepreneurial to be understood by ordinary investors.[4] Small shareholders are free riders to begin with, hoping to use other's entrepreneurship to make some money. If a large shareholder (generally the entrepreneur) must avoid merger and acquisitions that involve so-called conflicts of interest and the small shareholders have the final say, then it will be difficult to make a good decision. In reality, it is possible for a controlling shareholder (the entrepreneur) to harm the interests of small shareholders. Only people that do not understand entrepreneurship, however, will say that Li Ka-shing's huge wealth is the result of exploiting small shareholders.

Even regarding the conflict of interests between entrepreneurs and investors, it is not necessarily a "distribution problem" that traditional corporate governance theorists believe it is. As pointed out by Schumpeter, discussed in Chapter 2 of the current book, the entrepreneur has non-profit motives, including: (1) the dream to establish a commercial kingdom; (2) the will to conquer; and (3) the joy of

---

[4] Using both a theoretical model and historical cases, Lamoreaux and Rosenthal (2023) find that firms controlled by entrepreneurs can take on more difficult projects, and thus push the technological frontier out more rapidly, than firms controlled by investors. However, they still attribute the reason to the conflict of interests, not the conflict of cognitions. In their model, the conflict of interests comes from the "externalities" the entrepreneur enjoys but which the investors do not share, including enhancement of the entrepreneur's reputation, status, and job prospects, or perhaps just the feeling of achievement, whatever the outcome of the project.

creating. These three objectives are related to both the result and the process, both in positive and in negative aspects. We cannot say that anything non-profit oriented is inappropriate. If that were the case, many outstanding entrepreneurs would disappear. Schumpeter said: "Only with the first groups of motives is private property as the result of entrepreneurial activity an essential factor in making it operative. With the other two it is not" (Schumpeter, 1934, p. 94).

Non-profit motives are very important for someone to choose to be an entrepreneur. Traditional theories either ignore entrepreneurs' non-profit motive or dismiss it as a "moral hazard" problem that needs to be eliminated through the incentive mechanism. They do not see the positive role of non-profit motives, thus distorting our understanding of conflicts of interest or even mistaking conflicts of cognition for conflicts of interest. This is very regrettable!

Pure investors only care about return on investment but not about other goals pursued by entrepreneurs. This is especially the case for small outside shareholders. They only care about the result, not the process itself, because they do not obtain joy from the process itself. This inevitably leads to some conflicts, even if entrepreneurs do not steal or slack off. Due to the assumption that "shareholders are always right," traditional corporate governance and practice easily use the "fiduciary duty" of managers to negate entrepreneurship. The result is that the interests of investors are actually harmed.

The dual conflicts of interests and cognitions imply that corporate governance theory cannot assume that shareholders are always correct and thus entrepreneurs must obey them. Let me provide a few cases.

Case I: A milestone in corporate law was *Dodge v. Ford Motor Co.* in 1919.[5] At that time, Henry Ford owned 60% of Ford Motor Company, the Dodge brothers jointly owned 10%, and the rest was scattered among other shareholders. The company's accounts showed more than $10 million in undivided profits that could be used to pay dividends, but Ford did not pay any. Thus, the Dodge brothers went to court. Henry Ford's defense was that the company needed this money to expand. He was planning to build a second factory but did not want to pass the burden of growth on to the customers through higher prices. The prospects of the automobile market at the time were not

---

[5] *Dodge v. Ford Motor Co.*, 170 N.W.668 (Mich, 1919). See Robert C. Clark (1986).

great, but increasing investment was not without reason, because a company's investment decisions are not based on the current market situation. The decision was made on Ford's expectation and imagination of the future market.

The court ruled in favor of the Dodge brothers and made Ford pay the dividend. If we accept the uniqueness of entrepreneurial cognition, then perhaps the court's decision was a negation of Henry Ford's entrepreneurial judgment, not a defense of the fiduciary duty as argued by the judge. From that point on, Ford never trusted minority shareholders again, believing they had insufficient success and surplus failures, so he bought back all shares with cash. In hindsight, perhaps the court's decision harmed the interests of the Dodge brothers because they missed out on Ford Motor Company's explosive growth. There is a price to pay for stupidity!

Case II: Juan Trippe is an iconic figure in the history of aviation. He made a huge contribution to the entirety of human flight. Trippe founded Pan American Airlines in 1927 and served as the CEO. For a long time, basically, he had the final say in the major affairs of the company. The board of directors was filled with yes-men. Trippe's ambition was to "conquer the skies" by defeating the airships that dominated transatlantic flight at the time. He kept buying new airplanes and opening new routes (including South American, transpacific, and transatlantic routes), which made the company heavily indebted and resulted in the shareholders not receiving dividends for a long time. Trippe was convinced that this was the right thing to do over the long term and shareholders would be handsomely rewarded in the end. Trippe's ambitions were not understood by Cornelius "Sonny" Vanderbilt Whitney, the company's major shareholder. Mr. Whitney was a classmate of Trippe at Yale, was a playboy, and had invested in the film *Gone with the Wind*. During a board meeting in the spring of 1939, Whitney staged a coup. Within minutes, he had stripped Trippe of his power and took control of the company. Within a year, however, the company ran into trouble and the game was over for Whitney. The board of directors put Trippe back in control of the company. Whitney regretted his actions. After Trippe regained control, the company developed quite well. As it turned out, Trippe's strategy was correct and the shareholders were rewarded handsomely (Rose, 2020).

Case III: Investor stupidity left a deep impression on Steve Jobs. Steve Wozniak and Jobs founded Apple Computer Company in

1975, but Steve Jobs was driven out by the board of directors in 1985. The board members that drove him out included Mike Markkula and Arthur Rock, the first investors in Apple. They were fatherly figures to Jobs, but in the end sided with the CEO at the time, John Sculley. Twelve years later, when the company was facing bankruptcy, the board of directors had no choice but to invite Jobs back. Remembering the previous lesson, Jobs' condition for coming back was he would have the final say on new board members. The board agreed.

In January 1997, Jobs returned to the company as a "special advisor." In July 1997, the board of directors ousted CEO Gil Amelio. Interim CEO Fred Anderson said he "would work under the guidance of Steve Jobs."

Jobs quickly sought to remove the entire board of directors, with the exception of the chairman, Edgar Woolard. The board of directors complied. Among the people asked to resign was Markkula, the initial investor that had ousted him. With the help of Woolard, Jobs quickly assembled a new board of directors. Jobs once invited Arthur Levitt, the former Chairman of the Securities and Exchange Commission, to join the board. Levitt was excited and began to discuss his role on the board with Jobs. However, when Jobs read an article about corporate governance that Levitt published, he then rescinded the invitation. The viewpoint of the article was the board of directors should be strong and independent. Levitt was disappointed that Apple's board of directors was not designed to be independent of the CEO. That was correct, Jobs did not like a strong board of directors. He wanted the final say![6]

A board of directors pursues "collective decision-making" based on voting. In essence, collective decision-making is in conflict with entrepreneurship. In many cases, the collective is foolish, so entrepreneurial decision-making cannot be a crystallization of the collective wisdom. When we make individual decisions, we think about responsibility. When we make collective decisions, we think about avoiding responsibility. This leads to the "groupthink trap." A group of very rational and very intelligent people often make foolish decisions, bringing about huge disasters. Research by psychologists has shown that the more an organization emphasizes harmony and the absence of

---

[6] For the details of conflicts between Jobs and the board, see Isaacson (2011), chapters 22 and 23.

disagreement, the more likely it is to fall into the "groupthink trap," meaning make incorrect decisions.[7]

Of course, I am not advocating for entrepreneurs being unrestrained. If investors do not have a say, then they will lose their willingness to invest. There will be too many impersonators in the pool of would-be entrepreneurs. That is what I meant when I say the function of capitalists are the selection of entrepreneurs. You cannot do whatever you want with other people's money. You have lofty ideas and unique judgment, but these ideas and judgments might lead to disaster. So you must be constrained. Treating the capitalist as the principal and the entrepreneur as the agent is misleading, however. Traditional corporate governance theories and practices muddle managers and entrepreneurs. They focus too much on restraining managers. A good corporate governance cannot allow entrepreneurs to do whatever they want, but it also cannot shackle entrepreneurs. Good corporate governance should bring entrepreneurship into play to the maximum extent so that the most entrepreneurial people control the enterprise. In this view, one-share/one-vote might not be a good rule. Under that system, if shareholding is relatively dispersed or the entrepreneur is a minority shareholder, the most entrepreneurial person will not have a stable and enduring position. Using multiple classes of voting shares in favor of the entrepreneur may be preferred even from the point of view of the outside investors' interests. Therefore, corporate governance theories and practice should shift attention from managers to entrepreneurs.

Balancing the relationship between capitalists, investors, and entrepreneurs is the permanent theme of corporate governance. The greatest challenge corporate governance faces is the conflicts of cognition between entrepreneurs and investors, not conflicts of interest. We need an entrepreneur-centric corporate governance model. An effective corporate governance structure must put the most entrepreneurial people in control of the corporation, as well as incentivize them to innovate and create. We do not want to just select a few non-corrupt people and be done with it. A defect in the current corporate governance theory is it puts too much energy, law, and policy on constraining entrepreneurship and making corporations more bureaucratic and conservative, not more

---

[7] The term groupthink was coined by Irving L. Janis in his book *Groupthink: Psychological Studies of Policy Decisions and Fiascoes* (1982).

vibrant and creative. If we continue with the current corporate governance model, I believe our corporations might be less corrupt in the future, but at the same time will be less entrepreneurial. At that point, sustainable economic development is impossible. Companies exist to create value. They do not exist to not be corrupt. Entrepreneurs are the core of value creation. We must always remember that the best corporate governance is to ensure entrepreneurship plays the greatest role, instead of just preventing thieves. This all means that the legal rules of corporate governance must be general, flexible, and entrepreneur-friendly. As pointed out by Lamoreaux and Rosenthal (2023), no simple corporate governance rule is either normatively optimal or positively adopted. Any rule will fail the normative test because there will always be a range of disagreement between the entrepreneur and the investor, the two key stakeholders.

15 | *Protection of Rights versus Protection of Interests*

China needs innovation. China needs the rule of law. Innovation is inseparable from the rule of law. Innovation depends on entrepreneurs. These statements have become a consensus among most people, which is a good thing.

In my opinion, however, many people's understanding of the rule of law and innovation is still not in the right place. We could even say it is somewhat misplaced. For example, we often hear that the law should protect the interests of consumers, protect the interests of investors, protect the interests of minority shareholders, protect the interests of employees, and so on. These notions are misleading because – strictly speaking – there is no way to protect "interests." Protecting interests is not only incompatible with market competition, but also hinders innovation and leads to economic decline.

The rule of law should protect everyone's rights, but not anyone's interests.

Protecting Interests Is Incompatible with Market Competition

Market competition is essentially a race to see who can do better, who has lower costs, and who can create greater value for consumers. In market competition, there must be survival of the fittest. If the interests of some people are to be protected, then competition cannot be allowed. Moreover, protecting the interests of some people will inevitably infringe on the interests of other people at the same time.

For example, I might open a restaurant, and business is good. Suddenly, someone opens a new restaurant across the way with better food, lower prices, and more attentive service. The customers at my restaurant all go there, so my customer visits and profits decline. In the end, I go bankrupt. If my interests are to be protected, then that restaurant should be prohibited from operating. That would necessarily harm the interests of customers and the new restaurant owners.

Within the market, not only is there competition between producers, but also between consumers. There are some winners and some losers. For example, Moutai's production capacity is limited.[1] High-income earners have raised the price of Moutai to nearly ¥3,000, making it impossible for middle- and low-income earners to drink it. We could say that the high-income class has harmed the interests of the middle- and low-income classes. If we want to protect the interests of the middle- and low-income classes, we must prohibit the high-income class from purchasing Moutai, but doing so will harm the interests of the high-income class and Kweichow Moutai Company.

Producers lowering prices can also make some consumers feel that their interests have been harmed. For example, since Tesla's made-in-China Model 3 entered the market, the price has dropped four times in a row, from ¥358,000 to ¥249,000. It stands to reason that price cuts are good for consumers, but people that already own Model 3s will not believe this. Every time the prices dropped, existing car owners protested in front of the dealerships. This phenomenon is more prominent when new houses are sold at a reduced price. If the interests of previous customers are to be protected, then prices cannot be cut. However, this will harm the interests of new customers. Whose interests should be protected?

Even in non-market areas, the results of competition can hurt some people's interests. Suppose a university's economics department wants to recruit 10 graduate students, but 20 take the entrance test. The top 10 will harm the interests of the bottom 10, however. If the top 10 do not pass the test, then the bottom 10 now have a chance to be admitted. Since the number of spots is limited, those who do well on the test will always harm the interests of those who do not do well, and it is impossible to protect the interests of all candidates at the same time. Even a lottery will not solve the problem, because the lucky ones will harm the interests of the unlucky ones.

Therefore, interests cannot be universally protected. The so-called protection of interests, at best, is the protection of the interests of one group of people at the expense of another group.

---

[1] Moutai, or Maotai, is a distilled Chinese liquor (spirit), made in the town of Maotai in China's Guizhou province. It is a very popular drink at state functions and one of the country's most popular and highest priced spirits.

Protecting Interests Harms Innovation

I want to emphasize in particular that the interest protection concept is incompatible with innovation. Just as Schumpeter said, innovation is a type of creative destruction. It uses new products and new technologies to replace old products and old technologies. New enterprises replace old enterprises. Even new industries replace old industries. These all harm the vested interests of some people. Economic historian Joel Mokyr said that finding an example of a technological progress that did not reduce the value of some people's assets or capabilities is very difficult (Mokyr, 2002, p. 237). If we want to protect the interests of old products, old technologies, old enterprises, and old industries, then we cannot have innovation.

After Richard Arkwright invented the water frame, some manual producers of textiles went bankrupt. When the Stephensons invented the locomotive, the canals went out of use. Should the interests of the manual textile producers and canal companies have been protected?

Thomas Edison's invention of the electric lighting system destroyed the traditional gas lighting system. After the automobile appeared, the interests of those who originally raised horses, provided stables, built carriages, and drove carriages were all harmed. The success of the steamship pushed the original sailing ship out of the ocean transportation market. The invention of the printing press put hundreds of thousands of scribes out of work. The emergence of laser typesetting made hundreds of thousands of typesetters useless. Social media has made traditional print and television media outdated, even unsustainable. High-speed rail grounded many short-haul passenger flights. The list goes on and on. Should we protect the interests of all these losers? In fact, there is no way to protect them unless we reject any form of innovation.

The appearance of each new technology will harm the interests of some people. This has been the case since the ancient times to the present day. If we want to protect the interests of the harmed party, we must necessarily obstruct the progression of innovation. Therefore, we must acknowledge that interest protection and innovation are in conflict.

Historically, there has basically not been any innovation that has not been resisted or opposed. Resistance to innovation is enlarged by the asymmetry between those that are harmed and those that benefit (Mokyr, 1990, p. 256). Those harmed by innovation are primarily the producers of the traditional products and technologies that are being replaced. Their numbers are limited, but relatively concentrated in the same industry or location. They all know each other, and even have their own group (such as a guild or industry association) and spokespeople. Thus, they can easily voice opposition to gain attention.

Consumers benefit the most from innovation. Innovation allows them to have more choices and it continuously lowers prices. No innovation can succeed if an insufficient number of consumers obtain a large enough benefit. Consumers, however, are often just having fun silently. There is a large number of them but they do not know each other. They are hard to organize. Besides expressing their preference for new products through purchases, they cannot voice much support for innovation. The result is that the voices opposed to innovation are often louder than the voices supporting it.

The Rule of Law Must Protect Rights

The rule of law should not protect interests. The rule of law can only protect rights. Protecting interests is politics, not the rule of law. Politics emphasizes protecting interests, because the essence of politics is the balance of interests.

What are rights? Rights are not privileges enjoyed by some people, but instead are things that all people can enjoy equally according to universal rules.

Many rights in the real world evolved through human history. They were not the product of design. For example, when we line up, we defer to first come, first served. Why should the late-comers respect the rights of the people at the front of the line? If the late-comers do not respect the rights of the people in the front of the line, then their rights will be disrespected by the people that come even later. Their position in line will not mean anything (Sugden, 1989; Zhang, 2018b, chapter 12). Respecting rights is good for everyone.

Legally speaking, rights are the "categorical imperative" in Immanuel Kant's theories. A categorical imperative means that the rules must be universal instead of only applying to a few people. I am willing to view something as a right and also want others to view it as a right. This is true equal rights. The rule of law becoming a rule means that it applies to all concerned, thus a "categorical imperative."[2]

Kant's "categorical imperative" is similar to Confucius' statement made more than 2,000 years ago: "Do not do to others what you do not want to do to yourself." This is commonly called the "golden rule."[3]

Adam Smith's "impartial spectator" refers to evaluating fairness from the perspective of an independent third party, not the interests of the people involved.[4] The spectator's perspective is the result of the people involved considering the other party's perspective.

John Rawls, the great political philosopher of the twentieth century, has a classic metaphor: "The veil of ignorance" (Rawls, 1999). The rules of the game will be fair only when the parties are ignorant of their future position. Similar to when we divide a piece of cake, the pieces will be divided fairly when the person who divides the cake does not know who will get which piece. Otherwise, it is easy to be biased.

Therefore, rights are things people can enjoy equally. For example, doing business and providing goods and services to consumers is an equal right enjoyed by everyone. I have this right and so do others. As for who wins and who loses, only the customer (the market) can decide, because consumers' freedom to choose is also a right. No one has the right to deprive consumers of their freedom to choose. The reason forced buying or selling is illegal is not because it harms the interests of consumers, but because it harms the rights of consumers.

Of course, the reason rights are meaningful is because they affect the interests of the people involved. But rights and interests should not be confused. Rights can be protected and must be protected, but interests

---

[2] For Kant's concept of rights, see Mulholland (1990), chapter 2.

[3] The *Golden Rule* is the principle of treating others as one wants to be treated. Various expressions of this rule can be found in the tenets of most religions and creeds through the ages. It can be considered an ethic of reciprocity in some religions, although different religions treat it differently.

[4] See: Adam Smith's *Theory of Moral Sentiments* (1759). As Amartya Sen said: "Even though Smith's exposition of this idea is less remembered, there are substantial similarity between the Kantian and the Smithian approaches. In fact, Smith's analysis of the "impartial spectator" has some claim to being the pioneering idea in the enterprise of interpreting impartiality and formulating the standards of fairness which so engaged the world of the European Enlightenment" (Sen, 2009, p. 124).

Institutional Ecology of Entrepreneurship

cannot be protected. Only interests based on rights can be protected, and only interests based on rights should be protected.

Furthermore, the protection of interests is often in conflict with the protection of rights. Suppose a new merchant harms an existing merchant by offering a new product or service. If the government prohibits the new service, it is infringing on the rights of the new merchant and the customers.

Protecting Rights: A Matter of Rise and Fall of a Nation

In reality, people are concerned with not only the rule of law, but also politics. If political considerations outweigh rule of law considerations, protection of rights will give way to protection of interests. Of course, no country's laws only protect rights or only protect interests. The difference is a matter of degree, but degree matters!

A country's innovation ability, speed of progress, and even its rise and fall to a large degree depend upon whether the law protects rights or interests. For example, in the eighteenth century, science was more developed in France than Britain. France had more technological inventions, too. Even though Britain led in some of the most important technological advances, such as the steam engine, textiles, and iron production, many other inventions that made important contributions to the Industrial Revolution came from France and elsewhere. In Joel Mokyr's terminology: England was a net importer of macro-inventions but a net exporter of micro-inventions (Mokyr, 2009, p. 113). Chlorine bleaching technology, linen wet spinning, gas lighting, canned foods, jacquard looms, mechanical papermaking technology, and soda production technology were all major technologies invented by the French, but the British commercialized them (Ibid. chapter 7). Even the piston steam engine was originally invented by Denis Papin, a Frenchman.

Why did the Industrial Revolution happen first in Britain but not France? A major reason was that the French government mainly protected interests, whereas the British government mainly protected rights.

At that time, France was a highly centralized autocratic regime (Louis XIV's "I am the state"). The king had the absolute power to collect taxes without any form of restriction by the legislature. Doing business was a privilege and everything was forbidden without permission from the king. The main basis of French commerce was monopolies bought from the king. Mining anywhere required a concession. The nobility ruled French industry with little competition. During the reign of Louis XIV in the second half of the seventeenth century, the French government executed more than 16,000 entrepreneurs at once. Their only crime was importing and manufacturing cotton textiles in violation of Jean-Baptiste Colbert's industrial and trade policies (Hernando De Soto, 2000, p. 10).

The French government colluded with the guilds to tightly regulate commerce and inventions. The French guilds were very powerful. In order to protect vested interests, with the support of industrial officials, the guilds had detailed restrictions on all aspects of the production process and management. In the textile industry, for example, clothe dyeing had to comply with 317 regulations and be inspected by guild officials at any time. It was forbidden to use the British dyeing process. A textile enterprise could not own more than six looms. Workers could only be employed by guilds, not the enterprise. Guilds, in tandem with industry officials, set a minimum price for goods that no one could sell below. Under these circumstances, pressure groups could prevent the introduction of almost any new technology. The result was that although France did not lack inventions, it lacked innovation. The textile industry was stagnant, similar to other industries (Stark, 2007).

In contrast, the Monopoly Act was formally passed by the British Parliament as early as in 1624. In addition to establishing the patent system, it abolished other forms of franchise rights. Doing business became a universal right. After the Glorious Revolution, the government became a limited government. The power of the government was constrained by law. Locke's view of natural rights was deeply rooted in the hearts of people. Property rights were more effectively protected (Rosen, 2010, chapter 3). The power of English guilds was largely abolished, so even a barber like Richard Arkwright could transform into a cotton magnate. In France, a barber could not possibly become a spinner.

Traditional forces in Britain attempted to obstruct innovation, such as the "Luddite Movement" famous for destroying machines between 1811 and 1814. The British Parliament also enacted some prohibitions on the introduction of machinery in the early days. In general, though, the British government gave preference to the protection of rights (including patent rights). For example, in 1769, a law was passed to make destroying machinery a crime. In 1779, the government called in the army to suppress the machine-smashing riot in Lancashire. In 1780, Parliament rejected the cotton spinning workers' petition to prohibit cotton spinning machines. And other similar petitions were also rejected. In 1814, Parliament terminated the 250-year-old Statute of Artificers (Mokyr, 1990, pp. 257–258; Mokyr, 2002, p. 262). In England innovation continued to emerge in an endless stream and it was the first country to become industrialized. This was undoubtedly related to "rights taking precedence over interests" in England.

A large number of French inventions were first used by the British, precisely because France put "interests over rights" whereas Britain put "rights over interests." Mechanical papermaking is a typical example. In 1799, Frenchman Louis-Nicolas Robert applied for a patent for continuous papermaking technology. He got into a dispute with his boss, Saint-Léger Didot, over ownership of the invention. Didot believed England was a better place to develop the machine. Due to travel difficulties during the French Revolution, Didot sent his brother-in-law, John Gamble, to England. John Gamble was an Englishman living in Paris. After a series of introductions, Gamble was introduced to Sealy and Henry Fourdrinier, two brothers that owned a stationery store in London. They agreed to provide funding. Gamble obtained a British patent on October 20, 1801, known as the "Fourdrinier machine." By 1850, 90% of British paper production came from mechanical papermaking (Mokyr, 2009, p. 138).

Not only did England import French technology, it also "imported" French talents. England was a refuge for French entrepreneurs and inventors. In 1685, Louis XIV repealed the Edict of Nantes. Protestants were no longer tolerated. An estimated 80,000 Huguenots immigrated to England, most of them prominent entrepreneurs (Mokyr, 2016, p. 233). England's timepiece and instrument manufacturers primarily came from these Huguenots. The timepiece and instrument technicians made a major contribution to England's textile machinery industry. For example, the John Kay who helped Richard Arkwright invent the hydro-spinning machine (same name but different person from the John Kay who invented the flying shuttle), was a watchmaker.

England's most important talent imported from France was Marc Isambard Brunel. During the Revolution, he fled to the United States, then immigrated to England. He and his son, Isambard Kingdom

Brunel, were leading figures in British civil engineering during the first half of the nineteenth century. Marc Brunel is known for constructing the Thames Tunnel. Kingdom Brunel designed the first propeller-driven, ocean-going iron ship, the SS *Great Britain*. When it was launched in 1843, it was the largest passenger steamship ever built. He later designed and built the 22,000-ton SS *Great Eastern*, used later to lay the trans-Atlantic cable.[5] In the BBC's 2002 list of "100 Greatest Britons," Isambard Kingdom Brunel came in second place (behind Winston Churchill).

Britain's relative decline in innovation during the Second Industrial Revolution is related to its shift toward the protection of vested interests. After the middle of the nineteenth century, British skilled labor became increasingly hostile to new technologies. To obtain better wages, protect their special skills, and maintain superior working conditions, they successfully prevented the introduction of new machines in the production of shoes, carpets, printing, glass, and processed metals. The powerful trade unions in the textile industry successfully slowed the pace of innovation in the textile industry. They created a social atmosphere hostile to technological change. The ring spinning machine was prevented from replacing the traditional "mule machine." These issues caused England's flagship textile industry to lose international competitiveness (Lazonick, 1986, pp. 18–50; Mokyr, 2002, pp. 271–275; Mokyr, 1990, pp. 265–267).

Similarly, the United States losing ground in the automotive and steel industries to Japan in the 1970s and 1980s was largely the result of the United States protecting the vested interests of workers in those industries.

Innovation Should Have No Restricted Zone

I also want to emphasize further that innovation is an equal right enjoyed by everyone. There is no industry that cannot innovate. A rule of law society should not set domain limits on innovation, such as stipulating which fields are innovative and which are not. In fact, almost all innovations start from traditional fields. The Industrial Revolution that happened more than 200 years ago started in the

---

[5] See Chapter 2 of this book.

textile and metallurgy industries. These were very old industries but were similarly the most active fields of innovation.

Innovation grows out of an ecosystem. It is not planned. Ecology means that different species are interdependent, and no species is superfluous. It is highly possible that some entrepreneurs are only engaged in arbitrage activities, but they provide other entrepreneurs with opportunities and incentives to innovate. It is a mistake to believe that if real estate developers are banned, there will be a boom in high technology; or without the Internet, everyone will develop new materials.

From entrepreneurs' perspective, innovation solves a specific problem, especially when the starting point is resolving a technical issue. The end result of innovation, however, is unpredictable. Entrepreneurial innovation might start out just as a way to reduce production costs or to make the consumer experience better, not to change the world. In the end, however, it might truly change the world. The degree of change might be completely beyond anyone's initial imagination. Let me illustrate this using the steam engine as an example.

The original purpose of the steam engine was just to replace the manual winch for mine drainage. That remained the case for 70 years after Thomas Newcomen invented it and no one thought it had other uses. Even though James Watt's separated condensation tank greatly increased the efficiency of the steam engine, it was still a drainage tool. Later, with Boulton's encouragement, Watt transformed the steam engine from reciprocating motion to rotary motion, and the steam engine gradually replaced man power, horse power, wind power, and hydropower to become general power. Not only did it drive stone mills, but also drove textile machines and hammers. After Richard Trevithick invented the high-pressure steam engine, the steam engine became mobile power. Not only could it pull trains, but also drive ships. Watt himself opposed the high-pressure steam engine, believing it was too dangerous (Rosen, 2010, chapter 12). After the emergence of generators, steam engines could also turn generators to convert mechanical energy into electrical energy. The research on improvement of the steam engine led to thermodynamics, followed by new power engines such as internal combustion engines and steam turbines. With the internal combustion engine, there could be (gasoline-driven) automobiles and airplanes, as well as agricultural mechanization.

This type of evolution in the kinetic revolution does not mean that it was the only possible trajectory. The following hypothetical trajectory is also entirely possible. At first, someone attempted to replace the horse with a machine to pull a cart. The result was the invention of the steam engine, but it was too bulky to walk on its own. That innovation therefore failed, but someone used the steam engine to drive stone mills, and that innovation was successful. After the water pump was invented, someone used the steam engine to drive the pump that drained the mines, and that was also successful. After continuous improvement, the steam engine became general power, and finally replaced the horse for pulling carts until finally there was a steam carriage.

It is also necessary to point out that the diffusion of the steam engine was actually a very slow process (Rosenberg, 1976, pp. 174–182; Allen, 2009, pp. 177–181). The first Watt steam engine was put into use in 1776, but until 1830 waterpower still occupied half of England's fixed power. Between 1830 and 1870, the steam engine achieved an absolute advantage. Even during this period, however, hydropower usage increased by 44%. In the United States and continental Europe, the proliferation of the steam engine was even slower. By 1869, which was almost a century after Watt patented the steam engine, steam engines overtook hydropower in American manufacturing. In New England, steam power accounted for less than 30%.

The reason for the slow diffusion of the steam engine is related to the improvement of hydropower efficiency. Hydropower is a very traditional energy source. With the development of hydraulics over the 100 years between 1750 and 1850, hydraulic technology greatly improved. One of the biggest improvements was the replacement of the traditional over- and undershot water wheels with the breastshot water wheel in the 1750s. After that, there were some minor innovations to the breastshot. Another major improvement was the introduction of the French-invented water turbine in the 1840s. Before 1850, the steam engine did not have a very significant advantage over hydropower.

Waterwheel competition did not slow down the spread of the steam engine, but instead accelerated the progress of the steam engine. Just as biology evolves in competition, technology also progresses in competition. The steam engine continuously improved while competing with traditional hydropower. Fuel consumption and unit power costs dropped significantly. The steam engine finally replaced hydropower as the dominant power in the second half of the nineteenth century. It is conceivable that if legislation banned the waterwheel upon the emergence of the steam engine, then the steam engine would not have progressed so quickly. The water turbine later made hydroelectric power generation possible, which inspired the invention of the steam turbine. The steam turbine greatly improved the efficiency of steam utilization.

The debate between gasoline vehicles and electric vehicles is currently a hot topic. One inspiration from the competition between steam engines and hydropower is that the right of manufacturers to produce gasoline vehicles should be protected by law. Even if electric vehicles can achieve total victory over gasoline vehicles, using legal means to prohibit gasoline vehicles is inappropriate. Although banning gasoline vehicles would speed up the proliferation of electric vehicles, it would slow down the speed of technological progress for electric vehicles. Advocates of electric vehicles should realize that if electric vehicles were outlawed in the 1920s, they would be unlikely to make a comeback today.

Understanding innovation as "planting melons to eat melons, planting beans to eat beans" is a type of planned economy thought process.

In summary, the rule of law must protect rights, not interests. We should protect the rights of each person and allow each person's creativity to freely play a role. What a person thinks, says, and does is his own business. The only constraint is that the equal rights of others cannot be harmed. As long as we insist on this, the world will surely see endless innovations that change history, and we simply cannot imagine these innovations today.

16 | Challenges for Entrepreneurs from Conflicting Values

How Trade Brings Peace

There are three kinds of logic governing human history and reality. The first is the logic of the market. The second is the logic of power. The third is the logic of belief.

The logic of the market is benefiting others to benefit yourself with mutual cooperation and wealth creation. The logic of power is harming others to benefit yourself with plundered wealth. The thinking behind these two logics is different. Behind the logic of the market is the positive-sum game way of thinking. It is the belief that wealth is created, people can cooperate to achieve win-win, and both parties can be better off. Behind the logic of power is the zero-sum game way of thinking, or even the negative-sum game way of thinking. The belief is that there is a fixed amount of wealth. You being better off means I must be worse off. Conversely, if I want to live well, I must harm you.

The logic of belief is the idea that one's own belief is the only correct one. In an attempt to conquer others intellectually, you are even willing to use force. Many conflicts between people are not conflicts of interests, but instead conflicts of belief. Many disasters in human history were caused by conflicts of belief. The "belief" I am referring to here is broad. It includes religion, nationalism, ideology, values, etc. Below, I use the word "values" to encompass them all.

Does the logic of belief create wealth or destroy it? It depends on what you do believe or do not believe. For example, if you believe in the logic of the market, humanity will become more peaceful. If you believe in the logic of power, the world will become more conflicted.

In the long history of humanity, the logic of power was dominant. Only in modern times have we gradually transitioned toward the logic of the market. This transformation is related to globalization, especially the benefits brought by trade.

Adam Smith provided the moral foundation for the logic of the market. Before Adam Smith, personal gain was considered immoral. Adam Smith upended this traditional concept. He proved that the pursuit of self-interest is not inherently immoral. Rather, in the market economy, self-interest is the main driver of altruistic behavior. When exchange is done freely between people, personal gain can only come after others have benefited, so it is impossible to benefit oneself at the expense of others. The logic of the market not only enables people to change the way they realize their desire for wealth, but also makes it possible to replace the desire for power with the desire for wealth. Thus, cooperation replaces conquest. When people can gain wealth through exchange (the logic of the market), there is no need to plunder wealth by force (the logic of power).

The logic of the market not only applies to individuals, but also nations. Trade causes people and countries to be more interdependent and more likely to live in peace. An early advocate of the "trade peace theory" was French Enlightenment thinker Montesquieu. He said: "the natural effect of commerce is to lead to peace. Two nations that trade together become mutually dependent: if one has an interest in buying, the other has one in selling; and all unions are based on mutual needs."[1]

In a trade relationship, the seller does not want to go to war with the buyer's country. Neither does the buyer want to go to war with the seller's country. Therefore, there is a substitution relationship between commodities and militaries. Jean-Francois Melon, a good friend of Montesquieu, said: "The spirit of conquest and the spirit of commerce are mutually exclusive in a nation."[2] Michael Shermer wrote about Bastiat's Principle (referring to the nineteenth-century French liberal economist Frederic Bastiat): "Where goods do not cross frontiers, armies will, but where goods do cross frontiers, armies will not" (Shermer, 2015, p. 126).

In addition to the "trade–peace theory," Enlightenment thinkers also proposed the "democracy–peace theory." Immanuel Kant believed that the benefits of war go to the rulers, but the costs are borne by the common people, so only the rulers are interested in war. Democracy contributes to world peace because democratic governments' ability to

[1] Cited from Hirschman (2013), p. 80.   [2] Ibid.

raise money and recruit soldiers for war is restrained by voters, so the likelihood of war is lower.[3]

Over the past two or three decades, some scholars have done quantitative research on the relationship between trade, democracy, and war. For instance, Bruce Russett and John Oneal (2001) analyzed 2,300 international military conflicts between 1816 and 2001. They reached the following three conclusions:

(1) Democracies are less involved in wars. When two countries are fully democratic (a democracy score measuring between 1 and 10), disputes between them decreased by 50 percent, but when one member of a country pair was either a low-scoring democracy or a full autocracy, it doubled the chance of a quarrel between them.
(2) When trade factors are added, the likelihood of conflict is further reduced. Using democracy, relative military strength, national status, and economic growth as control variables, they found that countries with a high degree of trade dependence were less likely to be involved in military conflict. A country open to the world is less inclined to use force.
(3) Democracy peace only works when both countries are democracies, but trade peace works even when only one of the countries is a market economy. This means that trade contributes more to peace than democracy.

The Interests of Entrepreneurs Transcend Borders

What do entrepreneurs do? Entrepreneurs do business. Entrepreneurs are the practitioners of the market logic. Globalization over the past 500 years is largely the result of entrepreneurship. Every international trade route is created by entrepreneurs. Entrepreneurs not only want to make money, but also conquer the world. They have a dream of establishing a commercial empire. However, they do not use violence to conquer the world. Instead, they use better services or more affordable, high-quality products to conquer the consumer. A consumer is conquered when he is made better off, not when he fears violence. This is the difference between a commercial empire and a traditional political empire.

[3] Kant (1983 [1795]).

Karl Marx once said that capitalists have no homeland. Their home is anywhere they can make money. In other words, the interests of entrepreneurs go beyond national borders, religions, and nationalities. Of course, Marx also said that the working class has no homeland. The veracity of this statement, however, has not been proven.

This is precisely the reason entrepreneurs are a force for peace. When two nations have a conflict, merchant groups are often the buffers. Their pragmatic philosophy can defuse a lot of conflicts between nations.

We know that before China joined the World Trade Organization in 2001, the US Congress had to review every year whether it would continue to grant China "most-favored nation treatment." Before each review, many large American companies lobbied for China while American trade unions always opposed renewal.

During the May 30 Movement in 1925, the Chinese public boycotted foreign banks, causing a bank run. Some Chinese banks and money shops secretly aided British and Japanese banks through their difficulties.[4]

Similarly, in the summer of 1989, after the Tiananmen Event, there was a run on the Bank of China (Hong Kong) by Hong Kong residents, but HSBC, Standard Chartered, and other foreign banks provided funds to the Bank of China, ensuring the bank would not collapse.

In reality, entrepreneurs do have a homeland in ethnic, legal, and cultural senses. Nationalities do constrain entrepreneurs. No matter how much entrepreneurs' commercial interests transcend national borders, they will always be identified as entrepreneurs of a specific country not as entrepreneurs in general. If the values between two countries are different, especially when they are in a state of hostility, entrepreneurs might be in an awkward situation of "being unable to make anybody happy" even if they are just "in the business of doing business." If most people believe in the logic of power, it will be difficult for the logic of the market to succeed. In the age of nation-states, nationalist beliefs are a powerful force that influences consumer behavior and thus entrepreneurial choices. Nationalism is essentially the logic of power.

---

[4] The May Thirtieth Movement refers to Chinese labor and anti-imperialist movements in the mid- to late-1920s that sprung out of reaction to the Shanghai Municipal Police using deadly force to end a protest in the International Settlement on May 30, 1925.

In addition, most entrepreneurs also hold their own beliefs. Different entrepreneurs may have different beliefs. If your beliefs conflict with national beliefs, then it is inevitable that your business activities will be negatively affected.

A conflict of values can destroy a business or even an industry. Entrepreneurs are often helpless in this regard. Allow me to illustrate this point with the story of the airship.

Conflict of Values and the Destruction of the Airship Industry

Recall that, in Chapter 11, we discussed the history of airships in detail. The German entrepreneurs, Count Ferdinand Zeppelin and Hugo Eckener, are two of the most important figures in the history of airships. Zeppelin invented the airship. After his death in 1917, Eckener succeeded him. For both of them, airships were life. They hoped to seal the divisions between countries and bring peace and prosperity to mankind. They created a new industry, but in the end it failed.

Why did the airship ultimately lose out to the airplane? There are many technical reasons, of course, but nationalism and conflicting values also played an important role. The rise and fall of the airship industry highlights the challenges faced by entrepreneurs due to conflicting values.[5]

As an airship entrepreneur, Hugo Eckener faced three value conflicts. The first was the nationalism conflict between Germans and the victorious countries after World War I. The second was the conflict of his own values when compared with the values of Adolf Hitler. The third was the conflict between American values and Hitler's values.

As it relates to the first aspect, German nationalism actually helped Eckener. After World War I, the Treaty of Versailles distributed the remaining airships as war reparations to the victors (Britain, France, and the United States). As punishment, Germany was also prohibited from producing airships with a capacity of more than one million cubic feet. This almost sent Eckener's airship career up in smoke. Out of nationalistic feelings, however, German workers destroyed the airship that was meant as reparations for the United States. This gave his airship company a new chance at life. Eckener persuaded the

---

[5] The following materials are drawn from Rose (2020).

Americans to allow him to produce a new airship to compensate the United States. This temporarily sustained the airship company and its technology, production equipment, and talent. By 1925, the Allies finally ended the ban on German production of large airships. This could be considered Eckener's lucky break.

As it relates to the second aspect, Eckener's own values and Hitler's were out of step. Eckener had been the presidential candidate of the Social Democrats and he publicly criticized the Nazi Party, both of which made him intolerable to Hitler. After becoming chancellor, Hitler ordered Eckener's arrest, but President Hindenburg intervened. This stymied Hitler's passion for airships and Eckener had difficulty getting support for airships from the Nazi authorities. Given Eckener's lofty reputation in Germany and the international community (especially the United States), Hitler always had misgivings about dealing with Eckener. However, Hitler giving control of the company to Ernst August Lehmann, who sympathized with the Nazis, meant Eckener had to devote much of his time and energy to internal power struggles at the expense of the company's development.

In their conflict with Hitler, the Americans did Eckener a big favor. On March 7, 1936, Germany remilitarized the Rhineland, violating the Treaty of Versailles. Prior to this, Joseph Goebbels used the airships *Graf Zeppelin* and *Hindenburg* to promote a "referendum" in the Rhineland. Eckener opposed the use of airships for such political purposes. For this and his other disapproval of and disrespectful remarks toward the Nazis and Hitler, Goebbels "unpersoned" him. Being unpersoned meant he did not exist. Eckener's name could not appear in media. When the media mentioned him, they could only use "Lotte's father" (Lotte being the name of his daughter). Eckener had to turn to President Roosevelt for a chance to fly the *Hindenburg* (LZ-129) to New York for the first time. Roosevelt invited him to the White House. Out of respect for Roosevelt, the Nazi authorities removed Eckener from the "unpersoned" list. Because of this he was finally able to command the first flight of the *Hindenburg* airship to the United States.

Eckener could not escape the conflict of values between the Americans and Hitler, however. This conflict decimated his airship career.

Airships can use two types of gasses: hydrogen and helium. The biggest difference between the two is that hydrogen is much more flammable than helium. Due to an English airship incident in October 1930, Eckener decided to use helium when designing the *Hindenburg*, instead of the traditional hydrogen. At that time, however, only the United States had the ability to produce helium. The Helium Act of 1925 categorized helium as a "strategic material." Only helium unusable within the United States could be exported. Exports required unanimous consent from the Department of Commerce, Department of the Interior, State Department, War Department, the US Navy, and the president. It could not be used for military purposes.

When Eckener sought permission to purchase helium, the Commerce Department and State Department agreed. But Harold Ickes, the Secretary of the Interior, was a steadfast anti-Nazi. The application was held up by him. President Roosevelt wanted to avoid the wrath of German Americans and Jewish Americans, so he had an ambiguous attitude.

Eckener had no choice but to personally visit Ickes in Washington, D.C. When they met, Ickes had three conditions. The first was a written guarantee from Hitler or Goering that the imported helium would not be used for military purposes. Both of them knew, however, that the leader of a country could not give this kind of written guarantee to another country's department secretary. This matter went nowhere. Eckener could only abandon his original plan. The airship was redesigned to continue using hydrogen. The *Hindenburg* made its 11th flight to the United States in May 1937. That was the first flight to the United States of that year.

After the incident, both the United States and Germany reflected on it. Roosevelt and Hitler exchanged friendly letters. Many Americans expressed sympathy after the incident. They believed that America bore some responsibility for the incident. Not selling helium for airships used in civil aviation violated humanitarian principles.

A few days after the incident, President Roosevelt organized a "special cabinet committee." Members included the Secretary of the Interior, Secretary of Commerce, Secretary of the Navy, Secretary of War, and Secretary of State to discuss whether helium should be sold to Germany. When the committee met on May 19, they leaned toward agreeing to exports. Even Secretary Ickes softened his stance.

Eckener also went to Washington, D.C. and testified to the US Senate Committee on Naval Affairs, guaranteeing that airships would not be used, under any circumstances, by Germany for warfare.

On September 1, 1937, the US Congress revised the Helium Act. Export restrictions were loosened. The revised law mandated temporary permits issued by the Department of State, with approval from the National Munitions Control Board and final approval from the Secretary of the Interior.

At the time, the LZ-130 airship was near completion. According to the Zeppelin Company's plans, by 1940, there were to be no less than four airships operating between Europe and the Americas. The company was also considering passenger airships for India and Asia. If helium could be acquired, then the airship industry might have the opportunity to develop into something big.

In October 1937, the request to procure 18 million cubic feet of helium was submitted. Cordell Hull, the US Secretary of State at the time, approved it and the National Munitions Control Board did not oppose it.

Secretary of the Interior Ickes made three conditions. First, a written guarantee from Hitler or Goering that helium would not be used for military purposes. Second, the price per cubic foot must increase from $8.50 to $10. Third, a one-time $500,000 punitive deposit must be made. These three conditions were difficult for Germany to accept. Goering protested during a visit to the American ambassador and threatened to boycott the 1939 World Fair being held in New York.

Just as opinions on selling helium to Germany was split within the American government, Hitler became more aggressive. Ickes believed that as long as he could stall a little longer, Hitler would show his true face. At that point, he could leverage public opinion to oppose helium sales to Germany.

As expected, on March 12, 1938, Nazi Germany annexed Austria and began a purge against Jews. "Aryanization" was pushed forward in full. American public opinion began to change quickly. Opposition to selling helium to Germany became louder. Opposition organized by Jews and labor unions was especially fierce.

Under these circumstances, on May 14, 1938, Eckener again personally traveled to Washington, D.C. to visit Ickes as a final effort. The two of them got along, and Ickes had great respect for Eckener. During the talks, Eckener repeatedly explained to Ickes that helium had no military value. At the end of the talks, Ickes asked: "What guarantee can you give us that the Nazi regime will not seize the helium gas for other than peaceful purposes?"

Eckner was tested by his conscience. His words would determine the result. As long as he swore by the guarantee, he could obtain the helium he coveted. His airship career could continue. He knew very well the type of man Hitler was, however. Making such a promise was against his conscience. He made a moral choice: Stop his efforts in the airship business. He replied: "I can give you no such guarantee; in fact, my only fear is the same that you entertain."

After making this statement, Eckener knew that his airship career was over.

Seeing Eckener's pained expression, Ickes said that Congress might change the relevant law or his successor might have a different viewpoint. They both knew that was unlikely. The airship era was already over!

The Sino–US Conflict of Values

What point am I trying to explain with the airship example?

Value conflicts bring about a major challenge for entrepreneurs, both within a country and between countries. This type of challenge might come from the government or the public. Over the years, certain Korean, Japanese, and American firms have faced difficulties in China. Certain Chinese firms have had trouble in America. These are related to the value conflicts between countries. This point is especially worth the focus of today's entrepreneurs.

A serious conflict of values has always existed between China and the United States. The United States is a democratic country, valuing individual freedom, private property, and the rule of law. China is an authoritarian country, holding the opposite values. During the first 30 years of Reform and Opening, this conflict did not cause much difficulty for Chinese entrepreneurs. The reason was that Americans within the government, academia, and industry all believed that China's market reforms would certainly cause China's political system and values to inevitably move closer to those of the United States, so they were more than happy to transfer technology to China, invest in China, and train Chinese talent as a means to change China. China made the best of a mistake and took business as business. It even hoped the United States would change.

That was only wishful thinking for both sides. Now, both sides acknowledge that neither side's values will draw closer to the other's within the foreseeable future. The United States cannot change China, and China cannot change the United States either.

In the past, only China worried about US-driven peaceful evolution. Now, because China has become strong and aggressive, the United States has also begun to worry about Chinese-driven peaceful evolution. Therefore, over the next few decades, value conflicts will be the primary source of conflict between the two countries. It will be a common challenge faced by entrepreneurs from both countries.

Entrepreneurs engaged in international trade will face more and bigger challenges in the future than they originally have, especially because the entire industrial chain is interdependent. When doing business in a mine field, you can be blown to pieces at any time. In other words, it will be like walking at night after curfew and being asked for the passcode. If you do not know the passcode or say the wrong passcode, then you will be punished. It is also like having two heads of a work unit in conflict with each other. Who do you follow? If you follow one, the other will be upset. If you follow neither of them, both will be upset, so you will be at a loss.

This will be a tremendous challenge faced by American entrepreneurs, Chinese entrepreneurs, and other countries' entrepreneurs in the future. For both American and Chinese entrepreneurs, microchips are Eckener's highly demanded helium. The restriction on sale has been imposed. It can be expected more resources, technologies, and customers will be restricted. Things that could be bought in the past might not be purchasable in the future. Business that could be done in the past might not be doable in the future. There will be more and more entity lists. It will be more and more difficult to pass through national gates. Product quality and customers will no longer determine who you can and cannot sell to; instead, the government will.

The United States used the excuse that Huawei and ZTE did business with Iran to sanction them. In the future, firms might be punished for selling products in certain regions (such as Tibet and Xinjiang) of China. American firms might also be punished for this. Similarly, Chinese firms might be punished by the Chinese government for selling particular products to American firms.

Even if the government does not punish enterprises, the public, under the influence of nationalism, might punish firms. Entrepreneurs must recognize that nationalism will create a tremendous challenge for their business in the future. When nationalism is prevalent and a conflict occurs between nations, a common commercial practice might be labeled "treasonous" behavior. An entrepreneur might be condemned or boycotted by the public simply because of one politically incorrect sentence on their website or one offensive word in an advertisement.

Some people might say that a cold war cannot occur between the United States and China because they are so interdependent. I do not see it this way. The goal of a cold war is to cut off these relationships. The consistency of interests may not be able to defeat the conflict of values.

Of course, as I pointed out earlier in this chapter, trade is a force of peace. The logic of the market is an important driving force for the evolution and convergence of human values. As a practitioner of market logic, entrepreneurs can and should make a difference in resolving conflicts of values. In history, entrepreneurs are both creators of wealth and innovators of ideas. Many breakthroughs in traditional values are the result of the efforts of entrepreneurs. I believe that as long as entrepreneurs can persistently practice the logic of the market, human beings will have hope to move toward harmony. There is a long way to go!

Appendix A
My Journey Studying Entrepreneurs

To appreciate the importance of research on entrepreneurs, we must remember three things. The first is the cultural background. In traditional cultures, both East and West, religious and secular, merchants and entrepreneurial activities were despised. The New Testament says that "it is easier for a camel to go through the eye of a needle than for someone who is rich to enter the kingdom of heaven." Confucius said: "The mind of the superior man is conversant with righteousness; the mind of the mean man is conversant with gain."[1] The Chinese saying *"wu shang bu jian"* translates to: "all businessmen are dishonest." People's disdain for entrepreneurial activities is to a large degree based on perception, not interests. The second thing to remember is the theoretical background. Mainstream economics lacks the entrepreneur. The word "entrepreneur" is not even in the vocabulary of the textbook. Producer's decision-making in mainstream economics is a computational program, not entrepreneurial decision-making. Mainstream economics assumes that the market is always in an equilibrium state and the future is certain. This fundamentally excludes entrepreneurship. The third thing to remember is the institutional background. The essence of the planned economy is repudiation of entrepreneurship. It deprives individuals of the freedom to choose, start a business, and innovate. Central planning assumes the planning authorities grasp all required information about supply and demand. Entrepreneurship is not only unnecessary, but also harmful because it undermines the formation of the plan and interferes with the execution of the plan. Therefore, any country that implements a planned economy has no room for entrepreneurial activity.

---

[1] English translation by James Legge (1861).

Since writing my first essay in 1983, entrepreneurs have been the topic of my research over the last 40 years. Entrepreneurs make an appearance in most of my books and articles. The course of my research on entrepreneurs can be recapped in three phases:

The First Phase (1983–1989) Viewing the importance of entrepreneurship and changes in ideas from the perspective of economic and social change: The position of entrepreneurs in economic development; entrepreneurship and changes in social viewpoints; the relationship between entrepreneurs and the ownership system; the growth path of Chinese entrepreneurs.

The Second Phase (1990–2008) Opening the black box of the firm and understanding the enterprise system from an entrepreneurship perspective: Exploring the theory behind the origin of the capitalist firm and establishing "An Entrepreneurial/Contractual Theory of the Firm"; applying my theory of the firm to analysis of Chinese state-owned enterprise reform; analyzing the relationship between entrepreneurship and corporate governance.

The Third Phase (2008 to the Present) Understanding economic growth and market operations from the perspective of entrepreneur decision-making and competency to unify theories on entrepreneurs, economic growth, and the market: Understanding the relationship between entrepreneurs and China's economic growth; conceptualizing the "Smith–Schumpeterian Growth Model"; generalizing entrepreneurial functions as arbitrage and innovation; assessing how entrepreneurs as a discovery force as well as a creative force play a leading role in the market and growth; researching the mental model of entrepreneurial decision-making and thoroughly reflecting on the neoclassical economics paradigm.

The First Phase (1983–1989)

Viewing the importance of entrepreneurship and changes in ideas from the perspective of economic and social change

In November 1983, I wrote an article titled "The Core of Enterprise Quality is Entrepreneur Quality."[2] There were four core viewpoints. First, entrepreneurs are the soul of an enterprise. Second, entrepreneurs

---

[2] Unpublished.

are different from professional managers in that the function of professional managers is management, whereas the function of entrepreneurs
is "innovation." Third, risk-taking is one of the foundational qualities
of entrepreneurs. Fourth, a lack of risk-taking is a "common ailment"
of Chinese enterprise leaders.

Based on this essay, I participated in the national "reformers conference" held in Hefei, Anhui Province in May 1984. This conference was
initiated by the then well-known reformers such as Professor Wen
Yuankai of the Science and Technology University of China and
Bu Xinsheng (one of the then most famous businessmen). Attendance
at the conference was invite-only. I mailed Professor Wen my essay.
After reading it, he sent me an invitation. During a small-group discussion, I talked about entrepreneurship and received positive feedback
from other participants. Sanlian Press had recently published a translation of Robert "Bob" Considine's book *The Remarkable Life of
Armand Hammer* (1975). Wang Yan, the editor of *Dushu Magazine*,
heard my remarks and asked me to write a review of the book—that
became the article "The Times Require Entrepreneurs with an
Innovative Spirit" in September 1984. This would be the first published article about entrepreneurs in Chinese economic circles. The
three subheadings of this article are actually three important propos-
itions. First, entrepreneurs are the "kings" of economic growth.
Second, innovation is the basic function of entrepreneurs. And third,
risk-taking is one of the foundational qualities of entrepreneurs.

After the article was published, it aroused quite a large response
from readers. I was extremely lucky to get acquainted with Sheng Bin,
who was working at the Central Party School. His research dealt with
Chinese economic history, especially focusing on the history of Chinese
capitalism and modern Japanese history. Thus, he was very familiar
with the generation of Chinese entrepreneurs after the Westernization
Movement (such as Sheng Hsuan-huai and Chang Chien). My article
resonated with him, and the two of us hit it off, leading to our book *On
Entrepreneurs: The Kings of Economic Growth*. We submitted the
book to the People's Publishing House in 1987 and it was published
in early 1989 (a revised edition, titled *Entrepreneurs: The Kings of
Economic Growth*, was published by the Shanghai People's Press in
2014). There were five chapters in total and to this day it is still a
relatively complete description of entrepreneurs. We described the
social status of entrepreneurs, the function of entrepreneurs, the

qualities of entrepreneurs, and the social conditions that produce entrepreneurs. We also proposed two possible growth paths for Chinese entrepreneurs: peasant entrepreneurs and the entrepreneurization of bureaucratic managers.

Looking back, my views on entrepreneurs had a positive impact on changing people's concept of "entrepreneurs" from a negative connotation to a positive one. I remember after the conference in Hefei, Li Zhijiang at the *Beijing Daily* hoped I could write an article on entrepreneurs for his newspaper. However, after I wrote the article, it could not be published. One reason, Li told me, was the chief editor disagreed with two words. The first was '*qiyejia*' (entrepreneur) and the second was '*maoxian jingshen*' (risk-taking spirit). I asked: Then what can be used? He said I could use '*shiyejia*' (industrialist) and '*tanxian jingshen*' (adventure spirit). I disagreed but they deceived me and changed risk-taking to adventure spirit while keeping entrepreneur. Thus, "The Adventure Spirit is One of the Foundational Qualities of Entrepreneurs" was published by the *Beijing Daily* on June 13, 1984.

This incident shows that at the time "entrepreneur" was still a derogatory term in Chinese society, equivalent to "capitalist" and synonymous with exploiters. For China's reforms to truly succeed, people's traditional perceptions of entrepreneurs had to change. To change people's traditional perceptions of entrepreneurs, ideas needed to change. Ideas needed to modernize because entrepreneurs as a group is the product of modern ideas and the result of enlightenment. When I traveled the country during that time, the topic of my speeches was "Entrepreneurs and Modernization of Ideas." I proposed ten big concepts that needed to change, and have listed them below:

1. Wealth Concept: From Water in the Glass to Water in the Well ("Zero-Sum Games to Positive-Sum Games" in today's terms);
2. Time Concept: From Circular to Linear (Time is Money);
3. Equality Concept: From Equality of Outcome to Equality of Opportunity;
4. Labor Concept: From Physical Exhaustion to Intellectual Exertion (the value of knowledge and the absurd story of *The Foolish Old Man Removes the Mountains*);
5. Consumption View (Happiness View): From Reducing the Denominator (Desire) to Expanding the Numerator (Enjoyment);

6. Money Concept: From "The Root of All Evil" to "Social Reward";
7. Hero Concept: From "Studying to Become a Government Official" to "Studying to Become a Businessperson";
8. Moral Concept: Moral Judgment Cannot Replace Economic Calculation;
9. Native Land Concept: From "Loving the Countryside and Loving the Land" to "The World as Home" (Talent Mobility, Abolition of the Household Registration System);
10. Talent Concept: From Favoring Morals over Talent and Favoring Personal Virtue over Social Morality to Favoring Social Morality and Risk Taking.

These views were integrated into the (inaugural) 1985 first paper of *Guanli Shijie (Management World)*. At that time, China's most influential official news magazine was *Liaowang Zhoukang (Outlook Weekly)*. Its editor serialized my articles in five consecutive issues. . These essays played a relatively large role in changing people's opinions of entrepreneurs.

In September 1986, the *People's Daily* published my article titled "Bring Up True Entrepreneurs." The core concepts of this article were as follows. First, the commodity economy equals the market plus entrepreneurs (or the market economy equals prices plus entrepreneurs).[3] Second, a lack of entrepreneurs was the primary difficulty faced by reform, and thus the arduousness and persistence of reform. The objective of reform was to replace government officials with entrepreneurs as the main part of economic operation. Third, the contingent of entrepreneurs is the product of a specific arrangement of property rights. China's current property ownership system can only produce bureaucratic managers, not true entrepreneurs. Fourth, reform of the ownership system was key to create a contingent of entrepreneurs. Fifth, opening the market was the basic way to bring up entrepreneurs.

On this foundation, I further wrote a more systematic, much longer article, titled "Entrepreneurs and the Ownership System." This article was first internally published in the Economic System Reform Research Center of China's *Research Report No. 30* (December 10, 1986). This

---

[3] At the time, the term "market economy" was ideologically/politically incorrect. So, Chinese economists used the term "commodity economy" to refer to the market economy.

article has two major parts. In the first part, I proposed that modern companies are the disintegration of entrepreneurial functions, not the separation of ownership and control. In the second part, I proposed the theorem that entrepreneurs cannot exist under state ownership. The first section was openly published in the 1987 first issue of *Jingji Yanjiu* (*Economic Research Journal*). The second part of the article was cut out just before going to print by the journal editor because of ideological and political sensitivity.[4]

The Second Phase (1990–2008)

Opening the black box of the firm and investigating the enterprise system from an entrepreneurship perspective

I wrote "Bring Up True Entrepreneurs" and "Entrepreneurs and the Ownership System" because Chinese economics circles were avoiding the ownership system issue although the importance of entrepreneurs was gradually accepted. An official viewpoint was entrepreneurs are important, but the ownership system is not important because entrepreneurs can exist independent from the ownership system. These two articles were written in opposition to this type of viewpoint. However, I felt my thesis at the time was not thorough. I recognized in order to understand the relationship between entrepreneurs and the ownership system, we must clearly answer the question: "Why does capital hire labor?" When I attended Oxford University for my doctoral studies in 1990, I took this issue with me. After reading a large amount of literature, I discovered mainstream economics does not answer this question. Actually, in mainstream economics, it is inconsequential whether capital hires labor or labor hires capital. This is not surprising because in mainstream economics, the firm is just a production function with no role for the entrepreneur at all. I wanted to open the black box in an attempt to understand the firm from entrepreneurs' perspective. This was the origin of "An Entrepreneurial/Contractual Theory of the Firm," which was an exploration of the logical origin of the capitalist firm.

I believe the firm has value because differences exist in people's entrepreneurial ability. By allowing the people with the most

---

[4] A new campaign of "anti-bourgeois liberalization" was launched in January 1987, which led to Party General Secretary Hu Yaobang's dismissal.

entrepreneurial abilities to specialize in business decisions while the people with less entrepreneurial capabilities focus on production, the firm will create more value than having each person produce independently. However, for a firm to create value, it must resolve two key issues. The first is personnel selection, i.e. selecting entrepreneurial people to take control of the enterprise. The second is incentives, i.e. giving each member of the firm (including entrepreneurs) sufficient incentive to work. Based on the answers to these two issues, I proposed a very simple logical explanation for the capitalist enterprise system. The capitalist firm is a system of efficiently solving both the incentive and the selection of entrepreneurs.

First, I showed the most important and most likely to slack-off members of the firm should be owners of the firm (residual claimants). Not only are entrepreneurs the most important people, they can also slack-off the easiest, so entrepreneurs must be owners of the firm. Turning entrepreneurs into owners allows them to self-monitor, otherwise there is no way to implement effective monitoring.

Next, I showed capital hiring labor is a type of systematic arrangement to guarantee the most entrepreneurial people control the firm in situations where entrepreneurial ability is difficult to observe and cannot be measured with objective standards. Capitalists must assume risk. Therefore, the incapable people do not dare say they are capable under the capitalist system. In contrast, if public capital is invested, there will be a lot of pretend entrepreneurs. If a society eliminates private property, a logical inference is it will lose the self-selection mechanism of entrepreneurs.

The Chinese edition of my doctoral thesis was published by the Shanghai People's Press in 1995 as *Qiye de Qiyejia-Qiyue Lilun* (*An Entrepreneurial/Contractual Theory of the Firm*). Actually, that was the subheading of the original text. The English edition was published in 2018 as *The Origin of the Capitalist Firm* and the subheading was kept.

Even though my doctoral thesis was pure theory, its ideas can be clearly applied to analyze China's economic reforms. At the time, there was debate in theoretical circles. Some non-Chinese economists used statistics to show that state-owned enterprise reform increased enterprise performance, but Chinese scholars generally believed state-owned enterprise reform was not successful. Using my theories, I came to the following conclusion: "Decentralization of decision power and transfer of profits" reform can resolve managers' short-term incentive problem but cannot resolve long-term incentives. The reason long-term incentives could not be resolved is because the operator selection problem had not been resolved, meaning there was no way to guarantee that the state-owned enterprise is operated by the entrepreneurial people. Selection by bureaucrats is different from selection by capitalists. If capitalists choose the wrong person, they bear the risks. If bureaucrats choose the wrong person, they do not need to bear any cost. If the operator selection problem cannot be effectively resolved, then state-owned enterprise reform cannot truly succeed.

On June 6, 1995, my colleague Justin Yifu Lin and I had a debate at Peking University. The media hyped it up as "crossfire at Beida." Our speeches were published in the China Economic Research Center of Peking University's bulletin. Our primary disagreement was that Professor Lin believed the problem for state-owned enterprises was an unfair playing field, caused by heavy social burdens on state-owned enterprises, whereas I believed the ownership system was the root cause. A series of my articles on Chinese enterprise reform later formed the book *The Theory of the Firm and Chinese Enterprise Reform* (first published in 1999). For many years, this book has ranked as one of the most cited books in Chinese humanities and social sciences. *An Entrepreneurial/Contractual Theory of the Firm* also ranks among the most cited books in those categories.

After the year 2000, I began to focus more on the relationship between entrepreneurs and corporate governance. Traditional corporate governance theory centers around managerial incentive problems. The core issue discussed is how to motivate and discipline managers' behaviors. Stated simply, it is trying to prevent corruption (moral hazard). According to my theory, moral hazard is a secondary issue. The primary issue is selecting the best person and making entrepreneurship play a true role. In the market economy, "diligence" cannot substitute for "competency."

Therefore, I proposed that entrepreneurial selection is more important than managerial incentives. An "entrepreneur-centric corporate governance model" should be established. A landmark event in 2004 was the "Gu-Lang Dispute." Gu Cujun was an overseas-returned entrepreneur. By taking over a few insolvent state-owned enterprises and restructuring them, Gu became a famous billionaire. Professor Larry Lang, a Taiwanese finance professor from the Chinese

University of Hong Kong, repeatedly accused Gu of stealing state assets. Gu was eventually sentenced to 12 years in prison by a local court. State-owned enterprise reform was disrupted. The reason Lang's viewpoints were inflammatory and could change the course of state-owned enterprise reform is related to defects in mainstream corporate governance theory. The *Economic Observer* published my article titled "Be Kind to People that Contribute to Society" as a response. My view was that without an understanding of entrepreneurship, it is impossible to understand how an actual enterprise operates and how values are created by entrepreneurs. Without understanding how an actual enterprise operates, we will treat legitimate value-creating activities as illegal acts of exploiting small shareholders and embezzling state-owned assets.

During this period, I also explored the relationships between entrepreneurs and professional managers, between entrepreneurship and enterprise core competence, between entrepreneurs and government, as well as between entrepreneurs and public opinion. This research formed the main content of my books *Property Rights, Incentive and Corporate Governance*, published in 2005, and *Core Competence and Growth of the Firm*, published in 2006. The former book is a relatively systematic dissertation on corporate governance and explains corporate governance from the entrepreneur's perspective. In 2014, it was re-published as *Understanding Companies: Property Rights, Incentives and Governance*.

I summarized six misunderstandings of popular theories about corporate governance structure. The first mistaken belief is that competition can substitute for private ownership of property. The second mistaken belief is that perfect corporate governance can substitute for ownership incentives. The third mistaken belief is that stricter regulation leads to more effective governance. This often stifles entrepreneurship, instead. The fourth mistake is making corporate governance the business of the government, which damages the market's reputation mechanism. The fifth mistake is assuming small shareholders are always right and innocent, when actually they are free riders. The sixth mistake is assuming company problems are solely caused by the incentive mechanism and ignore problems caused by "ignorance."

Besides the books already mentioned, there are some other books related to the content discussed previously, including *Property Rights, Government, and Reputation* (2001), *Market and Government* (2014), and *The Power of Ideas* (2014).

The Third Phase (2008 to the Present)

Understanding economic growth and market operations from the perspective of entrepreneur decision-making and competency

The third phase began in 2008, which happened to be the 30-year anniversary of Reform and Opening. At that time, in a paper I prepared for a conference convened by Professor Ronald Coase of the University of Chicago, I proposed looking at what the most intelligent and entrepreneurial people are doing to understand a society's development. From this perspective, what was China's biggest change over the last 30 years? China's entrepreneurial talents were reconfigured. Originally, our most outstanding people joined the government. After the reforms, the most outstanding people gradually went into enterprises. The Confucian Analects tell us: "The good student should apply himself to be an officer" (*xue er you ze shi*). This changed to "The good student should apply himself to be a businessman" (*xue er you ze shang*).

I distinguished between the three generations of entrepreneurs that appeared after China's Reform and Opening. The first generation was peasant-background entrepreneurs. The second generation was bureaucrat-background entrepreneurs. The third generation of entrepreneurs were overseas-returnee students or those with an engineering background. We now have the fourth generation composed of people born in the 1980s and 1990s. These generations of entrepreneurs jointly and successively pushed forward China's rapid economic growth.

In 2012, I published the book *What Changes China* (Zhang, 2012). The answer is entrepreneurs![5] During this period, I conceptualized the "Smith–Schumpeterian Growth Model." Adam Smith proposed that market scale determines division of labor; division of labor determines technological progress; technological progress determines economic development. A positive and accelerating cycle is thus formed. However, this cycle requires entrepreneurs to push it along. I put the entrepreneurship emphasized by Schumpeter in the central position because each link is inseparable from every link. Markets are discovered and created by entrepreneurs. New divisions of labor and industries are created by entrepreneurs. Technological progress is even more the result of entrepreneurial innovation. Turning new income

[5] Weiying Zhang. 2012. *What Changes China (Shenma Gaibian Zhongguo)*. Beijing: CITIC Press.

into new markets also relies on entrepreneurs. Entrepreneur-driven growth is a positive feedback process.

Currently, economists generally utilize two types of theories to understand economic growth. The first is the neoclassical growth theory, which understands economic growth from the perspective of capital inputs and total factor productivity. The second is Keynesian macroeconomics, which explains economic growth through changes in aggregate demand. I believe these theories are futile and even lead to misled decisions because they both ignore entrepreneurs. I believe the Smith–Schumpeterian growth model allows us to better understand the real world's economic growth better than all other growth models, including the neoclassical growth model and the Keynesian short-term growth model.

I proposed a series of viewpoints about the two functions of entrepreneurs. The two functions of entrepreneurs are arbitrage and innovation. So-called arbitrage refers to finding profit-making opportunities and increasing the efficiency of resource allocation given technological circumstances. Innovation is pushing the production possibilities frontier outward by creating new products, new production methods, and new resources. I wrote this viewpoint into the book *Principles of Economics*, published in 2015. This was the first time entrepreneurship was systematically written into an economics textbook. Other economics textbooks lack the entrepreneur. They do not even have the word "entrepreneur" in the index because there is no place for the entrepreneur in neoclassical economics.

I used this framework to analyze China's economic growth, and I believe that the high growth rate over the last few decades was driven primarily by arbitrage-oriented entrepreneurs. The three generations of entrepreneurs of China, especially the first two, were basically arbitrage-oriented entrepreneurs. Now, there is less room for arbitrage. Future growth will primarily rely on innovation-oriented entrepreneurs. However, innovation is much more demanding of institutions. Systems and cultures suitable for arbitrage are not suitable for innovation. Innovation-oriented entrepreneurs have completely different requirements on the system. The reason is simple. Arbitrage is short-term behavior whereas innovation is long-term behavior. Therefore, without effective protections for intellectual property and stable expectations, it is difficult for entrepreneurs to have an incentive to innovate. For China to transition from growth driven by arbitrage entrepreneurs to growth driven by innovation entrepreneurs, a whole set of reforms must be initiated.

These views are reflected in my article titled "China's Future Growth Depends on Innovation Entrepreneurs."[6] and my co-authored book titled *Entrepreneurship and the Chinese Economy.*[7] This book was a collaboration between my students and I. It is a relatively systematic explanation, from many aspects of entrepreneurship, of the next steps in China's reforms.

During this period, I began to comprehensively reflect on mainstream economic theory. Mainstream economic theory is a static theory describing an unchanging circular economy. This is the reason it lacks entrepreneurs. Mainstream economics assumes each person is omniscient, the future is certain, risk can be calculated as probability, and resources, preferences, and technology are given. Entrepreneurship is not needed.

Both Chinese and English versions of my two articles titled "Reflections on Economics"[8] and "A Paradigmatic Change Is Needed"[9] have been published (2015 and 2021, respectively). The two paradigms refer to the neoclassical paradigm and the Austrian School paradigm. The key difference between the two is one includes entrepreneurs and the other does not. I believe neoclassical economics distorts our understanding of the market because it studies an imaginary market, not the real market. By comparison, the Austrian School of economics has a relatively better market theory because it studies the real market. Economics requires a paradigm change similar to astronomy's change from the geocentric theory to the heliocentric theory.

I recognized the key to understanding the market is understanding entrepreneurship. The key to understanding entrepreneurship is understanding human "ignorance" and the future's uncertainty and indeterminacy; that is, understanding the essence of knowledge. I became a disciple of Hayek. The market is the process of creating, discovering, and applying knowledge. Knowledge is essentially dispersed, subjective, difficult to use intensively, and limited. This is the reason we need entrepreneurs. Entrepreneurship is essential for efficient, orderly, and

---

[6] Weiying Zhang. 2017. "China's Future Growth Depends on Innovation Entrepreneurs." *Journal of Chinese Economic and Business Studies*, 15 (1): 19–40.

[7] Zhang, Weiying and Yong Wang. 2019. *Entrepreneurship and the Chinese Economy. (Qiyejia Jingshen yu Zhongguo Jingji).* Beijing: CITIC Press.

[8] Weiying Zhang. 2015. "Reflections on Economics: Market Failure or Market Theory Failure?" *China Economic Journal*, 8(2): 109–121.

[9] Weiying Zhang. 2021. "A Paradigmatic Change Is Needed for Understanding the Real Market." *China Economic Review* 66: 101602.

continuously changing markets. To understand entrepreneurship, we need to understand Ludwig von Mises, F. A. Hayek, Joseph Schumpeter, Israel Kirzner, and G.L.S. Shackle. Understanding entrepreneurship means knowing neoclassical economics is not a good market theory and not getting misled by Keynesianism. Understanding entrepreneurship means knowing that the so-called Market Failure theory is absurd. Understanding entrepreneurship means rejecting central planning and industrial policy in all its forms. Understanding entrepreneurship means knowing the role of economists is to defend the freedom and legal environment in which entrepreneurship flourishes, not coming up with ideas helping the government set policies that inhibit or distort entrepreneurship.

In a book I published in 1989,[10] I discussed "what entrepreneurship is." I must confess, however, that I believe I did not truly understand what entrepreneurship is until the last few years. For people that believe in science – especially people that have a formal education in economics – to truly understand what entrepreneurship is, I recognized that they must understand what entrepreneurship is not. This applies to scholars, bureaucrats, the average person, and even entrepreneurs. The following three points are particularly important. First, entrepreneurial decision-making is not scientific decision-making. It is not based on data and calculation but is instead based on imagination and judgment. Second, entrepreneurial decision-making is not finding a solution under given constraints but instead is changing the constraints. Third, profit is not the only goal of entrepreneurs. Instead, entrepreneurs have goals beyond profit.

The above is the path of my research on entrepreneurs over 40 years. My goal in studying entrepreneurs is to change people's views and improve the environment for entrepreneurs. My hope is to appeal to the government to implement true reforms that make our property rights system, legal environment, and cultural atmosphere more favorable to the role of entrepreneurship, starting a business, and innovation. This is the only way China, and even the whole world, will have more glorious prospects!

---

[10] Weiying Zhang and Sheng Bing. 2014(1989). *The Entrepreneur: The King of Economic Growth* (*Qiyejia: Jingji Zengzhang de Guowang*). Horizon Shanghai People's Press.

Appendix B
How I Came to Know the Austrian School of Economics

According to the teachings of Confucius, people know the "decrees of Heaven" only after turning 50 years old. I must admit that long before that point in my life, I believed I was a true neoclassical economist. During my graduate studies, I read some second-hand writings on the socialist calculation debate of the 1930s. Although I knew Ludwig von Mises and Friedrich von Hayek were steadfast opponents of the planned economy, my knowledge of the Austrian School of economics was limited, so let us not even talk of a systematic understanding.

A Staunch Defender of Neoclassical Economics: 1982–2008

During my undergraduate studies, I majored in political economy. After four years, I had a thorough understanding of the systemic reasoning and basic theories of traditional political economy, which is mainly Marxist economics. According to the standards of the time, I was an outstanding graduate. In February 1982, I was lucky to meet Mao Yushi and Yang Xiaokai at an academic conference held in Xi'an. Mao's "principles of optimal allocation" was refreshing. Yang's theories on the division of labor also opened my eyes. Meeting the two of them became a turning point in my academic career. Therefore, as soon as I entered graduate study, I decided to systematically study "Western economics," even though my graduate field of study was still political economy, where *Das Kapital* was a required subject. At that time, what we called "Western economics" was what we now call "mainstream economics." Actually, it is what the Western academic world calls "neoclassical economics."

At the time, some economics departments of Chinese universities established "Western economics majors." In fact, they studied Western economics as an academic school and took it as the target for criticism as "bourgeois philistine economics."[1] Graduates of these programs were broadly knowledgeable and could even vividly state a few anecdotes about famous Western economists, but they did not have a firm grasp of the foundational knowledge of economics. I once met some graduate students who majored in Western economics from prestigious Chinese universities but could not even understand the microeconomics curriculum when they went on to study at Western universities. In contrast, I took "Western economics" as true economic science. It is a tool for the analysis of practical economic problems. It is not a research object, nor is it the target of criticism. In my studies, I always attempted to grasp its analytical methods and systemic logic, not seek out its internal contradictions and fallacies.

The theoretical system of neoclassical economics has become extremely mathematical. In order to truly grasp this theoretical system, I also specifically enrolled in a few mathematics courses (including calculus, probability theory, and linear algebra) and participated in the "Seminar on Operation Research and Linear Programming" that was organized by several faculty members of the mathematics department. Because my university did not have an instructor with the background to teach mainstream economics, I organized a six-person reading club. Members included graduate students from the economics department and young instructors, as well as an undergraduate student from the mathematics department that eventually tested into the graduate economics program. I taught myself the subject matter, then volunteered to teach the other members of the group. In order to have credibility as an "instructor," I had to conduct rigorous mathematical derivation of every equation, every curve, and every theorem in the textbook. I benefited from this and concluded: The best way to learn is to be a teacher. When I received my master's degree in 1984, mainstream economics was the academic genetics of my way of thinking. Some people say that the articles I wrote were not at all like the writings of a graduate student of political economy. The writing was too "westernized."

There are different schools of thought in mainstream economics. The Chicago School is the classic form of neoclassical economics, and

---

[1] According to Marxism, Western economics after David Ricardo was all "bourgeois philistine economics," not scientific, and Marxist political economy was the only scientific economics.

I admired it. Milton Friedman's analysis of the superiority of the free price system and the defects of government intervention were extremely convincing. I read his *Freedom to Choose* multiple times. I have a series of papers on the Chinese economic transformation written in the spirit of Chicago. After I graduated in December 1984, I got a research job at the Economic System Reform Institute of China, which was newly established as a policy think tank for the then Prime Minister, Zhao Ziyang. Friedman's influence on me was so great, that a colleague there gave me the nickname "Milton Zhangman"! Of course, I knew that he disagreed with my neoclassical viewpoints, and we often argued.

In October 1987, my work unit sent me to Oxford University for 14 months of advanced studies. Three years later, I went back to Oxford University to pursue a Doctor of Philosophy in economics. I returned to China in August 1994, so I had spent five years at Oxford in total. After five years of training at Oxford, my theoretical foundation of neoclassical economics was much more solid. I also had a better understanding of the latest developments in mainstream economics (especially game theory and information economics). Almost all of the new theories in economics that I learned were developed on the neoclassical paradigm. For this reason, new economic theories (including new institutional economics, transaction cost theory, information economics, etc.) did not cause me to doubt the theoretical foundation of neoclassical economics, but instead strengthened the neoclassical style in my research. This point can be seen in my doctoral dissertation and later work. In my doctoral dissertation, I attempted to provide a new explanation for the "capital hiring labor" system of the capitalist firm, based on information economics. The Chinese version was published in 1995 by the Shanghai People's Press. An English version was published by Springer in 2018 as *The Origin of the Capitalist Firm: An Entrepreneurial/Contractual Theory of the Firm*. In an article published in *Jingji Yanjiu* (*Economic Research Journal*) in 2000, I used a mathematical model to show that power struggles within a firm are related to the institutional arrangement of property rights.[2] It is quite a pleasant thing to be able to analyze both an internal

[2] Weiying Zhang. 2000. "Property Rights Arrangement and Internal Power Struggle of the Firm" (Chanquan Anpai yu Qiye Neibu de Quanli Douzheng). *Economic Research Journal* (*Jingji Yanjiu*), 6: 41–50.

institutional arrangement and power struggles within a firm utilizing a rigorous mathematical model.

I had always been a strong defender of the neoclassical system! Of course, I knew, from time to time, that criticisms of neoclassical economics had come from the academic world. For a long time, however, like many other believers of neoclassical economics, I always considered critics as laymen who do not understand neoclassical economics. It was not worthwhile refuting them. The neoclassical cornerstone is unbreakable! Without this cornerstone, the market economy is without a theoretical foundation! It seems now that this is a fatal conceit. I had not realized that neoclassical economics can also provide theoretical support for the planned economy. The Lange model for economic planning is a neoclassical theory.[3]

Although I am convinced of the neoclassical economics system, it has always been like a piece of clothing that is too tight. It restricts movement. I had always thought I was traveling along the route directed by neoclassical economics. From time to time, I deviated from this path. For example, the entrepreneurship that I had always advocated was difficult to fit into the framework of the neoclassical paradigm. But before the summer of 2008, I had not realized it.

2008: Awakening to the Thinking of the Austrian School of Economics

In mid-July 2008, Professor Ronald Coase organized the Chicago Conference on China's Economic Transformation. I was invited to attend, and submitted a paper titled "The Reallocation of Entrepreneurial Talents and Economic Development in China."[4] As the title implies, this paper analyzed how entrepreneurs in China had come about over the last 30 years, and how they drove China's rapid economic growth. Lee Benham, the director of the Ronald Coase Institute, was a discussant of my paper. The first sentence he said was, "This paper is very Austrian." His statement made me suddenly realize

[3] Oskar Lange. 1938. "On the Economic Theory of Socialism." *On the Economic Theory of Socialism*. Edited by Benjamin E. Lippincott. Minneapolis: University of Minnesota Press.
[4] For the revised version, see Weiying Zhang, W. W. Cooper, Honghui Deng, Barnett R. Parker, and T. Ruefli. 2010. "Entrepreneurial Talents and Economic Development in China." *Socio-Economic Planning Sciences*, 44(4): 178–192.

that—all along—I had been more of an Austrian School economist than a neoclassical economist!

Lee Benham's statement made me reconsider my own academic career. As it so happened, at that point in time I was reading Mark Skousen's *Vienna and Chicago, Friends or Foes?*[5] This book made me realize even though I had always thought I was a disciple of the Chicago School of neoclassical economics, in fact, my way of thinking was closer to the Austrian School! My faith in the market is as thorough as that of Mises and Hayek. Milton Friedman and George Stigler often had some reservations. The Chicago School often brought government intervention in through the backdoor! Of course, compared to Keynesian neoclassical economics, the Chicago School and Austrian School are more like friends. Perhaps my limited knowledge of the Austrian School was the reason I aligned myself with the Chicago School for a long time.

During my graduate studies in 1984, I published two papers. One paper proposed the dual-track price reform. The other discussed the importance of entrepreneurs in economic development.[6] Looking back, these two papers could be seen as an application of Mises–Hayek theory. Due to incomplete information and dispersed knowledge, price rationalization can only happen through a continuous trial and error process. (This was the core viewpoint of Mises and Hayek in the great socialist calculation debate of the 1930s.) In the real world, free prices can only trend toward equilibrium, but cannot reach equilibrium. Precisely because I acknowledged this, I proposed transforming the price formation mechanism as the key to price reform. I did not propose using administrative means to adjust the price to the "rational" level. Instead, I proposed the policy of gradually liberalizing

---

[5] Mark Skousen. 2005. *Vienna & Chicago: Friends or Foes?* Washington, DC: Capital Press.

[6] My thoughts on the dual-track price system reform were put forward in the article "Yi Jiage Tizhi Gaige wei Zhongxin, Daidong Zhengge Jingji Tizhi de Gaige" (Taking Price Reform as the Center of Systemic Economic Reform), completed April 21, 1984. It was first published in June 1984 as part of *Expert Suggestions III*, an internal reference material for the Energy Group of the State Council Technology and Economic Research Center. An English version was included as an appendix chapter in Weiying Zhang. 2015.*The Logic of the Market* (Washington, DC: Cato Institute, pp. 265–282). My first article about entrepreneurs was titled "The Times Require Entrepreneurs with the Spirit of Innovation" (Shidai Xuyao Juyou Chuanxin Jingshen de Qiyejia) and was published in *Dushu* in 1984, Issue 9.

prices through the "dual track system." If we strictly followed the Chicago School's price theory, then price rationalization could either be achieved through one major adjustment or one 'big bang' liberalization. Similarly, I acknowledged the leading role that entrepreneurs have in the operation of the market and economic growth. That is precisely the reason I declared, "the times require entrepreneurs with the spirit of innovation." In 1989, Mr. Sheng Bin and I published the book *Jingji Zengzhang de Guowang: Lun Qiyejia* (*Entrepreneurs: Kings of Economic Growth*). Over the last 30 years, I have made entrepreneurship my primary research focus. Entrepreneurs are central to the Austrian School but have no place in neoclassical economics.

A reexamination of the paper I completed in April 1984 will find that the idea of dual-track reform I proposed is actually the evolutionary idea of F. A. Hayek. The "ignorance" of humans is the reason the price reform must be carried out in a step-by-step manner, rather than through adjustments by the government. It is impossible to know what a reasonable price is. In the original text, I wrote that the first reason why administrative price adjustment was not a solution to the problem was:

Prices represent a structure with infinite parameters. We cannot know the value of the parameters without knowing the supply-and-demand functions of every product. Instead, we know only that price changes cause a chain reaction, but we cannot know the specific degree of the chain reaction.[7]

I also wrote:

Unlike price adjustment, price system reform is a continuous process. The issue is not whether the first step attains a rational price, but whether there is a trend toward one.[8]

I had not read Hayek's work at that time, so I could be considered a Hayekian without knowing it.

Further, my thoughts on the dual-track price reform were related to my understanding of the role of entrepreneurs and the formation of the entrepreneurial contingent in the market economy. In the original text, when discussing the four obstacles to price reform, I wrote:

[7] Weiying Zhang. 2015. *The Logic of the Market: An Insider's View of Chinese Economic Reform*. Washington, DC: Cato Institute Press.
[8] Ibid. p. 275.

Enterprises are not accustomed to the market because we lack a generation
of entrepreneurs. In the past, we implemented the "state standard theory."
Enterprises were the servants of administrative bodies and dealt with fulfil-
ling production plans rather than making business decisions. In the current
flexible market, enterprises must transition from production units to business
operators; that is similar to asking a child who has never left home to live
independently. There must be a period of adjustment. Initially, it will be
difficult to avoid certain issues, and that difficulty will increase the friction
coefficient of reform. We should differentiate between the chaos caused by
defects in the market and the chaos caused by enterprises' misunderstandings
of the market mechanism. The defects of the market may need to be fixed by
planning, whereas enterprise adjustment to the market can be resolved only
by the market itself.

Entrepreneurs represent the soul of enterprises. The quality of an entrepreneur determines the quality of the enterprise. As enterprises transition, the
function of entrepreneurs will become more important. In some ways, the
coming era is the era of entrepreneurs. They must have the ability to (a)
absorb information, (b) discover investment opportunities, (c) raise capital,
(d) organize production, (e) implement technology, and (f) open new
markets. Those capabilities require them to have a spirit for risk taking.
The old system stifled the formation of that kind of entrepreneurial
group. The majority of people leading our enterprises are "safety first"
administrative bureaucrats, not entrepreneurs with the courage to explore.
It is hard to imagine that a market mechanism inserted into a planned
economy could operate smoothly without entrepreneurs. We can anticipate
that if we have a batch of new-era entrepreneurs, systemic reform will
be much smoother.[9]

After the Chicago Conference, I bought the great works of the
Austrian School from the Mises Institute website. I also bought every
Chinese translation of Austrian School literature that I could find.
I eagerly read these books and resented myself for not discovering
sooner the treasure that is the Austrian School. At the same time,
I was glad to have unconsciously deviated from the path of neoclassical
economics very early. If I had not deviated from neoclassical theory
first, I might not have been able to maintain the consistency of my
viewpoints. Regardless, from the perspective of a person with a lifelong
aspiration for economics and firm belief in the market, neglecting such

[9] Ibid. pp. 281–282.

an important school of thought is unforgivable. Moreover, it is the best market theory!

Just as I was concentrating on reading the work of Mises and Hayek, a financial crisis swept the globe. The Global Financial Crisis is considered the largest economic crisis since the Great Depression of the 1930s. After the crisis erupted, popular opinion almost unanimously blamed economic liberalization. Western pro-market mainstream economists kept their silence. Keynesian interventionist policies made a comeback as all types of bailout policies were implemented. However, one article I read noted that Mises and Hayek were the only two economists to predict the Great Depression. *The Economist* magazine also reported the Bank for International Settlements Chief Economist William White foresaw a financial crisis as early as in 2006. White is an Austrian School economist. Later, I met him at the Mont Pelerin Society Meeting held in Hong Kong in 2014.

After I put considerable effort into reading Hayek's *Prices and Production* (which is actually very difficult to follow), I understood how only Austrian School economists foresaw these two great crises. I recognized that the Austrian School's theory of the business cycle, which was originally proposed by Mises and later developed by Hayek, had the most convincing explanation of economic cycles. Simply put, economic and financial crises are not failures of the market. Instead, they are the inevitable consequence of the government's inflationary policy. Inflationary monetary policy causes interest rates to be lower than the normal level. This misleads entrepreneurial decisions. Entrepreneurs invest excessively and consumers consume excessively, which artificially distorts the structure of production. Bubbles occur in equity and real estate markets. However, because these types of inflationary policies are not sustainable, a crisis will certainly happen. Keynesian stimulus policies might mitigate the crisis in the short term, but it appears they create a bigger crisis in the long term. In light of this, I gave a speech in early 2009 titled "Completely Bury Keynesianism." It criticized China's ¥4 trillion stimulus package. Of course, even though my criticisms were later proved correct, very few people agreed with me at the time. People that understand the Mises–Hayek business cycle theory are rare. Hayek was awarded the 1974 Nobel Prize in Economics for his business cycle theory; however, very few mainstream economists are familiar with his business cycle theory. This is quite bewildering!

2009 to the Present: Systematic Reflections on Mainstream Economics and Constructing a Theory of Entrepreneurs

Starting in 2009, I began to systematically reflect on mainstream economics. From 2010 onwards, I gave a few speeches about "reflections on economics" and "the paradigmatic transformation of economics."[10] My basic viewpoint is, up to this point, the Austrian School of economics is the best market theory. It studies the real market. The way people behave is its starting point for understanding how the market operates. It understands the market as a continuous process of discovering and utilizing information. It gives entrepreneurship a central status. It understands economic growth as a continuous process of innovation. It can correctly foresee the unintended consequences of government interference in the market. It unites both microeconomics and macroeconomics. It can propose a logically consistent and factual interpretation of economic crises. By comparison, neoclassical economics is not a good market theory. It studies an imaginary market contained in the computers of economists. It understands the market as static, not a process of discovery and competition. Although it assumes people are self-interested (which is true), it overlooks the importance of ignorance and ideas. It ignores entrepreneurship. It cannot tell us the true cause of economic growth. It separates microeconomics and macroeconomics. It cannot explain economic crises, but still wants to proscribe a solution, overestimating the power of science and reason. It claims to have proven the Pareto efficiency of perfect competition markets, but provides a theoretical justification for unlimited government interference in the market. The reason for this is a free competition market cannot possibly have "perfect competition."

Neoclassical economics considers "perfect competition" to be the ideal model of the market economy. It is the benchmark for measuring market efficiency. According to this definition, so-called perfect competition refers to an infinite number of small firms producing equivalent products with equivalent technology and selling them at equivalent prices. Anyone who understands actual market operations knows that "perfect competition" defined in this way is the absence of competition,

---

[10] Weiying Zhang. 2015. "Reflections on Economics: Market Failure or Market Theory Failure?" *China Economic Journal*, 8(2): 109–121.

because it is incompatible with innovation and technological progress! We will not mention whether or not this is an ideal market that society should pursue. Interventionist policies that attempt to transform the real world into a "perfect competition market" can only bring about a series of disasters. Imagine setting monkeys as the standard for human beauty. Men and women would have to undergo painful plastic surgery to become "attractive." Unfortunately, criticisms from Austrian School economists like Mises and Hayek did not have the slightest impact on mainstream economists' faith in the "perfect competition" paradigm.

In the second half of 2016, Professor Lin Yifu and I started a debate on the efficiency and feasibility of industrial policy. This debate led me to further recognize how easy it is for neoclassical economics to lead people astray. Our disagreements about industrial policy are disagreements between the two different paradigms of the market. Professor Lin embraces the "neoclassical economics paradigm." I embrace the "Mises–Hayek paradigm."[11] All of Professor Lin's arguments are based on the market failure theories of neoclassical economics. However, so-called market failure is instead neoclassical economics market theory failure, not failure of the actual market. In order to prove the efficiency of the market, neoclassical economists made certain very strong—but unrealistic—assumptions (including perfect competition, perfect information, and economic activity without externalities). A natural logical inference is that since these assumptions are not satisfied in the real world, so-called market failure must have occurred. In fact, effective market operation in no way depends on the assumptions of neoclassical economics.

According to the Austrian School paradigm, market efficiency only depends on the following assumptions: (1) Not only are people self-interested, but are also ignorant; (2) human action is purposeful, and only individuals are capable of making decisions; and (3) competition is free when individual rights are effectively protected by the law. Among these three assumptions, the first two are very realistic. No one can deny these two axioms. Together, they mean the government cannot be better than competitive entrepreneurs at selecting

[11] For writings on the debate between the two sides, see Justin Yifu Lin. 2016. "Industrial Policy and Economic Development: Perspective from New Structural Economics." *Comparative Studies (Bijiao)*, 6: 163–173. Weiying Zhang. 2016. "Why I Oppose Industrial Policy: Debate with Justin Yifu Lin." *Comparative Studies (Bijiao)*, 6: 174–202. Chapter 12 of this book was mainly taken from my article.

industries and technology. Whether or not the third assumption exists depends on the government. Industrial policy often makes this assumption difficult to achieve. If the third assumption can also be achieved, then competitive entrepreneurs will continuously create new technologies, new products, and new industries. Market failure is the result of government intervention (including industrial policy), it does not constitute the reason for government intervention.

I have said that I have studied entrepreneurship for about 40 years, but only in the last few years have I understood what true entrepreneurship is. This is thanks to the writings of Ludwig von Mises, F. A. Hayek, Israel Kirzner, Jesús Huerta de Soto, and especially Hayek's theory of knowledge and epistemology (see Chapters 1–3 of this book). They gave me a new understanding of the market and strengthened my belief in the market. I realized that the greatest advantage of the market economy is not obtaining the optimal allocation of given resources. Instead, it is obtaining the most valuable exertion of human creativity (entrepreneurship) so that entrepreneurs can create wealth for society while not bringing disaster to humanity. When I wrote the original text of Chapter 2 of this book, I wanted to show that neoclassical economists are unable to understand entrepreneurs, thus they cannot understand the market economy. The market theories they develop are incorrect, or at least misleading. Many of their economic policy proposals are harmful.

My personal experience shows that Daniel Kahneman is right when he uses the "theory-induced blindness" to explain why even great scholars easily ignore the evident facts. The neoclassical misconception of the market can dominate economics for so long because economists on the whole believe it is right.

Overall, in order to have a correct understanding of the actual market, my current view is mainstream economics requires a paradigm shift. Specifically, it needs to absorb the Austrian School of economic thought. Of course, I also know that a paradigm shift is not an easy task. Even the smartest and most innovative people have difficulty freeing themselves from the old paradigm. Thomas Kuhn's book *The Structure of Scientific Revolutions* makes this point very clearly.[12] Not only was Albert Einstein the founder of the theory of relativity, but he also was the earliest scientist to propose the concept of quantum mechanics. However, because he

[12] Thomas S. Kuhn. 1970. *The Structure of Scientific Revolutions*. Second edition. University of Chicago Press.

always adhered to the strict causality and certainty paradigm of Newtonian mechanics, he stubbornly refused to accept the uncertainty principle of quantum mechanics until the very end of his life. Neoclassical economics has reigned over economics for over 100 years. Not only is it engrained in the mindsets of the majority of economists, but also their livelihoods depend on it. From an economist's perspective, it is difficult to publish research that was not done under the neoclassical paradigm. Finding a job is even harder. For this reason, many followers of Mises in Vienna and many followers of Hayek at the London School of Economics later parted ways with their instructors and joined the Keynesian camp. Some even became major figures of Keynesianism. Mises never received a salaried full-time position at a university for the rest of his life. However, major scientific progress always occurs along with a research paradigm shift. People that pursue truth are different from people that only pursue interests. Economists should seek out correct market theories, not just market theories that make it easy to find a job.

Lastly, I must emphasize that my criticisms of neoclassical economics do not mean I believe it is totally without merit. Similarly, my praise for the Austrian School of economics does not mean I believe it is perfect. Neoclassical economics is like a machine built by many generations of economists. Although it cannot perform the functions we expect, many of its components can be reused. The Austrian School of economics has been marginalized for a very long time. It has not received the intelligence or resource inputs it should have, so it is far behind neoclassical economics in terms of formalization. If we perceive the transformation of the economics paradigm as a long-term process, perhaps the first step should be to incorporate some major ideas of the Austrian School into mainstream economics textbooks. In fact, my publication of *Jingjixue Yuanli* (*Principles of Economics*) in 2015 was an attempt to do this.[13]

Unlike other textbooks, my *Principles of Economics* has a place for entrepreneurs. Entrepreneurship is not only a force that drives markets toward equilibrium but is also a source of economic growth. I also constructed the entrepreneur-centric "Smith–Schumpeterian growth model." As an explanation for economic growth, this model is far more convincing than the neoclassical growth model and the Keynesian growth model.

---

[13] Weiying Zhang. 2015. *Principles of Economics*. Xi'an: Northwest University Press. .

References

Abernathy, William J., Kim B. Clark, and Alan M. Kantrow. 1984. *Industrial Renaissance: Producing a Competitive Future for America*. New York: Basic Books.

Acemoglu, Daron. 1995. "Reward Structures and the Allocation of Talent." *European Economic Review*, 39(1): 17–33.

Acemoglu, Daron and James Robinson. 2012. *Why Nations Fail: The Origins of Power, Prosperity, and Poverty*. New York: Crown Business.

Acemoglu, Daron and Simon Johnson. 2023. *Power and Progress: Our Thousand-year Struggle over Technology and Prosperity*. Public Affairs.

Aghion, Philippe and Peter Howit. 1992. "A Mode of Growth through Creative Destruction." *Econometrica*, 60: 323–351.

Aghion, Philippe, Céline Antonin, and Simon Bunel. 2021. *The Power of Creative Destruction: Economic Upheaval and the Wealth of Nations*. Cambridge, MA: Belknap Press.

Aiyar, Swaminathan. 2016. "Twenty-Five Years of Indian Economic Reform: A Story of Private-Sector Success, Government Failure, and Institutional Weakness." *Cato Institute Policy Analysis*, (803).

Akerlof, George. 1970. "Market for Lemons: Quality Uncertainty and the Market Mechanism." *Quarterly Journal of Economics*, 83(4): 488–500.

Alicke, Mark D. and Ethan Zell. 2008. "Social Comparison and Envy." In *Envy: Theory and Research*. Edited by Richard Smith. Oxford: Oxford University Press.

Allen, Robert C. 2009. *The British Industrial Revolution in Global Perspective*. Cambridge: Cambridge University Press.

Alvarez, S.A. and J.B. Barney. 2007. "Discovery and Creation: Alternative Theories of Entrepreneurial Action." *Strategic Entrepreneurship Journal*, 1(1–2): 11–26.

2010. "Entrepreneurship and Epistemology: The Philosophical Underpinnings of the Study of Entrepreneurial Opportunities." *Academy of Management Annals*, 4(1): 557–583.

Amit, Raphael, Kenneth R. MacCrimmon, Charlene Zietsman, and John M. Oesch. 2000. "Does Money Matter? Wealth Attainment as the Motive for Initiating Growth-Oriented Technology Ventures." *Journal of Business Venturing*, 16(2): 119–143.

Arikan, A. M., I. Arikan, and I. Koparan. 2020. "Creation Opportunities: Entrepreneurial Curiosity, Generative Cognition, and Knightian Uncertainty." *Academy of Management Review*, 45(4): 808–824.

Arrow, K. J. 1951. "Alternative Approaches to the Theory of Choice in Risk-Taking Situations." *Econometrica*, 19: 404–437.

Astebro, Thomas, Holger Herz, Ramana Nanda, and Roberto A. Weber. 2014. "Seeking the Roots of Entrepreneurship: Insights from Behavioral Economics." *Journal of Economic Perspective*, 28(3): 49–70.

Bähr, Johannes. 2017. *Werner von Siemens: 1816–1892*. CH Beck.

Baldwin, Roberto. 2012. "Netflix Gambles on Big Data to Become the HBO of Streaming." *Wired Magazine*, November 29, 2012.

Baumol, William. 1959. *Business Behavior, Value and Growth*. New York: Macmillan.

   1994. *Entrepreneurship, Management, and the Structure of Payoffs*. Cambridge, MA: MIT Press.

Becker, Markus C., Thorbjorn Knudsen, and Richard Swedber (eds.). 2011. *The Entrepreneur: Classic Text by Joseph A. Schumpeter*. Stanford, CA: Stanford University Press.

Beinhocker, William Oliver. 2006. *The Origin of Wealth: Evolution, Complexity and Radical Remaking of Economics*. Boston: Harvard Business School Press.

Bennett, D. L. and B. Nikolaev. 2017. "On the Ambiguous Economic Freedom–Inequality Relationship." *Empirical Economics*, 53(2): 717–754.

Berglund, H., M. Bousfiha, and Y. Mansoori. 2020. "Opportunities as Artifacts and Entrepreneurship as Design." *Academy of Management Review*, 45(4): 825–846.

Berman, Sheri. 1998. *The Social Democratic Moment: Ideas and Politics in the Making of Interwar Europe*. Cambridge, MA: Harvard University Press.

Bernstein, William J. 2004. *The Birth of Plenty: How the Prosperity of the Modern World was Created*. New York: McGraw-Hill.

Bianchi, Tiago. 2023. "Global Market Share of Leading Search Engines 2015–2023." *Statista*, May 24, 2023. https://www.statista.com/statis tics/1381664/worldwide-all-devices-market-share-of-search-engines/.

Boyer, P. and M. B. Petersen. 2018. "Folk-Economic Beliefs: An Evolutionary Cognitive Model." *Behavioral and Brain Sciences*, 41: 1–51.

Buchanan, James M. and Viktor J. Vanberg. 1991. "The Market as a Creative Process." *Economics and Philosophy*, 7(1): 167–186.

Casson, Mark. 1982. *The Entrepreneur: An Economic Theory*. London: Martin Robertson & Co Ltd.

Chen Hai. 2012. *Jiu'er Pai: "Xin Shidafu" Qiyejia de Shangdao yu Lixiang.* Beijing, China: CITIC Press.

Chen Zhongshi. 1993. *Bai Lu Yuan.* Beijing, China: People's Literature Publishing House.

Christensen, Clayton. 1997. *The Innovator's Dilemma: When New Technologies Cause Great Firms to Fail.* Harvard Business Review Press.

Clark, Gregory. 2007. *A Farewell to Alms: A Brief Economic History of the World.* Princeton, NJ: Princeton University Press.

Clark, Robert C. 1986. *Corporate Law.* Boston, MA: Little, Brown & Company.

Coase, Ronald. 1960. "The Problem of Social Cost." *Journal of Law and Economics*, 3: 1–44.

Collins, Harry. 2010. *Tacit and Explicit Knowledge.* Chicago: University of Chicago Press.

Cooper, Arnold C., Carolyn Y. Woo, and William C. Dunkelberg. 1988. "Entrepreneurs' Perceived Chances for Success." *Journal of Business Venturing*, 3(2): 97–108.

Cosidine, Bob. 1975. *The Remarkable Life of Dr. Armand Hammer.* New York: Harper & Row.

David, Paul and Gavin Wright. 1996. "The Origin of American Resource Abundance." IISA working paper 96–15.

Dawkins, Richard. 2009. *The Greatest Show on Earth: The Evidence for Evolution.* New York: Free Press.

de Soto, Hernando. 2000. *The Mystery of Capital: Why Capitalism Triumphs in the West and Fails Everywhere Else.* New York: Basic Books.

de Soto, Jesús Huerta. 2010. *Socialism, Economic Calculation and Entrepreneurship.* Camberley, England: Edward Elgar.

Diamond, Jared. 1997. *Guns, Germs and Steel: The Fates of Human Societies.* New York: W. W. Norton & Co.

Djankov, S., R. La Porta, F. Lopez-De-Silanes, and A. Shleifer. 2002. "The Regulation of Entry." *The Quarterly Journal of Economics*, 117(1): 1–37.

Drucker, Peter. 1985. *Innovation and Entrepreneurship.* New York: Harper & Row.

Du Sha. 2018. *Du Sha and His Times (yi ge ren he ta de shidai).* Hong Kong: Open Page.

Easterly, William. 2013. *The Tyranny of Experts: Economists, Dictators, and the Forgotten Rights of the Poor.* New York: Basic Books.

Evans, David. 2003. "The Antitrust Economics of Multi-Sided Platform Markets." *Yale Journal on Regulation*, 20(2): 325–381.

Evans, David S. and Boyan Jovanovic. 1989. "An Estimated Model of Entrepreneurial Choice Under Liquidity Constraints." *Journal of Political Economy*, 97(4): 808–827.

Feather, N. T. 1989. "Attitudes Towards the Higher Achiever: The Fall of Tall Poppy." *Australian Journal of Psychology*, 41(3): 97–110.

Fontana, G. and B. Gerrard. 2004. "A post Keynesian theory of decision making under uncertainty." *Journal of Economic Psychology*, 25: 619–637.

Foss, Nicolai and Peter Klein. 2020. *Organizing Entrepreneurial Judgment: A New Approach to the Firm*. Cambridge University Press.

Garrison, Roger W. 2001. *Time and Money: The Macroeconomics of Capital Structure*. London: Routledge.

Gay, Peter. 1969. *Enlightenment: The Science of Freedom*. New York: W. W. Norton.

Gleason, D. P. 2016. "Money Men, Misdemeanors, and Motorcar Makers: The Uncompromising Vision of Henry Ford and Those He Left Behind." *Michigan Historical Review*, 42(2): 81–96.

Griffin, M. A. and G. Grote. 2020. "When Is More Uncertainty Better? A Model of Uncertainty Regulation and Effectiveness." *Academy of Management Review*, 45(4): 745–765.

Grossman, S. J. and Oliver D. Hart. 1986. "The Costs and Benefits of Ownership: A Theory of Vertical and Lateral Integration." *Journal of Political Economy*, 94(4): 691–719.

Grossman, Gene M. and Elhanan Helpman. 1991. *Innovation and Growth in the Global Economy*. Cambridge, MA: MIT Press.

Hammack, Bill. 2017. *Fatal Flight: The True Story of Britain's Last Great Airship*. New York: Articulate Noise Books.

Harada, Issaku. "China's Great Industrial Policy Debate Rages On," https://asia.nikkei.com/Economy/China-s-great-industrial-policy-debate-rages-on.

Hart, Oliver. 1995. *Firms, Contracts, and Financial Structure*. Oxford.: Clarendon Press.

Hauer, John. 2015. "Inventors, Entrepreneurs and Space in Between," https://techcrunch.com/2015/05/28/inventors-entrepreneurs-and-the-space-in-between

Hayek, F.A. 1931. *Prices and Production*. London: George Routledge.

  1935. *Collectivist Economic Planning*. London: Routledge & Sons. Reprinted by Augustus M. Kelley, 1975.

  1937. "Economics and Knowledge." (Republished in Hayek: *Individualism and Economic Order*, 1948.)

  1945. "The Use of Knowledge in Society." (Republished in Hayek: *Individualism and Economic Order*, 1948.)

  1946. "Individualism: True and False." (Republished in Hayek: *Individualism and Economic Order*, 1948).

  1948. *Individualism and Economic Order*. Chicago: University of Chicago Press.

1978. *New Studies in Philosophy, Politics, Economics and the History of Ideas*. Chicago: University of Chicago Press.

1991[1988]. *The Fatal Conceit: The Errors of Socialism. (The Collected Works of Friedrich August Hayek)*, Volume I. Edited by W. W. Bartley, III. Chicago: Chicago University Press and London: Routledge.

2011 [1960]. *The Constitution of Liberty*. Chicago: University of Chicago Press.

Hiam, C. Michael. 2014. *Dirigible Dreams: The Age of the Airship*. Lebanon, N.H.: ForeEdge.

Hirschman, Albert O. 2013. *The Passions and the Interests: Political Arguments for Capitalism before Its Triumph*. Princeton, NJ: Princeton University Press.

Hoogland, Charles E., Stephen Thielke, and Richard H. Smith. 2017. "Envy as an Evolving Episode." In *Envy at Work and in Organizations*. Edited by Richard H. Smith, Ugo Merlone, and Michelle K. Duffy. Oxford: Oxford University Press.

Hsieh, C. T. and P. J. Klenow. 2009. "Misallocation and Manufacturing TFP in China and India." *The Quarterly Journal of Economics*, 124(4): 1403–1448.

Hutton, E. (trans.) 2014. *Xunzi: The Complete Text*. Princeton, NJ: Princeton University Press, chapter 9.

Irvine, Janis L. 1982. *Groupthink: Psychological Studies of Policy Decisions and Fiascoes*. 2nd edn. Cengage Learning.

Isaacson, Walter. 2011. *Steve Jobs*. London: Simon & Schuster.

2014. *The Innovators: How a Group of Hackers, Geniuses, and Geeks Created the Digital Revolution*. London: Simon & Schuster.

Jacobs, Jane. 1970. *The Economy of Cities*. New York: Vintage Books.

Jewkes, John, David Sawers, and Richard Stillerman. 1969. *The Sources of Invention*. New York: W. W. Norton & Company.

Jiang, Xiaojuan. 1993. "Public Choice Issues on China's Promotion of Industrial Policy." (Zhonghuo Tuixing Chanye Zhengce Zhong de Gonggong Xuanze Wenti). *Economic Research Journal (Jingji Yanjiu)*, 1993(6): 3–18.

Jomo, Kwame Sundaram. 1990. *Growth and Structural Change in the Malaysian Economy*. London: Macmillan.

Johnson, Steven. 2014. *How We Got to Now: Six Innovations that Made the Modern World*. New York: Riverhead Books.

Juma, Calestous. 2016. *Innovation and Its Enemies: Why People Resist New Technologies*. New York: Oxford University Press.

Kahneman, Daniel. 2011. *Thinking, Fast and Slow*. New York: Farrar, Straus and Giroux.

Kan, Kaili. 2014. "Zhongguo Xu Fansi TD Juece Cuowu de Zhidu Genyuan." FTchinese.com. December 18, 2014.

Kant, Immanuel. 1983 (1795). "Perpetual Peace: A Philosophical Sketch." In *Perpetual Peace and Other Essays*. Ted Humphrey (trans.). Indianapolis: Hackett.

Kay, J. and M. King. 2020. *Radical Uncertainty: Decision-Making beyond the Numbers*. New York, NY: WW Norton & Company.

Kets de Vries, Manfred F. R. 1985. "The Dark Side of Entrepreneurship." *Harvard Business Review*, 63(6): 160–167.

Keynes, J. M. 1936. *The General Theory of Employment, Interest and Money*. London: Macmillan.

   1937. "The General Theory of Employment." *Quarterly Journal of Economics*, 51: 209–23.

Khan, Lina. 2016. "Amazon's Antitrust Paradox." *Yale Law Journal*, 126 (3): 710.

Khor, N. and J. Pencavel. 2006. "Income Mobility of Individuals in China and the United States." *Economics of Transition*, (3): 417–458.

Kirzner, Israel. 1973. *Competition and Entrepreneurship*. Chicago: University of Chicago Press.

   1979. *Perception, Opportunity and Profit*. Chicago: University of Chicago Press.

   1985. *Discovery and the Capitalist Process*. Chicago: University of Chicago Press.

   1992. *The Meaning of Market Process*. London: Routledge.

Kitch, Edmund W. 1983. "The Fire of Truth: A Remembrance of Law and Economics at Chicago, 1932–1970." *Journal of Law and Economics*, 26(1): 163–234.

Klein, Daniel. 1997. *Reputation: Studies in the Voluntary Elicitation of Good Conduct*. University of Michigan Press.

Knight, Frank. 1921. *Risk, Uncertainty, and Profit*. Boston: Houghton Mifflin.

Kohn, Meir. 2004. "Value and Exchange." *Cato Journal*, 24(3): 303–339.

Kornai, Janos. 1980. *The Economics of Shortage*. North Holland.

Kosacoff, Bernardo and Adrián Ramos. 1999. "The Industrial Policy Debate." *Cepal Review*, 68: 35–60.

Kreps, David. 1986. "Corporate Culture and Economic Theory." In *Technological Innovation and Business Strategy*. Edited by M. Tsuchiya. Nippon Keizai Shimbuunsha Press. Also, in *Rational Perspective on Political Science*. Edited by J. Alt and K. Shepsle. Cambridge, MA: Harvard University Press, 1999.

Krueger, Anne O. 1974. "The Political Economy of the Rent-Seeking Society." *American Economic Review*, 64(3): 291–303.

Kuhn, Thomas S. 1970. *The Structure of Scientific Revolutions*. Enlarged (2nd edn.). University of Chicago Press.

Kydland, Finn E. and Edward C. Prescott. 1982. "Time to Build and Aggregate Fluctuations." *Econometrica,* 50(6): 1345–1370.

Kymlicka, Will. 2002. *Contemporary Political Philosophy: An Introduction.* 2nd Edition. Oxford: Oxford University Press.

La Porta, Rafael, Florencio Lopez-de-Silanes, Andrei Shleifer, and Robert W Vishny. 1997. "Legal Determinants of External Finance." *Journal of Finance,* 52(3): 1131–1150.

Lachmann, Ludwig. 1976. "From Mises to Shackle: An Essay on Austrian Economics and the Kaleidic Society." *Journal of Economic Literature,* 14: 54–64.

1977. "Professor Shackle on the Economic Significance of Time." In *Capital, Expectation and the Market Process*. Kansas City, MO: Sheed Andrews and McMeel, pp. 81–93.

1986. *The Market as an Economic Process*. Oxford: Basil Blackwell.

Lall, Sanjaya. 2004. "Reinventing Industrial Strategy: The Role of Government Policy in Building Industrial Competitiveness." *Annals of Economics and Finance,* 14(2): 661–692.

Lamoreaux, N. R. and J. L. Rosenthal. 2023. *Do Entrepreneurs Want Control? And Should They Get What They Want? A Historical and Theoretical Exploration* (No. w31106). National Bureau of Economic Research.

Lampert, C. M., M. Kim, and F. Polidoro Jr. 2020. "Branching and Anchoring: Complementary Asset Configurations in Conditions of Knightian Uncertainty." *Academy of Management Review,* 45(4): 847–868.

Landes, David. 1969. *The Unbound Prometheus*. New York: Cambridge University Press.

Laricchia, Federica. 2023. "Quarterly Smartphone Market Share Worldwide by Vendor 2009–2023." *Statista,* Nov 8. https://www.statista.com/stat istics/271496/global-market-share-held-by-smartphone-vendors-since-4th-quarter-2009/

Lazonick, William. 1986. "The Cotton Industry." In *The Decline of the British Economy*. Edited by Bernard Elbaum and William Lazonick. New York: Oxford University Press.

Lecuna, Antonio. 2021. "Understanding Imagination in Entrepreneurship." *Entrepreneurship Research Journal.* https://doi.org/10.1515/erj-2021-0103

Legge, James. 1895. *The Chinese Classics: The Works of Mencius*. Volume II. Oxford: Clarendon Press.

Levenstein, Margaret. 1998. *Accounting for Growth: Information Systems and the Creation of the Large Corporation*. Stanford, CA: Stanford University Press.

Lewis, P. 2017. "Shackle on Choice, Imagination and Creativity: Hayekian Foundations." *Cambridge Journal of Economics*, 41(1): 1–24.

Lin, Jun. 2009. *Boiling for 15 years (Futeng Shiwu Nian)*. Beijing: Citic Press.

Lin, Justin Yifu. 2010. *Self-Selected Works (Lin Yifu Zixuan Ji)*. Shanxi Economic Press.

   2012. *New Structural Economics (Xin Jigou Jingjixue)*. Beijing: Peking University Press.

   2016. "Industrial Policy and Economic Development: Perspective from New Structural Economics." *Comparative Studies (Bijiao)*, 6: 163–173.

   2016. "Zhaoban Xifang Zhuliu Jingji Lilun shi Xing Butong de." *Qiushi*, 20: 57–59.

Littlechild, S. C. 1979. "Comment: Radical Subjectivism or Radical Subversion?" In *Time, Uncertainty and Disequilibrium*. Edited by M.J. Rizzo. Lexington, MA: Lexington Books.

Liu, He and Yang Weimin. 1999. *China's Industrial Policy: Theory and Practice (Zhongguo de Chanye Zhengce: Lilun yu Shijian)*. Beijing: Economic Press China.

Locke, John. 1690. *An Essay Concerning Human Understanding*. Book IV, chapter III.

Lucas, Robert E., Jr. 1978. "On the Size Distribution of Business Firms." *Bell Journal of Economics*, 9(2): 508–523.

   1988. "On the mechanics of Economic Development." *Journal of Monetary Economics*, 22(1): 3–42.

Ma, Yun. 2016. "In the Next 30 Years, the Planned Economy Will Become Bigger and Bigger." *The First Financial and Economic Daily (Diyi Caijing Ribao)*. November 20. Weblink: http://tech.sina.com.cn/i/2016-11-20/doc-ifxxwrwk1500894.shtml.

Maddison, Angus. 2007. *Contours of the World Economy, 1-2030 AD*. Oxford: Oxford University Press.

Mantoux, Paul. 1928[1964]. *The Industrial Revolution in the Eighteenth Century: An Outline of the Beginnings of the Modern Factory System in England*. Translated by Marjorie Vernon. London and New York: Routledge.

Marsh, Peter. 2012. *The New Industrial Revolution: Consumers, Globalization, and the End of Mass Production*. New Haven, CT: Yale University Press.

Marris, R. 1964. *The Economic Theory of Managerial Capitalism*. London: Macmillan.

Mayer-Schönberger, Viktor and Kenneth Cukier. 2013. *Big Data: A Revolution that Will Transform How We Live, Work, and Think*. Boston, MA: Houghton Mifflin Harcourt.

Maynard Smith, John. 1982. *Evolution and the Theory of Games*. Cambridge, U.K.: Cambridge University Press.

McCloskey, Deirdre N. 2006. *The Bourgeois Virtues: Ethics for an Age of Commerce*. Chicago: University of Chicago Press.

2023. "'Power and Progress' Review: Technology and the New Leviathan." *Wall Street Journal*. June 17, 2023. https://www.wsj.com/articles/power-and-progress-review-the-new-leviathan-39689d0c

Miller, Chris. 2022. *Chip War: The Fight for the World's Most Critical Technology*. London: Scribner.

Mises, Ludwig von. 1912 (1953). *Theory of Money and Credit*. 2nd Edition. New Haven: Yale University Press.

1972. *The Anti-Capitalistic Mentality*. Indianapolis: Liberty Fund.

2007(1949). *Human Action*. Indianapolis: Liberty Fund.

Mokyr, Joel. 1990. *The Lever of Riches: Technological Creativity and Economic Progress*. New York and Oxford: Oxford University Press.

2002. *The Gifts of Athena: Historical Origin of the Knowledge Economy*. Princeton, NJ: Princeton University Press.

2009. *The Enlightened Economy: An Economic History of Britain 1700–1850*. New Haven: Yale University Press.

2016. *A Culture of Growth: The Origin of the Modern Economy*. Princeton, NJ: Princeton University Press.

Montesquieu. 1750(1977). David Wallace Carrithers (ed.). *The Spirit of the Laws: A Compendium of the First English Edition*. Berkeley, CA: University of California Press.

Morgan, Kenneth. 2016. *The Birth of Industrial Britain: Economic Change 1750–1850*. London: Routledge.

Mulholland, Leslie Arthur. 1990. *Kant's System of Rights*. Columbia University Press.

Navarro. J. G. 2023. "Advertising Worldwide Statistics and Factors." *Statista*, August 3. https://www.statista.com/topics/990/global-advertising-market/#topicOverview

Nordhaus William D. 2004. "Schumpeterian Profits in the American Economy: Theory and Measurement." Yale University Cowles Foundation Discussion Paper No. 1457 (April 2004).

North, Douglass C. 1990. *Institutions, Institutional Change and Economic Performance*. New York: Cambridge University Press.

Nozick, Robert. 1998. "Why Do Intellectuals Oppose Capitalism?" *Cato Policy Report*, 20(1), 8–11.

Orole, Felix, Kamisan Gadar, and Kamarudin Nor. 2012. "The Role of Imagination in Entrepreneurial Innovation." Conference paper, 11th International Entrepreneurship Forum Kuala Lumpur, Malaysia, 4–6 September, 2012.

Olson, Mancur. 1982. *The Rise and Decline of Nations*. New Haven: Yale University Press.

Pack, Howard and Kamal Saggi. 2006. "Is There a Case for Industrial Policy? A Critical Survey." *The World Bank Research Observer*, 21 (2): 267–297.

Packard, M. D. and B. B. Clark. 2020. "On the Mitigability of Uncertainty and the Choice between Predictive and Nonpredictive Strategy." *Academy of Management Review*, 45(4): 766–786.

Perkins, Dwight and Thomas Rawski. 2008. "Forecasting China's Economic Growth to 2025." In *China's Great Economic Transformation*. Edited by Loren Brandt and Thomas Rawski. Cambridge: Cambridge University Press.

Perry, Mark J. 2018. "Only 53 US Companies Have Been on the Fortune 500 Since 1955, Thanks to the Creative Destruction that Fuels Economic Prosperity." AEIdeas.

Phelps, Edmund. 2015. *Mass Flourishing: How Grassroots Innovation Created Jobs, Challenge, and Change*. Princeton, NJ: Princeton University Press.

Phelps, Edmund, Raicho Bojilov, Hian Teck Hoon, and Gylfi Zoega. 2020. *Dynamism: The Values That Drive Innovation, Job Satisfaction, and Economic Growth*. Cambridge, MA: Harvard University Press.

Piketty, T. 2013. *Capital in the 21st Century*. Cambridge, MA: Harvard University Press.

Polanyi, Michael. 1958. *Personal Knowledge*. Chicago: University of Chicago Press.

1959. *The Study of Man*. Chicago: University of Chicago Press.

Pomeranz, Kenneth. 2000. *The Great Divergence: China, Europe, and the Making of the Modern World Economy*. Princeton, NJ: Princeton University Press.

Porter, Michael, Hirotaka Takeuchi, and Mariko Sakakibara. 2000. *Can Japan Compete?* Palgrave Macmillan.

Rand, Ayn. 1961. *For the New Intellectual: The Philosophy of Ayn Rand*. New York: Random House.

1962. "Check Your Premises." *The Objectivist Newsletter*. 1(1). Edited and published by Ayn Rand and Nathaniel Branden.

Rawls, John. 1999. *A Theory of Justice*. Revised Edition. Cambridge, MA: The Belknap Press of Harvard University Press.

Rindova, V. and Courtney, H. 2020. "To Shape or Adapt: Knowledge Problems, Epistemologies, and Strategic Postures under Knightian Uncertainty." *Academy of Management Review*, 45(4): 787–807.

Rindova, V. P. and Martins, L. L. 2018. "The Three Minds of the Strategist: Toward an Agentic Perspective in Behavioral Strategy." In *Advances in Strategic Management*, vol. 39. Edited by M. Augier, C. Fang, and V. P. Rindova. Bingley, U.K.: Emerald Publishing Limited.

Romer, Paul. 1986. "Increasing Returns and Long-Run Growth." *Journal of Political Economy*, 94: 1002–1037.

1990. "Endogenous Technological Change." *Journal of Political Economy*, 98 (5): S71–S102.

1994. "The Origins of Endogenous Growth." *The Journal of Economic Perspectives*, 8 (1): 3–22.

Rose, Alexander. 2020. *Empires of the Sky: Zeppelins, Airplanes, and Two Men's Epic Duel to Rule the World*. New York: Random House.

Rosen, Sherwin. 1982. "Authority, Control, and the Distribution of Earnings." *The Bell Journal of Economics*, 13(2): 311–323.

Rosen, William. 2010. *The Most Powerful Idea in the World: A Story of Steam, Industry, and Invention*. Random House.

Rosenberg, Nathan. 1976. *Perspectives on Technology*. New York: Cambridge University Press.

Rosenberg, Nathan. 1994. *Exploring the Black Box: Technology, Economics, and History*. Cambridge University Press.

2000. *Schumpeter and the Endogeneity of Technology*. London: Routledge.

Rothbard, Murray N. 1983. *America's Great Depression*. Fourth Edition. New York: Richardson & Snyder.

1995. *Classical Economics: An Austrian Perspective on the History of Economic Thought*. Volume II. Camberley, England: Edward Elgar.

Rubin, Paul. 2003. "Folk Economics." *Southern Journal of Economics*, 70 (1): 157–171.

Russett, Bruce and John Oneal. 2001. *Triangulating Peace: Democracy, Interdependence, and International Organizations*. New York: W. W. Norton & Company.

Sachs, Jeffrey. 2000. *The Ages of Globalization: Geography, Technology, and Institutions*. New York: Columbia University Press.

Samuelson, P. A. 1957. "Wages and Interest: A Modern Dissection of Marxian Economic Models." *The American Economic Review*, 47(6): 884–912.

Schoeck, Helmut. 1966. *Envy: A Theory of Social Behavior*. Indianapolis: Liberty Fund.

Schumpeter, Joseph. 1934. *The Theory of Economic Development: An Inquiry into Profits, Capital, Credit, Interest, and the Business Cycle*. Translated by Redvers Opie. Cambridge, MA: Harvard University Press.

2003 (1942). *Capitalism, Socialism, and Democracy*. London: Taylor & Francis.

2017(1939). *Business Cycles: A Theoretical, Historical, and Statistical Analysis of the Capitalist Process*. Eastford, CT: Martino Fine Books.

1943. "Capitalism in the Postwar World." In *Essays: On Entrepreneurs, Innovations, Business Cycles and the Evolution of Capitalism*. Edited by Richard Clemence. New Brunswick (United States) and London (UK): Transaction Publishers, 2008.

Scientific American. 1899. "Airship or Aeroplane—Which," December 9, 1899.

Scruton, Roger. 2006. "Hayek and Conservatism." *The Cambridge Companion to Hayek*. Edited by Edward Feser. Cambridge University Press.

Sen, Amartya. 2009. *The Idea of Justice*. New York: Penguin Books.

Shackle, G.L.S. [1972]1991. *Epistemics and Economics*. Cambridge University Press.

1979a. *Imagination and the Nature of Choice*. Cambridge University Press.

1979b. "Imagination, formalism and choice." In *Time, Uncertainty and Disequilibrium*. Edited by M.J. Rizzo. Lexington, MA: Lexington Books.

1983. "The Bounds of Unknowledge." In *Beyond Positive Economics*. Edited by J. Wiseman. London: Macmillan.

Shearmur, J. and D. Klein. 1997. "Good Conduct in the Great Society: Adam Smith and the Role of Reputation." *Reputation: Studies in the Voluntary Elicitation of Good Conduct*. Edited by D. Rizzo. Ann Arbor: University of Michigan Press.

Shermer, Michael. 2015. *The Moral Arc: How Science and Reason Lead Humanity toward Truth, Justice, and Freedom*. New York: Henry Holt & Company.

Shleifer, Andrei and Robert Vishny. 2002. *The Grabbing Hand: Government Pathologies and Their Cures*. Cambridge, MA: Harvard University Press.

Simpson, Brian. 2005. *Markets Don't Fail!* Lexington Books.

Skousen, Mark. 2005. *Vienna and Chicago: Friends or Foes?* Washington, DC: Capital Press.

Smil, Vaclav. 2005. *Creating the Twentieth Century: Technical Innovations of 1867–1914 and Their Lasting Impact*. New York: Oxford University Press.

2006. *Transforming the Twentieth Century: Technical Innovations and Their Consequences*. New York: Oxford University Press.

Smiles, Samuel. 1865. *Lives of Boulton and Watt*. London: John Murray.

Smith, Adam. 2002(1759). *Theory of Moral Sentiments*. Edited by Knud Haakonssen. Cambridge University Press.

Smith, Vernon L. 2008. *Rationality in Economics: Constructivist and Ecological Form*. Cambridge University Press.

Solow, Robert. 1956. "A Contribution to the Theory of Economic Growth." *Quarterly Journal of Economics*, 70: 65–94.

1957. "Technical Change and the Aggregate Production Function." *The Review of Economics and Statistics*, 39(3): 312–320.

Sowell, Thomas. 2012. *Intellectuals and Society*. New York: Basic Books.

2019. *Discrimination and Disparities*. New York: Basic Books.

Spencer, H. 1892. *Social Statics, Abridged and Revised; Together with the Man Versus the State*. D Appleton & Company. https://doi.org/10.1037/14113-000.

Stanley, Kenneth O. and Joel Lehman. 2015. *Why Greatness Cannot Be Planned: The Myth of the Objective*. London: Springer.

Stark, Rodney. 2007. *The Victory of Reason: How Christianity Led to Freedom, Capitalism, and Western Success*. London: Random House.

Stigler, George. 1951. "The Division of Labor Is Limited by the Extent of the Market." *The Journal of Political Economy*, 59(3): 185–193.

1971. "The Theory of Economic Regulation." *Bell Journal of Economics*, 2(1): 3–21.

Stiglitz, Joseph. 1994. *Whither Socialism?* Boston, MA: MIT Press.

2016. *The Great Divide: Unequal Societies and What We Can Do about Them*. New York: W. W. Norton & Company.

Sugden, Robert. 1989. "Spontaneous Order." *Journal of Economic Perspectives*, 3(4): 85–97.

Taylor, Mark Zachary. 2016. *The Politics of Innovation: Why Some Countries Are Better Than Others at Science & Technology*. Oxford University Press.

Tellis, Gerard J. and Peter N. Golder. 2002. *Will and Vision: How Latecomers Grow to Dominate Markets*. New York: McGraw-Hill.

Thiel, Peter and Blake Masters. 2014. *Zero to One: Notes on Startups, or How to Build the Future*. Crown Business.

Vance, Ashlee. 2015. *Elon Musk: Tesla, SpaceX, and the Quest for a Fantastic Future*. London: HarperCollins.

Vaz, Mark Cotta and John H. Hill. 2019. *Pan Am at War: How the Airline Secretly Helped America Fight World War II*. New York: Skyhorse Publishing.

Wang, Xiaolu, Fan Gang, and Liu Peng. 2009. "Transformation of China's Growth Pattern and Sustainability of Growth." (*Zhongguo Jingji Zengzhang Fangshi Zhuanhuan he Zengzhang Kechixuxing*). *Economic Research Journal* (Jingji Yanjiu), 44(1), 4–16.

Wang, Xiaolu, Fan Gang, and Yu Jingwen. 2017. *Marketization Index of China's Provinces (Zhongguo Fensheng Shichanghua Zhishu Baogao)*. Beijing: Social Sciences.

Warsh, David. 2007. *Knowledge and the Wealth of Nations: A Story of Economic Discovery*. New York and London: W. W. Norton & Company.

348

References

Watson, Burton. 1961. *Records of the Grand Historian of China: Translated from the Shi Chi of Ssu-Ma Chien.* Vol. II. Columbia University Press.

Weber, Max. 1905 [1930]. *The Protestant Ethic and the Spirit of Capitalism.* London: George Allen & Unwin.

Williams, Trevor I. 2000. *A History of Invention: From Stone Axes to Silicon Chips.* New York: Checkmark Books.

Williamson, Oliver E. 1964. *The Economics of Discretional Behavior: Managerial Objectives in a Theory of the Firm.* Englewood Cliff: Prentice Hall.

Wu, Si. 2003. *The Law of Blood Payment (Xue Chou Dinglu).* Workers Press.

Wu, Y. 2011. "Total Factor Productivity Growth in China: A Review." *Journal of Chinese Economic and Business Studies,* 9(2): 111–126.

Yang, Dongjin. 2013. "From Policy Support to Policy Shield: Process, Causes and Damage." (*Cong Zhengfu Fuzhi dao Zhengfu Biyin: Guocheng, Yuanyi ji qi Weihai—Jiyu Zhongguo Jiaoche Chanye de Tansuoxing Yanjiu*) *Industrial Economic Research (Chanye Jingji Yanjiu)* 2013(5): 1–9.

Yang, Xiaokai. 1988. "*A Microeconomics Approach to Modeling the Division of Labor Based on Increasing Return to Specialization.*" Ph. D. Dissertation. Department of Economics, Princeton University.

Yang, Xiaokai and Jeff Borland. 1991. "A Microeconomic Mechanism for Economic Growth." *Journal of Political Economy,* 99(3): 460–482.

Yang, Xiaokai, and Y-K Ng. 1993. *Specialization and Economic Organization: A New Classical Microeconomic Framework.* Amsterdam: North-Holland.

Young, Allyn. 1928. "Increasing Returns and Economic Progress." *Economic Journal,* 38(152): 527–542.

Yunogami, Takashi. 2015. *Lost Manufacture: The Failure of Japanese Manafacture (Shiqu de Zhizaoye: Riben Zhizaoye de Shibai).* Beijing: China Machine Press.

Zhang, Jie. 2016. "Xiaoxi Cheng Xin Nengyuan Qiche Pianbu Diaocha Jieguo Jiang Gongbu." *Beijing News.* May 16, 2016.

Zhang, Weiying. 1999. *Qiye Lilun yu Zhongguo Qiye Gaige.* (*The Theory of the Firm and Chinese Enterprise Reform*). Beijing: Peking University Press.

2006. "Shichang Jingji Zhong de Zhengfu Xingwei – Riben de Jingyan." *Jiage, Shichang yu Qiyejia (Price, Market, and Entrepreneur).* Beijing: Peking University Press.

2014. *Shichang yu Zhengfu (Market and Government).* Northwestern University of China Press.

2015a. "Reflections on Economics: Market Failure or Market Theory Failure?" *China Economic Journal,* 8 (2): 109–121.

2015b. *The Logic of the Market: An Insider's View of Chinese Economic Reform*. Translated by Matthew Dale. Washington, DC: Cato Institute Press.

2017a. "China's Future Growth Depends on Innovation Entrepreneurs." *Journal of Chinese Economic and Business Studies*, 15(1): 19–40.

2017b. *The Road Leading to the Market*. London: Routledge.

2018a. *The Origin of the Capitalist Firm: An Entrepreneurial/Contractual Theory of the Firm*. Singapore: Springer Nature.

2018b. *Game Theory and Society*. Translated by Matthew Dale. London and New York: Routledge.

2018c. "Six Understandings of Corporate Governance Structure in the Context of China." *The European Journal of Finance*, 24(16): 1375–1387.

2019. "The China Model View Is Factually False." *Journal of Chinese Economic and Business Studies*, 17(3): 287–311.

2020. *Ideas for China's Future*. Translated by Matthew Dale. Singapore: Palgrave Macmillan.

2021a. "A Paradigmatic Change is Needed for Understanding the Real Market." *China Economic Review*, 66: 101602.

2021b. "Market Economy and China's 'Common Prosperity' Campaign." *Journal of Chinese Economic and Business Studies*, 4: 323–337.

Zhang, Weiying, W. W. Cooper, Honghui Deng, Barnett R. Parker, and T. Ruefli. 2010. "Entrepreneurial Talents and Economic Development in China." *Socio-Economic Planning Sciences*, 44(4): 178–192.

Zhang, Weiying and Sheng Bing. 2014 (1989). *The Entrepreneur: The King of Economic Growth*. (Qiyejia: Jingji Zengzhang de Guowang) Horizon Shanghai People's Press.

Zhang, Zhen and Richard Arvey. 2009. "Rule Breaking in Adolescence and Entrepreneurial Status: An Empirical Investigation." *Journal of Business Venturing*, 24(5): 436–447.

Zhou, Hang. 2018. *Chongxin Lijie Chuangye: Yige Chuangyezhe de Tuzhong Sikao*. Beijing: CITIC Publishing Group.

Zhou, Hongyi and Fan Haitao. 2017. *Subverter: Autobiography of Zhou Hongyi*. (*Dianfuzhe: Zhou Hongyi Zizhuan*). Beijing: Beijing United Press.

Zhou, Hua. 2015. *A Biography of Chu Shijian* (*Chu Shijian Zhuan*). Beijing: CITIC Publishing Group.

Zhou, Zhenghua. 2022. "Qumei Da Shuju, Lijie Qiyejia" ("Disenchanting Big Data and Understanding Entrepreneurs"). *Management Insights*, 31: 96–98.

Zhu, Xiaodong. 2012. "Understanding China's Growth: Past, Present and Future." *The Journal of Economic Perspectives*, 26 (4): 103–124.

Zitelmann, Rainer. 2018. *The Wealth Elite: A Groundbreaking Study of the Psychology of the Super Rich*. London: LID Publishing.

2019. *The Power of Capitalism*. London: LID Publishing.

2020. *The Rich in Public Opinion: What We Think When We Think about Wealth*. Washington, DC: Cato Institute.

2023. *In Defence of Capitalism: Debunking the Myths*. Oxford: Management Books.

Zweig, Stefan. 2015. *Shooting Stars: Ten Historical Miniatures*. Translated by Anthea Bell. Pushkin Press.

Index

Printed in the United States
by Baker & Taylor Publisher Services

Printed in the United States
by Baker & Taylor Publisher Services